The Official (ISC)²® Guide to the CCSP℠ CBK®

Second Edition

ADAM GORDON
CISSP-ISSAP, CISSP-ISSMP, SSCP, CCSP, CISA,
CRISC, MCSE PRIVATE CLOUD, VCP-CLOUD

A Wiley Brand

The Official (ISC)2® Guide to the CCSP℠ CBK®, Second Edition

Published by
John Wiley & Sons, Inc.
10475 Crosspoint Boulevard
Indianapolis, IN 46256
www.wiley.com

Published by John Wiley & Sons, Inc., Indianapolis, Indiana
Published simultaneously in Canada

ISBN: 978-1-119-27672-2
ISBN: 978-1-119-27673-9 (ebk)
ISBN: 978-1-119-27674-6 (ebk)

Manufactured in the United States of America

10 9 8 7 6 5 4 3 2 1

For general information on our other products and services please contact our Customer Care Department within the United States at (877) 762-2974, outside the United States at (317) 572-3993 or fax (317) 572-4002.

Wiley publishes in a variety of print and electronic formats and by print-on-demand. Some material included with standard print versions of this book may not be included in e-books or in print-on-demand. If this book refers to media such as a CD or DVD that is not included in the version you purchased, you may download this material at http://booksupport.wiley.com. For more information about Wiley products, visit www.wiley.com.

Library of Congress Control Number: 2016935632

About the Author

 With more than 25 years of experience as both an educator and an IT professional, Adam Gordon holds numerous professional IT certifications, including CISSP, CISA, CRISC, CHFI, CEH, SCNA, VCP, and VCI. He is the author of several books and has earned numerous awards, including EC-Council Instructor of Excellence, 2006 -2007 and Top Technical Instructor Worldwide, 2002 -2003. Adam holds his bachelor's degree in international relations and his master's degree in international political affairs from Florida International University.

Adam has held a number of positions during his professional career, including CISO, CTO, consultant, and solutions architect. He has worked on many large implementations involving multiple customer program teams for delivery.

Adam has been invited to lead projects for companies such as Microsoft, Citrix, Lloyds Bank TSB, Campus Management, US Southern Command (SOUTHCOM), Amadeus, World Fuel Services, and Seaboard Marine.

Credits

Project Editors
Gill Editorial Services
Kelly Talbot

Technical Editor
Rob Shimonski

Production Manager
Kathleen Wisor

Copy Editor
Kezia Endsley

**Manager of Content Development &
Assembly**
Mary Beth Wakefield

Marketing Manager
Carrie Sherrill

**Professional Technology & Strategy
Director**
Barry Pruett

Business Manager
Amy Knies

Executive Editor
Jim Minatel

Project Coordinator, Cover
Brent Savage

Proofreader
Kim Wimpsett

Indexer
Johnna VanHoose Dinse

Cover Designer
Mike Trent

Cover Image
Mike Trent

Contents

Foreword

EVERY DAY AROUND THE WORLD, organizations are taking steps to leverage cloud infrastructure, software, and services. This is a substantial undertaking that also heightens the complexity of protecting and securing data. As powerful as cloud computing is to organizations, it's essential to have qualified people who understand information security risks and mitigation strategies for the cloud. As the largest not-for-profit membership body of certified information security professionals worldwide, (ISC)² recognizes the need to identify and validate information security competency in securing cloud services.

To help facilitate the knowledge you need to ensure strong information security in the cloud, I'm pleased to present the *Official (ISC)² Guide to the CCSP CBK*. Drawing from a comprehensive, up-to-date global body of knowledge, the *CCSP CBK* ensures that you have the right information security knowledge and skills to be successful and prepares you to achieve the Certified Cloud Security Professional (CCSP) credential.

(ISC)² is proud to collaborate with the Cloud Security Alliance (CSA) to build a unique credential that reflects the most current and comprehensive best practices for securing and optimizing cloud computing environments. To attain CCSP certification, candidates must have a minimum of five years' experience in IT, of which three years must be in information security and one year in cloud computing. All CCSP candidates must be able to demonstrate capabilities found in each of the six Common Body of Knowledge (CBK) domains:

- Architectural Concepts and Design Requirements
- Cloud Data Security
- Cloud Platform and Infrastructure Security

- Cloud Application Security
- Operations
- Legal and Compliance

The CCSP credential represents advanced knowledge and competency in cloud security design, implementation, architecture, operations, controls, and immediate and long-term responses.

Cloud computing has emerged as a critical area within IT that requires further security considerations. According to the 2015 (ISC)² Global Information Security Workforce Study, cloud computing is identified as the top area for information security, with a growing demand for education and training within the next three years. In correlation to the demand for education and training, 73 percent of more than 13,000 survey respondents believe that cloud computing will require information security professionals to develop new skills.

If you are ready to take control of the cloud, *The Official (ISC)² Guide to the CCSP CBK* prepares you to securely implement and manage cloud services within your organization's information technology (IT) strategy and governance requirements. CCSP credential holders will achieve the highest standard for cloud security expertise—managing the power of cloud computing while keeping sensitive data secure.

The recognized leader in the field of information security education and certification, (ISC)² promotes the development of information security professionals throughout the world. As a CCSP with all the benefits of (ISC)² membership, you would join a global network of more than 110,000 certified professionals who are working to inspire a safe and secure cyber world.

Qualified people are the key to cloud security. This is your opportunity to gain the knowledge and skills you need to protect and secure data in the cloud.

Regards,

David P. Shearer
CEO
(ISC)²

Introduction

THERE ARE TWO MAIN requirements that must be met to achieve the status of Certified Cloud Security Professional (CCSP); one must take and pass the certification exam and be able to demonstrate a minimum of five years of cumulative paid full-time information technology experience, of which three years must be in information security and one year must be in one of the six domains of the CCSP examination. A firm understanding of what the six domains of the CCSP Common Body of Knowledge (CBK) are and how they relate to the landscape of business is a vital element in successfully being able to meet both requirements and claim the CCSP credential. The mapping of the six domains of the CCSP CBK to the job responsibilities of the information security professional in today's world can take many paths based on a variety of factors, such as industry vertical, regulatory oversight and compliance, geography, and public versus private versus military as the overarching framework for employment in the first place. In addition, considerations such as cultural practices and differences in language and meaning can play a substantive role in the interpretation of what aspects of the CBK will mean and how they will be implemented in any given workplace.

It is not the purpose of this book to attempt to address all these issues or provide a definitive prescription as to "the" path forward in all areas. Rather, it is to provide the official guide to the CCSP CBK and, in so doing, to lay out the information necessary to understand what the CBK is and how it is used to build the foundation for the CCSP and its role in business today. Being able to map the CCSP CBK to your knowledge, experience, and understanding is the way that you will be able to translate the CBK into actionable and tangible elements for both the business and its users that you represent.

1. The Architectural Concepts and Design Requirements domain focuses on the building blocks of cloud-based systems. The CCSP needs an understanding of cloud computing concepts such as definitions based on the ISO/IEC 17788 standard; roles like the cloud service customer, provider, and partner; characteristics such as multitenancy, measured services, and rapid elasticity and scalability; and building block technologies of the cloud such as virtualization, storage, and networking. The cloud reference architecture will

need to be described and understood, focusing on areas such as cloud computing activities (as described in ISO/IEC 17789), clause 9, cloud service capabilities, categories, deployment models, and the cross-cutting aspects of cloud platform architecture and design, such as interoperability, portability, governance, service levels, and performance. In addition, the CCSP should have a clear understanding of the relevant security and design principles for cloud computing, such as cryptography, access control, virtualization security, functional security requirements like vendor lock-in and interoperability, what a secure data life cycle is for cloud-based data, and how to carry out a cost-benefit analysis of cloud-based systems. The ability to identify what a trusted cloud service is and what role certification against criteria plays in that identification—using standards such as the Common Criteria and FIPS 140-2—are further areas of focus for this domain.

2. The Cloud Data Security domain contains the concepts, principles, structures, and standards used to design, implement, monitor, and secure operating systems (OSs), equipment, networks, applications, and those controls used to enforce various levels of confidentiality, integrity, and availability. The CCSP needs to understand and implement data discovery and classification technologies pertinent to cloud platforms, as well as be able to design and implement relevant jurisdictional data protections for personally identifiable information (PII), such as data privacy acts and the ability to map and define controls within the cloud. Designing and implementing digital rights management (DRM) solutions with the appropriate tools and planning for the implementation of data retention, deletion, and archiving policies are activities that a CCSP will need to understand how to undertake.

3. The Cloud Platform and Infrastructure Security domain covers knowledge of the cloud infrastructure components—both the physical and virtual—existing threats, and mitigating and developing plans to deal with those threats. Risk management is the identification, measurement, and control of loss associated with adverse events. It includes overall security review, risk analysis, selection and evaluation of safeguards, cost-benefit analysis, management decisions, safeguard implementation, and effectiveness review. The CCSP is expected to understand risk management, including risk analysis, threats and vulnerabilities, asset identification, and risk management tools and techniques. In addition, the candidate needs to understand how to design and plan for the use of security controls such as audit mechanisms, physical and environmental protection, and the management of identification, authentication, and authorization solutions within the cloud infrastructures she manages. Business continuity planning (BCP) facilitates the rapid recovery of business operations to reduce the overall impact of the disaster by ensuring continuity of the critical business functions. Disaster recovery planning includes procedures for emergency response, extended backup operations, and postdisaster recovery when the computer installation suffers loss of computer resources and physical facilities. The CCSP is expected to understand how to prepare a business continuity or disaster recovery plan (DRP), techniques and concepts, identification of critical data and systems, and the recovery of lost data within cloud infrastructures.

4. The Cloud Application Security domain focuses on issues to ensure that the need for training and awareness in application security, the processes involved with cloud software assurance and validation, and the use of verified secure software are understood. The domain refers to the controls that are included within systems and applications software and the steps used in their development (such as software development life cycle). The CCSP should fully understand the security and controls of the development process, system life cycle, application controls, change controls, program interfaces, and concepts used to ensure data and application integrity, security, and availability. In addition, the need to understand how to design appropriate identity and access management (IAM) solutions for cloud-based systems is important.

5. The Operations domain is used to identify critical information and the execution of selected measures that eliminate or reduce adversary exploitation of critical information. The domain examines the requirements of the cloud architecture, from planning of the data center design and implementation of the physical and logical infrastructure for the cloud environment to running and managing that infrastructure. It includes the definition of the controls over hardware, media, and the operators with access privileges to any of these resources. Auditing and monitoring are the mechanisms, tools, and facilities that permit the understanding of security events and subsequent actions to identify the key elements and report the pertinent information to the appropriate individual, group, or process. The need for compliance with regulations and controls through the applications of frameworks such as ITIL and ISO/IEC 20000 is also discussed. In addition, the importance of risk assessment across both the logical and the physical infrastructures and the management of communication with all relevant parties are focused on. The CCSP is expected to know the resources that must be protected, the privileges that must be restricted, the control mechanisms that are available, the potential for abuse of access, the appropriate controls, and the principles of good practice.

6. The Legal and Compliance domain addresses ethical behavior and compliance with regulatory frameworks. It includes the investigative measures and techniques that can be used to determine if a crime has been committed and methods used to gather evidence (including legal controls, e-discovery, and forensics). This domain also includes an understanding of privacy issues and audit processes and methodologies required for a cloud environment, such as internal and external audit controls, assurance issues associated with virtualization and the cloud, and the types of audit reporting specific to the cloud, such as the Statement on Standards for Attestation Engagements (SSAE) No. 16, and the International Standards for Assurance Engagements (ISAE) No. 3402.[1] Further, examining and understanding the implications that cloud environments have in relation to enterprise risk management and the impact of outsourcing for design and hosting of these systems are important considerations that many organizations face today.

---

[1] Many service organizations that previously had a SAS 70 service auditor's examination (SAS 70 audit) performed converted to the SSAE No.16 standard in 2011 and now have an SSAE 16 report instead. This is also referred to as a Service Organization Controls (SOC) 1 report.

CONVENTIONS

To help you get the most from the text, we've used a number of conventions throughout the book.

WARNING Warnings draw attention to important information that is directly relevant to the surrounding text.

NOTE Notes discuss helpful information related to the current discussion.

As for styles in the text, we show URLs within the text like so: `www.wiley.com`.

Architectural Concepts and Design Requirements

THE GOAL OF THE Architectural Concepts and Design Requirements domain is to provide you with knowledge of the building blocks necessary to develop cloud-based systems.

You will be introduced to such cloud computing concepts as the customer, provider, partner, measured services, scalability, virtualization, storage, and networking. You will be able to understand the cloud reference architecture based on activities defined by industry-standard documents.

Lastly, you will gain knowledge in relevant security and design principles for cloud computing, including secure data lifecycle and cost-benefit analysis of cloud-based systems.

DOMAIN OBJECTIVES

After completing this domain, you will be able to do the following:

❑ Define the various roles, characteristics, and technologies as they relate to cloud computing concepts

❑ Describe cloud computing concepts as they relate to cloud computing activities, capabilities, categories, models, and cross-cutting aspects

❑ Identify the design principles necessary for secure cloud computing

❑ Define the various design principles for the different types of cloud categories

❑ Describe the design principles for secure cloud computing

❑ Identify criteria specific to national, international, and industry for certifying trusted cloud services

❑ Identify criteria specific to the system and subsystem product certification

INTRODUCTION

> *"Cloud computing is a model for enabling ubiquitous, convenient, on-demand network access to a shared pool of configurable computing resources (e.g., networks, servers, storage, applications, and services) that can be rapidly provisioned and released with minimal management effort or service provider interaction."*
>
> "The NIST Definition of Cloud Computing"[1]

Cloud computing (*Figure 1.1*) is the use of Internet-based computing resources, typically "as a service," to allow internal or external customers to consume where scalable and elastic information technology (IT)-enabled capabilities are provided.

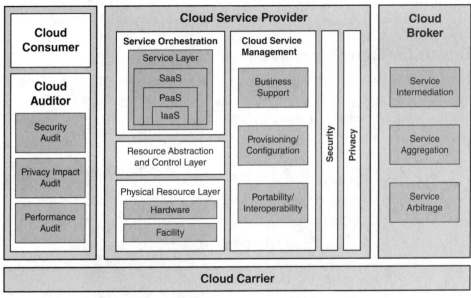

FIGURE 1.1 **Cloud computing overview.**

Cloud computing, or cloud, means many things to many people. There are indeed various definitions for cloud computing and what it means from many of the leading standards bodies. The previous National Institute of Standards and Technology (NIST) definition is the most commonly utilized, cited by professionals and others alike to clarify what the term *cloud* means.

It's important to note the difference between a cloud service provider (CSP) and a managed service provider (MSP). The main difference is to be found in the control exerted over the data and process and by who. With an MSP, the consumer dictates the technology and operating procedures. According to the MSP Alliance, MSPs typically have the following distinguishing characteristics:[2]

- Some form of network operations center (NOC) service

- Some form of help desk service

- Remote monitoring and management of all or most of the objects for the customer

- Proactive maintenance of the objects under management for the customer

- Delivery of these solutions with some form of predictable billing model, where the customer knows with great accuracy what the regular IT management expense will be

With a CSP, the service provider dictates both the technology and the operational procedures being made available to the cloud consumer. This means that the CSP is offering some or all of the components of cloud computing through a software as a service (SaaS), infrastructure as a service (IaaS), or platform as a service (PaaS) model.

Drivers for Cloud Computing

There are many drivers that may move a company to consider cloud computing. These may include the costs associated with the ownership of their current IT infrastructure solutions as well as projected costs to continue to maintain these solutions year in and year out (*Figure 1.2*).

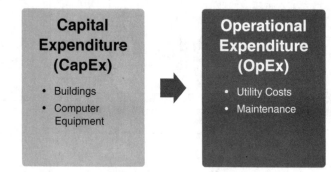

FIGURE 1.2 **Drivers that move companies toward cloud computing.**

Additional drivers include but are not limited to the following:

- The desire to reduce IT complexity

  - **Risk reduction:** Users can use the cloud to test ideas and concepts before making major investments in technology.

  - **Scalability:** Users have access to a large number of resources that scale based on user demand.

- - **Elasticity:** The environment transparently manages a user's resource utilization based on dynamically changing needs.
- Consumption-based pricing
  - **Virtualization:** Each user has a single view of the available resources, independent of their arrangement in terms of physical devices.
  - **Cost:** The pay-per-usage model allows an organization to pay only for the resources it needs with basically no investment in the physical resources available in the cloud. There are no infrastructure maintenance or upgrade costs.
- Business agility
  - **Mobility:** Users can access data and applications from around the globe.
  - **Collaboration and innovation:** Users are starting to see the cloud as a way to work simultaneously on common data and information.

Security, Risks, and Benefits

You cannot bring up or discuss the topic of cloud computing without hearing the words *security*, *risk*, and *compliance*. In truth, cloud computing does pose challenges and represents a paradigm shift in the way in which technology solutions are being delivered. As with any notable change, this brings about questions and a requirement for clear and concise understandings and interpretations to be obtained, from both a customer and a provider perspective. The Certified Cloud Security Professional (CCSP) must play a key role in the dialogue within the organization as it pertains to cloud computing, its role, the opportunity costs, and the associated risks (*Figure 1.3*).

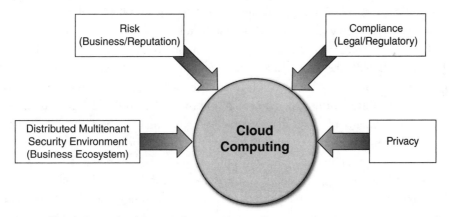

FIGURE 1.3 **Cloud computing issues and concerns.**

Risk can take many forms in an organization. The organization needs to carefully weigh all the risks associated with a business decision before engaging in an activity to minimize the risk impact associated with an activity. There are many approaches and frameworks that can be used to address risk in an organization, such as the Control Objectives for Information and Related Technology (COBIT) framework, The Committee of Sponsoring Organizations of the Treadway Commission (COSO) Enterprise Risk Management Integrated Framework, and the NIST Risk Management Framework. Organizations need to become risk aware in general, focusing on risks within and around the organization that may cause harm to the reputation of the business. Reputational risk can be defined as "the loss of value of a brand or the ability of an organization to persuade."[3] To manage reputational risk, an organization should consider the following items:

- Strategic alignment
  - Effective board oversight
  - Integration of risk into strategy setting and business planning
- Cultural alignment
  - Strong corporate values and a focus on compliance
- Operational focus
  - Strong control environment

Although many people think of cloud technologies as less secure or carrying greater risk, this is simply not possible or acceptable to say unless making a direct and measured comparison against a specified environment or service. For instance, it would be incorrect to simply assume or state that cloud computing is less secure as a service modality for the delivery of a customer relationship management (CRM) platform than a more traditional CRM application model, calling for an on-premise installation of the CRM application and its supporting infrastructure and databases. To assess the true level of security and risk associated with each model of ownership and consumption, the two platforms would need to be compared across a range of factors and issues, allowing for a side-by-side comparison of the key deliverables and issues associated with each model.

In truth, the cloud may be more or less secure than your organization's environment and current security controls depending on any number of factors, which include technological components; risk management processes; preventative, detective, and corrective controls; governance and oversight processes; resilience and continuity capabilities; defense in depth; and multifactor authentication.

Therefore, the approach to security varies depending on the provider and the ability for your organization to alter and amend its overall security posture prior to, during, and after migration or utilization of cloud services.

In the same way that no two organizations or entities are the same, neither are two CSPs. A one-size-fits-all approach is never good for security, so do not settle for it when utilizing cloud-based services.

The extensive use of automation within the cloud enables real-time monitoring and reporting on security control points, allowing for the establishment of continuous security monitoring regimes, enhancing the overall security posture of the organization consuming the cloud services. The benefits realized by the organization can include greater security visibility, enhanced policy and governance enforcement, and a better framework for management of the extended business ecosystem through a transition from an infrastructure-centric to a data-centric security model.

CLOUD COMPUTING DEFINITIONS

The following list forms a common set of terms and phrases you will need to become familiar with as a CCSP. Having an understanding of these items puts you in a strong position to communicate and understand technologies, deployments, solutions, and architectures within the organization as needed. This list is not comprehensive and should be used along with the vocabulary terms in Appendix B, "Glossary," to form as complete a picture as possible of the language of cloud computing.

- **Anything as a service (XaaS):** The growing diversity of services available over the Internet via cloud computing as opposed to being provided locally or on premises.

- **Apache CloudStack:** An open source cloud computing and IaaS platform developed to help make creating, deploying, and managing cloud services easier by providing a complete stack of features and components for cloud environments.

- **Business continuity:** The capability of the organization to continue delivery of products or services at acceptable predefined levels following a loss of service.

- **Business continuity management:** A holistic management process that identifies potential threats to an organization and the impacts to business operations those threats, if realized, might cause. It provides a framework for building organizational resilience with the capability of an effective response that safeguards the interests of its key stakeholders, reputation, brand, and value-creating activities.

- **Business continuity plan:** The creation of a strategy through the recognition of threats and risks facing a company, with an eye to ensure that personnel and assets are protected and able to function in the event of a disaster.

- **Cloud app:** Short for cloud application, cloud app describes a software application that is never installed on a local computer. Instead, it is accessed via the Internet.

- **Cloud Application Management for Platforms (CAMP):** CAMP is a specification designed to ease management of applications—including packaging and deployment—across public and private cloud computing platforms.

- **Cloud backup:** Cloud backup, or cloud computer backup, refers to backing up data to a remote, cloud-based server. As a form of cloud storage, cloud backup data is stored in and accessible from multiple distributed and connected resources that comprise a cloud.

- **Cloud backup solutions:** Cloud backup solutions enable enterprises or individuals to store their data and computer files on the Internet using a storage service provider rather than storing the data locally on a physical disk, such as a hard drive or tape backup.

- **Cloud computing:** A type of computing, comparable to grid computing, that relies on sharing computing resources and using a network of remote servers to store, manage, and process data instead of using a local server or a personal computer.

- **Cloud computing accounting software:** Cloud computing accounting software is accounting software that is hosted on remote servers. It provides accounting capabilities to businesses in a fashion similar to the SaaS business model. Data is sent into the cloud, where it is processed and returned to the user. All application functions are performed offsite, not on the user's desktop.

- **Cloud database:** A database accessible to clients from the cloud and delivered to users on demand via the Internet. Also referred to as database as a service (DBaaS), cloud databases can use cloud computing to achieve optimized scaling, high availability, multitenancy, and effective resource allocation.

- **Cloud enablement:** The process of making available one or more of the following services and infrastructures to create a public cloud computing environment: CSP, client, and application.

- **Cloud management:** Software and technologies designed for operating and monitoring the applications, data, and services residing in the cloud. Cloud management tools help ensure a company's cloud computing–based resources are working optimally and properly interacting with users and other services.

- **Cloud migration:** The process of transitioning all or part of a company's data, applications, and services from onsite premises behind the firewall to the cloud, where the information can be provided over the Internet on an on-demand basis.

- **Cloud OS:** A phrase frequently used in place of PaaS to denote an association to cloud computing.

- **Cloud portability:** In cloud computing terminology, this refers to the ability to move applications and their associated data between one CSP and another—or between public and private cloud environments.

- **Cloud provisioning:** The deployment of a company's cloud computing strategy, which typically first involves selecting which applications and services will reside in the public cloud and which will remain onsite behind the firewall or in the private cloud. Cloud provisioning also entails developing the processes for interfacing with the cloud's applications and services as well as auditing and monitoring who accesses and utilizes the resources.

- **Cloud server hosting:** A type of hosting in which hosting services are made available to customers on demand via the Internet. Rather than being provided by a single server or virtual server, cloud server hosting services are provided by multiple connected servers that comprise a cloud.

- **Cloud storage:** The storage of data online in the cloud, whereby a company's data is stored in and accessible from multiple distributed and connected resources that comprise a cloud.

- **Cloud testing:** Load and performance testing conducted on the applications and services provided via cloud computing—particularly the capability to access these services—to ensure optimal performance and scalability under a variety of conditions.

- **Desktop as a service:** A form of virtual desktop infrastructure (VDI) in which the VDI is outsourced and handled by a third party. Also called hosted desktop services, desktop as a service is frequently delivered as a cloud service along with the apps needed for use on the virtual desktop.

- **Enterprise application:** Describes applications—or software—that a business uses to assist the organization in solving enterprise problems. When the word *enterprise* is combined with *application*, it usually refers to a software platform that is too large and complex for individual or small business use.

- **Enterprise cloud backup:** Enterprise-grade cloud backup solutions typically add essential features such as archiving and disaster recovery (DR) to cloud backup solutions.

- **Eucalyptus:** An open source cloud computing and IaaS platform for enabling AWS-compatible private and hybrid clouds.

- **Event:** A change of state that has significance for the management of an IT service or other configuration item. The term can also be used to mean an alert or notification created by an IT service, configuration item, or monitoring tool. Events often require IT operations staff to take actions and lead to incidents being logged.

- **Host:** A device providing a service.

- **Hybrid cloud storage:** A combination of public cloud storage and private cloud storage in which some critical data resides in the enterprise's private cloud and other data is stored and accessible from a public cloud storage provider.

- **IaaS:** IaaS is defined as computer infrastructure, such as virtualization, being delivered as a service. IaaS is popular in the data center where software and servers are purchased as a fully outsourced service and usually billed on usage and how much of the resource is used—compared with the traditional method of buying software and servers outright.

- **Incident:** An unplanned interruption to an IT service or reduction in the quality of an IT service.

- **Managed service provider:** An IT service provider in which the customer dictates both the technology and the operational procedures.

- **Mean time between failure (MTBF):** The measure of the average time between failures of a specific component or part of a system.

- **Mean time to repair (MTTR):** The measure of the average time it should take to repair a failed component or part of a system.

- **Mobile cloud storage:** A form of cloud storage that applies to storing an individual's mobile device data in the cloud and providing the individual with access to the data from anywhere.

- **Multitenant:** In cloud computing, multitenant is the phrase used to describe multiple customers using the same public cloud.

- **Node:** A physical connection.

- **Online backup:** In storage technology, online backup means to back up data from your hard drive to a remote server or computer using a network connection. Online backup technology leverages the Internet and cloud computing to create an attractive offsite storage solution with few hardware requirements for any business of any size.

- **PaaS:** The process of deploying onto the cloud infrastructure consumer-created or acquired applications that are created using programming languages, libraries, services, and tools supported by the provider. The consumer does not manage or control the underlying cloud infrastructure including network, servers, operating systems (OSs), or storage but has control over the deployed applications and possibly the configuration settings for the application-hosting environment.

- **Personal cloud storage:** A form of cloud storage that applies to storing an individual's data in the cloud and providing the individual with access to the data from anywhere. Personal cloud storage also often enables syncing and sharing stored data across multiple devices such as mobile phones and tablet computers.

- **Private cloud:** Describes a cloud computing platform that is implemented within the corporate firewall, under the control of the IT department. A private cloud is designed to offer the same features and benefits of cloud systems but removes a number of objections to the cloud computing model, including control over enterprise and customer data, worries about security, and issues connected to regulatory compliance.

- **Private cloud project:** Companies initiate private cloud projects to enable their IT infrastructure to become more capable of quickly adapting to continually evolving business needs and requirements. Private cloud projects can also be connected to public clouds to create hybrid clouds.

- **Private cloud security:** A private cloud implementation aims to avoid many of the objections regarding cloud computing security. Because a private cloud setup is implemented safely within the corporate firewall, it remains under the control of the IT department.

- **Private cloud storage:** A form of cloud storage in which both the enterprise data and the cloud storage resources reside within the enterprise's data center and behind the firewall.

- **Problem:** The unknown cause of one or more incidents, often identified as a result of multiple similar incidents.

- **Public cloud storage:** A form of cloud storage in which the enterprise and storage service provider are separate and the data is stored outside of the enterprise's data center.

- **Recovery point objective (RPO):** The RPO helps determine how much information must be recovered and restored. Another way of looking at the RPO is to ask yourself, "How much data can the company afford to lose?"

- **Recovery time objective (RTO):** A time measure of how fast you need each system to be up and running in the event of a disaster or critical failure.

- **SaaS:** A software delivery method that provides access to software and its functions remotely as a web-based service. SaaS allows organizations to access business functionality at a cost typically less than paying for licensed applications since SaaS pricing is based on a monthly fee.

- **Storage cloud:** Refers to the collection of multiple distributed and connected resources responsible for storing and managing data online in the cloud.

- **Vertical cloud computing:** Describes the optimization of cloud computing and cloud services for a particular vertical (for example, a specific industry) or specific-use application.

- **Virtual host:** A software implementation of a physical host.

CLOUD COMPUTING ROLES

The following groups form the key roles and functions associated with cloud computing. They do not constitute an exhaustive list but highlight the main roles and functions within cloud computing:

- **Cloud backup service provider:** A third-party entity that manages and holds operational responsibilities for cloud-based data backup services and solutions to customers from a central data center.

- **Cloud computing reseller:** A company that purchases hosting services from a cloud server hosting or cloud computing provider and then resells them to its own customers.

- **Cloud customer:** An individual or entity that utilizes or subscribes to cloud-based services or resources.

- **Cloud service auditor**: A third-party organization that verifies attainment of service-level agreements (SLAs).

- **Cloud services brokerage (CSB):** Typically a third-party entity or company that looks to extend or enhance value to multiple customers of cloud-based services through relationships with multiple CSPs. It acts as a liaison between cloud services customers and CSPs, selecting the best provider for each customer and monitoring the services. The CSB can be utilized as a middleman to broker the best deal and customize services to the customer's requirements. The CSB may also resell cloud services.

- **CSP:** A company that provides cloud-based platform, infrastructure, application, or storage services to other organizations or individuals, usually for a fee; otherwise known to clients "as a service."

KEY CLOUD COMPUTING CHARACTERISTICS

Think of the following as a rulebook or a set of laws when dealing with cloud computing. *If a service or solution does not meet all of the following key characteristics, it is not true cloud computing.*

- **On-demand self-service:** The cloud service provided that enables the provision of cloud resources on demand (whenever and wherever they are required). From a security perspective, this has introduced challenges to governing the use and provisioning of cloud-based services, which may violate organizational policies.

By its nature, on-demand self-service does not require procurement, provisioning, or approval from finance, and as such, it can be provisioned by almost anyone with a credit card. For enterprise customers, this is most likely the least important characteristic because self-service for the majority of end users is not of utmost importance.

- **Broad network access:** The cloud, by its nature, is an always on and always accessible offering for users to have widespread access to resources, data, and other assets. Think convenience—access what you want, when you need it, from any location.

In theory, all you should require is Internet access and relevant credentials and tokens, which give you access to the resources.

The mobile device and smart device revolution that is altering the way organizations fundamentally operate has introduced an interesting dynamic into the cloud conversation within many organizations. These devices should also be able to access the relevant resources that a user may require; however, compatibility issues, the inability to apply security controls effectively, and nonstandardization of platforms and software systems has stemmed this somewhat.

- **Resource pooling:** Lies at the heart of all that is good about cloud computing. More often than not, traditional, noncloud systems may see utilization rates for their resources between 80 percent and 90 percent for a few hours a week and rates at an average of 10 percent to 20 percent for the remainder. What the cloud looks to do is group (pool) resources for use across the user landscape or multiple clients, which can then scale and adjust to the user's or client's needs, based on their workload or resource requirements. CSPs typically have large numbers of resources available, from hundreds to thousands of servers, network devices, applications, and so on, which can accommodate large volumes of customers and can prioritize and facilitate appropriate resourcing for each client.

- **Rapid elasticity:** Allows the user to obtain additional resources, storage, compute power, and so on, as the user's need or workload requires. This is more often transparent to the user, with more resources added as necessary seamlessly.

Because cloud services utilize the pay-per-use concept, you pay for what you use. This is of particular benefit to seasonal or event-type businesses utilizing cloud services.

Think of a provider selling 100,000 tickets for a major sporting event or concert. Leading up to the ticket release date, little to no compute resources are needed; however, when the tickets go on sale, they may need to accommodate 100,000 users in the space of 30–40 minutes. This is where rapid elasticity and cloud computing can really be beneficial, compared with traditional IT deployments, which would have to invest heavily using capital expenditure (CapEx) to support such demand.

- **Measured service:** Cloud computing offers a unique and important component that traditional IT deployments have struggled to provide—resource usage can be measured, controlled, reported, and alerted upon, which results in multiple benefits and overall transparency between the provider and the client. In the same way you may have a metered electricity service or a mobile phone that you top up with credit, these services allow you to control and be aware of costs. Essentially, you pay for what you use and have the ability to get an itemized bill or breakdown of usage.

  A key benefit being availed by many proactive organizations is the ability to charge departments or business units for their use of services, thus allowing IT and finance to quantify exact usage and costs per department or by business function—something that was incredibly difficult to achieve in traditional IT environments.

In theory and in practice, cloud computing should have large resource pools to enable swift scaling, rapid movement, and flexibility to meet your needs at any given time within the bounds of your service subscription.

Without all these characteristics, it is simply not possible for the user to be confident and assured that the delivery and continuity of services will be maintained in line with potential growth or sudden scaling (either upward or downward). Without pooling and measured services, you cannot implement the cloud computing economic model.

CLOUD TRANSITION SCENARIO

Consider the following scenario.

Due to competitive pressures, XYZ Corp is hoping to better leverage the economic and scalable nature of cloud computing. These policies have driven XYZ Corp toward the consideration of a hybrid cloud model that consists of enterprise private and public cloud use. Although security risk has driven many of the conversations, a risk management approach has allowed the company to separate its data assets into two segments: sensitive and nonsensitive. IT governance guidelines must now be applied across the entire cloud platform and infrastructure security environment. This also affects infrastructure operational options. XYZ Corp must now apply cloud architectural concepts and design requirements that would best align with corporate business and security goals.

As a CCSP, you have several issues to address to guide XYZ Corp through its planned transition to a cloud architecture.

- What cloud deployment model(s) would need to be assessed to select the appropriate ones for the enterprise architecture?
  a. Based on the choice(s) made, additional issues may become apparent, such as these:
     i. Who will the audiences be?
     ii. What types of data will they be using and storing?
     iii. How will secure access to the cloud be enabled, audited, managed, and removed?
     iv. When and where will access be granted to the cloud? Under what constraints (time, location, platform, and so on)?
- What cloud service model(s) would need to be chosen for the enterprise architecture?
  a. Based on the choice(s) made, additional issues may become apparent, such as these:
     i. Who will the audiences be?
     ii. What types of data will they be using and storing?
     iii. How will secure access to the cloud service be enabled, audited, managed, and removed?
     iv. When and where will access be granted to the cloud service? Under what constraints (time, location, platform, and so on)?

Dealing with a scenario such as this requires the CCSP to work with the stakeholders in XYZ Corp to seek answers to the questions posed. In addition, the CCSP should carefully consider the information in Table 1.1 to craft a solution.

TABLE 1.1 **Possible Solutions**

INFORMATION ITEM	POSSIBLE SOLUTION
Hybrid cloud model	Outsourced hosting in partnership with on-premise IT support
Risk-management-driven data separation	Data classification scheme implemented company wide
IT governance guidelines	Coordination of all governance, risk, and compliance (GRC) activities within XYZ Corp through a chief risk officer (CRO) role
Cloud architecture alignment with business requirements	Requirements gathering and documentation exercise driven by a project management office (PMO) or a business analyst (BA) function

BUILDING BLOCKS

The building blocks of cloud computing are composed of random access memory (RAM), the central processing unit (CPU), storage, and networking. IaaS has the most fundamental building blocks of any cloud service: the processing, storage, and network infrastructure upon which all cloud applications are built. In a typical IaaS scenario, the service provider delivers the server, storage, and networking hardware and its virtualization, and then it's up to the customer to implement the OSs, middleware, and applications required.

CLOUD COMPUTING FUNCTIONS

As with traditional computing and technology environments, a number of functions are essential for creating, designing, implementing, testing, auditing, and maintaining the relevant assets. The same is true for cloud computing, with the following key roles representing a sample of the fundamental components and personnel required to operate cloud environments:

- **Cloud administrator:** This individual is typically responsible for the implementation, monitoring, and maintenance of the cloud within the organization or on behalf of an organization (acting as a third party).

  Most notably, this role involves the implementation of policies, permissions, access to resources, and so on. The cloud administrator works directly with system, network, and cloud storage administrators.

- **Cloud application architect:** This person is typically responsible for adapting, porting, or deploying an application to a target cloud environment.

  The main focus of this role is to work closely and alongside development and other design and implementation resources to ensure that an application's performance, reliability, and security are all maintained throughout the lifecycle of the application. This requires continuous assessment, verification, and testing throughout the various phases of both the software and systems development lifecycles.

  Most architects represent a mix or blend of system administration experience and domain-specific expertise—giving insight to the OS, domain, and other components, while identifying potential reasons the application may be experiencing performance degradation or other negative impacts.

- **Cloud architect:** This role determines when and how a private cloud meets the policies and needs of an organization's strategic goals and contractual requirements from a technical perspective.

  The cloud architect is also responsible for designing the private cloud, is involved in hybrid cloud deployments and instances, and has a key role in understanding and evaluating technologies, vendors, services, and other skillsets needed to deploy the private cloud or to establish and function the hybrid cloud components.

- **Cloud data architect:** This individual is similar to the cloud architect. The data architect's role is to ensure the various storage types and mechanisms utilized within the cloud environment meet and conform to the relevant SLAs and that the storage components are functioning according to their specified requirements.

- **Cloud developer:** This person focuses on development for the cloud infrastructure itself. This role can vary from client tools or solutions engagements to systems components. Although developers can operate independently or as part of a team, regular interactions with cloud administrators and security practitioners are required for debugging, code reviews, and relevant security assessment remediation requirements.

- **Cloud operator:** This individual is responsible for daily operational tasks and duties that focus on cloud maintenance and monitoring activities.

- **Cloud service manager:** This person is typically responsible for policy design, business agreement, pricing model, and some elements of the SLA (not necessarily the legal components or amendments that require contractual amendments). This role works closely with cloud management and customers to reach agreement and alongside the cloud administrator to implement SLAs and policies on behalf of the customers.

- **Cloud storage administrator:** This role focuses on the mapping, segregations, bandwidth, and reliability of storage volumes assigned. Additionally, this role may require ensuring that conformance to relevant SLAs continues to be met, working with and alongside network and cloud administrators.

CLOUD SERVICE CATEGORIES

Cloud service categories fall into three main groups: IaaS, PaaS, and SaaS. Each is discussed in the following sections.

IaaS

According to "The NIST Definition of Cloud Computing," in IaaS, "the capability provided to the consumer is to provision processing, storage, networks, and other fundamental computing resources where the consumer is able to deploy and run arbitrary software, which can include OSs and applications. The consumer does not manage or control the underlying cloud infrastructure but has control over OSs, storage, and deployed applications; and possibly limited control of select networking components (e.g., host firewalls)."[4]

Traditionally, infrastructure has always been the focal point for ensuring which capabilities and organization requirements could be met versus those that were restricted. It also represented possibly the most significant investments in terms of CapEx and skilled resources made by the organization. The emergence of the cloud has changed this traditional view of infrastructure's role significantly by commoditizing it and allowing it to be consumed through an on-demand, pay-as-you-go model.

IaaS Key Components and Characteristics

The following form the basis for the IaaS service model:

- **Scale:** The requirement for automation and tools to support the potentially significant workloads of either internal users or those across multiple cloud deployments (dependent on which cloud service offering) is a key component of IaaS. Users and customers require optimal levels of visibility, control, and assurances related to the infrastructure and its ability to satisfy their requirements.

- **Converged network and IT capacity pool:** This follows from the scale focus, but it looks to drill into the virtualization and service management components required to cover and provide appropriate levels of service across network boundaries.

  From a customer or user perspective, the pool appears seamless and endless (no visible barriers or restrictions, along with minimal requirement to initiate additional resources) for both the servers and the network. These are (or should be) driven and focused at all times in supporting and meeting relevant platform and application SLAs.

- **Self-service and on-demand capacity:** This requires an online resource or customer portal that allows the customers to have complete visibility and awareness of the virtual IaaS environment they currently utilize. It additionally allows customers to acquire, remove, manage, and report on resources, without the need to engage or speak with resources internally or with the provider.

- **High reliability and resilience:** To be effective, the requirement for automated distribution across the virtualized infrastructure is increasing and affording resilience, while enforcing and meeting SLA requirements.

IaaS Key Benefits

IaaS has a number of key benefits for organizations, which include but are not limited to the following:

- Usage metered and priced on the basis of units (or instances) consumed. This can also be billed back to specific departments or functions.

- The ability to scale up and down infrastructure services based on actual usage. This is particularly useful and beneficial when there are significant spikes and dips within the usage curve for infrastructure.

- Reduced cost of ownership. There is no need to buy assets for everyday use, no loss of asset value over time, and reduced costs of maintenance and support.

- Reduced energy and cooling costs along with "green IT" environment effect with optimum use of IT resources and systems.

Significant and notable providers in the IaaS space include Amazon, AT&T, Rackspace, Verizon/Terremark, and HP, among others.

PaaS

According to "The NIST Definition of Cloud Computing," in PaaS, "the capability provided to the consumer is to deploy onto the cloud infrastructure consumer-created or acquired applications created using programming languages, libraries, services, and tools supported by the provider. The consumer does not manage or control the underlying cloud infrastructure, including network, servers, OSs, or storage, but has control over the deployed applications and possibly configuration settings for the application-hosting environment."[5]

PaaS and the cloud platform components have revolutionized the manner in which development and software has been delivered to customers and users over the past few years. The barrier for entry in terms of costs, resources, capabilities, and ease of use have dramatically reduced time to market—promoting and harvesting the innovative culture within many organizations.

PaaS Key Capabilities and Characteristics

Outside of the key benefits, PaaS should have the following key capabilities and characteristics:

- **Support multiple languages and frameworks:** PaaS should support multiple programming languages and frameworks, thus enabling the developers to code in whichever language they prefer or whatever the design requirements specify.

  In recent times, significant strides and efforts have been taken to ensure that open source stacks are both supported and utilized, thus reducing lock-in or issues with interoperability when changing CSPs.

- **Multiple hosting environments:** The ability to support a wide choice and variety of underlying hosting environments for the platform is key to meeting customer requirements and demands. Whether public cloud, private cloud, local hypervisor, or bare metal, supporting multiple hosting environments allows the application developer or administrator to migrate the application when and as required. This can also be used as a form of contingency and continuity and to ensure ongoing availability.

- **Flexibility:** Traditionally, platform providers provided features and requirements that they felt suited the client requirements, along with what suited their service offering and positioned them as the provider of choice, with limited options for the customers to move easily.

  This has changed drastically, with extensibility and flexibility now offered to meet the needs and requirements of developer audiences. This has been heavily influenced by open source, which allows relevant plug-ins to be quickly and efficiently introduced into the platform.

- **Allow choice and reduce lock-in:** Learning from previous horror stories and restrictions, proprietary meant red tape, barriers, and restrictions on what developers could do when it came to migration or adding features and components to the platform. Although the requirement to code to specific application programming interfaces (APIs) was made available by the provider, developers could run their apps in various environments based on commonality and standard API structures, ensuring a level of consistency and quality for customers and users.

- **Ability to auto-scale:** This enables the application to seamlessly scale up and down as required to accommodate the cyclical demands of users. The platform will allocate resources and assign these to the application, as required. This serves as a key driver for any seasonal organizations that experience spikes and drops in usage.

PaaS Key Benefits

PaaS has a number of key benefits for developers, which include but are not limited to these:

- OSs can be changed and upgraded frequently, including associated features and system services.

- Globally distributed development teams are able to work together on software development projects within the same environment.

- Services are available and can be obtained from diverse sources that cross national and international boundaries.

- Upfront and recurring or ongoing costs can be significantly reduced by utilizing a single vendor instead of maintaining multiple hardware facilities and environments.

Significant and notable providers in the PaaS space include Microsoft, OpenStack, and Google, among others.

SaaS

According to "The NIST Definition of Cloud Computing," in SaaS, "The capability provided to the consumer is to use the provider's applications running on a cloud infrastructure. The applications are accessible from various client devices through either a thin client interface, such as a web browser (e.g., web-based email), or a program interface. The consumer does not manage or control the underlying cloud infrastructure including networks, servers, operating systems, storage, or even individual application capabilities, with the possible exception of limited user-specific application configuration settings."[6]

SaaS Delivery Models

Within SaaS, two delivery models are currently used:

- **Hosted application management (hosted AM):** The provider hosts commercially available software for customers and delivers it over the Web (Internet).

- **Software on demand:** The CSP gives customers network-based access to a single copy of an application created specifically for SaaS distribution (typically within the same network segment).

SaaS Benefits

Cloud computing provides significant and potentially limitless possibilities for organizations to run programs and applications that may previously have not been practical or feasible given the limitations of their own systems, infrastructure, or resources.

When utilizing and deploying the right middleware and associated components, the ability to run and execute programs with the flexibility, scalability, and on-demand self-service capabilities can present massive incentives and benefits for scalability, usability, reliability, productivity, and cost savings.

Clients can access their applications and data from anywhere at any time. They can access the cloud computing system using any computer linked to the Internet. Other capabilities and benefits related to the application include these:

- **Overall reduction of costs:** Cloud deployments reduce the need for advanced hardware to be deployed on the client side. Essentially, requirements to purchase high specification systems, redundancy, storage, and so on, to support applications are no longer necessary. From a customer perspective, a device to connect to the relevant application with the appropriate middleware is all that should be required.

- **Application and software licensing:** Customers no longer need to purchase licenses, support, and associated costs because licensing is leased and is relevant only when in use (covered by the provider). Additionally, purchasing of bulk licensing and the associated CapEx is removed and replaced by a pay-per-use licensing model.

- **Reduced support costs:** Customers save money on support issues because the relevant CSP handles them. Appropriately managed, owned, and operated streamlined hardware would, in theory, have fewer problems than a network of heterogeneous machines and OSs.

SaaS has a number of key benefits for organizations, which include but are not limited to these:

- Ease of use and limited administration.
- Automatic updates and patch management. The user is always running the latest version and most up-to-date deployment of the software release as well as any relevant security updates (no manual patching required).
- Standardization and compatibility. All users have the same version of the software release.
- Global accessibility.

Significant and notable providers in the SaaS space include Microsoft, Google, Salesforce.com, Oracle, and SAP, among others.

CLOUD DEPLOYMENT MODELS

Cloud deployment models fall into four main types of clouds: public, private, hybrid, and community.

Now that you are equipped with an understanding and appreciation of the cloud service types, you will learn how these services are merged into the relevant deployment models. The selection of a cloud deployment model will depend on any number of factors and may be heavily influenced by your organization's risk appetite, cost, compliance and regulatory requirements, and legal obligations, along with other internal business decisions and strategy.

The Public Cloud Model

According to NIST, "the cloud infrastructure is provisioned for open use by the general public. It may be owned, managed, and operated by a business, academic, or government organization, or some combination of them. It exists on the premises of the cloud provider."[7]

Public Cloud Benefits

The following are typical key drivers or benefits of a public cloud:

- Easy and inexpensive setup because the provider covers hardware, application, and bandwidth costs

- Streamlined and easy-to-provision resources

- Scalability to meet customer needs

- No wasted resources—pay as you consume

Given the increasing demands for public cloud services, many providers are now offering and remodeling their services as public cloud offerings. Significant and notable providers in the public cloud space include Amazon, Microsoft, Salesforce, and Google, among others.

The Private Cloud Model

According to NIST, "the cloud infrastructure is provisioned for exclusive use by a single organization comprising multiple consumers (e.g., business units). It may be owned, managed, and operated by the organization, a third party, or some combination of them, and it may exist on or off premises."[8]

A private cloud is typically managed by the organization it serves; however, outsourcing the general management of this to trusted third parties may also be an option. A private cloud is typically available only to the entity or organization, its employees, contractors, and selected third parties.

The private cloud is also sometimes referred to as the *internal* or *organizational cloud*.

Private Cloud Benefits

Key drivers or benefits of a private cloud typically include these:

- Increased control over data, underlying systems, and applications

- Ownership and retention of governance controls

- Assurance over data location and removal of multiple jurisdiction legal and compliance requirements

Private clouds are typically more popular among large, complex organizations with legacy systems and heavily customized environments. Additionally, where significant technology investment has been made, it may be more financially viable to utilize and incorporate these investments within a private cloud environment than to discard or retire such devices.

The Hybrid Cloud Model

According to NIST, "the cloud infrastructure is a composition of two or more distinct cloud infrastructures (private, community, or public) that remain unique entities, but are bound together by standardized or proprietary technology that enables data and application portability (e.g., cloud bursting for load balancing between clouds)."[9]

Hybrid cloud computing is gaining in popularity because it enables organizations to retain control of their IT environments, coupled with the convenience of allowing organizations to use public cloud service to fulfill non-mission-critical workloads and taking advantage of flexibility, scalability, and cost savings.

Hybrid Cloud Benefits

Key drivers or benefits of hybrid cloud deployments include these:

- Retain ownership and oversight of critical tasks and processes related to technology.

- Reuse previous investments in technology within the organization.

- Control the most critical business components and systems.

- Act as a cost-effective means of fulfilling noncritical business functions (utilizing public cloud components).

- Enhance cloud bursting and DR by hybrid cloud deployments. Cloud bursting allows for public cloud resources to be utilized when a private cloud workload has reached maximum capacity.

The Community Cloud Model

According to NIST, "the cloud infrastructure is provisioned for exclusive use by a specific community of consumers from organizations that have shared concerns (e.g., mission, security requirements, policy, and compliance considerations). It may be owned, managed, and operated by one or more of the organizations in the community, a third party, or some combination of them, and it may exist on or off premises."[10]

Community clouds can be on-premises or offsite and should give the benefits of a public cloud deployment, while providing heightened levels of privacy, security, and regulatory compliance.

CLOUD CROSS-CUTTING ASPECTS

The deployment of cloud solutions, by its nature, is often deemed a technology decision; however, it's truly a business alignment decision. Although cloud computing no doubt enables technology to be delivered and utilized in a unique manner, potentially unleashing multiple benefits, the choice to deploy and consume cloud services should be a business decision, taken in line with the business or organization's overall strategy.

Why is it a business decision, you ask? Two distinct reasons:

- All technology decisions should be made with the overall business direction and strategy at the core.
- When it comes to funding and creating opportunities, these should be made at a business level.

A cloud transition's ability to directly support organizational business or mission goals and to express that message in a business manner is the difference between a successful project and a failed project in the eyes of the organization.

Architecture Overview

The architect is a planner, strategist, and consultant who sees the "big picture" of the organization. He understands current needs, thinks strategically, and plans long into the future. Perhaps the most important role of the architect today is to understand the business and how to design the systems that the business will require. This allows the architect to determine which system types, development, and configurations meet the identified business requirements while addressing any security concerns.

Enterprise security architecture provides the conceptual design of network security infrastructure and related security mechanisms, policies, and procedures. It links components of the security infrastructure as a cohesive unit with the goal of protecting corporate information. The Cloud Security Alliance (CSA) provides a general enterprise architecture (*Figure 1.4*). The CSA Enterprise Architecture is located at `https://cloudsecurityalliance.org/`.

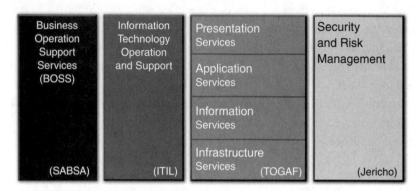

FIGURE 1.4 **CSA Enterprise Architecture.**

See the following sections for a starting point to reference the building blocks of the CSA Enterprise Architecture.

Sherwood Applied Business Security Architecture

Sherwood Applied Business Security Architecture (SABSA)[11] includes the following components, which can be used separately or together:

- Business Requirements Engineering Framework
- Risk and Opportunity Management Framework
- Policy Architecture Framework
- Security Services-Oriented Architecture Framework
- Governance Framework
- Security Domain Framework
- Through-Life Security Service Management and Performance Management Framework

Information Technology Infrastructure Library

Information Technology Infrastructure Library (ITIL)[12] is a group of documents that are used in implementing a framework for IT service management. ITIL forms a customizable framework that defines how service management is applied throughout an organization. ITIL is organized into a series of five volumes: Service Strategy, Service Design, Service Transition, Service Operation, and Continual Service Improvement.

The Open Group Architecture Framework

The Open Group Architecture Framework (TOGAF)[13] is one of many frameworks available to the cloud security professional for developing an enterprise architecture. TOGAF provides a standardized approach that can be used to address business needs by providing a common lexicon for business communication. TOGAF is based on open methods and approaches to enterprise architecture, allowing the business to avoid a lock-in scenario from the use of proprietary approaches. TOGAF also provides for the ability to quantifiably measure return on investment (ROI) so that the business can use resources more efficiently.

Jericho/Open Group

The Jericho forum now is part of the Open Group Security Forum.[14] You can find the Jericho Forum Cloud Cube Model at `https://collaboration.opengroup.org/ jericho/cloud_cube_model_v1.0.pdf`

Key Principles of an Enterprise Architecture

The following principles should be adhered to at all times:

- Define protections that enable trust in the cloud.
- Develop cross-platform capabilities and patterns for proprietary and open source providers.
- Facilitate trusted and efficient access, administration, and resiliency to the customer or consumer.
- Provide direction to secure information that is protected by regulations.
- Facilitate proper and efficient identification, authentication, authorization, administration, and auditability.
- Centralize security policy, maintenance operation, and oversight functions.
- Make access to information both secure and easy to obtain.
- Delegate or federate access control where appropriate.
- Ensure ease of adoption and consumption, supporting the design of security patterns.
- Make the architecture elastic, flexible, and resilient, supporting multitenant, multilandlord platforms.
- Ensure the architecture addresses and supports multiple levels of protection, including network, OS, and application security needs.

The NIST Cloud Technology Roadmap

The NIST Cloud Technology Roadmap helps CSPs develop industry-recommended, secure, and interoperable identity, access, and compliance management configurations and practices. It offers guidance and recommendations for enabling security architects, enterprise architects, and risk-management professionals to leverage a common set of solutions that fulfill their common needs to be able to assess where their internal IT and CSPs are in terms of security capabilities and to plan a roadmap to meet the security needs of their business.[15]

There are a number of key components that the cloud security professional should comprehensively review and understand to determine which controls and techniques may be required to adequately address the requirements discussed in the following sections.

Interoperability

Interoperability defines how easy it is to move and reuse application components regardless of the provider, platform, OS, infrastructure, location, storage, format of data or APIs, how well applications work together, and how well new applications work with other solutions present in the business, organization, or provider's existing architecture.

Standards-based products, processes, and services are essential for entities to ensure the following:

- Investments do not become prematurely technologically obsolete.

- Organizations are able to easily change CSPs to flexibly and cost effectively support their mission.

- Organizations can economically acquire commercial and develop private clouds using standards-based products, processes, and services.

Interoperability mandates that those components should be replaceable by new or different components from different providers and continue to work, as should the exchange of data between systems.

Portability

Portability is a key aspect to consider when selecting CSPs because it can both help prevent vendor lock-in and deliver business benefits by allowing identical cloud deployments to occur in different CSP solutions, either for the purposes of DR or for the global deployment of a distributed single solution.

Availability

Systems and resource availability defines the success or failure of a cloud-based service. As a single point of failure (SPOF) for cloud-based services, where the service or cloud deployment loses availability, the customer is unable to access target assets or resources, resulting in downtime.

In many cases, CSPs are required to provide upward of 99.9 percent availability as per the SLA. Failure to do so can result in penalties, reimbursement of fees, loss of customers, loss of confidence, and ultimately brand and reputational damage.

Security

For many customers and potential cloud users, security remains the biggest concern, with security continuing to act as a barrier preventing them from engaging with cloud services.

As with any successful security program, the ability to measure, obtain assurance, and integrate contractual obligations to minimum levels of security are the keys to success.

Many CSPs now list their typical or minimum levels of security but will not list or publicly state specific security controls for fear of being targeted by attackers who would have the knowledge necessary to successfully compromise their networks.

Where such contracts and engagements require specific security controls and techniques to be applied, these are typically seen as extras. They incur additional costs and require that the relevant nondisclosure agreements (NDAs) be completed before engaging in active discussions.

In many cases, for smaller organizations, a move to cloud-based services significantly enhances their security controls, given that they may not have access to or possess the relevant security capabilities of a large-scale cloud computing provider.

The general rule of thumb for security controls and requirements in cloud-based environments is based on "if you want additional security, additional cost will be incurred." You can have almost whatever you want when it comes to cloud security—just as long as you can find the right provider and you are willing to pay for it.

Privacy

In the world of cloud computing, privacy presents a major challenge for both customers and providers alike. The reason for this is simple: no uniform or international privacy directives, laws, regulations, or controls exist, leading to a separate, disparate, and segmented mesh of laws and regulations being applicable depending on the geographic location where the information may reside (data at rest) or be transmitted (data in transit).

Although many of the leading providers of cloud services make provisions to ensure the location and legislative requirements (including contractual obligations) are met, this should never be taken as a given and should be specified within relevant SLAs and contracts. Given the true global nature and various international locations of cloud computing data centers, the potential for data to reside in two, three, or more locations around the world at any given time is a real possibility.

For many European entities and organizations, failure to ensure appropriate provisions and controls have been applied can violate EU data protection laws and obligations that can lead to various issues and implications.

Within Europe, privacy is seen as a human right and as such should be treated with the utmost respect. Not bypassing the various state laws across the United States and other geographic locations can make the job of the cloud architect extremely complex, requiring an intricate level of knowledge and controls to ensure that no such violations or breaches of privacy and data protection occur.

Resiliency

Cloud resiliency represents the ability of a cloud services data center and its associated components, including servers, storage, and so on, to continue operating in the event of a disruption, which may be equipment failure, power outage, or a natural disaster.

Given that most CSPs have a significantly higher number of devices and redundancy in place than a standard in-house IT team, resiliency should typically be far higher, with equipment and capabilities being ready to fail over, multiple layers of redundancy, and enhanced exercises to test such capabilities.

Performance

Cloud computing and high performance should go hand in hand at all times. Let's face it—if the performance is poor, you may not be a customer for very long. For optimum performance to be experienced through the use of cloud services, the provisioning, elasticity, and other associated components should always focus on performance.

The speed at which you can travel by boat depends on the engine and the boat design. The same applies for performance, which at all times should be focused on the network, the computer, the storage, and the data.

With these four elements influencing the design, integration, and development activities, performance should be boosted and enhanced throughout. It is always harder to refine and amend performance once design and development have been completed.

Governance

The term *governance* relating to processes and decisions looks to define actions, assign responsibilities, and verify performance. The same can be said and adopted for cloud services and environments, where the goal is to secure applications and data when in transit and at rest. In many cases, cloud governance is an extension of the existing organizational or traditional business process governance, with a slightly altered risk and controls landscape.

Although governance is required from the commencement of a cloud strategy or cloud migration roadmap, it is seen as a recurring activity and should be performed on an ongoing basis.

A key benefit of many cloud-based services is the ability to access relevant reporting, metrics, and up-to-date statistics related to usage, actions, activities, downtime, outages, updates, and so on. This may enhance and streamline governance and oversight activities with the addition of scheduled and automated reporting.

Note that processes, procedures, and activities may require revision postmigration or movement to a cloud-based environment. Not all processes remain the same, with segregation of duties, reporting, and incident management forming a sample of processes that may require revision after the cloud migration.

SLAs

Think of a rulebook and legal contract all rolled into one document—that's what you have in terms of an SLA. In the SLA, the minimum levels of service, availability, security, controls, processes, communications, support, and many other crucial business elements are stated and agreed upon by both parties.

Many may argue that the SLAs are heavily weighted in favor of the CSP, but there are several key benefits when compared with traditional-based environments or in-house IT. These include downtime, upgrades, updates, patching, vulnerability testing, application coding, test and development, support, and release management. Many of these require the provider to take these areas and activities seriously; failing to do so affects their bottom line.

Note that not all SLAs cover the areas or focus points with which you may have issues or concerns. When this is not the case, every effort should be made to obtain clarity prior to engaging with the CSP services.

Auditability

Auditability allows for users and the organization to access, report, and obtain evidence of actions, controls, and processes that were performed or run by a specified user.

Similar to standard audit trails and systems logging, systems auditing and reporting are offered as standard by many of the leading CSPs.

From a customer perspective, increased confidence and the ability to have evidence to support audits, reviews, or assessments of object-level or systems-level access form key drivers.

From a stakeholder, management, and assessment perspective, auditability provides mechanisms to review, assess, and report user and systems activities. Auditability in non-cloud environments can focus on financial reporting, whereas cloud-based auditability focuses on actions and activities of users and systems.

Regulatory Compliance

Regulatory compliance is an organization's requirement to adhere to relevant laws, regulations, guidelines, and specifications relevant to its business, specifically dictated by the nature, operations, and functions it provides or utilizes to its customers. When the organization fails to meet or violates regulatory compliance regulations, punishment can include legal actions, fines, and, in limited cases, halting business operations or practices.

Key regulatory areas that are often included in cloud-based environments include but are not limited to the Payment Card Industry Data Security Standard (PCI DSS), the Health Insurance Portability and Accountability Act (HIPAA), the Federal Information Security Management Act (FISMA), and the Sarbanes-Oxley Act (SOX).

NETWORK SECURITY AND PERIMETER

Network security looks to cover all relevant security components of the underlying physical environment and the logical security controls that are inherent in the service or available to be consumed as a service (SaaS, PaaS, and IaaS). Two key elements need to be drawn out at this point:

- Physical environment security ensures that access to the cloud service is adequately distributed, monitored, and protected by underlying physical resources within which the service is built.
- Logical network security controls consist of link, protocol, and application layer services.

As a cloud customer and a CSP, both data and systems security are of utmost importance. The goal from both sides is to ensure the ongoing availability, integrity, and confidentiality of all systems and resources. Failure to do so has a negative impact from a customer, confidence, brand awareness, and overall security posture standpoint.

Taking into account that cloud computing requires a high volume of constant connections to and from the network devices, the always on and always available elements are necessary and essential.

In the cloud environments, the classic definition of a network perimeter takes on different meanings under different guises and deployment models.

- For many cloud networks, the perimeter is clearly the demarcation point.

- For other cloud networks, the perimeter transforms into a series of highly dynamic micro-borders around individual customer solutions or services (to the level of certain data sets and flows within a solution) within the same cloud, consisting of virtual network components.

- In other cloud networks, there is no clear perimeter at all. Although the network may be typically viewed as a perimeter and a number of devices within those perimeters communicating both internally and externally, this may be somewhat less clear and segregated in cloud computing networks.

Next, you will look at some of the add-on components that strengthen and enhance the overall security posture of cloud-based networks. You will see how to utilize them and learn why they play a fundamental function in technology deployments today.

CRYPTOGRAPHY

The need for the use of cryptography and encryption is universal for the provisioning and protection of confidentiality services in the enterprise. In support of that goal, the CCSP should ensure that he understands how to deploy and use cryptography services in a cloud environment. In addition, it's important to integrate strong key management services and a secure key management lifecycle into the cryptography solution.

Encryption

The need for confidentiality along with the requirement to apply additional security controls and mechanisms to protect information and communications is great. Whether it is encryption to a military standard or simply the use of self-signed certificates, everyone has different requirements and definitions of what a secure communications and cryptography-based infrastructure looks like. As with many areas of security, encryption can be subjective when you drill down into the algorithms, strengths, ciphers, implementation methods, and so on.

As a general rule of thumb, encryption mechanisms should be selected based on the information and data they protect, while taking into account requirements for access and general functions. The critical success factor for encryption is to enable secure and legitimate access to resources, while protecting and enforcing controls against unauthorized access.

The cloud architect and administrator should explore the appropriate encryption and access measures to ensure that proper separation of tenants' information and access is deployed within public cloud environments. Additionally, encryption and relevant controls need to be applied to private and hybrid cloud deployments to adequately and sufficiently protect communications between hosts and services across various network components and systems.

Data in Transit (Data in Motion)

Also described or termed *data in motion*, data in transit focuses on information or data while in transmission across systems and components typically across internal and external (untrusted) networks. Where information is crossing or traversing trusted and untrusted networks, the opportunity for interception, sniffing, or unauthorized access is heightened.

Data in transit can include the following scenarios:

- Data transiting from an end user endpoint (laptop, desktop, smart device, and so on) on the Internet to a web-facing service in the cloud
- Data moving between machines within the cloud (including between different cloud services), such as between a web virtual machine (VM) and a database
- Data traversing trusted and untrusted networks (cloud- and non-cloud-based environments)

Typically, the cloud architect is responsible for reviewing the way data in transit will be protected or secured at the design phase. Special consideration should be focused on how the cloud will integrate, communicate, and allow for interoperability across boundaries and hybrid technologies. Once implemented, the ongoing management and responsibility of data in transit resides in the correct application of security controls, including the relevant cryptography processes to handle key management.

Perhaps the best-known use of cryptography for the data in transit scenario is secure sockets layer (SSL) and transport layer security (TLS). TLS provides a transport layer–encrypted "tunnel" between email servers or message transfer agents (MTAs), whereas SSL certificates encrypt private communications over the Internet using private and public keys.

These cryptographic protocols have been in use for many years in the form of hypertext transfer protocol secure (HTTPS), typically to provide communication security over the Internet, but it has now become the standard and de facto encryption approach for browser-to-web host and host-to-host communications in both cloud and noncloud environments.

Recent increases show a number of cloud-based providers using multiple factors of encryption, coupled with the ability for users to encrypt their own data at rest within the cloud environment. The use of symmetric cryptography for key exchange followed by symmetric encryption for content confidentiality is also increasing.

This approach looks to bolster and enhance standard encryption levels and strengths of encryption. Additionally, IP security (IPSec), which has been used extensively, is a transit encryption protocol widely used and adopted for virtual private network (VPN) tunnels; it makes use of cryptography algorithms such as Triple DES (3DES) and Advanced Encryption Standard (AES).

Data at Rest

Data at rest focuses on information or data while stagnant or at rest (typically not in use) within systems, networks, or storage volumes. When data is at rest, appropriate and suitable security controls need to be applied to ensure the ongoing confidentiality and integrity of information.

Encryption of stored data, or data at rest, continues to gain traction for both cloud-based and non-cloud-based environments. The cloud architect is typically responsible for the design and assessment of encryption algorithms for use within cloud environments. Of key importance for both security and performance is the deployment and implementation of encryption on the target hosts and platforms.

The selection and testing of encryption form an essential component prior to ensuring performance impacts. In some cases, encryption can affect performance.

User interface (UI) response times and processor capabilities are up to a quarter or even half of the processor in an unencrypted environment. This varies depending on the type, strength, and algorithm. In high-performing environments with significant processor and utilization requirements, encryption of data at rest may not be included or utilized as standard.

Encryption of data at rest provides, assists, and assures organizations that opportunities for unauthorized access or viewing of data through information spills or residual data are further reduced.

Note that when information is encrypted on the CSP side and in the event of discrepancies or disputes with the providers, it may prove challenging to obtain or extract your data.

Key Management

In the old traditional banking environments, two people with keys were required to open the safe; this led to a reduced number of thefts, crimes, and bank robberies. Encryption, as with bank processes, should never be handled or addressed by a single person.

Encryption and segregation of duties should always go hand in hand. Key management should be separated from the provider hosting the data, and the data owners should be positioned to make decisions (these may be in line with organizational policies) but ultimately should be in a position to apply encryption, control, and manage key management processes, select the storage location for the encryption keys (on-premises in an isolated location is typically the best security option), and retain ownership and responsibilities for key management.

The Importance of Key Management

From a security perspective, you remove the dependency or assumption that the CSP is handling the encryption processes and controls correctly.

Also, you are not bound or restricted by shared keys or data spillage within the cloud environments because you have a unique and separate encryption mechanism to apply an additional level of security and confidentiality at a data and transport level.

Common Approaches to Key Management

For cloud computing key management services, the following two approaches are most commonly utilized:

- **Remote Key Management Service (KMS):** This is where the customer maintains the KMS on-premises. Ideally, the customer will own, operate, and maintain the KMS. This way the customer can control the information confidentiality, and the CSP can focus on the hosting, processing, and availability of services.

  Note that hybrid connectivity is required between the CSP and the cloud customer for the encryption and decryption to function.

- **Client-Side Key Management:** Similarly to the remote KMS approach, the client-side approach looks to put the customer or cloud user in complete control of the encryption and decryption keys.

  The main difference here is that most of the processing and control is done on the customer side. The CSP provides the KMS; however, the KMS resides on the customer's premises, where the customer generates, holds, and retains the keys. Note that this approach is typically utilized for SaaS environments and cloud deployments.

As with most areas of technology, access control is merging and aligning with other combined activities. Some of these are automated using single sign-on capabilities; others operate in a standalone, segregated fashion.

The combination of access control and effective management of those technologies, processes, and controls has given rise to identity and access management (IAM). In a nutshell, IAM includes people, processes, and systems that manage access to enterprise resources. This is achieved by ensuring that the identity of an entity is verified (who are they, can they prove who they are) and then granting the correct level of access based on the assets, services, and protected resources being accessed.

IAM typically looks to utilize a minimum of two—preferably three or more—factors of authentication. Within cloud environments, services should include strong authentication mechanisms for validating users' identities and credentials. In line with best practice, one-time passwords should be utilized as a risk reduction and mitigation technique.

The key phases that form the basis and foundation for IAM in the enterprise include the following:

- Provisioning and deprovisioning
- Centralized directory services
- Privileged user management
- Authentication and access management

Each is discussed in the following sections.

Provisioning and Deprovisioning

Provisioning and deprovisioning are critical aspects of access management. Think of setting up and removing users. In the same way as you would set up an account for a user entering your organization requiring access to resources, provisioning is the process of creating accounts to allow users to access appropriate systems and resources within the cloud environment.

The ultimate goal of user provisioning is to standardize, streamline, and create an efficient account creation process, while creating a consistent, measurable, traceable, and auditable framework for providing access to end users.

Deprovisioning is the process whereby a user account is disabled when the user no longer requires access to the cloud-based services and resources. This is not just limited to a user leaving the organization but may also be due to a user changing a role, function, or department.

Deprovisioning is a risk-mitigation technique to ensure that authorization creep or additional and historical privileges are not retained, thus granting access to data, assets, and resources that are not necessary to fulfill the job role.

Centralized Directory Services

As when building a house or large structure, the foundation is key. In the world of IAM, the directory service forms the foundation for IAM and security both in an enterprise environment and within a cloud deployment. A directory service stores, processes, and facilitates a structured repository of information stored, coupled with unique identifiers and locations.

The primary protocol in relation to centralized directory services is Lightweight Directory Access Protocol (LDAP), built and focused on the X.500 standard.[16] LDAP works as an application protocol for querying and modifying items in directory service providers like Active Directory. Active Directory is a database-based system that offers authentication, directory, policy, and other services to a network.

Essentially, LDAP acts as a communication protocol to interact with Active Directory. LDAP directory servers store their data hierarchically (similar to domain name system [DNS] trees and UNIX file structures) with a directory record's distinguished name (DN) read from the individual entries back through the tree, up to the top level.

Each entry in an LDAP directory server is identified through a DN access to directory services, should be part of the IAM solution, and should be as robust as the core authentication modes used.

The use of privileged identity management (PIM) features is strongly encouraged for managing access of the administrators of the directory. If these are hosted locally rather than in the cloud, the IAM service requires connectivity to the local LDAP servers, in addition to any applications and services for which it is managing access.

Within cloud environments, directory services are heavily utilized and depended upon as the go-to trusted source by the IAM framework as a security repository of identity and access information. The same can be said for federated environments. Again, trust and confidence in the accuracy and integrity of the directory services are must-haves.

Privileged User Management

As the names implies, privileged user management focuses on the process and ongoing requirements to manage the lifecycle of user accounts with highest privileges in a system. Privileged accounts typically carry the highest risk and impact because compromised privileged user accounts can lead to significant permissions and access rights being obtained, thus allowing the user or attacker to access resources and assets that may negatively affect the organization.

The key components from a security perspective relating to privileged user management should, at a minimum, include the ability to track usage, authentication successes and failures, and authorization times and dates; log successful and failed events; enforce password management; and contain sufficient levels of auditing and reporting related to privileged user accounts.

Many organizations monitor this level of information for standard or general users, which would be beneficial and useful in the event of an investigation; however, the privileged accounts should capture this level of detail by default because attackers often target and compromise a general or standard user, with the view to escalating privileges to a more privileged or admin account. Not forgetting that a number of these components are technical by nature, the overall requirements that are used to manage these should be driven by organizational policies and procedures.

Note that segregation of duties can form an extremely effective mitigation and risk-reduction technique around privileged users and their ability to effect major changes.

Authorization and Access Management

Access to devices, systems, and resources forms a key driver for use of cloud services (broad network access); without it, the overall benefits that the service may provide are reduced to the enterprise, and legitimate business or organizational users are isolated from their resources and assets.

In the same way that users require authorization and access management to be operating and functioning to access the required resources, security requires these service components to be functional, operational, and trusted to enforce security within cloud environments.

In its simplest form, authorization determines the user's right to access a certain resource. (Think of entry onto a plane with your reserved seat or when you may be visiting an official residence or government agency to visit a specified person.)

Access management is focused on the manner and way in which users can access relevant resources, based on their credentials and characteristics of their identity. (Think of a bank or highly secure venue—only certain employees or personnel can access the main safe or highly sensitive areas.)

Note that both authorization and access management are point-in-time activities that rely on the accuracy and ongoing availability of resources and functioning processes, segregation of duties, privileged user management, password management, and so on, to operate and provide the desired levels of security. If one of the mentioned activities is not carried out regularly as part of an ongoing managed process, it can weaken the overall security posture.

DATA AND MEDIA SANITIZATION

By its nature, cloud-based environments are typically hosting multiple types, structures, and components of data among various resources, components, and services for users to access. If you want to leave or migrate from one CSP to another, this may be possible with little hassle, although other entities have experienced significant challenges in removing and exporting their large amounts of structured data from one provider to another. This is where vendor lock-in and interoperability elements come to the fore. It's also necessary to consider data and media sanitization. The ability to safely remove all data from a system or media, rendering it inaccessible, is critical to ensuring confidentiality and to managing a secure lifecycle for data in the cloud.

Vendor Lock-In

Vendor lock-in highlights where a customer may be unable to leave, migrate, or transfer to an alternate provider because of technical or nontechnical constraints. Typically, this could be based on the technology, platforms, or system design that may be proprietary or because of a dispute between the provider and the customer. Vendor lock-in poses a real risk for an organization that may not be in a position to leave the current provider or indeed continue with business operations and services.

Additionally, where a specific proprietary service or structure has been used to store your vast amounts of information, this may not support the intelligent export into a structured format. For example, how many organizations would be pleased with 100,000 records being exported into a flat-based text file? Open APIs are being strongly championed as a mechanism to reduce this challenge.

Aside from the hassle and general issues associated with reconstructing and formatting large data sets into a format that could be imported and integrated into a new cloud service or CSP, the challenge related to secure deletion or the sanitization of digital media remains a largely unsolved issue among CSPs and cloud customers alike.

Most organizations have failed to assess or factor in this challenge in the absence of a cloud computing strategy, and ultimately many have not put highly sensitive or regulated data in cloud-based environments as yet. This is likely to change with the shift toward compliant clouds and cloud-based environments aligned with certification standards such as ISO 27001/2, SOC 2, and PCI DSS among other international frameworks.

In the absence of degaussing, which is not a practical or realistic option for cloud environments, the approach for rendering data unreadable should be the first option taken (assuming the physical destruction of storage areas is not feasible). Adopting a security mind-set, if you can restrict the availability, integrity, and confidentiality of the data, you can then make the information unreadable, which will act as the next best method to secure deletion. How might you achieve this in cloud-based environments?

Cryptographic Erasure

A fairly reliable way to sanitize a device is to erase or overwrite the data it contains. With the recent developments in storage devices, most now contain built-in sanitize commands that enable users and custodians to sanitize media in a simple and convenient format. Although these commands are mostly effective when implemented and initiated correctly, like all technological commands, it is essential to verify their effectiveness and accuracy.

Where possible (this may not apply to all cloud-based environments), erase each block, overwrite all with a known pattern, and erase them again.

When done correctly, a complete erasure of the storage media eliminates risks related to key recovery (where stored locally—yes, this is a common mistake), side-channel attacks on controller to recover information about the destroyed key, and future attacks on the cryptosystem.

Note that key destruction on its own is not a comprehensive approach because the key may be recovered using forensic techniques.

Data Overwriting

Although it is not inherently secure and does not make the data irretrievable, overwriting data multiple times can make the task of retrieval far more complex, challenging, and time consuming. This technique may not be sufficient if you are hosting highly sensitive, confidential, or regulated information within cloud deployments.

When you delete files and data, they become invisible to the user; however, the space they inhabit in the storage media is made available for other information and data to be written to by the system and storage components as part of normal usage of the storage media. The challenge and risk with this is that forensic investigators and relevant toolsets can retrieve this information in a matter of minutes, hours, or days.

Where possible, overwriting data multiple times helps extend the time and efforts required to retrieve the relevant information and may make the storage components or partitions unattractive to potential attackers or those focused on retrieving the information.

WARNING Given enough time, effort, and resources in the absence of degaussing media, these approaches may not be sufficient to evade a determined attacker or reviewer from retrieving relevant information. What it may do is dissuade or make the task too challenging for a novice, intermediate, or opportunist attacker, who could decide to target easier locations or storage mediums.

VIRTUALIZATION SECURITY

Virtualization technologies enable cloud computing to become a real and scalable service offering due to the savings, sharing, and allocations of resources across multiple tenants and environments. As with all enabling technologies, the specified deployment and manner in which the solution is deployed may allow attackers to target relevant components and functions with the view to obtain unauthorized access to data, systems, and resources.

In the world of cloud computing, virtualization represents one of the key targets for the attackers. Specifically, although virtualization may introduce technical vulnerabilities based on the solution, the single most critical component to enable the technology to function in the manner for which it was developed, along with enforcing the relevant technical and nontechnical security controls, is the hypervisor.

The Hypervisor

The role of the hypervisor is a simple one: to allow multiple OSs to share a single hardware host (with each OS appearing to have the host's processor, memory, and resources to itself).

Think of a management console. Effectively, this is what the hypervisor does—intelligently controlling the host processor and resources, prioritizing and allocating what is needed to each OS, while ensuring there are no crashes and the neighbors do not upset each other.

Now you will dig a little deeper, with the goal of learning the security elements associated with VMs.

- **Type 1 hypervisor:** There are many accounts, definitions, and versions of what the distinctions between Type 1 and Type 2 hypervisors are (and are not), but with the view to keeping it simple, this book refers to Type 1 hypervisors as those running directly on the hardware with VM (guest operating system) resources provided by the hypervisor.

  These are also referred to as bare metal hypervisors. Examples of these include VMware ESXi and Citrix XenServer.

- **Type 2 hypervisor:** Type 2 hypervisors run on a host OS to provide virtualization services. Examples of Type 2 are VMware Workstation and Virtual Box.

In summary, Type 1 relates to hardware, and Type 2 relates to an OS.

Security Types

From a security perspective, you'll now explore which of the hypervisors provides a more robust security posture and which is more targeted by attackers.

- **Type 1 security:** Type 1 hypervisors significantly reduce the attack surface over Type 2 hypervisors. Type 1 hypervisor vendors also control relevant software that comprise and form the hypervisor package, including the virtualization functions and OS functions, such as devices drivers and input/output (I/O) stacks.

  Because the vendors have control over the relevant packages, they can reduce the likelihood of malicious software being introduced into the hypervisor foundation and introducing or exposing the hypervisor layer.

  The limited access and strong control over the embedded OS greatly increase the reliability and robustness of Type 1 hypervisors.

- **Type 2 security:** Because Type 2 hypervisors are OS based, they are more attractive to attackers, given that there are far more vulnerabilities associated with the OS as well as other applications that reside within the OS layer.

  A lack of standardization on the OS and other layers can open up additional opportunities and exposures that might make the hypervisor susceptible to attack and compromise.

Where technology, hardware, and software standardization can be used effectively, this can significantly reduce the risk landscape and increase the security posture.

COMMON THREATS

Threats form a real and ever-evolving challenge for organizations to counteract and defend against. Whether they are cloud specific or general disruptions to business and technology, threats can cause significant issues, outages, poor performance, and catastrophic impacts should they materialize.

Many of the top risks identified in the research paper *The Notorious Nine: Cloud Computing Top Threats in 2013*, published by the Cloud Security Alliance's Top Threats Working Group, remain a challenge for non-cloud-based environments and organizations alike. What this illustrates is the consistent challenges faced by entities today, altered and amplified by different technology deployments, such as cloud computing.[17]

Data Breaches

Not new to the security practitioner and company leaders, this age-old challenge continues to dominate headlines and new stories around the world. Whether it is a lost laptop that is unencrypted or side channel timing attacks on VMs, what cloud computing has done is widen the scope and coverage for data breaches.

Given the nature of cloud deployments and multitenancy, VMs, shared databases, application design, integration, APIs, cryptography deployments, key management, and multiple locations of data all combine to provide a highly amplified and dispersed attack surface, leading to greater opportunity for data breaches.

Cloud security professionals can expect to be facing far more data breaches and loss of organizational and personal information as the adoption of the cloud and further use of mobile devices continue to increase. This is in large measure due to the rise of smart devices, tablets, increased workforce mobility, bring your own device (BYOD), and other factors, such as the historical challenge of lost devices, compromised systems, and traditional forms of attacks, coupled with the previously listed factors related to the cloud.

Depending on the data and information classification types, any data breaches or suspected breaches of systems security controls may require mandatory breach reporting to relevant agencies, entities, or bodies. This can include healthcare information (HIPAA), personally identifiable information (Directive 95/46/EC of the European Parliament and of the Council on the protection of individuals with regard to the processing of personal data and on the free movement of such data), and credit card information (PCI DSS). Significant fines may be imposed on organizations that cannot illustrate sufficient duty of care or security controls being implemented to prevent such data breaches. These vary greatly depending on the industry, sector, geographic location, and nature of the information.

Data Loss

Not to be confused with a data breach, data loss refers to the loss of information, deletion, overwriting, corruption, or integrity related to the information stored, processed, or transmitted within cloud environments.

Data loss within cloud environments can present a significant threat and challenge to organizations. The reasons for this can be illustrated by the following questions:

- Does the provider or customer have responsibility for data backup?
- If backup media containing the data is obtained, does this include all data or only a portion of the information?
- Where data has become corrupt or overwritten, can an import or restore be performed?
- Where accidental data deletion has occurred from the customer side, will the provider facilitate the restoration of systems and information in multitenancy environments or on shared platforms?

Note that when the customer uploads encrypted information to the cloud environment, the encryption keys become a critical component to ensure data is not lost and remains available. The loss of the relevant encryption keys constitutes data loss because the information will no longer be available for use in the absence of the keys.

Security can from time to time come back to haunt you if it is not owned, operated, and maintained effectively and efficiently.

Account or Service Traffic Hijacking

This is not a cloud-specific threat but one that has been a constant thorn and challenge for relevant security professionals to combat through the years. Account and service traffic hijacking has long been targeted by attackers, using methods such as phishing, more recently smishing (SMS phishing), spear phishing (targeted phishing attacks), and exploitation of software and other application-related vulnerabilities.

The key component of these attack methods, when successful, allows for the attackers to monitor and eavesdrop on communications, sniff and track traffic, capture relevant credentials, and access and alter account and user profile characteristics (changing passwords and more).

Of late, attackers are utilizing compromised systems, accounts, and domains as a smokescreen to launch attacks against other organizations and entities, making the source of the attack appear to be from suppliers, third parties, competitors, or other legitimate organizations that have no knowledge or awareness of having been compromised.

Insecure Interfaces and APIs

For users to access cloud computing assets and resources, they utilize the APIs made available by the CSP. Key functions of the APIs, including the provisioning, management, and monitoring, are performed utilizing the provider interfaces. For the security controls and availability of resources to function in the way that they were designed, use of the provider APIs is required to prevent against deliberate and accidental attempts to circumvent policies and controls.

Sounds simple enough, right? In an ideal world, that may be true, but for the modern and evolving cloud landscape, that challenge is amplified with relevant third parties, organizations, and customers (depending on deployment) building additional interfaces and "bolt on" components to the API, which significantly increase the complexity, resulting in a multilayered API. This can result in credentials being passed to third parties or consumed insecurely across the API and relevant stack components.

Note that most providers make concerted efforts to ensure the security of their interfaces and APIs; however, any variations or additional components added on from the consumer or other providers can reduce the overall security posture and stance.

Denial of Service

By their nature, denial-of-service (DoS) attacks prevent users from accessing services and resources from a specified system or location. This can be done using any number of attack vectors available but typically look to target buffers, memory, network bandwidth, or processor power.

With cloud services relying ultimately on availability to service and enable connectivity to resources from customers, when DoS attacks are targeted at cloud environments, they can create significant challenges for the provider and customer alike.

Distributed denial-of-service (DDoS) attacks are launched from multiple locations against a single target. Work with the cloud security architect to ensure that system design and implementation do not create an SPOF that can expose an entire system to failure if a DoS or DDoS attack is successfully launched against a system.

Note that although it's widely touted by the media and feared by organizations worldwide, many believe that DoS attacks require large volumes of traffic to be successful. This is not always the case; asymmetric application-level payload attacks have measured success with as little at 100–150Kbps packets.

Malicious Insiders

When looking to secure the key assets of any organization, three primary components are essential—people, processes, and technology. People tend to present the single largest challenge to security due to the possibility of a disgruntled, rogue, or simply careless employee or contractor exposing sensitive data either by accident or on purpose.

According to CERT, malicious insider threats to an organization can come from "a current or former employee, contractor, or other business partner who has or had authorized access to an organization's network, system, or data and intentionally exceeded or misused that access in a manner that negatively affected the confidentiality, integrity, or availability of the organization's information or information systems."[18]

Abuse of Cloud Services

Think of the ability to have previously unobtainable and unaffordable computing resources available for a couple of dollars an hour. Well, that is exactly what cloud computing provides—an opportunity for businesses to have almost unlimited scalability and flexibility. The challenge for many organizations is that this scalability and flexibility are provided across the same platforms or resources that attackers can access and use to execute dictionary attacks, execute DoS attacks, crack encryption passwords, or host illegal software and materials for widespread distribution. Note that the power of the cloud is not always used in the manner for which it is offered to users.

Insufficient Due Diligence

Cloud computing has created a revolution among many users and companies with regard to how they utilize technology-based solutions and architectures. As with many such technology changes and revolutions, some have acted before giving the appropriate thought and due care to what a secure architecture would look like and what would be required to implement one.

Cloud computing has, for many organizations, become that rash decision—intentionally or unintentionally. The change in roles, focus, governance, auditing, reporting, strategy, and other operational elements requires a considerable investment on the part of the business in a thorough risk-review process, as well as amendments to business processes.

Given the immaturity of the cloud computing market, many entities and providers are still altering and refining the way they operate. There will be acquisitions, changes, amendments, and revisions in the way in which entities offer services, which can influence both customers and partners.

Finally, when the dust settles in the race for cloud space, pricing may vary significantly, rates and offerings may be reduced or inflated, and cyber attacks could force customers to review and revise their selection of a CSP. Should your provider go bankrupt, are you in a position to change CSPs in a timely and seamless manner?

It is incumbent upon the cloud security professional to ensure that both due care and due diligence are being exercised in the drive to the cloud.

- **Due diligence** is the act of investigating and understanding the risks a company faces.

- **Due care** is the development and implementation of policies and procedures to aid in protecting the company, its assets, and its people from threats.

Note that cloud companies may merge, be acquired, go bust, change services, and ultimately change their pricing model. Those that fail to carry out the appropriate due diligence activities may in fact be left with nowhere to go or turn to unless they introduce compensating controls to offset such risks (potentially resulting in less financial benefit).

Shared Technology Vulnerabilities

For CSPs to effectively and efficiently deliver their services in a scalable way, they share infrastructure, platforms, and applications among tenants and potentially with other providers. This can include the underlying components of the infrastructure, resulting in shared threats and vulnerabilities.

Where possible, providers should implement a layered approach to securing the various components. A defense-in-depth strategy should include compute, storage, network, application, and user security enforcement and monitoring. This should be universal, regardless of whether the service model is IaaS, PaaS, or SaaS.

SECURITY CONSIDERATIONS FOR DIFFERENT CLOUD CATEGORIES

Security can be a subjective issue, viewed differently across different industries, companies, and users, based on their needs, desires, and requirements. Many of these actions and security appetites are strongly influenced by compliance and other regulatory requirements.

IaaS Security

Within IaaS, a key emphasis and focus must be placed on the various layers and components stemming from the architecture to the virtual components. Given the reliance and focus placed on the widespread use of virtualization and the associated hypervisor components, this must be a key focus as an attack vector to gain access to or disrupt a cloud service.

The hypervisor acts as the abstraction layer that provides the management functions for required hardware resources among VMs.

- **VM attacks:** Cloud servers contain tens of VMs. These VMs may be active or offline and, regardless of state, are susceptible to attacks. Active VMs are vulnerable to all traditional attacks that can affect physical servers.

  Once a VM is compromised, VMs on the same physical server can attack each other because they share the same hardware and software resources, including memory, device drivers, storage, and hypervisor software.

- **Virtual network:** The virtual network contains the virtual switch software that controls the movement of traffic between the virtual network interface cards (NICs) of the installed VMs and the physical NICs of the host.

- **Hypervisor attacks:** Malicious hackers consider the hypervisor a potential target because of the greater control afforded by lower layers in the system. Compromising the hypervisor enables control over the installed VMs, the physical system, and the hosted applications.

  Common attacks include hyperjacking (installing a rogue hypervisor that can take complete control of a server), such as SubVir, Blue Pill (hypervisor rootkit using AMD secure virtual machine [SVM]), Vitriol (hypervisor rootkit using Intel VT-x), and direct kernel structure manipulation (DKSM).

  Another common attack is the VM escape, which is done by crashing the guest OS to get out of it and running an arbitrary code on the host OS. This allows malicious VMs to take complete control of the host OS.

- **VM-based rootkits (VMBRs):** These rootkits act by inserting a malicious hypervisor on the fly or modifying the installed hypervisor to gain control over the host workload.

- **Virtual switch attacks:** The virtual switch is vulnerable to a wide range of layer II attacks such as manipulation or modification of the virtual switch's configuration, VLANs and trust zones, and ARP tables.

- **DoS attacks:** DoS attacks in a virtual environment form a critical threat to VMs, along with all other dependent and associated services.

  Note that not all DoS attacks are from external attackers.

  These attacks can be the direct result of misconfigurations at the hypervisor, which allows a single VM instance to consume and utilize all available resources. In the same manner as a DoS attack renders resources unavailable to users attempting to access them, misconfigurations at the hypervisor restrict any other VM running on the same physical machine. This prevents network hosts from functioning appropriately because of the resources being consumed and utilized by a single device.

  Hypervisors prevent any VM from gaining 100 percent usage of any shared hardware resources, including CPU, RAM, network bandwidth, and other memory. Appropriately configured hypervisors detect instances of resource hogging and take appropriate actions, such as restarting the VM in an effort to stabilize or halt any processes that may be causing the abuse.

- **Colocation:** Multiple VMs residing on a single server and sharing the same resources increase the attack surface and the risk of VM-to-VM or VM-to-hypervisor compromise. On the other hand, when a physical server is off, it is safe from attacks. However, when a VM comes offline, it is still available as VM image files that are susceptible to malware infections and patching.

Provisioning tools and VM templates are exposed to different attacks that attempt to create new unauthorized VMs or patch the VM templates. This infects the other VMs that will be cloned from this template.

These new categories of security threats are a result of the new, complex, and dynamic nature of the cloud virtual infrastructure, as follows:

- **Multitenancy:** By design, different users within a cloud share the same applications and the physical hardware to run their VMs. As a result, information leakage as well as an increase in the attack surface and the risk of VM-to-VM or VM-to-hypervisor compromise can occur.

- **Loss of control:** Users are typically not aware of the location of their data and services, whereas the CSPs host and run VMs without being aware of their contents.

- **Network topology:** Cloud architecture is dynamic due to the fact that existing workloads change over time because of the creation and removal of VMs. In addition, the abilities of VMs to migrate from one host to another leads to the rise of nonpredefined network topologies.

- **Logical network segmentation:** Within IaaS, the requirement for isolation alongside the hypervisor remains a key and fundamental activity to reduce external sniffing, monitoring, and interception of communications and others within the relevant segments.

  When assessing relevant security configurations and connectivity models, VLANs, NATs, bridging, and segregation provide viable options to ensure the overall security posture remains strong, flexible, and constant, as opposed to other mitigation controls that may affect the overall performance.

- **No physical endpoints:** Due to server and network virtualization, the number of physical endpoints (such as switches, servers, and NICs) is reduced. These physical endpoints are traditionally used in defining, managing, and protecting IT assets.

- **Single point of access (SPOA) or SPOF:** Hosts have a limited number of access points (NICs) available to all VMs.

  This represents a critical security vulnerability: compromising these access points opens the door to compromise the VMs, the hypervisor, or the virtual switch.

The Cloud Security Alliance Common Controls Matrix (CCM) provides a good go-to guide for specific risks for SaaS, PaaS, and IaaS.[19]

PaaS Security

PaaS security involves four main areas, each of which is discussed in the following sections.

System and Resource Isolation

PaaS tenants should not have shell access to the servers running their instances (even when virtualized). The rationale behind this is to limit the chance and likelihood of configuration or system changes affecting multiple tenants. Where possible, administration facilities should be restricted to siloed containers to reduce this risk.

Careful consideration should be given before access is provided to the underlying infrastructure hosting a PaaS instance. In enterprises, this may have less to do with malicious behavior and more to do with efficient cost control; it takes time and effort to undo tenant-related fixes to their environments.

User-Level Permissions

Each instance of a service should have its own notion of user-level entitlements (permissions). If the instances share common policies, appropriate countermeasures and controls should be enabled by the cloud security professional to reduce authorization creep or the inheritance of permissions over time.

However, it is not all a challenge; the effective implementation of distinct and common permissions can yield significant benefits when implemented across multiple applications within the cloud environment.

User Access Management

User access management enables users to access IT services, resources, data, and other assets. Access management helps to protect the availability, integrity, and confidentiality (AIC) of these assets and resources, ensuring that only those authorized to use or access these are permitted access.

In recent years, traditional standalone access control methods have become less utilized, with more holistic approaches to unify the authentication of users becoming favored. (This includes single sign-on.) For user access management processes and controls to function effectively, a key emphasis is placed on the agreement, implementation of the rules, and organizational policies for access to data and assets.

The key components of user access management include but are not limited to the following:

- **Intelligence:** Requires collection, analysis, auditing, and reporting against rule-based criteria, typically based on organizational policies.

- **Administration:** The ability to perform onboarding or changing account access on systems and applications.

  These solutions or toolsets should enable automation of tasks that were typically or historically performed by personnel within the operations or security function.

- **Authentication:** Provides assurance and verification in real time as to the user being who she claims to be, accompanied by relevant credentials (such as passwords).

- **Authorization:** Determines the level of access to grant each user based on policies, roles, rules, and attributes. The principle of least privilege should always be applied (that is, only what is specifically required to fulfill the job functions).

Note that User Access Management enables organizations to avail benefits across the areas of security, operational efficiencies, user administration, auditing, and reporting along with other onboarding components; however, it can be difficult to implement for historical components or environments.

Protection Against Malware, Backdoors, and Trojans

Traditionally, development and other teams create backdoors to enable administrative tasks to be performed.

The challenge with these is that once backdoors are created, they provide a constant vector for attackers to target and potentially gain access to the relevant PaaS resources. You have heard of the story in which attackers gained access through a backdoor, only to create additional backdoors while removing the legitimate backdoors, essentially holding the systems, resources, and associated services hostage.

More recently, attackers have utilized embedded and hardcoded malware as a method of obtaining unauthorized access and retaining this access for a prolonged and extended period. Most notably, malware has been placed in point-of-sale (PoS) devices, handheld card-processing devices, and other platforms, thereby divulging large amounts of sensitive data (including credit card numbers, customer details, and so on).

As with SaaS, web application and development reviews should go hand in hand. Code reviews and other software development lifecycle checks are essential to ensure that the likelihood of malware, backdoors, Trojans, and other potentially harmful vectors is reduced significantly.

SaaS Security

SaaS security involves three main areas, each of which is discussed in the following sections.

Data Segregation

Multitenancy is one of the major characteristics of cloud computing. As a result of multitenancy, multiple users can store their data using the applications that SaaS provides. Within these architectures, the data of various users will reside at the same location or across multiple locations and sites. With the appropriate permissions or using attack methods, the data of customers may become visible or possible to access.

Typically, in SaaS environments, this can be achieved by exploiting code vulnerabilities or injecting code within the SaaS application. If the application executes this code without verification, there is a high potential of success for the attacker to access or view other customers' or tenants' data.

A SaaS model should therefore ensure a clear segregation for each user's data. The segregation must be ensured not only at the physical level but also at the application level. The service should be intelligent enough to segregate the data from different users. A malicious user can use application vulnerabilities to hand-craft parameters that bypass security checks and access sensitive data of other tenants.

Data Access and Policies

When allowing and reviewing access to customer data, the key aspect to structuring a measurable and scalable approach begins with the correct identification, customization, implementation, and repeated assessments of the security policies for accessing data.

The challenge associated with this is to map existing security policies, processes, and standards to meet and match the policies that the CSP enforces. This may mean revising existing internal policies or adopting new practices whereby users can only access data and resources relevant to their job function and role.

The cloud must adhere to these security policies to avoid intrusion or unauthorized users viewing or accessing data.

The challenge from a CSP perspective is to offer a solution and service that is flexible enough to incorporate the specific organizational policies put forward by the organization, while also being positioned to provide a boundary and segregation among the multiple organizations and customers within a single cloud environment.

Web Application Security

Because SaaS resources are required to be always on and availability disruptions kept to a minimum, security vulnerabilities within the web application(s) carry significant risk and potential impact for the enterprise. Vulnerabilities, no matter what risk categorization, present challenges for CSPs and customers alike. Given the large volume of shared and colocated tenants within SaaS environments, if a vulnerability is exploited, both the cloud customer and the service provider may experience catastrophic consequences.

As with traditional web application technologies, cloud services rely on a robust, hardened, and regularly assessed web application to deliver services to its users. The fundamental difference with cloud-based services versus traditional web applications is their footprint and the attack surface they will present.

In the same way that web application security assessments and code reviews are performed on applications prior to release, this becomes even more crucial when dealing with cloud services. The failure to carry out web application security assessments and code reviews may result in unauthorized access, corruption, or other integrity issues affecting the data, along with a loss of availability.

Finally, web applications introduce new and specific security risks that may not be counteracted or defended against by traditional network security solutions (firewalls, intrusion detection systems [IDSs], intrusion prevention systems [IPSs], and so on). The nature and manner in which web application vulnerabilities and exploits operate may not be identified or may appear legitimate to the network security devices designed for non-cloud architectures.

OPEN WEB APPLICATION SECURITY PROJECT TOP TEN SECURITY THREATS

The Open Web Application Security Project (OWASP) has provided the 10 most critical web application security threats that should serve as a minimum level for application security assessments and testing.

The OWASP top 10 covers the following categories:

- "A1—**Injection:** Injection flaws, such as SQL, OS, and LDAP injection occur when untrusted data is sent to an interpreter as part of a command or query. The attacker's hostile data can trick the interpreter into executing unintended commands or accessing data without proper authorization.

- "A2—**Broken Authentication and Session Management:** Application functions related to authentication and session management are often not implemented correctly, allowing attackers to compromise passwords, keys, or session tokens, or to exploit other implementation flaws to assume other users' identities.

- "A3—**Cross-Site Scripting (XSS):** XSS flaws occur whenever an application takes untrusted data and sends it to a web browser without proper validation or escaping. XSS allows attackers to execute scripts in the victim's browser, which can hijack user sessions, deface websites, or redirect the user to malicious sites.

- "A4—**Insecure Direct Object References:** A direct object reference occurs when a developer exposes a reference to an internal implementation object, such as a file, directory, or database key. Without an access control check or other protection, attackers can manipulate these references to access unauthorized data.

- "A5—**Security Misconfiguration:** Good security requires having a secure configuration defined and deployed for the application, frameworks, application server, web server, database server, and platform. Secure settings should be defined, implemented, and maintained, as defaults are often insecure. Additionally, software should be kept up to date.

- **"A6—Sensitive Data Exposure:** Many web applications do not properly protect sensitive data, such as credit cards, tax IDs, and authentication credentials. Attackers may steal or modify such weakly protected data to conduct credit card fraud, identity theft, or other crimes. Sensitive data deserves extra protection such as encryption at rest or in transit, as well as special precautions when exchanged with the browser.

- **"A7—Missing Function Level Access Control:** Most web applications verify function-level access rights before making that functionality visible in the UI. However, applications need to perform the same access control checks on the server when each function is accessed. If requests are not verified, attackers will be able to forge requests in order to access functionality without proper authorization.

- **"A8—Cross-Site Request Forgery (CSRF):** A CSRF attack forces a logged-on victim's browser to send a forged HTTP request, including the victim's session cookie and any other automatically included authentication information, to a vulnerable web application. This allows the attacker to force the victim's browser to generate requests the vulnerable application thinks are legitimate requests from the victim.

- **"A9—Using Components with Known Vulnerabilities:** Components, such as libraries, frameworks, and other software modules, almost always run with full privileges. If a vulnerable component is exploited, such an attack can facilitate serious data loss or server takeover. Applications using components with known vulnerabilities may undermine application defences and enable a range of possible attacks and impacts.

- **"A10—Unvalidated Redirects and Forwards:** Web applications frequently redirect and forward users to other pages and websites, and use untrusted data to determine the destination pages. Without proper validation, attackers can redirect victims to phishing or malware sites, or use forwards to access unauthorized pages."[20]

CLOUD SECURE DATA LIFECYCLE

Data is the single most valuable asset for most organizations. Depending on the value of the information to their operations, security controls should be applied accordingly.

As with systems and other organizational assets, data should have a defined and managed lifecycle across the following key stages (*Figure 1.5*). According to Securosis, the data lifecycle is comprised of six phases, from creation to destruction.

- **Create:** New digital content is generated or existing content is modified.
- **Store:** Data is committed to a storage repository, which typically occurs directly after creation.
- **Use:** Data is viewed, processed, or otherwise used in some sort of activity (not including modification).
- **Share:** Information is made accessible to others—users, partners, customers, and so on.
- **Archive:** Data leaves active use and enters long-term storage.
- **Destroy:** Data is permanently destroyed using physical or digital means.

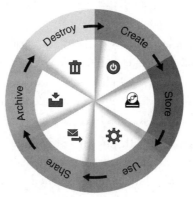

FIGURE 1.5 Key stages of the data lifecycle.

The lifecycle is not a single linear operation but a series of smaller lifecycles running in different environments. At all times, it is important to be aware of the logical and physical location of the data to satisfy audit, compliance, and other control requirements.

In addition to the location of the data, it is important to know who is accessing the data and how they are accessing it.

NOTE Different devices have specific security characteristics or limitations (BYOD, and so on).

INFORMATION AND DATA GOVERNANCE TYPES

Table 1.2 lists a sample of information and data governance types. Note that this may vary depending on your organization, geographic location, risk appetite, and so on.

TABLE 1.2 Information and Data Governance Types

FEATURE	DESCRIPTION
Information classification	What is the high-level description of valuable information categories (such as highly confidential, regulated)?
Information management policies	What activities are allowed for different information types?
Location and jurisdictional policies	Where can data be geographically located? What are the legal and regulatory implications or ramifications?
Authorizations	Who is allowed to access different types of information?
Custodianship	Who is responsible for managing the information at the bequest of the owner?

BUSINESS CONTINUITY AND DISASTER RECOVERY PLANNING

Business continuity management is the process by which risks and threats to the ongoing availability of services, business functions, and the organization are actively reviewed and managed at set intervals as part of the overall risk-management process. The goal is to keep the business operating and functioning in the event of a disruption.

Disaster recovery planning (DRP) is the process by which suitable plans and measures are taken to ensure that, in the event of a disaster (flood, storm, tornado, and so on), the business can respond appropriately with the view to recovering critical and essential operations (even somewhat limited) to a state of partial or full level of service in as little time as possible. The goal is to quickly establish, reestablish, or recover affected areas or elements of the business following a disaster.

Note that DR and business continuity are often confused or used interchangeably in some organizations. Wherever possible, be sure to use the correct terminology and highlight the differences between them.

Business Continuity Elements

From the perspective of the cloud customer, business continuity elements include the relevant security pillars of availability, integrity, and confidentiality.

The availability of the relevant resources and services is often the key requirement, along with the uptime and ability to access these on demand. Failure to ensure this results in significant impacts, including loss of earnings, loss of opportunities, and loss of confidence for the customer and provider.

Many security professionals struggle to keep their business continuity processes current once they have started to utilize cloud-based services. Equally, many fail to adequately update, amend, and keep their business continuity plans up to date in terms of complete coverage of services. This may be due to a number of factors; however, the key component contributing to this is that business continuity is operated mainly at set intervals and is not integrated fully into ongoing business operations. That is, business continuity activities are performed only annually or biannually, which may not take into account notable changes in business operations (such as the cloud) within relevant business units, sections, or systems.

Note that not all assets or services are equal! What are the key or fundamental components required to ensure the business or service can continue to be delivered? The answer to this question should shape and structure your business continuity and disaster recovery (BCDR) practices.

Critical Success Factors

Two critical success factors for business continuity when utilizing cloud-based services are as follows:

- Understand your responsibilities versus the CSP's responsibilities.
  - Customer responsibilities
  - CSP responsibilities
  - Understanding any interdependencies or third parties (supply chain risks)
  - Order of restoration (priority)
  - Appropriate frameworks and certifications held by the facility, services, and processes
  - Right to audit and make regular assessments of continuity capabilities
  - Communications of any issues or limited services
  - Identification of need for backups to be held onsite or offsite or with another CSP
- Clearly state and ensure the SLA addresses which components of business continuity and disaster recovery are covered and to what degree they are covered.
  - Penalties and compensation for loss of service
  - RTOs and RPOs
  - Loss of integrity or confidentiality
  - Points of contact and escalation processes

- Failover to maintain compliance

- Changes being communicated in a timely manner

- Clearly defined responsibilities

- Where usage of third parties is required per the agreed-upon SLA

The cloud customer should be in agreement with and fully satisfied with all the details relating to BCDR (including recovery times, responsibilities, and more) prior to signing any documentation or agreements that signify acceptance of the terms for system operation.

The customer typically pays for the associated time and costs of requesting amendments or changes to the relevant SLA.

Important SLA Components

Finally, regarding DR, the cloud customer should take a similar approach to ensure the following are fully understood and acted upon, prior to signing relevant SLAs and contracts:

- Undocumented single points of failure should not exist.

- Migration to alternate providers should be possible within agreed-upon timeframes.

- All components need to be supported by alternate CSPs in the event of a failover; if not, onsite services may be required as a fallback solution.

- Automated controls should be enabled to allow customers to verify data integrity.

- Where data backups are included, incremental backups should allow the user to select the desired settings, including coverage, frequency, and ease of use for recovery point restoration options.

- Regular assessment of the SLA and any changes that may affect the customer's ability to utilize cloud computing components for DR should be captured at regular and set intervals.

Although it's impossible to plan for every event or disaster that may occur, relevant plans and continuity measure should cover a number of logical groupings, which could be applied for unforeseen or unplanned incidents.

As cloud adoption and migration continue to expand, all affected or associated areas of business (technology and otherwise) should be reviewed under BCDR plans, thus ensuring that any changes for the customer or provider are captured and acted upon. Imagine the challenges of trying to restore or act upon a loss of availability, when processes, controls, or technologies have changed without the plans being updated or amended to reflect such changes.

The following ISO/IEC documents may be of use to CCSPs as they are considering what items an SLA will need to address:

- ISO/IEC DIS 19086-1, "Information Technology—Cloud Computing—Service Level Agreement (SLA) Framework—Part 1: Overview and Concepts"

- ISO/IEC NP 19086-2, "Information Technology—Cloud Computing—Service Level Agreement (SLA) Framework and Technology—Part 2: Metrics"

- ISO/IEC CD 19086-3, "Information Technology –Cloud Computing—Service Level Agreement (SLA) Framework and Technology—Part 3: Core Requirements"

- ISO/IEC AWI 19941, "Information Technology –Cloud Computing—Interoperability and Portability"

- ISO/IEC CD 19944, "Information Technology—Cloud Computing—Data and Their Flow Across Devices and Cloud Services"

- ISO/IEC FDIS 20933, "Information Technology—Distributed Application Platforms and Services (DAPS)—Access Systems"

COST-BENEFIT ANALYSIS

Cost is often identified as a key driver for the adoption of cloud computing. The challenge with decisions being made solely or exclusively on cost savings can come back to haunt the organization or entity that failed to take a risk-based view and factor in the relevant effects that may materialize.

- **Resource pooling:** Resource sharing is essential to the attainment of significant cost savings when adopting a cloud computing strategy. This is often coupled with pooled resources being used by different consumer groups at different times.

- **Shift from CapEx to OpEx:** The shift from capital expenditure (CapEx) to operational expenditure (OpEx) is seen as a key factor for many organizations as their requirement to make significant purchases of systems and resources is minimized. Given the constant evolution of technology and computing power, memory, capabilities, and functionality, many traditional systems purchased lose value almost instantly.

- **Factor in time and efficiencies:** Given that organizations rarely acquire used technology or servers, almost all purchases are of new and recently developed technology. But it's not just technology investment savings. Time and efficiencies achieved can be the greatest savings achieved when utilizing cloud computing.

- **Include depreciation:** When you purchase a new car, the value deteriorates the moment you drive the car off the showroom floor. The same applies for IT, only with newer and more desirable cars, technologies, and models being released every few months or years. Using this analogy clearly highlights why so many organizations are now opting to lease cloud services as opposed to constantly investing in technologies that become outdated in relatively short periods.

- **Reduction in maintenance and configuration time:** Remember all those days, weeks, months, and years spent maintaining, operating, patching, updating, supporting, engineering, rebuilding, and generally making sure everything needed was done to the systems and applications required by the business users? Well, given that the CSP now handles a large portion of those duties (if not all—depending on which cloud service you are using), the ability to free up, utilize, and reallocate resources to other technology or related tasks could prove to be invaluable.

- **Shift in focus:** Technology and business personnel being able to focus on the key elements of their role, instead of the daily firefighting and responding to issues and technology components, comes as a welcome change to those professionals serious about their functions.

- **Utilities costs:** Outside of the technology and operational elements, from a utilities cost perspective, massive savings can be achieved with the reduced requirement for power, cooling, support agreements, data center space, racks, cabinets, and so on. Large organizations that have migrated big portions of the data center components to cloud-based environments have reported tens of thousands to hundreds of thousands in direct savings from the utilities elements. Green IT is very much at the fore of many global organizations, and cloud computing plays toward that focus in a strong way.

- **Software and licensing costs:** Software and relevant licensing costs present a major cost saving as well because you only pay for the licensing used versus the bulk or enterprise licensing levels of traditional non-cloud-based infrastructure models.

- **Pay per usage:** As outlined by the CapEx versus OpEx discussion earlier in this section, cloud computing gives businesses a new and clear benefit: pay per usage. In terms of traditional IT functions, when systems and infrastructure assets were acquired, they were seen as a "necessary or required spend" for the organization; however, with cloud computing, they can now be monitored, categorized, and billed to specified functions or departments based on usage. This is a significant win and driver for IT departments because it releases pressure to reduce spending and allows for billing of usage for relevant cost bases directly to those, as opposed to absorbing the costs themselves as a business requirement.

With departments and business units now able to track costs and usage, it's easy to work out the amount of money spent versus the amount saved in traditional type computing. Sounds pretty straightforward, right?

- **Other factors:** What about new technologies, new or revised roles, legal costs, contract and SLA negotiations, additional governance requirements, training required, CSP interactions, and reporting? All these may impact and alter the price you see versus the price you pay, otherwise known as the total cost of ownership (TCO).

Many organizations have not factored in such costs to date. As such, their view of cost savings may be skewed or misguided somewhat.

CERTIFICATION AGAINST CRITERIA

If it cannot be measured, it cannot be managed.

This is a statement that any auditor and security professional should abide by regardless of his focus. How can someone have confidence, awareness, and assurances that he and the CSP are taking the correct steps to ensure that data is secured properly? Frameworks and standards hold the key here.

Why are users and entities still unconvinced that cloud computing is a good option, particularly from a security perspective? The reason is simple: no international cloud computing standards or security standards exist.

In the absence of cloud-specific security standards that are universally accepted by providers and customers alike, you'll deal with a patchwork of security standards, frameworks, and controls that are being applied to cloud environments. These include but are not limited to the following:

- ISO/IEC 27001:2013[21]
- ISO/IEC 27002:2013
- ISO/IEC 27017:2015
- SOC 1/SOC 2/SOC 3
- NIST SP 800-53
- PCI DSS

Possibly the most widely known and accepted information security standard, ISO 27001 was originally developed and created by the British Standards Institute, under the name of BS 7799. The standard was adopted by the International Organization for Standardization (ISO) and rebranded ISO 27001. ISO 27001 is the standard to which organizations certify, as opposed to ISO 27002, which is the best practice framework to which many others align.

ISO 27001:2005 consisted of 133 controls across 11 domains of security, focusing on the protection of information assets in their various forms (digital, paper, and so on). Since September 2013, ISO 27001 has been updated to ISO 27001:2013 and now consists of 35 control objectives and 114 controls spread over 14 domains.

Domains include these:

1. Information Security Policies
2. Organization of Information Security
3. Human Resources Security
4. Asset Management
5. Access Control
6. Cryptographic
7. Physical and Environmental Security
8. Operations Security
9. Communications Security
10. System Acquisition, Development, and Maintenance
11. Supplier Relationship
12. Information Security Incident Management
13. Information Security Business Continuity Management
14. Compliance

By its nature, ISO 27001 is designed to be vendor and technology agnostic (that is, it does not view them differently). As such, it looks for the information security management system (ISMS) to address the relevant risks and components in a manner that is appropriate and adequate based on the risks.

Even though ISO 27001 is the most advanced security standard widely used today, it does not specifically look at the risks associated with cloud computing. As such, it cannot be deemed as fully comprehensive when measuring security in cloud-based environments.

All standards and frameworks assist in the structure and standardization of security practices; however, they cannot be applied across multiple environments (of differing natures), deployments, and other components with 100 percent confidence and completeness, given the variations and specialized elements associated with cloud computing.

Due to its importance overall, ISO 27001 will continue to be used by CSPs and required by cloud customers as one of the key security frameworks for cloud environments.

ARCHITECTURAL CONCEPTS
AND DESIGN REQUIREMENTS

ISO/IEC 27002:2013

ISO/IEC 27002:2013 provides guidelines for organizational information security standards including the selection, implementation, and management of controls taking into consideration the organization's information security risk environments. It is designed to be used by organizations that intend to select controls within the process of implementing an ISMS based on ISO/IEC 27001. It can also be used by organizations to implement commonly accepted information security controls and develop their own information security management guidelines.

ISO/IEC 27017:2015

ISO/IEC 27017:2015 offers guidelines for information security controls applicable to the provision and use of cloud services by providing additional implementation guidance for relevant controls specified in ISO/IEC 27002 and additional controls with implementation guidance that specifically relate to cloud services. ISO 27017 provides controls and implementation guidance for both CSPs and cloud service customers.

SOC 1/SOC 2/SOC 3[22]

The Statement on Auditing Standards 70 (SAS 70) was replaced by Service Organization Control (SOC) Type 1 and Type 2 reports in 2011 following changes and a more comprehensive approach to auditing being demanded by customers and clients alike. For years, SAS 70 was seen as the de facto standard for data center customers to obtain independent assurance that their data center service provider had effective internal controls in place for managing the design, implementation, and execution of customer information.

SAS 70 consisted of Type 1 and Type 2 audits. The Type 1 audit was designed to assess the sufficiency of the service provider's controls as of a particular date, and the Type 2 audit was designed to assess the effectiveness of the controls as of a certain date (point-in-time assessment).

Like many other frameworks, SAS 70 audits focused on verifying that the controls had been implemented and followed but did not focus on the overall completeness or effectiveness of the controls implemented. Think of having an alarm but not checking whether it was effective, functioning, or correctly installed.

SOC reports are performed in accordance with Statement on Standards for Attestation Engagements (SSAE) 16, Reporting on Controls at a Service Organization.

- SOC 1 reports focus solely on controls at a service provider that are likely to be relevant to an audit of a subscriber's financial statements.

- SOC 2 and SOC 3 reports address controls of the service provider that relate to operations and compliance.

There are some key distinctions between SOC 1, SOC 2, and SOC 3:

SOC 1 SOC 1 reports can be one of two types:

- A Type 1 report presents the auditors' opinion regarding the accuracy and completeness of management's description of the system or service as well as the suitability of the design of controls as of a specific date.

- Type 2 reports include the Type 1 criteria and audit of the operating effectiveness of the controls throughout a declared period, generally between 6 months and 1 year.

SOC 2 SOC 2 reporting was specifically designed for IT-managed service providers and cloud computing. The report specifically addresses any number of the five so-called Trust Services principles, which follow:

- **Security:** The system is protected against unauthorized access, both physical and logical.

- **Availability:** The system is available for operation and use as committed or agreed.

- **Processing Integrity:** System processing is complete, accurate, timely, and authorized.

- **Confidentiality:** Information designated as confidential is protected as committed or agreed.

- **Privacy:** Personal information is collected, used, retained, disclosed, and disposed of in conformity with the provider's privacy policy.

SOC 3 Reporting also uses the Trust Services principles but provides only the auditor's report on whether the system achieved the specified principle, without disclosing relevant details and sensitive information.

A key difference between a SOC 2 report and a SOC 3 report is that a SOC 2 report is generally restricted in distribution and coverage (due to the information it contains), and a SOC 3 report is broadly available, with limited information and details included within it (often used to instill confidence in perspective clients or for marketing purposes).

To review:

- **SOC 1:** This is intended for those interested in financial statements.

- **SOC 2:** Information technology personnel will be interested.

- **SOC 3:** This is used to illustrate conformity, compliance, and security efforts to current or potential subscribers and customers of cloud services.

NIST SP 800-53

NIST is an agency of the U.S. government that makes measurements and sets standards as needed for industry or government programs. The primary goal and objective of the 800-53[23] standard is to ensure that appropriate security requirements and security controls are applied to all U.S. federal government information and information management systems.

The standard requires that risk be assessed and the determination made whether additional controls are needed to protect organizational operations (including mission, functions, image, or reputation), organizational assets, individuals, other organizations, or the nation.

The 800-53 standard—"Security and Privacy Controls for Federal Information Systems and Organizations"—underwent its fourth revision in April 2013.

Primary updates and amendments include these:

- Assumptions relating to security control baseline development
- Expanded, updated, and streamlined tailoring guidance
- Additional assignment and selection statement options for security and privacy controls
- Descriptive names for security and privacy control enhancements
- Consolidated security controls and control enhancements by family with baseline allocations
- Tables for security controls that support development, evaluation, and operational assurance
- Mapping tables for international security standard ISO/IEC 15408 (Common Criteria)

Although the NIST Risk Management Framework provides the pieces and parts for an effective security program, it is aimed at government agencies focusing on the following key components:

2.1 Multitiered Risk Management

2.2 Security Control Structure

2.3 Security Control Baselines

2.4 Security Control Designations

2.5 External Service Partners

2.6 Assurance and Trustworthiness

2.7 Revisions and Extensions

3.1 Selecting Security Control Baselines

3.2 Tailoring Security Control Baselines

3.3 Creating Overlays

3.4 Document the Control Selection Process

3.5 New Development and Legacy Systems

One major issue that corporate security teams encounter when trying to base a program on the NIST SP 800-53 Risk Management Framework is that publicly traded organizations are not bound by the same security assumptions and requirements as government agencies. Government organizations are established to fulfill legislated missions and are required to collect, store, manipulate, and report sensitive data. Finally, a large percentage of these activities in a publicly traded organization is governed by cost-benefit analysis, boards of directors, and shareholder opinion, as opposed to government direction and influence.

For those looking to understand the similarities and overlaps with NIST SP 800-53 and ISO 27001/2, there is a mapping matrix listed within the 800-53 Revision 4 document.

PCI DSS

Visa, MasterCard, and American Express established PCI DSS[24] as a security standard to which all organizations or merchants that accept, transmit, or store cardholder data, regardless of size or number of transactions, must comply.

PCI DSS was established following a number of significant credit card breaches. It is a comprehensive and intensive security standard that lists both technical and nontechnical requirements based on the number of credit card transactions for the applicable entities.

Merchant Levels Based on Transactions

Table 1.3 illustrates the various merchant levels based on the number of transactions.

TABLE 1.3 **Merchant Levels Based on Transactions**

MERCHANT LEVEL	DESCRIPTION
1	Any merchant—regardless of acceptance channel—processing more than 6 million transactions per year. Any merchant that the credit card issuer, at its sole discretion, determines should meet the Level 1 merchant requirements to minimize risk to the credit card issuer's system.
2	Any merchant—regardless of acceptance channel—processing 1–6 million credit card transactions per year.
3	Any merchant processing 20,000 to 1 million credit card e-commerce transactions per year.
4	Any merchant processing fewer than 20,000 credit card e-commerce transactions per year and all other merchants—regardless of acceptance channel—processing up to 1 million credit card transactions per year.

For specific information and requirements, be sure to check with the PCI Security Standard Council.

Merchant Requirements

All merchants, regardless of level and relevant service providers, are required to comply with the following 12 domains/requirements:

- Install and maintain a firewall configuration to protect cardholder data.
- Avoid using vendor-supplied defaults for system passwords and other security parameters.
- Protect stored cardholder data.
- Encrypt transmission of cardholder data across open, public networks.
- Use and regularly update antivirus software.
- Develop and maintain secure systems and applications.
- Restrict access to cardholder data by business need-to-know.
- Assign a unique ID to each person with computer access.
- Restrict physical access to cardholder data.
- Track and monitor all access to network resources and cardholder data.
- Regularly test security systems and processes.
- Maintain a policy that addresses information security.

The 12 requirements list more than 200 controls that specify required and minimum security requirements for the merchants and service providers to meet their compliance obligations.

Failure to meet and satisfy the PCI DSS requirements (based on merchant level and processing levels) can result in significant financial penalties, suspension of credit cards as a payment channel, escalation to a higher merchant level, and potentially greater assurances and compliance requirements in the event of a breach in which credit card details may have be compromised or disclosed.

Since its establishment, PCI DSS has undergone a number of significant updates, through to the current version.

Due to the more technical and more black-and-white nature of its controls, many see PCI DSS as a reasonable and sufficient technical security standard. People believe that if it is good enough to protect their credit card and financial information, it should be a good baseline for cloud security.

SYSTEM AND SUBSYSTEM PRODUCT CERTIFICATION

System and subsystem product certification is used to evaluate the security claims made for a system and its components. Although there have been several evaluation frameworks available for use over the years, such as the Trusted Computer System Evaluation Criteria (TCSEC) developed by the United States Department of Defense, the Common Criteria (CC), discussed next, is the one that is internationally accepted and used most often.

CC

The CC[25] is an international set of guidelines and specifications (ISO/IEC 15408) developed for evaluating information security products, with the view to ensuring they meet an agreed-upon security standard for government entities and agencies.

CC Components

Officially, the CC is known as the "Common Criteria for Information Technology Security Evaluation." Until 2005, it was known as "The Trusted Computer System Evaluation Criteria." The CC is updated periodically.

Distinctly, the CC has two key components:

- **Protection profiles:** Define a standard set of security requirements for a specific type of product, such as a firewall, IDS, or unified threat management (UTM).

- **The evaluation assurance levels (EALs):** Define how thoroughly the product is tested. EALs are rated using a sliding scale from 1–7, with 1 being the lowest-level evaluation and 7 being the highest.

   The higher the level of evaluation, the more quality assurance (QA) tests the product would have undergone.

NOTE   Undergoing more tests does not necessarily mean the product is more secure.

The seven EALs are as follows:

- **EAL1:** Functionally tested
- **EAL2:** Structurally tested
- **EAL3:** Methodically tested and checked
- **EAL4:** Methodically designed, tested, and reviewed
- **EAL5:** Semiformally designed and tested
- **EAL6:** Semiformally verified design and tested
- **EAL7:** Formally verified design and tested

ARCHITECTURAL CONCEPTS AND DESIGN REQUIREMENTS

CC Evaluation Process

The goal of CC certification is to ensure customers that the products they are buying have been evaluated and that a vendor-neutral third party has verified the vendor's claims.

To submit a product for evaluation, follow these steps:

1. The vendor must complete a Security Target (ST) description that provides an overview of the product's security features.

2. A certified laboratory then tests the product to evaluate how well it meets the specifications defined in the protection profile.

3. A successful evaluation leads to an official certification of the product.

Note that CC looks at certifying a product only and does not include administrative or business processes.

FIPS 140-2

To maintain ongoing confidentiality and integrity of relevant information and data, you can use encryption and cryptography as a primary choice, specifically in various cloud computing deployment service types.

Federal Information Processing Standard (FIPS)[26] 140 Publication Series was issued by NIST to coordinate the requirements and standards for cryptography modules covering both hardware and software components for cloud and traditional computing environments.

The FIPS 140-2 standard provides four distinct levels of security intended to cover a range of potential applications and environments with emphasis on secure design and implementation of a cryptographic module.

Relevant specifications include these:

- Cryptographic module specification
- Cryptographic module ports
- Interfaces, roles, and services
- Authentication
- Physical security
- Operational environment
- Cryptographic key management
- Design assurance
- Controls and mitigating techniques against attacks

FIPS 140-2 Goal

The primary goal for the FIPS 140-2 standard is to accredit and distinguish secure and well-architected cryptographic modules produced by private sector vendors who seek to or are in the process of having their solutions and services certified for use in U.S. government departments and regulated industries (this includes financial services and healthcare) that collect, store, transfer, or share data that is deemed to be sensitive but not classified (that is, top secret).

Finally, when assessing the level of controls, FIPS is measured using a Level 1 to Level 4 rating. Despite the ratings and their associated requirements, FIPS does not state what level of certification is required by specific systems, applications, or data types.

FIPS Levels

The breakdown of the levels follows:

- **Security Level 1:** The lowest level of security. To meet Level 1 requirements, basic cryptographic module requirements are specified for at least one approved security function or approved algorithm. Encryption of a PC board presents an example of a Level 1 rating.

- **Security Level 2:** Enhances the required physical security mechanisms listed within Level 1 and requires that capabilities exist to illustrate evidence of tampering, including locks that are tamper proof on perimeter and internal covers to prevent unauthorized physical access to encryption keys.

- **Security Level 3:** Looks to develop the basis of Level 1 and Level 2 to include preventing the intruder from gaining access to information and data held within the cryptographic module. Additionally, physical security controls required at Level 3 should move toward detecting access attempts and responding appropriately to protect the cryptographic module.

- **Security Level 4:** Represents the highest rating. Security Level 4 provides the highest level of security, with mechanisms providing complete protection around the cryptographic module with the intent of detecting and responding to all unauthorized attempts at physical access. Upon detection, immediate zeroization of all plaintext critical security parameters (*also known as CSPs but not to be confused with cloud service providers*).[27] Security Level 4 undergoes rigid testing to ensure its adequacy, completeness, and effectiveness.

All testing is performed by accredited third-party laboratories and is subject to strict guidelines and quality standards. Upon completion of testing, all ratings are provided, along with an overall rating on the vendor's independent validation certificate.

From a cloud computing perspective, these requirements form a necessary and required baseline for all U.S. government agencies that may be looking to utilize or avail cloud-based services. Outside of the United States, FIPS does not typically act as a driver or a requirement; however, other governments and enterprises tend to recognize the FIPS validation as an enabler or differentiator over other technologies that have not undergone independent assessments or certification.

SUMMARY

Cloud computing covers a wide range of topics focused on the concepts, principles, structures, and standards used to monitor and secure assets and those controls used to enforce various levels of AIC across IT services throughout the enterprise. Security practitioners focused on cloud security must use and apply standards to ensure that the systems under their protection are maintained and supported properly. Today's environment of highly interconnected, interdependent systems necessitates the requirement to understand the linkage between information technology and meeting business objectives. Information security management communicates the risks accepted by the organization due to the currently implemented security controls and continually works to cost effectively enhance the controls to minimize the risk to the company's information assets.

REVIEW QUESTIONS

1. Which of the following are attributes of cloud computing?

   A. Minimal management effort and shared resources

   B. High cost and unique resources

   C. Rapid provisioning and slow release of resources

   D. Limited access and service provider interaction

2. Which of the following are distinguishing characteristics of a managed service provider?

   A. Have some form of a NOC but no help desk.

   B. Be able to remotely monitor and manage objects for the customer and reactively maintain these objects under management.

   C. Have some form of a help desk but no NOC.

   D. Be able to remotely monitor and manage objects for the customer and proactively maintain these objects under management.

3. Which of the following are cloud computing roles?

   A. Cloud customer and financial auditor

   B. CSP and backup service provider

   C. Cloud service broker and user

   D. Cloud service auditor and object

4. Which of the following are essential characteristics of cloud computing? (Choose two.)

   A. On-demand self-service

   B. Unmeasured service

   C. Resource isolation

   D. Broad network access

5. Which of the following are considered to be the building blocks of cloud computing?

   A. Data, access control, virtualization, and services

   B. Storage, networking, printing, and virtualization

   C. CPU, RAM, storage, and networking

   D. Data, CPU, RAM, and access control

6. When using an IaaS solution, what is the capability provided to the customer?

A. To provision processing, storage, networks, and other fundamental computing resources where the consumer is not able to deploy and run arbitrary software, which can include OSs and applications

B. To provision processing, storage, networks, and other fundamental computing resources where the provider is able to deploy and run arbitrary software, which can include OSs and applications

C. To provision processing, storage, networks, and other fundamental computing resources where the auditor is able to deploy and run arbitrary software, which can include OSs and applications

D. To provision processing, storage, networks, and other fundamental computing resources where the consumer is able to deploy and run arbitrary software, which can include OSs and applications

7. When using an IaaS solution, what is a key benefit provided to the customer?

A. Metered and priced usage on the basis of units consumed

B. The ability to scale up infrastructure services based on projected usage

C. Increased energy and cooling system efficiencies

D. Transferred cost of ownership

8. When using a PaaS solution, what is the capability provided to the customer?

A. To deploy onto the cloud infrastructure provider-created or acquired applications created using programming languages, libraries, services, and tools that the provider supports. The consumer does not manage or control the underlying cloud infrastructure, including network, servers, operating systems, or storage, but has control over the deployed applications and possibly configuration settings for the application-hosting environment.

B. To deploy onto the cloud infrastructure consumer-created or acquired applications created using programming languages, libraries, services, and tools that the provider supports. The provider does not manage or control the underlying cloud infrastructure, including network, servers, operating systems, or storage, but has control over the deployed applications and possibly configuration settings for the application-hosting environment.

C. To deploy onto the cloud infrastructure consumer-created or acquired applications created using programming languages, libraries, services, and tools that the provider supports. The consumer does not manage or control the underlying cloud infrastructure, including network, servers, operating systems, or storage, but has control over the deployed applications and possibly configuration settings for the application-hosting environment.

D. To deploy onto the cloud infrastructure consumer-created or acquired applications created using programming languages, libraries, services, and tools that the consumer supports. The consumer does not manage or control the underlying cloud infrastructure, including network, servers, operating systems, or storage, but has control over the deployed applications and possibly configuration settings for the application-hosting environment.

9. What is a key capability or characteristic of PaaS?

   A. Support for a homogenous hosting environment

   B. Ability to reduce lock-in

   C. Support for a single programming language

   D. Ability to manually scale

10. When using a SaaS solution, what is the capability provided to the customer?

    A. To use the provider's applications running on a cloud infrastructure. The applications are accessible from various client devices through either a thin client interface, such as a web browser (for example, web-based email), or a program interface. The consumer does not manage or control the underlying cloud infrastructure, including network, servers, operating systems, storage, or even individual application capabilities, with the possible exception of limited user-specific application configuration settings.

    B. To use the provider's applications running on a cloud infrastructure. The applications are accessible from various client devices through either a thin client interface, such as a web browser (for example, web-based email), or a program interface. The consumer does manage or control the underlying cloud infrastructure, including network, servers, operating systems, storage, or even individual application capabilities, with the possible exception of limited user-specific application configuration settings.

    C. To use the consumer's applications running on a cloud infrastructure. The applications are accessible from various client devices through either a thin client interface, such as a web browser (for example, web-based email), or a program interface. The consumer does not manage or control the underlying cloud infrastructure, including network, servers, operating systems, storage, or even individual application capabilities, with the possible exception of limited user-specific application configuration settings.

    D. To use the consumer's applications running on a cloud infrastructure. The applications are accessible from various client devices through either a thin client interface, such as a web browser (for example, web-based email), or a program interface. The consumer does manage or control the underlying cloud infrastructure, including network, servers, operating systems, storage, or even individual application capabilities, with the possible exception of limited user-specific application configuration settings.

11. What are the four cloud deployment models?

    A. Public, internal, hybrid, and community

    B. External, private, hybrid, and community

    C. Public, private, joint, and community

    D. Public, private, hybrid, and community

12. What are the six stages of the cloud secure data lifecycle?

    A. Create, use, store, share, archive, and destroy

    B. Create, store, use, share, archive, and destroy

    C. Create, share, store, archive, use, and destroy

    D. Create, archive, use, share, store, and destroy

13. What are SOC 1/SOC 2/SOC 3?

    A. Risk management frameworks

    B. Access controls

    C. Audit reports

    D. Software development phases

14. What are the five Trust Services principles?

    A. Security, Availability, Processing Integrity, Confidentiality, and Privacy

    B. Security, Auditability, Processing Integrity, Confidentiality, and Privacy

    C. Security, Availability, Customer Integrity, Confidentiality, and Privacy

    D. Security, Availability, Processing Integrity, Confidentiality, and Nonrepudiation

15. What is a security-related concern for a PaaS solution?

    A. Virtual machine attacks

    B. Web application security

    C. Data access and policies

    D. System and resource isolation

NOTES

[1] http://nvlpubs.nist.gov/nistpubs/Legacy/SP/nistspecialpublication800-145.pdf (p. 6)

[2] http://www.mspalliance.com/

[3] *Governance Reimagined: Organizational Design, Risk and Value Creation,* by David R. Koenig, John Wiley & Sons, Inc., p. 160.

[4] http://nvlpubs.nist.gov/nistpubs/Legacy/SP/nistspecialpublication800-145.pdf (p. 7)

[5] http://nvlpubs.nist.gov/nistpubs/Legacy/SP/nistspecialpublication800-145.pdf (p. 6)

[6] http://nvlpubs.nist.gov/nistpubs/Legacy/SP/nistspecialpublication800-145.pdf (p. 6)

[7] http://nvlpubs.nist.gov/nistpubs/Legacy/SP/nistspecialpublication800-145.pdf (p. 7)

[8] http://nvlpubs.nist.gov/nistpubs/Legacy/SP/nistspecialpublication800-145.pdf (p. 7)

[9] http://nvlpubs.nist.gov/nistpubs/Legacy/SP/nistspecialpublication800-145.pdf (p. 7)

[10] http://nvlpubs.nist.gov/nistpubs/Legacy/SP/nistspecialpublication800-145.pdf (p. 7)

[11] http://www.sabsa.org/

[12] https://www.axelos.com/itil

[13] http://www.opengroup.org/subjectareas/enterprise/togaf

[14] http://www.opengroup.org/subjectareas/platform3.0/cloudcomputing

[15] See the following for the October 22, 2014 announcement by NIST of the final publication release of the roadmap: http://www.nist.gov/itl/antd/cloud-102214.cfm

[16] See the following for the LDAP X.500 RFC: https://tools.ietf.org/html/rfc2247

[17] https://downloads.cloudsecurityalliance.org/initiatives/top_threats/The_Notorious_Nine_Cloud_Computing_Top_Threats_in_2013.pdf

[18] http://www.cert.org/insider-threat/

[19] See the following for more information: https://cloudsecurityalliance.org/research/ccm/

[20] https://www.owasp.org/index.php/Category:OWASP_Top_Ten_Project

[21] http://www.iso.org/iso/catalogue_detail?csnumber=54534

[22] https://www.ssae-16.com/

[23] http://nvlpubs.nist.gov/nistpubs/SpecialPublications/NIST.SP.800-53r4.pdf

[24] https://www.pcisecuritystandards.org/documents/PCI_DSS_v3.pdf

[25] http://www.commoncriteriaportal.org/files/ccfiles/CCPART1V3.1R4.pdf

[26] http://csrc.nist.gov/groups/STM/cmvp/standards.html

[27] In cryptography, zeroization is the practice of erasing sensitive parameters (electronically stored data, cryptographic keys, and CSPs) from a cryptographic module to prevent their disclosure if the equipment is captured.

DOMAIN 2

Cloud Data Security

THE GOAL OF THE Cloud Data Security domain is to inform you of the types of controls necessary to administer various levels of availability, integrity, and confidentiality (AIC) to secure data in the cloud.

You will gain knowledge on topics of data discovery and classification techniques; digital rights management; privacy of data; data retention, deletion, and archiving; data event logging, chain of custody and nonrepudiation; and the strategic use of security information and event management.

DOMAIN OBJECTIVES

After completing this domain, you will be able to do the following:

- ❑ Describe the cloud data lifecycle based on the Cloud Security Alliance (CSA) guidance

- ❑ Describe the design and implementation of cloud data storage architectures with regard to storage types, threats, and available technologies

- ❑ Identify the necessary data security strategies for securing cloud data

- ❑ Define the implementation processes for data discovery and classification technologies

- ❑ Identify the relevant jurisdictional data protections as they relate to personally identifiable information

- ❑ Define digital rights management (DRM) with regard to objectives and the available tools

- ❑ Identify the required data policies specific to retention, deletion, and archiving

- ❑ Describe various data events and know how to design and implement processes for auditability, traceability, and accountability

INTRODUCTION

Data security is a core element of cloud security (*Figure 2.1*). Cloud service providers (CSPs) often share the responsibility for security with the customer. Roles such as the chief information security officer (CISO), chief security officer (CSO), chief technology officer (CTO), enterprise architect, and network administrator may all play a part in providing elements of a security solution for the enterprise.

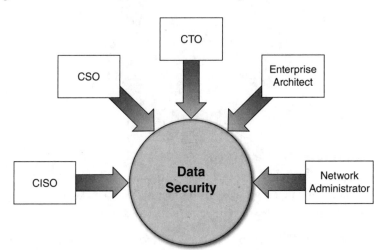

FIGURE 2.1 **Many roles are involved in providing data security.**

The data security lifecycle, as introduced by the Securosis Blog and then incorporated into the CSA guidance, enables the organization to map the different phases in the data lifecycle against the required controls that are relevant to each phase.[1]

The lifecycle contains the following steps:

1. Map the different lifecycle phases.

2. Integrate the different data locations and access types.

3. Map into functions, actors, and controls.

The data lifecycle guidance provides a framework to map relevant use cases for data access, while assisting in the development of appropriate controls within each lifecycle stage.

The lifecycle model serves as a reference and framework to provide a standardized approach for data lifecycle and data security. Not all implementations or situations align fully or comprehensively.

THE CLOUD DATA LIFECYCLE PHASES

According to Securosis, the data lifecycle is composed of six phases, from creation to destruction (*Figure 2.2*).

FIGURE 2.2 **The six phases of the data lifecycle.**

While the lifecycle is described as a linear process, data may skip certain stages or indeed switch back and forth between the different phases:

1. **Create:** The generation or acquisition of new digital content, or the altering or updating of existing content. This phase can happen internally in the cloud or externally. The creation phase is the preferred time to classify content according to its sensitivity and value to the organization. Careful classification is important because poor security controls can be implemented if content is classified incorrectly.

2. **Store:** The act of committing the digital data to some sort of storage repository. Typically occurs nearly simultaneously with creation. When storing the data, it should be protected in accordance with its classification level. Controls such as encryption, access policy, monitoring, logging, and backups should be implemented to avoid data threats. Content can be vulnerable to attackers if access control lists (ACLs) are not implemented well, files are not scanned for threats, or files are classified incorrectly.

3. **Use:** Data being viewed, processed, or otherwise used in some sort of activity, not including modification. Data in use is most vulnerable because it might be transported into unsecure locations such as workstations, and to be processed, it must be unencrypted. Controls such as data loss prevention (DLP), information rights management (IRM), and database and file access monitors should be implemented to audit data access and prevent unauthorized access.

4. **Share:** Information being made accessible to others, such as between users, to customers, and to partners. Not all data should be shared, and not all sharing should present a threat. But because data that is shared is no longer at the organization control, maintaining security can be difficult. Technologies such as DLP can be used to detect unauthorized sharing, and IRM technologies can be used to maintain control over the information.

5. **Archive:** Data leaving active use and entering long-term storage. Archiving data for a long period of time can be challenging. Cost versus availability considerations can affect data access procedures. Imagine if data is stored on a magnetic tape and needs to be retrieved 15 years later. Will the technology still exist to read the tape? Data placed in archive must still be protected according to its classification. Regulatory requirements must also be addressed. Different tools and providers might be part of this phase.

6. **Destroy:** Data being removed from the CSP. The destroy phase can be interpreted into different technical meanings according to usage, data content, and applications used. Data destruction can mean logically erasing pointers or permanently destroying data using physical or digital means. Consideration should be made according to regulation, type of cloud being used (infrastructure as a service [IaaS] versus software as a service [SaaS]), and the classification of the data.

LOCATION AND ACCESS OF DATA

Although the lifecycle does not require specification of the data location, who can access it, and from where, as a Certified Cloud Security Professional (CCSP), you need to fully understand and incorporate this into your planning to manage the lifecycle effectively within the enterprise.

Location

Data is a portable resource, capable of moving swiftly and easily between different locations, both inside and outside the enterprise. It can be generated in the internal network, be moved into the cloud for processing, and then be moved to a different provider for backup or archival storage.

The opportunity for portions of the data to be exported or imported to different systems at alternate locations cannot be discounted or overlooked.

The CCSP should pose the following questions alongside the relevant lifecycle phases:

■ Who are the actors that potentially have access to data that should be protected?

■ What are the potential locations for data that should be protected?

■ What are the controls in each of those locations?

- At what phases in each lifecycle can data move between locations?
- How does data move between locations (via what channels)?
- Where are these actors coming from? (What locations, and are they trusted or untrusted?)

Access

The traditional data lifecycle model does not specify requirements for who can access relevant data, nor how they are able to access it (device and channels). Mobile computing; the manner in which data can be accessed; and the wide variety of mechanisms and channels for storing, processing, and transmitting data across the enterprise have all amplified the impact of this lack of requirements.

FUNCTIONS, ACTORS, AND CONTROLS OF THE DATA

Upon completion of mapping the various data phases, data locations, and device access, it is necessary to identify what can be done with the data (that is, data functions) and who can access the data (that is, the actors). Once this has been established and understood, you need to check the controls to validate which actors have permissions to perform the relevant functions of the data (*Figure 2.3*).

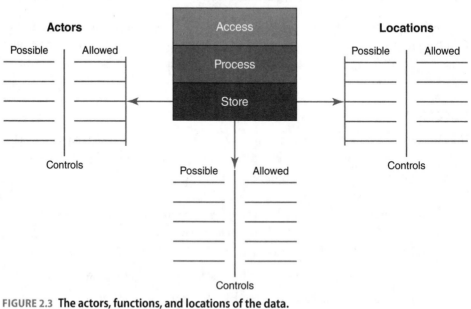

FIGURE 2.3 **The actors, functions, and locations of the data.**
SOURCE: https://securosis.com/tag/data+security+lifecycle

Key Data Functions

According to Securosis, the following illustrates key functions that can be performed with data in cloud-based environments:

- **"Access:** View/access the data, including copying, file transfers, and other exchanges of information
- **"Process:** Perform a transaction on the data. Update it, use it in a business processing transaction, and so on
- **"Store:** Store the data (in a file, database, etc.)"[2]

Take a look at how these functions map to the data lifecycle (*Figure 2.4*).

	Create	Store	Use	Share	Archive	Destroy
Access	X	X	X	X	X	X
Process	X		X			
Store		X			X	

FIGURE 2.4 Data functions mapping to the data lifecycle.
SOURCE: `https://securosis.com/tag/data+security+lifecycle`

Each of these functions is performed in a location by an actor (person).

Controls

Essentially, a control acts as a mechanism to restrict a list of possible actions to allowed or permitted actions. For example, encryption can be used to restrict the unauthorized viewing or use of data, application controls to restrict processing via authorization, and digital rights management (DRM) storage to prevent untrusted or unauthorized parties from copying or accessing data.

To determine the necessary controls to be deployed, you must first understand the following:

- Functions of the data
- Locations of the data
- Actors upon the data

After you have documented and understand these three items, you can design the appropriate controls and apply them to the system to safeguard data and control access to it. These controls can be of a preventative, detective (monitoring), or corrective nature.

Process Overview

You can use the table in *Figure 2.5* to walk through an overview of the process.

Function		Actor		Location	
Possible	Allowed	Possible	Allowed	Possible	Allowed

FIGURE 2.5 **Process overview.**

SOURCE: `https://securosis.com/tag/data+security+lifecycle`

Fill in the Function, Actor, and Location areas, signifying whether the item is possible to carry out with a Yes or a No.

- A No/No designation identifies items that are not available at this time within the organization.

- A Yes (possibility)/No (allowed) designation identifies items you could potentially negotiate with the organization to decide to allow at some point in the future.

- A Yes/Yes designation identifies items that are available and should be allowed. You may have to negotiate with the organization to formalize a plan for deployment and use of the function in question, along with the creation of the required policies and procedures to allow for the function's operation.

Tying It Together

At this point, we are able to produce a high-level mapping of data flow, including device access and data locations. For each location, we can determine the relevant function and actors. Once this is mapped, we can better define what to restrict from which actor and by which control (*Figure 2.6*).

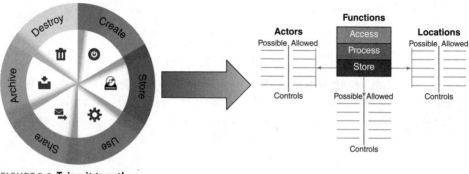

FIGURE 2.6 **Tying it together.**

CLOUD SERVICES, PRODUCTS, AND SOLUTIONS

At the core of all cloud services, products, and solutions are software tools with three underlying pillars of functionality:

- Processing data and running applications (compute servers)

- Moving data (networking)

- Preserving or storing data (storage)

Cloud storage is basically defined as data storage that is made available as a service via a network. Products and solutions are the most common cloud storage service–building blocks of physical storage systems. Private cloud and public services from SaaS and IaaS to platform as a service (PaaS) leverage tiered storage, including solid-state drives (SSDs) and hard disc drives (HDDs).

Similar to traditional enterprise storage environments, cloud services and solution providers exploit a mix of storage technology tiers that meet different service-level objective (SLO) and service-level agreement (SLA) requirements. For example, using fast SSDs for dense input/output (I/O) consolidation—supporting database journals and indices, metadata for fast lookup, and other transactional data—enables more work to be performed with less energy in a denser and more cost-effective manner.

Using a mixture of ultra-fast SSDs along with high-capacity HDDs provides a balance of performance and capacity to meet other service requirements with different service cost options. With cloud services, instead of specifying what type of physical drive to buy, CSPs cater to that by providing various availability, cost, capacity, functionality, and performance options to meet different SLA and SLO requirements.

DATA STORAGE

Data storage has to be considered for each of the cloud service models. IaaS, SaaS, and PaaS all need access to storage so they can provide services, but the type of storage technology used and the issues associated with each vary by service model. IaaS uses volume and object storage, whereas PaaS uses structured and unstructured storage. SaaS can use the widest array of storage types, including ephemeral, raw, and long-term storage. The following sections delve into these points in greater detail.

IaaS

Cloud infrastructure services, known as Infrastructure as a Service (IaaS), are self-service models for accessing, monitoring, and managing remote data center infrastructures, such as compute (virtualized or bare metal), storage, and networking services.

Instead of having to purchase hardware outright, users can purchase IaaS based on consumption. IaaS users are responsible for managing applications, data, runtime, middleware, and operating systems (OSs). Providers still manage virtualization, servers, hard drives, storage, and networking.

IaaS uses the following storage types (*Figure 2.7*):

- **Volume storage:** A virtual hard drive that can be attached to a virtual machine instance and be used to host data within a file system. Volumes attached to IaaS instances behave just like a physical drive or an array does. Examples include VMware Virtual Machine File System (VMFS), Amazon Elastic Block Store (EBS), RackSpace Redundant Array of Independent Disks(RAID), and Open-Stack Cinder.

- **Object storage:** Similar to a file share accessed via APIs or a web interface. Examples include Amazon S3 and Rackspace cloud files.

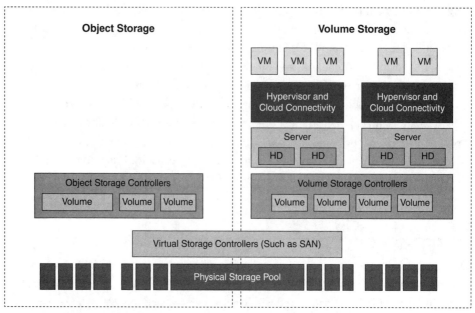

FIGURE 2.7 IaaS storage types.
SOURCE: https://securosis.com/assets/library/reports/Defending-Cloud-Data-with-Encryption.pdf

PaaS

Cloud platform services, or PaaS, are used for applications and other development while providing cloud components to software. What developers gain with PaaS is a framework they can build upon to develop or customize applications. PaaS makes the development, testing, and deployment of applications quick, simple, and cost effective. With this technology, enterprise operations or a third-party provider can manage OSs, virtualization, servers, storage, networking, and the PaaS software itself. Developers, however, manage the applications.

PaaS utilizes the following data storage types:

- **Structured:** Information with a high degree of organization, such that inclusion in a relational database is seamless and readily searchable by simple, straightforward search engine algorithms or other search operations.

- **Unstructured:** Information that does not reside in a traditional row-column database. Unstructured data files often include text and multimedia content. Examples include email messages, word processing documents, videos, photos, audio files, presentations, web pages, and many other kinds of business documents. Although these sorts of files may have an internal structure, they are still considered unstructured because the data they contain does not fit neatly in a database.

SaaS

Cloud application services, or SaaS, use the Web to deliver applications that are managed by a third-party vendor with interfaces being accessed on the client's side via one or more APIs.

Many SaaS applications can be run directly from a web browser without downloads or installations required, although some require small plug-ins. With SaaS, it is easy for enterprises to streamline their maintenance and support because vendors can manage everything: applications, runtime, data, middleware, OSs, virtualization, servers, storage, and networking. Popular SaaS offering types include email and collaboration, customer relationship management (CRM), and healthcare-related applications.

SaaS utilizes the following data storage types:

- **Information storage and management:** Data is entered into the system via the web interface and stored within the SaaS application (usually a back-end database). This data storage utilizes databases, which in turn are installed on object or volume storage.

- **Content and file storage:** File-based content is stored within the application.

  Other types of storage that may be utilized include these:

- **Ephemeral storage:** This type of storage is relevant for IaaS instances and exists only as long as its instance is up. It is typically used for swap files and other temporary storage needs and is terminated with its instance.

- **Content delivery network (CDN):** Content is stored in object storage, which is then distributed to multiple geographically distributed nodes to improve Internet consumption speed.

- **Raw storage:** Raw device mapping (RDM) is an option in the VMware server virtualization environment that enables a storage logical unit number (LUN) to be directly connected to a virtual machine (VM) from the storage area network (SAN). In Microsoft's Hyper-V platform, this is accomplished using pass-through disks.

- **Long-term storage:** Some vendors offer a cloud storage service tailored to the needs of data archiving. Typical data archiving needs include search, guaranteed immutability, and data lifecycle management. One example of this is the HP Autonomy Digital Safe archiving service, which uses an on-premises appliance that connects to customers' data stores via application programming interfaces (APIs) and allows user to search. Digital Safe provides read-only, write once read many (WORM), legal hold, e-discovery, and all the features associated with enterprise archiving. Its appliance carries out data deduplication prior to transmission to the data repository.

Threats to Storage Types

Data storage is subject to the following key threats:

- **Unauthorized usage:** In the cloud, data storage can be manipulated into unauthorized usage, such as by account hijacking or uploading illegal content. The multitenancy of the cloud storage makes tracking unauthorized usage more challenging.

- **Unauthorized access:** Unauthorized access can happen due to hacking, improper permissions in a multitenant's environment, or an internal CSP employee.

- **Liability due to regulatory noncompliance:** Specific controls (that is, encryption) might be required to ensure compliance with certain regulations. Not all cloud services enable all relevant data controls.

- **Denial-of-service (DoS) and distributed denial-of-service (DDoS) attacks on storage:** Availability is a strong concern for cloud storage. Without data, no instances can launch.

- **Corruption, modification, and destruction of data:** This can be caused by various sources: human error, hardware or software failure, events such as fire or flood, or intentional hacks. It can also affect a certain portion of the storage or the entire array.

- **Data leakage and breaches:** Consumers should always be aware that cloud data is exposed to data breaches. It can be external or coming from a CSP employee with storage access. Data tends to be replicated and moved in the cloud, which increases the likelihood of a leak.

- **Theft or accidental loss of media:** This threat applies to portable storage, but as cloud data centers grow and storage devices become smaller, there are increasingly more vectors for them to experience theft or similar threats.

- **Malware attack or introduction:** The goal of almost every malware is eventually reaching the data storage.

- **Improper treatment or sanitization after end of use:** End of use is challenging in cloud computing because usually we cannot enforce physical destruction of media. But the dynamic nature of data, where data is kept in different storages with multiple tenants, mitigates the risk that digital remnants can be located.

Technologies Available to Address Threats

You need to leverage different technologies to address the varied threats that may face the enterprise with regard to the safe storage and use of its data in the cloud (*Figure 2.8*).

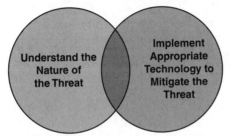

FIGURE 2.8 Basic approach to addressing a data threat.

The circumstances of each threat will be different. As a result, the key to success will be your ability to understand the nature of the threat you are facing, combined with your ability to implement the appropriate technology to mitigate the threat.

RELEVANT DATA SECURITY TECHNOLOGIES

It is important to be aware of the relevant data security technologies you may need to deploy or work with to ensure the AIC of data in the cloud.

Potential controls and solutions can include the following:

- **DLP:** For auditing and preventing unauthorized data exfiltration

- **Encryption:** For preventing unauthorized data viewing

- **Obfuscation, anonymization, tokenization, and masking:** Different alternatives for protecting data without encryption

Before working with these controls and solutions, it is important to understand how data dispersion is used in the cloud.

Data Dispersion in Cloud Storage

To provide high availability for data, assurance, and performance, storage applications often use the data dispersion technique. Data dispersion is similar to a RAID solution, but it is implemented differently. Storage blocks are replicated to multiple physical locations across the cloud. In a private cloud, you can set up and configure data dispersion yourself. Users of a public cloud do not have the capability to set up and configure data dispersion, although their data may benefit from the CSP using data dispersion.

The underlying architecture of this technology involves the use of erasure coding, which chunks a data object (think of a file with self-describing metadata) into segments. Each segment is encrypted, cut into slices, and dispersed across an organization's network to reside on different hard drives and servers. If the organization loses access to one drive, the original data can still be put back together. If the data is generally static with few rewrites, such as media files and archive logs, creating and distributing the data is a one-time cost. If the data is dynamic, the erasure codes have to be re-created and the resulting data blocks redistributed.

DLP

DLP, also known as data leakage prevention or data loss protection, describes the controls put in place by an organization to ensure that certain types of data (structured and unstructured) remain under organizational controls, in line with policies, standards, and procedures.

Controls to protect data form the foundation of organizational security and enable the organization to meet regulatory requirements and relevant legislation (that is, EU data-protection directives, U.S. privacy act, Health Insurance Portability and Accountability Act [HIPAA], and Payment Card Industry Data Security Standard [PCI DSS]). DLP technologies and processes play important roles when building those controls. The appropriate implementation and use of DLP reduces both security and regulatory risks for the organization.

DLP strategy presents a wide and varied set of components and controls that need to be contextually applied by the organization, often requiring changes to the enterprise security architecture. It is for this reason that many organizations do not adopt a full-blown DLP strategy across the enterprise.

For hybrid cloud users or those utilizing cloud-based services partially within their organizations, it is beneficial to ensure that DLP is understood and is appropriately structured across both cloud and noncloud environments. Failure to do so can result in segmented and nonstandardized levels of security—leading to increased risks.

DLP Components

DLP consists of three components:

- **Discovery and classification:** This is the first stage of a DLP implementation and an ongoing and recurring process. The majority of cloud-based DLP technologies are predominantly focused on this component. The discovery process usually maps data in cloud storage services and databases and enables classification based on data categories (regulated data, credit card data, public data, and more).

- **Monitoring:** Data usage monitoring for both ingress- and egress-based traffic flows forms the key function of DLP. Effective DLP strategies monitor the usage of data across locations and platforms while enabling administrators to define one or more usage policies. The ability to monitor data can be executed on gateways, servers, and storage as well as workstations and endpoint devices. Recently, the adoption of external services to assist with DLP "as a service" has increased, along with many cloud-based DLP solutions. The monitoring application should be able to cover most sharing options available for users (email applications, portable media, and Internet browsing) and alert them to policy violations.

- **Enforcement:** Many DLP tools provide the capability to interrogate data and compare its location, use, or transmission destination against a set of policies to prevent data loss. If a policy violation is detected, specified relevant enforcement actions can automatically be performed. Enforcement options can include the ability to alert and log, block data transfers or reroute them for additional validation, or encrypt the data prior to leaving the organizational boundaries.

DLP Architecture

DLP tool implementations typically conform to the following topologies:

- **Data in motion (DIM):** Sometimes referred to as network-based or gateway DLP. In this topology, the monitoring engine is deployed near the organizational gateway to monitor outgoing protocols such as hypertext transfer protocol (HTTP), hypertext transfer protocol secure (HTTPS), simple mail transfer protocol (SMTP), and file transfer protocol (FTP). The topology can be a mixture of proxy based, bridge, network tapping, or SMTP relays. To scan encrypted HTTPS traffic, appropriate mechanisms to enable SSL interception and broker are required to be integrated into the system architecture.

- **Data at rest (DAR):** Sometimes referred to as storage-based data. In this topology, the DLP engine is installed where the data is at rest, usually one or more storage subsystems, as well as file and application servers. This topology is effective for data discovery and for tracking usage but may require integration with network- or endpoint-based DLP for policy enforcement.

- **Data in use (DIU):** Sometimes referred to as client or endpoint based. The DLP application is installed on a user's workstations and endpoint devices. This topology offers insights into how users use the data, with the ability to add protection that the network DLP may not be able to provide. The challenge with client-based DLP is the complexity, time, and resources to implement across all endpoint devices, often across multiple locations and significant numbers of users.

Cloud-Based DLP Considerations

The following are some important considerations for cloud-based DLP:

- **Data in the cloud tends to move and replicate:** Whether it is between locations, data centers, backups, or back and forth into the organizations, the replication and movement can present a challenge to any DLP implementation.

- **Administrative access for enterprise data in the cloud could be tricky:** Make sure you understand how to perform discovery and classification within cloud-based storage.

- **DLP technology can affect overall performance:** Network or gateway DLP, which scans all traffic for predefined content, might have an effect on network performance. Client-based DLPs scan all workstation access to data, which can affect the workstation's operation. The overall impact must be considered during testing.

Leading Practices

Start with the data discovery and classification process. Those processes are more mature within the cloud deployments and present value to the data security process.

Cloud DLP policy should address the following:

- What kind of data is permitted to be stored in the cloud?

- Where can the data be stored (which jurisdictions)?

- How should it be stored (encryption and storage access consideration)?

- What kind of data access is permitted? Which devices and what networks? Which applications? Which tunnel?

- Under what conditions is data allowed to leave the cloud?

Encryption methods should be carefully examined based on the format of the data. Format-preserving encryption such as IRM is getting more popular in document storage applications; however, other data types may require vendor-agnostic solutions.

When implementing restrictions or controls to block or quarantine data items, it is essential to create procedures that prevent business process damage due to false positive events or indeed hinder legitimate transactions or processes from being performed.

DLP can be an effective tool when planning or assessing a potential migration to cloud applications. DLP discovery analyzes the data going to the cloud for content, and the DLP detection engine can discover policy violations during data migration.

Encryption

Encryption is an important technology to consider and use when implementing systems that allow for secure data storage and usage from the cloud. Although having encryption enabled on all data across the enterprise architecture reduces the risks associated with unauthorized data access and exposure, there are performance constraints and concerns to be addressed.

It is your responsibility as a CCSP to implement encryption within the enterprise in such a way that it provides the most security benefits, safeguarding the most mission-critical data while minimizing system performance issues as a result of the encryption.

Encryption Implementation

Encryption can be implemented within different phases of the data lifecycle:

- **DIM:** Technologies for encrypting data in motion are mature and well defined and include Internet protocol (IP) security protocol (IPSec), virtual private network (VPN), transport layer security/secure sockets layer (TLS/SSL), and other wire-level protocols.

- **DAR:** When the data is archived or stored, different encryption techniques should be used. The encryption mechanism itself may well vary in the manner in which it is deployed, dependent on the timeframe or indeed the period for which the data is stored. Examples of this include extended retention versus short-term storage, data located in a database versus a file system, and so on. This module discusses mostly DAR encryption scenarios.

- **DIU:** Data that is being shared, processed, or viewed. This stage of the data life-cycle is less mature than other data encryption techniques and typically focuses on IRM and DRM solutions.

Sample Use Cases for Encryption

The following are some use cases for encryption:

- When data moves in and out of the cloud—for processing, archiving, or sharing. Encryption will be used for data in motion techniques such as SSL/TLS or VPN to avoid information exposure or data leakage while in motion.

- Protecting data at rest such as file storage, database information, application components, archiving, and backup applications.

- Files or objects that must be protected when stored, used, or shared in the cloud.

- When complying with regulations such as HIPAA and PCI DSS, which in turn requires relevant protection of data traversing untrusted networks and protection of certain data types.

- Protection from third-party access via subpoena or lawful interception.

- Creating enhanced or increased mechanisms for logical separation between different customers' data in the cloud.

- Logical destruction of data when physical destruction is not feasible or technically possible.

Cloud Encryption Challenges

There are myriad factors influencing encryption considerations and associated implementations in the enterprise. Using encryption should always be directly related to business considerations, regulatory requirements, and any additional constraints that the organization may have to address. Different techniques will be used based on the location of data—whether at rest, in transit, or in use—while in the cloud.

Different options might apply when dealing with specific threats, such as protecting personally identifiable information (PII) or legally regulated information, or when defending against unauthorized access and viewing from systems and platform administrators.

Encryption Challenges

The following challenges are associated with encryption:

- The integrity of encryption is heavily dependent on control and management of the relevant encryption keys, including how they are secured. If the CSP holds the keys, not all data threats are mitigated against because unauthorized actors may gain access to the data through acquisition of the keys via a search warrant, legal ruling, or theft and misappropriation. Equally, if the customer is holding the encryption keys, this presents different challenges to ensure they are protected from unauthorized usage as well as compromise.

- Encryption can be challenging to implement effectively when a CSP is required to process the encrypted data. This is true even for simple tasks such as indexing and the gathering of metadata.

- Data in the cloud is highly portable. It replicates, is copied, and is backed up extensively, making encryption and key management challenging.

- Multitenant cloud environments and the shared use of physical hardware present challenges for the safeguarding of keys in volatile memory such as random access memory (RAM) caches.

- Secure hardware for encrypting keys may not exist in cloud environments, with software-based key storage often being more vulnerable.

- Storage-level encryption is typically less complex and can be more easily exploited and compromised, given sufficient time and resources. The higher you go up toward the application level, the more challenging the complexity to deploy and implement encryption becomes. However, encryption implemented at the application level is typically more effective at protecting the confidentiality of the relevant assets or resources.

- Encryption can negatively affect performance, especially high-performance data processing mechanisms such as data warehouses and data cubes.

- The nature of cloud environments typically requires you to manage more keys than traditional environments (access keys, API keys, encryption keys, and shared keys, among others).

- Some cloud encryption implementations require all users and service traffic to go through an encryption engine. This can result in availability and performance issues both to end users and to providers.

- Throughout the data lifecycle, data can change locations, format, encryption, and encryption keys. Using the data security lifecycle can help document and map all those different aspects.

- Encryption affects data availability. Encryption complicates data availability controls such as backups, disaster recovery planning (DRP), and colocations because expanding encryption into these areas increases the likelihood that keys may become compromised. In addition, if encryption is applied incorrectly within any of these areas, the data may become inaccessible when needed.

- Encryption does not solve data integrity threats. Data can be encrypted and yet be subject to tampering or file replacement attacks. In this case, supplementary cryptographic controls such as digital signatures need to be applied, along with nonrepudiation for transaction-based activities.

Encryption Architecture

Encryption architecture is very much dependent on the goals of the encryption solutions, along with the cloud delivery mechanism. Protecting DAR from local compromise or unauthorized access differs significantly from protecting DIM into the cloud. Adding controls to protect the integrity and availability of data can further complicate the process.

Typically, the following components are associated with encryption deployments:

- **The data:** This is the data object or objects that need to be encrypted.

- **Encryption engine:** This performs the encryption operation.

- **Encryption keys:** All encryption is based on keys. Safe-guarding the keys is a crucial activity, necessary for ensuring the ongoing integrity of the encryption implementation and its algorithms.

Data Encryption in IaaS

Keeping data private and secure is a key concern for those looking to move to the cloud. Data encryption can provide confidentiality protection for data stored in the cloud. In IaaS, encryption encompasses both volume and object storage solutions.

Basic Storage-Level Encryption

Where storage-level encryption is utilized, the encryption engine is located on the storage management level, with the keys usually held by the CSP. The engine encrypts data written to the storage and decrypts it when exiting the storage (that is, for use).

This type of encryption is relevant to both object and volume storage, but it only protects from hardware theft or loss. It does not protect from CSP administrator access or any unauthorized access coming from the layers above the storage.

Volume Storage Encryption

Volume storage encryption requires that the encrypted data reside on volume storage. This is typically done through an encrypted container, which is mapped as a folder or volume.

Instance-based encryption allows access to data only through the volume OS and therefore provides protection against the following:

- Physical loss or theft
- External administrator(s) accessing the storage
- Snapshots and storage-level backups being taken and removed from the system

Volume storage encryption does not provide protection against access made through the instance or an attack that is manipulating or operating within the application running on the instance.

Two methods can be used to implement volume storage encryption:

- **Instance-based encryption:** When instance-based encryption is used, the encryption engine is located on the instance itself. Keys can be guarded locally but should be managed external to the instance.

- **Proxy-based encryption:** When proxy-based encryption is used, the encryption engine is running on a proxy instance or appliance. The proxy instance is a secure machine that handles all cryptographic actions, including key management and storage. The proxy maps the data on the volume storage while providing access to the instances. Keys can be stored on the proxy or via the external key storage (recommended), with the proxy providing the key exchanges and required safeguarding of keys in memory.

Object Storage Encryption

The majority of object storage services offer server-side storage-level encryption, as described previously. This kind of encryption offers limited effectiveness, with the recommendation for external mechanisms to encrypt the data prior to its arrival within the cloud environments.

Potential external mechanisms include the following:

- **File-level encryption:** Examples include IRM and DRM solutions, both of which can be effective when used in conjunction with file hosting and sharing services that typically rely on object storage. The encryption engine is commonly implemented at the client side and preserves the format of the original file.

- **Application-level encryption:** The encryption engine resides in the application that is utilizing the object storage. It can be integrated into the application component or by a proxy that is responsible for encrypting the data before going to the cloud. The proxy can be implemented on the customer gateway or as a service residing at the external provider.

Database Encryption

For database encryption, the following options should be understood:

- **File-level encryption:** Database servers typically reside on volume storage. For this deployment, you are encrypting the volume or folder of the database, with the encryption engine and keys residing on the instances attached to the volume.

External file system encryption protects from media theft, lost backups, and external attack but does not protect against attacks with access to the application layer, the instances OS, or the database itself.

- **Transparent encryption:** Many database management systems contain the ability to encrypt the entire database or specific portions, such as tables. The encryption engine resides within the database, and it is transparent to the application. Keys usually reside within the instance, although processing and managing them may also be offloaded to an external Key Management Service (KMS). This encryption can provide effective protection from media theft, backup system intrusions, and certain database and application-level attacks.

- **Application-level encryption:** In application-level encryption, the encryption engine resides at the application that is utilizing the database.

Application encryption can act as a robust mechanism to protect against a range of threats, such as compromised administrative accounts and other database and application-level attacks. Because the data is encrypted before reaching the database, it is challenging to perform indexing, searches, and metadata collection. Encrypting at the application layer can be challenging based on the expertise requirements for cryptographic development and integration.

Key Management

Key management is one of the most challenging components of any encryption implementation. Even though new standards such as Key Management Interoperability Protocol (KMIP) are emerging, safeguarding keys and appropriately managing those keys are still the most complicated tasks you will need to engage in when planning cloud data security.

Following are some common challenges with key management:

- **Access to the keys:** Leading practices coupled with regulatory requirements may set specific criteria for key access, along with restricting or not permitting access to keys by CSP employees or personnel.

- **Key storage:** Secure storage for the keys is essential to safeguarding the data. In traditional in-house environments, keys were able to be stored in secure dedicated hardware. This may not always be possible in cloud environments.

- **Backup and replication:** The nature of the cloud results in data backups and replication across a number of different formats. This can affect the ability for long- and short-term key management to be maintained and managed effectively.

Key Management Considerations

Here are some considerations when planning key management:

- Random number generation should be conducted as a trusted process.
- Throughout the lifecycle, cryptographic keys should never be transmitted in the clear; they should always remain in a trusted environment.
- When considering key escrow or key management "as a service," carefully plan to take into account all relevant laws, regulations, and jurisdictional requirements.
- Lack of access to the encryption keys will result in lack of access to the data. This should be considered when discussing confidentiality threats versus availability threats.
- Where possible, key management functions should be conducted separately from the CSP to enforce separation of duties and force collusion to occur if unauthorized data access is attempted.

Key Storage in the Cloud

Key storage in the cloud is typically implemented using one or more of the following approaches:

- **Internally managed:** In this method, the keys are stored on the virtual machine or application component that is also acting as the encryption engine. This type of key management is typically used in storage-level encryption, internal database encryption, or backup application encryption. This approach can be helpful for mitigating against the risks associated with lost media.
- **Externally managed:** In this method, keys are maintained separate from the encryption engine and data. They can be on the same cloud platform, internally within the organization, or on a different cloud. The actual storage can be a separate instance (hardened especially for this specific task) or on a hardware security module (HSM). When implementing external key storage, consider how the key management system is integrated with the encryption engine and how the entire lifecycle of key creation through retirement is managed.
- **Managed by a third party:** This is when a trusted third party provides key escrow services. Key management providers use specifically developed secure infrastructure and integration services for key management. You must evaluate any third-party key storage services provider that may be contracted by the organization to ensure that the risks of allowing a third party to hold encryption keys is well understood and documented.

Key Management in Software Environments

Typically, CSPs protect keys using software-based solutions to avoid the additional cost and overhead of hardware-based security models.

Software-based key management solutions do not meet the physical security requirements specified in the National Institute of Standards and Technology (NIST) Federal Information Processing Standards Publication (FIPS) 140-2 or 140-3 specifications.[3] The ability for software to provide evidence of tampering is unlikely. The lack of FIPS certification for encryption may be an issue for U.S. federal government agencies and other organizations.

Masking, Obfuscation, Anonymization, and Tokenization

The need to provide confidentiality protection for data in cloud environments is a serious concern for organizations. The ability to use encryption is not always a realistic option for various reasons including performance, cost, and technical abilities. As a result, additional mechanisms need to be employed to ensure that data confidentiality can be achieved. Masking, obfuscation, anonymization, and tokenization can be used in this regard.

Data Masking

Data masking, or data obfuscation, is the process of hiding, replacing, or omitting sensitive information from a specific data set.

Data masking is typically used to protect specific data sets such as PII or commercially sensitive data or to comply with certain regulations such as HIPAA or PCI DSS. Data masking or obfuscation is also widely used for test platforms where suitable test data is not available. Both techniques are typically applied when migrating tests or development environments to the cloud or when protecting production environments from threats such as data exposure by insiders or outsiders.

Common approaches to data masking include these:

- **Random substitution:** The value is replaced (or appended) with a random value.
- **Algorithmic substitution:** The value is replaced (or appended) with an algorithm-generated value. (This typically allows for two-way substitution.)
- **Shuffle:** This shuffles different values from the data set. It is usually from the same column.
- **Masking:** This uses specific characters to hide certain parts of the data. It usually applies to credit card data formats: XXXX XXXX XX65 5432.
- **Deletion:** This simply uses a null value or deletes the data.

These are the primary methods of masking data:

- **Static:** In static masking, a new copy of the data is created with the masked values. Static masking is typically efficient when creating clean nonproduction environments.

- **Dynamic:** Dynamic masking, sometimes referred to as on-the-fly masking, adds a layer of masking between the application and the database. The masking layer is responsible for masking the information in the database on the fly when the presentation layer accesses it. This type of masking is efficient when protecting production environments. It can hide the full credit card number from customer service representatives, but the data remains available for processing.

Data Anonymization

Direct identifiers and indirect identifiers form two primary components for identification of individuals, users, or indeed personal information.

Direct identifiers are fields that uniquely identify the subject (usually name, address, and so on) and are usually referred to as PII. Masking solutions are typically used to protect direct identifiers.

Indirect identifiers typically consist of demographic or socioeconomic information, dates, or events. Although each standalone indirect identifier cannot identify the individual, the risk is that combining a number of indirect identifiers with external data can result in exposing the subject of the information. For example, imagine a scenario in which users were able to combine search engine data, coupled with online streaming recommendations to tie back posts and recommendations to individual users on a website.

Anonymization is the process of removing the indirect identifiers to prevent data analysis tools or other intelligent mechanisms from collating or pulling data from multiple sources to identify individual or sensitive information. The process of anonymization is similar to masking and includes identifying the relevant information to anonymize and choosing a relevant method for obscuring the data.

The challenge with indirect identifiers is the ability for this type of data to be integrated in free text fields that tend to be less structured than direct identifiers, thus complicating the process.

Tokenization

Tokenization is the process of substituting a sensitive data element with a nonsensitive equivalent, referred to as a token. The token is usually a collection of random values with the shape and form of the original data placeholder and mapped back to the original data by the tokenization application or solution.

Tokenization is not encryption and presents different challenges and different benefits. Encryption is using a key to obfuscate data, while tokenization removes the data entirely from the database, replacing it with a mechanism to identify and access the resources.

Tokenization is used to safeguard the sensitive data in a secure, protected, or regulated environment.

Tokenization can be implemented internally where there is a need to secure sensitive data centrally or externally using a tokenization service.

Tokenization can assist with each of these:

- Complying with regulations or laws
- Reducing the cost of compliance
- Mitigating risks of storing sensitive data and reducing attack vectors on that data

The basic tokenization architecture involves the following six steps (*Figure 2.9*):

1. An application collects or generates a piece of sensitive data.
2. Data is sent to the tokenization server; it is not stored locally.
3. The tokenization server generates the token. The sensitive data and the token are stored in the token database.
4. The tokenization server returns the token to the application.
5. The application stores the token rather than the original data.
6. When the sensitive data is needed, an authorized application or user can request it.

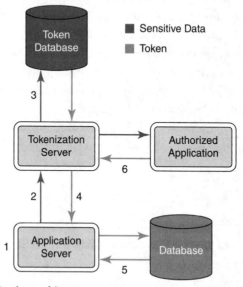

Basic Tokenization Architecture

FIGURE 2.9 **Basic tokenization architecture.**
SOURCE: https://securosis.com/Research/Publication/understanding-and-selecting-a-tokenization-solution

Keep the following tokenization and cloud considerations in mind:

- When using tokenization as a service, it is imperative to ensure the provider's and solution's ability to protect your data. Note that you cannot outsource accountability.

- When using tokenization as a service, special attention should be paid to the process of authenticating the application when storing or retrieving the sensitive data. Where external tokenization is used, appropriate encryption of communications should be applied to data in motion.

- As always, evaluate your compliance requirements before considering a cloud-based tokenization solution. You need to weigh the risks of having to interact with different jurisdictions and different compliance requirements.

APPLICATION OF SECURITY STRATEGY TECHNOLOGIES

When applying security strategies, it is important to consider the whole picture. Technologies may have dependencies or cost implications, and the larger organizational goals should be considered (such as time of storage versus encryption needs).

Table 2.1 shows the steps that you should consider when planning for data governance in the cloud.

TABLE 2.1 Data Security Strategies

PHASE	EXAMPLES
Understand data type	Regulated data, PII, business or commercial data, collaborative data
Understand data structure and format	Structured, unstructured data, and file types
Understand the cloud service module	IaaS, PaaS, SaaS
Understand the cloud storage options	Object storage, volume storage, database storage
Understand CSP data residency offering	Location Movement across borders Access
Plan data discovery and classification	Watermark, tag, or index all files and locations

(continues)

TABLE 2.1 *(continued)*

PHASE	EXAMPLES
Define data ownership	Define roles, entitlement, and access controls
Plan protection of data controls	Use of encryption or encryption alternatives (tokenization)
	Definition of data in motion encryption
	Protection of data controls also include backup and restore, DRP, secure disposal, and so on
Plan for ongoing monitoring	Periodic data extraction for backup
	Periodic backup and restore testing
	Ongoing event monitoring—audit data access events, detect malicious attempts, scan application-level vulnerabilities
	Periodic audits

EMERGING TECHNOLOGIES

It often seems that the cloud and the technologies that make it possible are evolving in many directions all at once. It can be hard to keep up with all the new and innovative technology solutions that are being implemented across the cloud landscape. Some examples of these exciting technologies, bit splitting and homomorphic encryption, are discussed in the following sections.

Bit Splitting

Bit splitting usually involves splitting up and storing encrypted information across different cloud storage services. Depending on how the bit splitting system is implemented, some or all of the data set is required to be available to unencrypt and read the data.

If a RAID 5 solution is used as part of the implementation, then the system is able to provide data redundancy as well as confidentiality protection, while making sure that a single CSP does not have access to the entire data set.

The benefits of bit splitting follow:

- Data security is enhanced due to the use of stronger confidentiality mechanisms.

- Bit splitting between different geographies and jurisdictions may make it harder to gain access to the complete data set via a subpoena or other legal processes.

- It can be scalable, can be incorporated into secured cloud storage API technologies, and can reduce the risk of vendor lock-in.

Although providing a useful solution to you, bit splitting also presents the following challenges:

- Processing and reprocessing the information to encrypt and decrypt the bits is a CPU-intensive activity.

- The whole data set may not be required to be used within the same geographies that the CSP stores and processes the bits within, leading to the need to ensure data security on the wire as part of the security architecture for the system.

- Storage requirements and costs are usually higher with a bit splitting system. Depending on the implementation, bit splitting can generate availability risks because all parts of the data may need to be available when decrypting the information.

Bit splitting can utilize different methods, a large percentage of which are based on secret sharing cryptographic algorithms:

- **Secret Sharing Made Short (SSMS):** Uses a three-phase process—encryption of information; use of information dispersal algorithm (IDA), which is designed to efficiently split the data using erasure coding into fragments; and splitting the encryption key using the secret sharing algorithm. The different fragments of data and encryption keys are then signed and distributed to different cloud storage services. The user can reconstruct the original data by accessing only m (lower than n) arbitrarily chosen fragments of the data and encryption key. An adversary has to compromise (m) cloud storage services and recover both the encrypted information and the encryption key that is also split.[4]

- **All-or-Nothing-Transform with Reed-Solomon (AONT-RS):** Integrates the AONT and erasure coding. This method first encrypts and transforms the information and the encryption key into blocks in a way that the information cannot be recovered without using all the blocks, and then it uses the IDA to split the blocks into m shares that are distributed to different cloud storage services (the same as in SSMS).[5]

Homomorphic Encryption

Homomorphic encryption enables processing of encrypted data without the need to decrypt the data. It allows the cloud customer to upload data to a CSP for processing without the requirement to decipher the data first.

The advantages of homomorphic encryption are sizeable, with cloud-based services benefitting most because it enables organizations to safeguard data in the cloud for processing while eliminating the majority of confidentiality concerns.

Note that homomorphic encryption is a developing area and does not represent a mature offering for most use cases. Many of the current implementations represent partial implementations of homomorphic encryption; however, these are typically limited to specific use cases involving small amounts or volumes of data.

DATA DISCOVERY

Data discovery is a departure from traditional business intelligence in that it emphasizes interactive, visual analytics rather than static reporting. The goal of data discovery is to work with and enable people to use their intuition to find meaningful and important information in data. This process usually consists of asking questions of the data in some way, seeing results visually, and refining the questions.

Contrast this with the traditional approach, which is for information consumers to ask questions. This approach causes reports to be developed, which are then fed to the consumer. This in turn generates more questions, which then generates more reports.

Data Discovery Approaches

Progressive companies consider data to be a strategic asset and understand its importance to drive innovation, differentiation, and growth. But leveraging data and transforming it into real business value requires a holistic approach to business intelligence and analytics. This is dramatically different from the business intelligence (BI) platforms of years past. It means going beyond the scope of most data visualization tools.

The continuing evolution of data discovery in the enterprise and the cloud is being driven by these trends:

- **Big data:** On big data projects, data discovery is more important and more challenging. Not only is the volume of data that must be efficiently processed for discovery larger, but the diversity of sources and formats presents challenges that make many traditional methods of data discovery fail. Cases in which big data initiatives also involve rapid profiling of high-velocity big data make data profiling harder and less feasible using existing toolsets.

- **Real-time analytics:** The ongoing shift toward (nearly) real-time analytics has created a new class of use cases for data discovery. These use cases are valuable but require data discovery tools that are faster, more automated, and more adaptive.

- **Agile analytics and agile business intelligence:** Data scientists and business intelligence teams are adopting more agile, iterative methods of turning data into business value. They perform data discovery processes more often and in more diverse ways, for example, when profiling new data sets for integration, seeking answers to new questions emerging this week based on last week's new analysis, or finding alerts about emerging trends that may warrant new analysis work streams.

Different Data Discovery Techniques

Data discovery tools differ by technique and data matching abilities. Assume you wanted to find credit card numbers. Data discovery tools for databases use a couple of methods to find and then identify information. Most use special login credentials to scan internal database structures, itemize tables and columns, and then analyze what was found. Three basic analysis methods are employed:

- **Metadata:** This is data that describes data. All relational databases store metadata that describes tables and column attributes. In the credit card example, you would examine column attributes to determine whether the name of the column or the size and data type resembles a credit card number. If the column is a 16-digit number or the name is something like CreditCard or CC#, then there's a high likelihood of a match. Of course, the effectiveness of each product will vary depending on how well the analysis rules are implemented. This remains the most common analysis technique.

- **Labels:** This is marked by data elements being grouped with a tag that describes the data. This can be done at the time the data is created, or tags can be added over time to provide additional information and references to describe the data. In many ways, it is just like metadata but slightly less formal. Some relational database platforms provide mechanisms to create data labels, but this method is more commonly used with flat files, becoming increasingly useful as more firms move to Indexed Sequential Access Method (ISAM) or quasi-relational data storage, such as Amazon's simpleDB, to handle fast-growing data sets. This form of discovery is similar to a Google search, with the greater the number of similar labels, the greater likelihood of a match. Effectiveness is dependent on the use of labels. ISAM is a file management system developed at IBM that allows records to be accessed either sequentially (in the order they were entered) or randomly (with an index). Each index defines a different ordering of the records.

- **Content analysis:** In this form of analysis, the data itself is analyzed by employing pattern matching, hashing, statistical, lexical, or other forms of probability analysis. In the case of the credit card example, when you find a number that resembles a credit card number, a common method is to perform a Luhn check on the number itself. This is a simple numeric checksum used by credit card companies to verify if a number is valid. If the number you discover passes the Luhn check, the probability is high that you have discovered a credit card number. The Luhn formula, which is also known as the modulus 10, or mod 10 algorithm, generates and validates the accuracy of credit card numbers. Content analysis is a growing trend and one that's being used successfully in DLP and web content analysis products.

Data Discovery Issues

You need to be aware of the following issues relating to data discovery:

- **Poor data quality:** Data visualization tools are only as good as the information that is inputted. If organizations lack an enterprise-wide data governance policy, they might be relying on inaccurate or incomplete information to create their charts and dashboards.

  Having an enterprise-wide data governance policy helps to mitigate the risk of a data breach. This includes defining rules and processes related to dashboard creation, ownership, distribution, and usage; creating restrictions on who can access what data; and ensuring that employees follow their organizations' data usage policies.

- **Dashboards:** With every dashboard, you have to wonder. Is the data accurate? Is the analytical method correct? Most importantly, can critical business decisions be based on this information?

  Users modify data and change fields with no audit trail and no way to tell who changed what. This disconnect can lead to inconsistent insight and flawed decisions, drive up administration costs, and inevitably create multiple versions of the truth.

  Security also poses a problem with data discovery tools. Information technology (IT) staff typically have little or no control over these types of solutions, which means they cannot protect sensitive information. This can result in unencrypted data being cached locally and viewed by or shared with unauthorized users.

- **Hidden costs:** A common data discovery technique is to put all the data into server RAM to take advantage of the inherent input/output rate improvements over disk. This technique has been successful and spawned a trend of using in-memory analytics for increased BI performance. Here's the catch, though: in-memory analytic solutions can struggle to maintain performance as the size of the data goes beyond the fixed amount of server RAM. For in-memory solutions, companies really need to hire someone with the right technical skills and background or purchase prebuilt appliances—both are unforeseen added costs. An integrated approach as part of an existing business intelligence platform delivers a self-managing environment that is a more cost-effective option. This is of interest especially for companies that are experiencing lagging query responses due to large data volumes or a high volume of ad hoc queries.

Challenges with Data Discovery in the Cloud

The challenges with data discovery in the cloud are threefold. They include identifying where your data is, accessing the data, and performing preservation and maintenance.

- **Identifying where your data is:** The ability to have data available on demand, across almost any platform and access mechanism, is an incredible advancement with regard to end user productivity and collaboration. However, at the same time, the security implications of this level of access confound both the enterprise or CCSP and the CSP, challenging all to find ways to secure the data that users are accessing in real time, from multiple locations, across multiple platforms.

  Not knowing where data is, where it is going, and where it will be at any given moment with assurance presents significant security concerns for enterprise data and the AIC that is required to be provided by the CCSP.

- **Accessing the data:** Not all data stored in the cloud can be accessed easily. Sometimes customers do not have the necessary administrative rights to access their data on demand, or long-term data can be visible to the customer but not accessible to download in acceptable formats for use offline.

  The lack of data access might require special configurations for the data discovery process, which in turn might result in additional time and expense for the organization. Data access requirements and capabilities can also change during the data lifecycle. Archiving, DR, and backup sets tend to offer less control and flexibility for the end user. In addition, metadata such as indexes and labels might not be accessible.

  When planning data discovery architectures, you should make sure you will have access to the data in a usable way and that metadata is accessible and in place. The required conditions for access to the data should be documented in the CSP SLA.

  There needs to be agreement ahead of time on issues such as the following:

  - Limits on the volume of data that will be accessible
  - The ability to collect and examine large amounts of data
  - Whether any related metadata will be preserved

  Other areas to examine and agree about ahead of time include storage costs, networking capabilities and bandwidth limitations, scalability during peak periods of usage, and any additional administrative issues that the CSP would need to bear responsibility for versus the customer.

- **Performing preservation and maintenance:** Who has the obligation to preserve data? It is up to you to make sure preservation requirements are clearly documented for, and supported by, the CSP as part of the SLA.

If the time requirement for preservation exceeds what has been documented in the provider SLA, the data may be lost. Long-term preservation of data is possible and can be managed via an SLA with a provider. However, the issues of data granularity, access, and visibility need to be considered when planning for data discovery against long-term stored data sets.

DATA CLASSIFICATION

Data classification as part of the information lifecycle management (ILM) process can be defined as a tool for categorization of data to help an organization effectively answer the following questions:

- What data types are available?
- Where is certain data located?
- What access levels are implemented?
- What protection level is implemented, and does it adhere to compliance regulations?

A data classification process is recommended for implementing data controls such as DLP and encryption. Data classification is also a requirement of certain regulations and standards, such ISO 27001 and PCI DSS.

Data Classification Categories

There are different reasons for implementing data classification and therefore many different parameters and categories for the classified data.

Some of the commonly used classification categories follow:

- Data type (format, structure)
- Jurisdiction (of origin, domiciled) and other legal constraints
- Context
- Ownership
- Contractual or business constraints
- Trust levels and source of origin
- Value, sensitivity, and criticality (to the organization or to a third party)
- Obligation for retention and preservation

The classification categories should match the data controls to be used. For example, when using encryption, data can be classified as "to encrypt" or "not to encrypt." For

DLP, other categories such as "internal use" and "limited sharing" are required to correctly classify the data.

The relationship between data classification and data labeling is important. Data labeling is usually referred to as tagging the data with additional information (department, location, and creator). One of the labeling options can be classification according to certain criteria: top secret, secret, classified. Classification is usually considered part of data labeling. It can be manual (a task usually assigned to the user creating the data) or automatic based on policy rules (according to location, creator, content, and so on).

Challenges with Cloud Data

Cloud data has some challenges:

- **Data creation:** The CCSP needs to ensure that proper security controls are in place so that whoever creates or modifies data must classify or update the data as part of the creation or modification process.

- **Classification controls:** Controls can be administrative (as guidelines for users who are creating the data), preventive, or compensating.

- **Metadata:** Classifications can sometimes be made based on the metadata that is attached to the file, such as owner or location. This metadata should be accessible to the classification process to make the proper decisions.

- **Classification data transformation:** Controls should be placed to make sure the relevant property or metadata can survive data object format changes and cloud imports and exports.

- **Reclassification consideration:** Cloud applications must support a reclassification process based on the data lifecycle. Sometimes the new classification of a data object may mean enabling new controls such as encryption or retention and disposal (for example, customer records moving from the marketing department to the loan department).

DATA PRIVACY ACTS

Privacy and data protection (P&DP) matters are often cited as a concern for cloud computing scenarios. The P&DP regulations affect not just those whose personal data is processed in the cloud (the data subjects) but also those (the cloud service customers) using cloud computing to process others' personal data and indeed those providing cloud services used to process that data (the service providers).

The key questions follow:

- What information in the cloud is regulated under data protection laws?
- Who is responsible for personal data in the cloud?
- Whose laws apply in a dispute?
- Where is personal data processed?

The global economy is undergoing an information explosion; there has been a massive growth in the complexity and volume of global data services. Personal data is now crucial material, and its protection and privacy have become important factors enabling the acceptance of cloud computing services.

The following is an overview of some of the ways in which different countries and regions around the world are addressing the varied legal and regulatory issues they face.

Global P&DP Laws in the United States

The United States has many sector-specific privacy and data security laws, both at the federal and the state levels. There is no official national Privacy Data Protection Authority; however, the Federal Trade Commission (FTC) has jurisdiction over most commercial entities and has authority to issue and enforce privacy regulations in specific areas (such as for telemarketing, spamming, and children's privacy). In addition to the FTC, a wide range of sector-specific regulators, particularly those in the healthcare and financial services sectors, have authority to issue and enforce privacy regulations.

Generally, the processing of personal data is subject to opt-out consent from the data subject, whereas the opt-in rule applies in special cases, such as the processing of sensitive or health data.

However, it is interesting to note that currently no specific geographic personal data transfer restrictions apply.

Regarding the accessibility of data stored within cloud services, it is important to underline that the Fourth Amendment to the U.S. Constitution applies; it protects people from unreasonable searches and seizures by the government. The Fourth Amendment, however, is not a guarantee against all searches and seizures, but only those that are deemed unreasonable under the law. Whether a particular type of search is considered reasonable in the eyes of the law is determined by balancing two important interests. On one side is the intrusion on an individual's Fourth Amendment rights; on the other side are legitimate government interests, such as public safety.

In 2012, the Obama Administration unveiled a Consumer Privacy Bill of Rights as part of a comprehensive blueprint to protect individual privacy rights and give users more control over how their information is handled in the United States.[6]

Global P&DP Laws in the European Union

The data protection and privacy laws in the EU member states are constrained by the EU directives, regulations, and decisions enacted by the European Union.

The main piece of legislation is the EU directive 95/46/EC "on the protection of individuals with regard to the processing of personal data and on the free movement of such data."[7]

These provisions apply in all the business and social sectors; thus, they cover the processing of personal data in cloud computing services. Furthermore, the European Union enacted a privacy directive (e-privacy directive) 2002/58/EC "concerning the processing of personal data and the protection of privacy in the electronic communications sector." This directive contains provisions concerning data breaches and the use of cookies.[8]

On March 12, 2014, the European Parliament formally adopted the text of the proposed EU General Data Protection Regulation for replacing the actual EU privacy directive 95/46/EC and of a new specific directive for privacy in the Police and Criminal Justice sector.[9]

The next steps for both the regulation and the directive are for the EU Council of Ministers to formulate a position and for trilateral negotiations between the European Commission, Parliament, and Council to begin. Entry into force is not expected before 2017.

Latin American as well as North Africa and medium-size Asian countries have privacy and data-protection legislation largely influenced by the EU privacy laws.

Global P&DP Laws in APEC

The Asia-Pacific Economic Cooperation council, or APEC, is becoming an essential point of reference for the data protection and privacy regulations of the region.

The APEC Ministers have endorsed the APEC privacy framework, recognizing the importance of the development of effective privacy protections that avoid barriers to information flows, ensure continued trade, and ensure economic growth in the APEC region. The APEC privacy framework promotes a flexible approach to information privacy protection across APEC member economies, while avoiding the creation of unnecessary barriers to information flows.

Differences Between Jurisdiction and Applicable Law

For privacy and data protection, it is particularly important to distinguish between these two concepts:

- **Applicable law:** This determines the legal standing of a case or issue.
- **Jurisdiction:** This usually determines the ability of a national court to decide a case or enforce a judgment or order.

The applicable law and the jurisdiction in relation to any given issue may not always be the same. This can be particularly true in the cloud services environment because of the complex nature of cloud hosting models and the ability to geolocate data across multiple jurisdictions.

Essential Requirements in P&DP Laws

The ultimate goal of P&DP laws is to provide safeguards to the individuals (data subjects) for the processing of their personal data in the respect of their privacy and will. This is achieved with the definitions of principles and rules to be fulfilled by the operators involved in the data processing. These operators who process the data are playing the role of data controller or data processor.

TYPICAL MEANINGS FOR COMMON PRIVACY TERMS

The following are common privacy terms and their basic meanings:

- **Data subject:** A subject who can be identified, directly or indirectly, in particular by reference to an identification number or to one or more factors specific to his physical, physiological, mental, economic, cultural, or social identity (such as telephone number or IP address).

- **Personal data:** Any information relating to an identified or identifiable natural person. There are many types of personal data, such as sensitive and health data and biometric data. According to the type of personal data, the P&DP laws usually set out specific privacy and data-protection obligations (such as security measures and data subject's consent for the processing).

- **Processing:** Operations that are performed upon personal data, whether or not by automatic means, such as collection, recording, organization, storage, adaptation, alteration, retrieval, consultation, use, disclosure by transmission, dissemination or otherwise making available, alignment or combination, blocking, erasure, or destruction. Processing is undertaken for specific purposes and scopes; as a result, the P&DP laws usually set out specific privacy and data-protection obligations, such as security measures and data subject's consent for the processing.

- **Controller:** The natural or legal person, public authority, agency, or any other body that alone or jointly with others determines the purposes and means of the processing of personal data. Where the purposes and means of processing are determined by national or community laws or regulations, the controller or the specific criteria for his nomination may be designated by national or community law.

- **Processor:** A natural or legal person, public authority, agency, or any other body that processes personal data on behalf of the controller.

PRIVACY ROLES FOR CUSTOMERS AND SERVICE PROVIDERS

The customer determines the ultimate purpose of the processing and decides on the outsourcing or the delegation of all or part of the concerned activities to external organizations. Therefore, the customer acts as a controller. In this role, the customer is responsible and subject to all the legal duties that are addressed in the P&DP laws applicable to the controller's role. The customer may task the service provider with choosing the methods and the technical or organizational measures to be used to achieve the purposes of the controller.

When the service provider supplies the means and the platform, acting on behalf of the customer, it is considered to be a data processor.

As a matter of fact, sometimes a service provider is considered either a joint controller or a controller in his own right, depending on concrete circumstances. However, even in complex data processing environments in which different controllers play a role in processing personal data, compliance with data-protection rules and responsibilities for possible breaches must be clearly allocated to avoid the protection of personal data being reduced to a negative conflict of competence.

In the current cloud computing scenario, customers may not have room to maneuver when negotiating the contractual terms of use of the cloud services because standardized offers are a feature of many cloud computing services. Nevertheless, it is ultimately the customer who decides on the allocation of part or the totality of processing operations to cloud services for specific purposes.

The imbalance in the contractual power of a small controller or customer with respect to large service providers should not be considered a justification for the controller to accept clauses and terms of contracts that are not in compliance with P&DP applicable to him.

In a cloud services environment, it is not always easy to properly identify and assign the roles of controller and processor between the customer and the service provider. However, this is a central factor of P&DP because all liabilities are assigned to the controller role, and its country of establishment mainly determines the applicable P&DP law and jurisdiction.

RESPONSIBILITY DEPENDING ON THE TYPE OF CLOUD SERVICES

The responsibilities of each role are dependent on the type of cloud service, as follows (*Figure 2.10*):

- **SaaS:** The customer determines and collects the data to be processed with a cloud service, whereas the service provider essentially makes the decisions of how to carry out the processing and implement specific security controls. It is not always possible to negotiate the terms of the service between the customer and the service provider.

- **PaaS:** The customer has higher possibility to determine the instruments of processing, although the terms of the services are not usually negotiable.

- **IaaS:** The customer has a high level of control for data, processing functionalities, tools, and related operational management, thus achieving a high level of responsibility in determining purposes and means of processing.

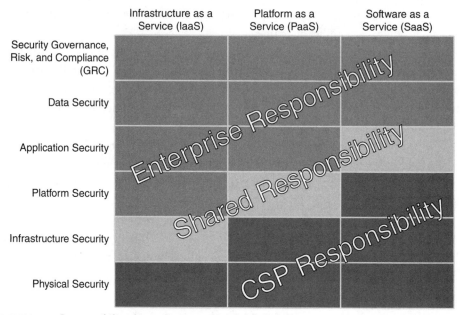

FIGURE 2.10 Responsibility depending on type of cloud service.

Therefore, although the main rule for identifying a controller is to search who determines purpose and scope of processing, in the SaaS and PaaS types, the service provider can also be considered a controller or joint controller with the customer. The proper identification of the controller and processor roles is essential for clarifying the P&DP liabilities of customer and service provider, as well as the applicable law.

Note that the cloud services agreement between the customer and the service provider should incorporate proper clauses and attachments to clarify the privacy roles and identify the applicable data protection, privacy measures, and consequent allocations of duties to ensure effective fulfillments as required by the applicable P&DP laws.

A guide that may be helpful to use for a proper identification of controller and processor roles in a cloud services environment in terms of SaaS, PaaS, and IaaS is NIST document SP800-145, "The NIST Definition of Cloud Computing."[10]

IMPLEMENTATION OF DATA DISCOVERY

The implementation of data discovery solutions provides an operative foundation for effective application and governance for any of the P&DP fulfillments.

- **From the customer's perspective:** The customer, in his role of data controller, has full responsibility for compliance with the P&DP laws obligations. Therefore, the implementation of data discovery solutions with data classification techniques provide a sound basis for operatively specifying to the service provider the requirements to be fulfilled and for performing effective periodic audit according to the applicable P&DP laws. They also demonstrate, to the competent privacy authorities, the customer's due accountability according to the applicable P&DP laws.

- **From the service provider's perspective:** The service providers, in the role of data processor, must implement and be able to demonstrate they have implemented in a clear and objective way the rules and the security measures to be applied in the processing of personal data on behalf of the controller. Thus, data discovery solutions with data classification techniques provide an effective enabler factor for their ability to comply with the controller P&DP instructions.

Furthermore, the service provider particularly benefits from this approach:

- For its duty to detect, promptly report to the controller, and properly manage the personal data breaches with respect to the applicable P&DP obligations.

- When the service provider involves subservice providers, to clearly trace and operatively transfer to them the P&DP requirements according to the processing assigned.

- When the service provider has to support the controller in any of the P&DP obligations concerning the application of rules and prohibitions of personal data transfer through multiple countries.

- For its duty to operatively support the controller when a data subject exercises his rights; thus, it is required information about which data is processed or to implement actions on this data (correct or destroy the data).

Implementation of data discovery with data classification techniques represents the foundation of DLP and data protection, which is applied to personal data processing to operate in compliance with the P&DP laws.

CLASSIFICATION OF DISCOVERED SENSITIVE DATA

Classification of data for the purpose of compliance with the applicable P&DP laws plays an essential role in the operative control of those elements that are the feeds of the P&DP fulfillments. This means that not only the nature of the data should be traced with classification but also its relationship to the P&DP law context in which the data itself should be processed.

In fact, the P&DP fulfillments, and especially the security measures required by these laws, can always be expressed at least in terms of a set of primary entities:

- **Scope and purpose of the processing:** This generally represents the main footprint that influences the whole set of typical P&DP fulfillments. For example, processing for administrative and accounting purposes requires fewer fulfillments in terms of security measures and obligations toward the data subjects and the DPAs compared with the processing of traffic telephone or Internet data for the purpose of mobile payment services. That's because the cluster of data processed (personal data of the subscriber, his billing data, the kind of purchased objects) assumes a more critical value for all the stakeholders involved and the P&DP laws consequently require more obligations and a higher level of protection.

- **Categories of the personal data to be processed:** Note that the category of the data means the type of data as identified for the purpose of a P&DP law. Usually this is quite different from the nature of the data—that is, its intrinsic and objective value. In this sense, data categories include these:

  - Personal data

  - Sensitive data (health, religious belief, political belief, sexuality, and so on)

  - Biometric data

  - Telephone or Internet data

  - Categories of the processing to be performed

  From the point of view of the P&DP laws, processing means an operation or a set of combined operations that can be materially applied to data; therefore, in this sense processing can be one or more of the following operations:

  - Collection

  - Recording

  - Organization

- Selection
- Retrieval
- Comparison
- Communication
- Dissemination
- Erasure

In derivation of these, a secondary set of entities is relevant for P&DP fulfillments:

- The geographic data locations are allowed to be considered and used for hosting of data.
- According to the applicable P&DP laws, there are constraints and prohibitions to be observed, and this should be properly reflected in the classification of data to act as a driver in allowing or blocking the moving of data from one location to another one.

- **Categories of users allowed:** Accessibility of data for a specific category of users is another essential feature for the P&DP laws. For example, the role of backup operator should not be able to read any data in the system even though the operator role needs to be able to interact with all system data to back it up.

- **Data-retention constraints:** The majority of the categories of data processed for specific scopes and purposes must be retained for a determined period of time (and then erased or anonymized) according to the applicable P&DP laws. For example, there are data-retention periods to be respected for access logs concerning the accesses made by the role of system administrator, and there are data retention periods to be respected for the details concerning the profiles defined from the online behavior of Internet users for the purpose of marketing. Once the retention period has ended, the legal ground for retention of the data disappears; therefore, any additional processing or handling of the data becomes unlawful.

- **Security measures to be ensured:** The type of security measures can vary widely depending on the purpose and data to be processed. Typically, they are expressed in terms of the following:
  - Basic security measures to ensure a minimum level of security regardless of the type of purpose, data, or processing
  - Specific measures according to the type of purpose, data, or processing
  - Measures identified in terms of output from a risk analysis process, to be operated by the controller or processor considering the risks of a specific context (technical, operational) that cannot be mitigated with the measures of the previous points

Proper classification of the data in terms of security measures provides the basis for any approach of control based on data leakage prevention and data protection processes.

- **Data breach constraints:** Several P&DP laws around the world already provide for specific obligations in terms of data breach. These obligations essentially require one to do the following:
  - Notify the competent DPA within tighter time limits.
  - Notify, in some specific cases set forth by law, the data subjects.
  - Follow a specific process of incident management, including activation of measures aimed at limiting the damages to the concerned data subjects.
  - Handle a secure archive concerning the occurred data breach.

  Therefore, data classification that can take into account the operational requirements coming from the data breach constraints becomes essential, especially in the cloud services context.

- **Status:** As a consequence of events such as a data breach, data can be left in a specific state that may require a number of necessary actions or a state where certain actions are prohibited. The clear identification of this status in terms of data classification can direct and oversee any further processing of the data according to the applicable laws.

Table 2.2 provides a quick recap of the main input entities for data classification with regard to P&DP.

TABLE 2.2 Main Input Entities for Data Classification for P&DP Purposes

SETS	INPUT ENTITIES
Primary set	P&DP law
	Scope and purpose of the processing
	Categories of the personal data to be processed
	Categories of the processing to be performed
Secondary set	Data location allowed
	Categories of users allowed
	Data retention constraints
	Security measures to be ensured
	Data breach constraints
	Status

✔ Note About Methods to Perform Classification

Data classification can be accomplished in different ways ranging from tagging the data by using other external information to extrapolating the classification from the content of the data. The latter one, however, may raise some concerns because, according to the laws of some jurisdictions, this can result in prohibited monitoring actions on the content belonging to data subjects (for example, the laws that restrict or prohibit access to the content of email in employer-employee relationships).

The use of classification methods should be properly outlined in the cloud service agreements between the customer and the service provider to achieve efficacy in classification within the limits set out by the laws governing the access to the data content.

MAPPING AND DEFINITION OF CONTROLS

All the P&DP requirements are important in a cloud service context; however, it is appropriate to bear in mind the key privacy cloud service factors (*Figure 2.11*).

Applicable Law
The law of the country or countries where customer/controller is established

Relationships - Customer/Service Provider/Subcontractor
Essential clarifications: ☑ Responsibility allocation for law compliance purposes ☑ How to operatively allow the exercise of data subjects

Fundamental Principles		
Transparency	**Purpose - Specification and Limitation**	**Data Retention and Erasure**
☑ Between customer and data subjects ☑ Between customer and service provider ☑ Clear and complete agreement	☑ Risk from the presence of many service providers and subcontractors ☑ Technological and organizational measures and contractual obligations	☑ Necessary reliability in these operations ☑ Technological and orginizational measures and contractual obligations

Contractual Safeguards and Data Transfers in Third Countries
☑ Agreements are necessary between customer and service provider for specification of obligations concerning privacy and data protection fulfillments ☑ Special focus to lawfully perform data transfer

FIGURE 2.11 **Key privacy cloud service factors.**

These key privacy cloud service factors stem from the "Opinion 5/2012 on Cloud Computing" adopted by the WP 29; this working party was set up under Article 29 of Directive 95/46/EC, and it is an independent European advisory body on data protection and privacy, essentially formed by the representatives of all the EU data protection authorities.[11]

These factors show that the primary need is to properly clarify in terms of contractual obligations the privacy and data protection requirements between the customer and the CSP.

PRIVACY LEVEL AGREEMENT

In this context, the CSA has defined baselines for compliance with data protection legislation and leading practices with the realization of a standard format named by the Privacy Level Agreement (PLA). By means of the PLA, the service provider declares the level of personal data protection and security that it sustains for the relevant data processing.

The PLA, as defined by the CSA, does the following:

- Provides a clear and effective way to communicate the level of personal data protection offered by a service provider

- Works as a tool to assess the level of a service provider's compliance with data protection legislative requirements and leading practices

- Provides a way to offer contractual protection against possible financial damages due to lack of compliance

PLA VERSUS ESSENTIAL P&DP REQUIREMENTS ACTIVITY

The various PLAs are documented by the CSA on its website. Table 2.3 provides a schematic outline of the PLA expected content and a mapping on the aforementioned essential P&DP requirements. Review Table 2.3 to identify the key differences between the PLA and the essential P&DP requirements.

TABLE 2.3 Key Differences Between the PLA and the Essential P&DP Requirements

| CSA PLA OUTLINE ANNEX I (*) | ESSENTIAL P&DP REQUIREMENTS | | | |
	FULFILLMENTS TOWARD THE DATA SUBJECTS	FULFILLMENTS TOWARD THE DATA PROTECTION AUTHORITY (DPA)	ORGANIZATIONAL-CONTRACTUAL MEASURES	TECHNICAL-PROCEDURAL MEASURES
1. Identify the Cloud Services Privacy Role Contact Data of Relevant Privacy Persons		X (Some of this information may be needed for the DPA notification, when due according to the applicable P&DP law)	X	
2. Categories of Personal Data That the Customer Is Prohibited from Sending to or Processing in the Cloud				X (Regarding the data transfer fulfillments)
3. Ways in Which the Data Will Be Processed (Details concerning personal data location, subcontractors, installation of software on cloud customers' systems)	X		X	X
4. Data Transfer (Details on the legal instruments to be used for lawfully transferring the data, locations of the data servers)	X (Information to data subject has to be consistent with data transfer info)		X	X

(continues)

TABLE 2.3 *(continued)*

	ESSENTIAL P&DP REQUIREMENTS			
CSA PLA OUTLINE ANNEX I (*)	FULFILLMENTS TOWARD THE DATA SUBJECTS	FULFILLMENTS TOWARD THE DATA PROTECTION AUTHORITY (DPA)	ORGANIZATIONAL-CONTRACTUAL MEASURES	TECHNICAL-PROCEDURAL MEASURES
5. Data Security Measures (Details concerning the technical, procedural, organizational, and physical measures for ensuring data: availability, integrity, confidentiality, transparency, purpose limitation Specify as applicable the security framework and certifications schema: CSA CCM, ISO/IEC 27001, NIST SP 800 53)			X	X
6. Monitoring		X		
7. Third-Party Audits	X		X	X
8. Personal Data Breach Notification (From the provider to the customer)			X	X
9. Data Portability, Migration, and Transfer Back Assistance			X	X
10. Data Retention, Restitution, and Deletion			X	X

| CSA PLA OUTLINE ANNEX I (*) | ESSENTIAL P&DP REQUIREMENTS | | | |
	FULFILLMENTS TOWARD THE DATA SUBJECTS	FULFILLMENTS TOWARD THE DATA PROTECTION AUTHORITY (DPA)	ORGANIZATIONAL-CONTRACTUAL MEASURES	TECHNICAL-PROCEDURAL MEASURES
11. Accountability (Details on how the provider [its subcontractors] can demonstrate compliance with the applicable P&DP laws)			X	X
12. Cooperation (Details on how the provider supports the customer to ensure compliance with applicable data protection provisions)	X	X		
13. Law Enforcement Access (Details on the process for managing the request to disclose personal data by law enforcement authorities)	X (**)	X (**)	X (**)	X (**)
14. Remedies (In case of breaches to the PLA)	X (**)	X (**)	X (**)	X (**)
15. Complaint; Dispute Resolution	X (**)	X (**)	X (**)	X (**)

(continues)

TABLE 2.3 *(continued)*

| CSA PLA OUTLINE ANNEX I (*) | ESSENTIAL P&DP REQUIREMENTS | | | |
	FULFILLMENTS TOWARD THE DATA SUBJECTS	FULFILLMENTS TOWARD THE DATA PROTECTION AUTHORITY (DPA)	ORGANIZATIONAL-CONTRACTUAL MEASURES	TECHNICAL-PROCEDURAL MEASURES
16. CSP Insurance Policy (Details on the provider's cyber insurance policy, if any, including insurance regarding security breaches)	X (**)	X (**)	X (**)	X (**)

(*) `https://cloudsecurityalliance.org/download/privacy-level-agreement-pla-outline-annex/`

(**) It can involve and receive impacts with regard to the relevant P&DP fulfillments.

The DLP techniques, already described in the previous modules, provide an effective basis to prevent unauthorized use, access, and transfer of data. As such, they are essential elements in the strategy to achieve compliance with the requirements specified in the PLA. A detailed description of the DLP techniques for cloud service purposes can be found within the resources made available by the Cloud Security Alliance on its website: `https://cloudsecurityalliance.org`.

APPLICATION OF DEFINED CONTROLS FOR PII

The operative application of defined controls for the protection of PII is widely affected by the cluster of providers and subproviders involved in the operation of a specific cloud service; therefore, any attempt to provide guidelines for this can be made only at the general level.

Because the application of data-protection measures has the ultimate goal of fulfilling the P&DP laws applicable to the controller, any constraints arising from specific arrangements of a cloud service operation shall be made clear by the service provider to avoid consequences for unlawful personal data processing. For example, with regard to servers located across several countries, it would be difficult to ensure the proper application of measures such as encryption for sensitive data on all systems.

In this context, the previously mentioned PLAs play an essential role. Furthermore, the service providers can benefit from making explicit reference to standardized frameworks of security controls expressly defined for cloud services. One such example is the Trust Services Principles and Criteria for Security, Availability, Processing Integrity, Confidentiality, and Privacy (TSP100) that the American Institute of CPAs (AICPA) has developed. The Trust Services are a set of professional attestation and advisory services that address risk. According to AICPA, the following principles should be used in the performance of Trust Services engagements:

- **Security.** The system is protected against unauthorized access (both physical and logical).

- **Availability.** The system is available for operation and use as agreed.

- **Processing Integrity.** System processing is complete, accurate, timely, and authorized.

- **Confidentiality.** Information designated as confidential is protected as agreed.

- **Privacy.** Personal information is collected, used, retained, disclosed, and destroyed in conformity with the commitments in the entity's privacy notice and with criteria set forth in Generally Accepted Privacy Principles.

Cloud Security Alliance Cloud Controls Matrix

In this sense, the Cloud Security Alliance Cloud Controls Matrix (CCM) is an essential and up-to-date security controls framework that is addressed to the cloud community and stakeholders. A fundamental richness of the CCM is its ability to provide mapping and cross relationships with the main industry-accepted security standards, regulations, and controls frameworks, such as the ISO 27001/27002, ISACA's COBIT, and PCI DSS.

The CCM can be seen as an inventory of cloud service security controls, arranged in the following separate security domains:

- Application and Interface Security
- Audit Assurance and Compliance
- Business Continuity Management and Operational Resilience
- Change Control and Configuration Management

- Data Security and Information Lifecycle Management
- Data Center Security
- Encryption and Key Management
- Governance and Risk Management
- Human Resources
- Identity and Access Management
- Infrastructure and Virtualization Security
- Interoperability and Portability
- Mobile Security
- Security Incident Management, E-Discovery, and Cloud
- Supply Chain Management, Transparency, and Accountability
- Threat and Vulnerability Management

Although all the CCM security controls can be considered applicable in a specific cloud services context, from the privacy and data-protection perspective, some of them have greater relevance to the P&DP fulfillments.

Therefore, the selection and implementation of controls for a specific cloud service involving processing of personal data shall be performed in the following ways:

- Within the context of an information security managed system. This requires at least the identification of law requirements, risk analysis, design and implementation of security policies, and related assessment and reviews.
- Considering the typical set of data protection and privacy measures required by the P&DP laws.

Table 2.4 shows a schematic representation of such relevance.

TABLE 2.4 Main Relevance of CCM Security Domains for P&DP Fulfillments

	FULFILLMENTS TOWARD THE DATA SUBJECTS			FULFILLMENTS TOWARD THE DATA PROTECTION AUTHORITY (DPA)			ORGANIZATIONAL-CONTRACTUAL MEASURES			TECHNICAL-PROCEDURAL MEASURES		
	Notice	Consent	Exercise of rights	Notification for specific processing or for specific data breach cases	DPA prior checking for specific cases of privacy risks	Authorization for specific processing	Controller-processor privacy agreement	Data transfer agreement	Training, appointment, and control for personnel in charge of data processing	Technical/procedural security measures	Data breach identification and management	Data retention requirements for specific processing
Application and Interface Security										X		
Audit Assurance and Compliance							X					
Business Continuity Management and Operational Resilience										X	X	X
Change Control and Configuration Management										X		
Data Security and Information Lifecycle Management							X			X		
Data Center Security							X					
Encryption and Key Management							X			X		
Governance and Risk Management							X	X				
Human Resources							X	X	X			

(continues)

TABLE 2.4 *(continued)*

	FULFILLMENTS TOWARD THE DATA SUBJECTS			FULFILLMENTS TOWARD THE DATA PROTECTION AUTHORITY (DPA)			ORGANIZATIONAL-CONTRACTUAL MEASURES			TECHNICAL-PROCEDURAL MEASURES		
	Notice	Consent	Exercise of rights	Notification for specific processing or for specific data breach cases	DPA prior checking for specific cases of privacy risks	Authorization for specific processing	Controller-processor privacy agreement	Data transfer agreement	Training, appointment, and control for personnel in charge of data processing	Technical/procedural security measures	Data breach identification and management	Data retention requirements for specific processing
Identity and Access Management									X	X	X	
Infrastructure and Virtualization Security									X	X		
Interoperability and Portability										X		
Mobile Security									X	X		
Security Incident Management, E-Discovery, and Cloud Forensics				X					X		X	
Supply Chain Management, Transparency, and Accountability							X			X		
Threat and Vulnerability Management										X		

Management Control for Privacy and Data-Protection Measures

There is a need to have management oversight and control for privacy and data protection measures. *Figure 2.12* illustrates the typical process flow that identifies issues and external variables to consider during the designing of policies. The designing and implementing of security policies is carried out with input from senior management and reference to any of the issues identified. Assessment and review of the policy is also carried out with a reference to issues identified and input from senior management. Risk analysis is performed to ensure that all policies are understood in the context of the risks they may introduce into the organization. The outcome of this assessment is shared with senior management and is used to weigh the applicability and usability of the policy within the organization. Adjustments or changes required to be implemented as a result of the assessment to adjust the policy in any way are fed back into the policy cycle to drive implementation of the changes.

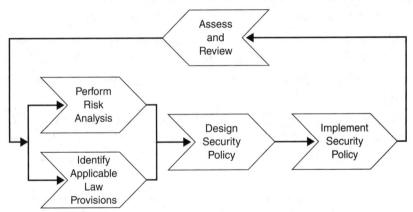

FIGURE 2.12 Management control for privacy and data-protection measures.

When implementing a security policy, typical data protection and privacy measures include the following:

- Segregation of roles and appointments
- Training and instructions
- Authentication techniques and procedures
- Authorization techniques and procedures
- Control on the time validity of assigned authorization profiles
- Vulnerability control (patches and hardening)
- Intrusion and malware detection and relevant countermeasures
- Backup plans, techniques, and procedures

- Data recovery plans, techniques, and procedures
- Additional measures according to the criticality of the personal data or the purpose of processing (strong authentication techniques and encryption)
- Personal data breach management plans, techniques, and procedures
- Log activities according to the criticality of personal data or the purpose of processing
- Data-retention control according to the purpose of processing
- Secure disposal of personal data and of processing equipment when no longer necessary

DATA RIGHTS MANAGEMENT OBJECTIVES

IRM is not just the use of standard encryption technologies to provide confidentiality for data—it is much more. Here is a short list of some of its features and use cases:

- IRM adds an extra layer of access controls on top of the data object or document. The ACL determines who can open the document and what they can do with it and provides granularity that flows down to printing, copying, saving, and similar options.
- Because IRM contains ACLs and is embedded into the original file, IRM is agnostic to the location of the data, unlike other preventive controls that depended on file location. IRM protection travels with the file and provides continuous protection.
- IRM is useful for protecting sensitive organization content such as financial documents. However, it is not limited to documents; IRM can be implemented to protect emails, web pages, database columns, and other data objects.
- IRM is useful for setting up a baseline for the default Information Protection Policy; that is, all documents created by a certain user, at a certain location, receive a specific policy.

IRM Cloud Challenges

IRM requires that all users with data access have matching encryption keys. This requirement means strong identity infrastructure is a must when implementing IRM, and the identity infrastructure should expand to customers, partners, and any other organizations with which data is shared.

- IRM requires that each resource be provisioned with an access policy. Each user accessing the resource is provisioned with an account and keys. Provisions should be made securely and efficiently for the implementation to be successful. Automation of provisioning of IRM resource access policy can help in implementing that goal. Automated policy provision can be based on file location, keywords, or origin of the document.

- Access to resources can be granted on a per-user basis or according to user role using a role-based access control (RBAC) model. Provisioning of users and roles should be integrated into IRM policies. Because in IRM most of the classification is in the user responsibility, or based on automated policy, implementing the right RBAC policy is crucial.

- Identity infrastructure can be implemented by creating a single location where users are created and authenticated or by creating federation and trust between different repositories of user identities in different systems. Carefully consider the most appropriate method based on the security requirements of the data.

- Most IRM implementations force end users to install a local IRM agent either for key storage or for authenticating and retrieving the IRM content. This feature may limit certain implementations that involve external users and should be considered part of the architecture planning prior to deployment.

- When reading IRM-protected files, the reader software should be IRM aware. The latest versions of Adobe and Microsoft products have good IRM support, but other readers could encounter compatibility issues and should be tested prior to deployment.

- The challenges of IRM compatibility with different OSs and different document readers increase when the data needs to be read on mobile devices. The usage of mobile platforms and IRM should also be tested carefully.

- IRM can integrate into other security controls such as DLP and document discovery tools, adding extra benefits.

IRM Solutions

Following are the key capabilities common to IRM solutions:

- **Persistent protection:** Ensures that documents, messages, and attachments are protected at rest, in transit, and even after they're distributed to recipients

- **Dynamic policy control:** Allows content owners to define and change user permissions (view, forward, copy, or print) and recall or expire content even after distribution

- **Automatic expiration:** Provides the ability to automatically revoke access to documents, emails, and attachments at any point, thus allowing information security policies to be enforced wherever content is distributed or stored

- **Continuous audit trail:** Provides confirmation that content was delivered and viewed and offers proof of compliance with your organization's information security policies

- **Support for existing authentication security infrastructure:** Reduces administrator involvement and speeds deployment by leveraging user and group information that exists in directories and authentication systems

- **Mapping for repository ACLs:** Automatically maps the ACL-based permissions into policies that control the content outside the repository

- **Integration with all third-party email filtering engines:** Allows organizations to automatically secure outgoing email messages in compliance with corporate information security policies and federal regulatory requirements

- **Additional security and protection capabilities:** Allows users additional capabilities such as these:

  - Determining who can access a document

  - Prohibiting printing of an entire document or selected portions

  - Disabling copy, paste, and screen capture capabilities

  - Watermarking pages if printing privileges are granted

  - Expiring or revoking document access at any time

  - Tracking all document activity through a complete audit trail

- **Support for email applications:** Provides interface and support for email programs such as Microsoft Outlook and IBM Lotus Notes

- **Support for other document types:** Other document types, besides Microsoft Office and Adobe PDF, can be supported as well

DATA-PROTECTION POLICIES

Data-protection policies should include guidelines for the different data lifecycle phases. In the cloud, the following three policies should receive proper adjustments and attention:

- Data retention

- Data deletion

- Data archiving

Data-Retention Policies

A data-retention policy is an organization's established protocol for keeping information for operational or regulatory compliance needs. The objectives of a data-retention policy are to keep important information for future use or reference, to organize information so it can be searched and accessed at a later date, and to dispose of information that is no longer needed. The policy balances the legal, regulation, and business data archival requirements against data storage costs, complexity, and other data considerations.

A good data-retention policy should define each of the following:

- Retention periods
- Data formats
- Data security
- Data-retrieval procedures for the enterprise

A data-retention policy for cloud services should contain the following components:

- **Legislation, regulation, and standards requirements:** Data-retention considerations depend heavily on the data type and the required compliance regimes associated with it. For example, according to the Basel II Accords for Financial Data, the retention period for financial transactions should be between three and seven years, whereas according to the PCI DSS version 3.1 Requirement 10.7, all access to network resources and cardholder data and credit card transaction data should be kept available for at least a year with at least three months available online.[12]

- **Data mapping:** This is the process of mapping all relevant data to understand data types (structured and unstructured), data formats, file types, and data locations (network drives, databases, object, or volume storage).

- **Data classification:** This involves classifying the data based on locations, compliance requirements, ownership, or business usage — in other words, its value. Classification is also used to decide on the proper retention procedures for the enterprise.

- **Data-retention procedure:** For each data category, the data-retention procedures should be followed based on the appropriate data retention policy that governs the data type. How long the data is to be kept, where (physical location, and jurisdiction), and how (which technology and format) should all be spelled out in the policy and implemented via the procedure. The procedure should also include backup options, retrieval requirements, and restore procedures, as required and necessary for the data types being managed.

- **Monitoring and maintenance:** These are procedures for making sure the entire process is working, including review of the policy and requirements to make sure there are no changes.

Data-Deletion Procedures and Mechanisms

A key part of data-protection procedures is the safe disposal of data once it is no longer needed. Failure to do so may result in data breaches or compliance failures. Safe-disposal procedures are designed to ensure that there are no files, pointers, or data remnants left behind in a system that could be used to restore the original data.

A data-deletion policy is sometimes required for the following reasons:

- **Regulation or legislation:** Certain laws and regulations require specific degrees of safe disposal for certain records.

- **Business and technical requirements:** Business policy may require safe disposal of data. Also, processes such as encryption might require safe disposal of the clear text data after creating the encrypted copy.

Restoring deleted data in a cloud environment is not an easy task for an attacker because cloud-based data is scattered, typically being stored in different physical locations with unique pointers. Achieving any level of physical access to the media is a challenge.

Nevertheless, it is still an existing attack vector that you should consider when evaluating the business requirements for data disposal.

Disposal Options

To safely dispose of electronic records, the following options are available:

- **Physical destruction:** Physically destroying the media by incineration, shredding, or other means.

- **Degaussing:** Using strong magnets for scrambling data on magnetic media such as hard drive and tapes.

- **Overwriting:** Writing random data over the actual data. The more times the overwriting process occurs, the more thorough the destruction of the data is considered to be.

- **Encryption:** Using an encryption method to rewrite the data in an encrypted format to make it unreadable without the encryption key.

Crypto-Shredding

Because the first three options are not fully applicable to cloud computing, the only reasonable method remaining is encrypting the data. The process of encrypting the data to dispose of it is called digital shredding or crypto-shredding.

Crypto-shredding is the process of deliberately destroying the encryption keys that were used to encrypt the data originally. The data is encrypted with the keys, so the data is rendered unreadable (at least until the encryption protocol used can be broken or is capable of being brute-forced by an attacker).

To perform proper crypto-shredding, consider the following:

- The data should be encrypted completely without leaving clear text remaining.
- The technique must make sure that the encryption keys are completely unrecoverable. This can be hard to accomplish if an external CSP or other third party manages the keys.

Data-Archiving Procedures and Mechanisms

Data archiving is the process of identifying and moving inactive data out of current production systems and into specialized long-term archival storage systems. Moving inactive data out of production systems optimizes the performance of resources needed there. Specialized archival systems store information more cost effectively and provide for retrieval when needed.

A data-archiving policy for the cloud should contain the following elements:

- **Data-encryption procedures:** Long-term data archiving with an encryption can present a challenge for the organization with regard to key management. The encryption policy should consider which media is used, what the restoral options are, and what threats should be mitigated by the encryption. Bad key management can lead to the destruction of the entire archive; therefore, it requires attention.

- **Data-monitoring procedures:** Data stored in the cloud tends to be replicated and moved. To maintain data governance, it is required that all data access and movements be tracked and logged to make sure that all security controls are being applied properly throughout the data lifecycle.

- **Ability to perform e-discovery and granular retrieval:** Archive data may be subject to retrieval according to certain parameters such as dates, subjects, and authors. The archiving platform should provide the ability to perform e-discovery on the data to determine which data should be retrieved.[13]

- **Backup and DR options:** All requirements for data backup and restore should be specified and clearly documented. It is important to ensure that the business continuity and disaster recovery (BCDR) plans are updated and aligned with whatever procedures are implemented.

- **Data format and media type:** The format of the data is an important consideration because it may be kept for an extended period of time. Proprietary formats can change, thereby leaving data in a useless state, so choosing the right format is important. The same consideration must be made for media storage types.

- **Data restoration procedures:** Data restoral testing should be initiated periodically to make sure the process is working. The trial data restore should be made into an isolated environment to mitigate risks, such as restoring an old virus or accidently overwriting existing data.

EVENTS

As a CCSP, you have tools at your disposal that can help you filter the large number of events that take place continuously within the cloud infrastructure, allowing you to selectively focus on those that are most relevant and important. Event sources are monitored to provide the raw data on events that will be used to paint a picture of a system being monitored. Event attributes are used to specify the kind of data or information associated with an event that you want to capture for analysis. Depending on the number of events and attributes being tracked, a large volume of data is produced. This data must be stored and then analyzed to uncover patterns of activity that may indicate threats or vulnerabilities are present in the system that have to be addressed. A security information and event management (SIEM) system can be used to gather and analyze the data flows from multiple systems, allowing for the automation of this process.

Event Sources

The relevant event sources you will draw data from will vary according to the cloud services modules that the organization is consuming. These include Saas, PaaS, and IaaS.

SaaS Event Sources

In SaaS environments, you typically have minimal control of, and access to, event and diagnostic data. Most infrastructure-level logs are not visible to the CCSP, and they will be limited to high-level, application-generated logs that are located on a client endpoint. In order to maintain reasonable investigation capabilities, auditability, and traceability of data, it is recommended to specify required data access requirements in the cloud SLA or contract with the CSP.

The following data sources play an important role in event investigation and documentation:

- Webserver logs
- Application server logs
- Database logs
- Guest OS logs

- Host access logs
- Virtualization platform logs and SaaS portal logs
- Network captures
- Billing records

PaaS Event Sources

In PaaS environments, you typically have control of and access to event and diagnostic data. Some infrastructure-level logs are visible to the CCSP, along with detailed application logs. Because the applications to be monitored are being built and designed by the organization directly, the level of application data that can be extracted and monitored is up to the developers.

To maintain reasonable investigation capabilities, auditability, and traceability of data, it is recommended that you work with the development team to understand the capabilities of the applications under development and to help design and implement monitoring regimes that maximize the organization's visibility into the applications and their data streams.

OWASP recommends that the following application events be logged:[14]

- Input validation failures, such as protocol violations, unacceptable encodings, and invalid parameter names and values
- Output validation failures, such as database record set mismatch and invalid data encoding
- Authentication successes and failures
- Authorization (access control) failures
- Session management failures, such as cookie session identification value modification
- Application errors and system events, such as syntax and runtime errors, connectivity problems, performance issues, third-party service error messages, file system errors, file upload virus detection, and configuration changes
- Application and related systems startups and shutdowns, and logging initialization (starting, stopping, or pausing)
- Use of higher-risk functionality, such as network connections, addition or deletion of users, changes to privileges, assigning users to tokens, adding or deleting tokens, use of systems administrative privileges, access by application administrators, all actions by users with administrative privileges, access to payment cardholder data, use of data encrypting keys, key changes, creation and deletion of system-level objects, data import and export including screen-based reports, and submission of user-generated content, especially file uploads

- Legal and other opt-ins, such as permissions for mobile phone capabilities, terms of use, personal data usage consent, and permission to receive marketing communications

IaaS Event Sources

In IaaS environments, the CCSP typically has control of and access to event and diagnostic data. Almost all infrastructure-level logs are visible to the CCSP, as are detailed application logs. To maintain reasonable investigation capabilities, auditability, and traceability of data, it is recommended that you specify data access requirements in the cloud SLA or contract with the CSP.

The following logs might be important to examine at some point but might not be available by default:

- Cloud or network provider perimeter network logs
- Logs from DNS servers
- Virtual machine manager (VMM) logs
- Host OS and hypervisor logs
- API access logs
- Management portal logs
- Packet captures
- Billing records

Identifying Event Attribute Requirements

So that you can perform effective audits and investigations, the event log should contain as much of the relevant data for the processes being examined as possible. OWASP recommends the following data event logging and event attributes to be integrated into event data.[15]

When:

- Log date and time (international format).
- Event date and time. The event time stamp may be different from the time of logging; for example, in server logging the client application is hosted on a remote device that is only periodically or intermittently online.
- Interaction identifier.

  Where:

- Application identifier, such as name and version
- Application address, such as cluster/host name or server IPv4 or IPv6 address and port number, workstation identity, and local device identifier
- Service name and protocol
- Geolocation
- Window, form, or page, such as entry point uniform resource locator (URL) and HTTP method for a web application and dialog box name
- Code location, including the script and module name

Who (human or machine user):

- Source address, including the user's device machine identifier, user's IP address, cell tower ID, and mobile telephone number
- User identity (if authenticated or otherwise known), including the user database table primary key value, username, and license number

What:

- Type of event
- Severity of event (0=emergency, 1=alert, …, 7=debug), (fatal, error, warning, info, debug, and trace)
- Security-relevant event flag (if the logs contain nonsecurity event data, too)
- Description

Additional considerations:

- Secondary time source (Global Positioning System [GPS]) event date and time.
- Action, which is the original intended purpose of the request. Examples are log in, refresh session ID, log out, and update profile.
- Object, such as the affected component or other object (user account, data resource, or file), URL, session ID, user account, or file.
- Result status. Whether the action aimed at the object was successful (can be Success, Fail, or Defer).
- Reason. Why the status occurred. Examples might be that the user was not authenticated in the database check or had incorrect credentials.
- HTTP status code (for web applications only). The status code returned to the user (often 200 or 301).

- Request HTTP headers or HTTP user agent (web applications only).

- User type classification, such as public, authenticated user, CMS user, search engine, authorized penetration tester, and uptime monitor.

- Analytical confidence in the event detection, such as low, medium, high, or a numeric value.

- Responses seen by the user or taken by the application, such as status code, custom text messages, session termination, and administrator alerts.

- Extended details, such as stack trace, system error messages, debug information, HTTP request body, and HTTP response headers and body.

- Internal classifications, such as responsibility and compliance references.

- External classifications, such as NIST Security Content Automation Protocol (SCAP) and Mitre Common Attack Pattern Enumeration and Classification (CAPEC).[16]

Storage and Analysis of Data Events

Event and log data can become costly to archive and maintain depending on the volume of data being gathered. Carefully consider these issues as well as the business and regulatory requirements and responsibilities of the organizations when planning for event data preservation.

Preservation is defined by ISO 27037:2012 as the "process to maintain and safeguard the integrity and/or original condition of the potential digital evidence."[17]

Evidence preservation helps ensure admissibility in a court of law. However, digital evidence is notoriously fragile and is easily changed or destroyed. Given that the backlog in many forensic laboratories ranges from six months to a year (and that the legal system might create further delays), potential digital evidence may spend a significant period of time in storage before it is analyzed or used in a legal proceeding. Storage requires strict access controls to protect the items from accidental or deliberate modification, as well as appropriate environment controls.

Also note that certain regulations and standards require that event logging mechanisms be tamper-proof to avoid the risks of faked event logs.

The gathering, analysis, storage, and archiving of event and log data is not limited to the forensic investigative process, however. In all organizations, you are called on to execute these activities on an ongoing basis for a variety of reasons during the normal flow of enterprise operations. Whether it is to examine a firewall log, diagnose an application installation error, validate access controls, understand network traffic flows, or manage resource consumption, the use of event data and logs is a standard practice.

SIEM

What you need to concern yourself with is how you can collect the volumes of logged event data available and manage it from a centralized location. That is where SIEM systems come in (*Figure 2.13*).

FIGURE 2.13 **The SIEM system.**

SIEM is a term for software products and services combining security information management (SIM) and security event management (SEM). SIEM technology provides real-time analysis of security alerts generated by network hardware and applications.

SIEM is sold as software, appliances, or managed services and is used to log security data and generate reports for compliance purposes.

The acronyms SEM, SIM, and SIEM are sometimes used interchangeably. The segment of security management that deals with real-time monitoring, correlation of events, notifications, and console views is commonly known as SEM. The second area provides long-term storage, analysis, and reporting of log data and is known as SIM.

SIEM systems typically provide the following capabilities:

- **Data aggregation:** Log management aggregates data from many sources, including network, security, servers, databases, and applications, providing the ability to consolidate monitored data to help avoid missing crucial events.

- **Correlation:** This involves looking for common attributes and linking events into meaningful bundles. This technology provides the ability to perform a variety of correlation techniques to integrate different sources to turn data into useful information. Correlation is typically a function of the SEM portion of a full SIEM solution.

- **Alerting:** This is the automated analysis of correlated events and production of alerts to notify recipients of immediate issues. Alerting can be to a dashboard or via third-party channels such as email.

- **Dashboards:** Tools can take event data and turn it into informational charts to assist in seeing patterns or identifying activity that is not forming a standard pattern.

- **Compliance:** Applications can be employed to automate the gathering of compliance data, producing reports that adapt to existing security, governance, and auditing processes.

- **Retention:** This involves employing long-term storage of historical data to facilitate correlation of data over time and to provide the retention necessary for compliance requirements. Long-term log data retention is critical in forensic investigations because it is unlikely that discovery of a network breach will coincide with the breach occurring.

- **Forensic analysis:** This is the ability to search across logs on different nodes and time periods based on specific criteria. It mitigates having to aggregate log information in your head or having to search through thousands and thousands of logs.

However, there are challenges with SIEM systems in the cloud that have to be considered when deciding whether this technology makes sense for the organization. Turning over internal security data to a CSP requires trust, and many users of cloud services desire more clarity on the provider's security precautions before being willing to trust a provider with this kind of information.

Another problem with pushing SIEM into the cloud is that targeted attack detection requires in-depth knowledge of internal systems—the kind found in corporate security teams. Cloud-based SIEM services may have trouble with recognizing the low-and-slow attacks. Often in targeted attacks, when organizations are breached, attackers create a relatively small amount of activity while carrying out their attacks. To see that evidence, the customer must have access to the data gathered by the CSP's monitoring infrastructure. That access to monitoring data needs to be specified as part of the SLA and may be difficult to gain access to, depending on the contract terms enforced.

SUPPORTING CONTINUOUS OPERATIONS

To support continuous operations, the following principles should be adopted as part of the security operations policies:

- **Audit logging:** Higher levels of assurance are required for protection, retention, and lifecycle management of audit logs. They must adhere to the applicable legal, statutory, or regulatory compliance obligations and provide unique user access accountability to detect potentially suspicious network behaviors or file integrity anomalies through forensic investigative capabilities in the event of a security breach. The continuous operation of audit logging is composed of three important processes.

- **New event detection:** The goal of auditing is to detect information security events. Policies should be created that define what a security event is and how to address it.

- **Adding new rules:** Rules are built to allow detection of new events. Rules allow for the mapping of expected values to log files and detect events. In continuous operation mode, rules have to be updated to address new risks.

- **Reduction of false positives:** The quality of the continuous operations audit logging depends on the ability to gradually reduce the number of false positives to maintain operational efficiency. This requires constant improvement of the rule set in use.

- **Contract and authority maintenance:** Points of contact for applicable regulatory authorities, national and local law enforcement, and other legal jurisdictional authorities should be maintained and regularly updated as per the business need (that is, a change in impacted scope or a change in a compliance obligation). This ensures that direct compliance liaisons have been established and will prepare the organization for a forensic investigation requiring rapid engagement with law enforcement.

- **Secure disposal:** Policies and procedures must be established with supporting business processes and technical measures implemented for the secure disposal and complete removal of data from all storage media. This is to ensure that the data is not recoverable by any computer forensic means.

- **Incident response legal preparation:** If a follow-up action concerning a person or organization after an information security incident requires legal action, proper forensic procedures, including chain of custody, should be required for preservation and presentation of evidence to support potential legal action subject to the relevant jurisdictions. Upon notification, impacted customers (tenants) or other external business relationships of a security breach should be given the opportunity to participate as is legally permissible in the forensic investigation.

CHAIN OF CUSTODY AND NONREPUDIATION

Chain of custody is the preservation and protection of evidence from the time it is collected until the time it is presented in court. For evidence to be considered admissible in court, documentation should exist for the collection, possession, condition, location, transfer, access to, and analysis performed on an item from acquisition through eventual final disposition. This concept is referred to as the chain of custody of evidence.

Creating a verifiable chain of custody for evidence within a cloud computing environment where there are multiple data centers spread across different jurisdictions can become challenging. Sometimes the only way to provide for a chain of custody is to include this provision in the service contract and ensure that the CSP will comply with requests pertaining to chain of custody issues.

SUMMARY

As has been discussed, cloud data security covers a range of topics focused on the concepts, principles, structures, and standards used to monitor and secure assets and those controls used to enforce various levels of AIC across IT services throughout the enterprise. CCSPs must use and apply standards to ensure that the systems under their protection are maintained and supported properly. The struggle for the CCSP is that the lack of standards specific to cloud environments can cause confusion and concern as to what path to follow and how to achieve the best possible outcome for the customer. As standards continue to be developed and emerge, it is incumbent on the CCSP to stay vigilant as well as be skeptical—vigilance to ensure awareness of the changing landscape of cloud security and skepticism to ensure that the appropriate questions are asked and answers are documented before a change to the existing policies and procedures of the organization is allowed. Security practitioners understand the different security frameworks, standards, and best practices leveraged by numerous methodologies and how they may be used together to provide stronger systems. Information security governance and risk management have enabled information technology to be used safely, responsibly, and securely in environments never before possible. The ability to establish strong system protections based on standards and policy and to assess the level and efficacy of that protection through auditing and monitoring are vital to the success of cloud computing security.

REVIEW QUESTIONS

1. What are the three things that you must understand before you can determine the necessary controls to deploy for data protection in a cloud environment?

   A. Management, provisioning, and location

   B. Function, location, and actors

   C. Actors, policies, and procedures

   D. Lifecycle, function, and cost

2. Which of the following are storage types used with an IaaS solution?

   A. Volume and block

   B. Structured and object

   C. Unstructured and ephemeral

   D. Volume and object

3. Which of the following are data storage types used with a PaaS solution?

   A. Raw and block

   B. Structured and unstructured

   C. Unstructured and ephemeral

   D. Tabular and object

4. Which of the following can be deployed to help ensure the confidentiality of data in the cloud? (Choose two.)

   A. Encryption

   B. SLAs

   C. Masking

   D. Continuous monitoring

5. Where would the monitoring engine be deployed when using a network-based DLP system?

   A. On a user's workstation

   B. In the storage system

   C. Near the organizational gateway

   D. On a VLAN

6. When using transparent encryption of a database, where does the encryption engine reside?

   A. At the application using the database

   B. On the instances attached to the volume

   C. In a key management system

   D. Within the database

7. What are three analysis methods used with data discovery techniques?

   A. Metadata, labels, and content analysis

   B. Metadata, structural analysis, and labels

   C. Statistical analysis, labels, and content analysis

   D. Bit splitting, labels, and content analysis

8. In the context of privacy and data protection, what is a controller?

   A. One who cannot be identified, directly or indirectly, in particular by reference to an identification number or to one or more factors specific to his physical, physiological, mental, economic, cultural, or social identity

   B. One who can be identified, directly or indirectly, in particular by reference to an identification number or to one or more factors specific to his physical, physiological, mental, economic, cultural, or social identity

   C. The natural or legal person, public authority, agency, or any other body that alone or jointly with others determines the purposes and means of the processing of personal data

   D. A natural or legal person, public authority, agency, or any other body that processes personal data on behalf of the customer

9. What is the CSA CCM?

   A. A set of regulatory requirements for CSPs

   B. An inventory of cloud service security controls that are arranged into separate security domains

   C. A set of software development lifecycle requirements for CSPs

   D. An inventory of cloud service security controls that are arranged into a hierarchy of security domains

10. Which of the following are common capabilities of IRM solutions?

    A. Persistent protection, dynamic policy control, automatic expiration, continuous audit trail, and support for existing authentication infrastructure

B. Persistent protection, static policy control, automatic expiration, continuous audit trail, and support for existing authentication infrastructure

C. Persistent protection, dynamic policy control, manual expiration, continuous audit trail, and support for existing authentication infrastructure

D. Persistent protection, dynamic policy control, automatic expiration, intermittent audit trail, and support for existing authentication infrastructure

11. What are the four elements that a data retention policy should define?

   A. Retention periods, data access methods, data security, and data retrieval procedures

   B. Retention periods, data formats, data security, and data destruction procedures

   C. Retention periods, data formats, data security, and data communication procedures

   D. Retention periods, data formats, data security, and data retrieval procedures

12. Which of the following methods for the safe disposal of electronic records can always be used within a cloud environment?

   A. Physical destruction

   B. Encryption

   C. Overwriting

   D. Degaussing

13. To support continuous operations, which of the following principles should be adopted as part of the security operations policies?

   A. Application logging, contract and authority maintenance, secure disposal, and business continuity preparation

   B. Audit logging, contract and authority maintenance, secure usage, and incident response legal preparation

   C. Audit logging, contract and authority maintenance, secure disposal, and incident response legal preparation

   D. Transaction logging, contract and authority maintenance, secure disposal, and DR preparation

NOTES

[1] Original Securosis blog entry for the data security life cycle can be found here: https://securosis.com/tag/data+security+lifecycle

The Cloud Security Alliance Guidance document can be downloaded here: https://downloads.cloudsecurityalliance.org/initiatives/guidance/csaguide.v3.0.pdf

[2] https://securosis.com/tag/data+security+lifecycle

[3] See the following for FIPS 140-2:
http://csrc.nist.gov/publications/fips/fips140-2/fips1402.pdf

See the following for FIPS 140-3:
http://csrc.nist.gov/groups/ST/FIPS140_3/#current-development

[4] See the following for background on Secret Sharing Made Short (SSMS): https://archive.org/stream/Hackin9Open52013/Hackin9%20Open%20-%205-2013_djvu.txt

[5] See the following for background on All-or-Nothing-Transform with Reed-Solomon (AONT-RS): https://www.usenix.org/legacy/event/fast11/tech/full_papers/Resch.pdf

[6] See the following for the text of the Consumer Protection Bill of Rights:
https://www.whitehouse.gov/sites/default/files/omb/legislative/letters/cpbr-act-of-2015-discussion-draft.pdf

[7] See the following for the full text of the EU directive 95/46/EC:
https://www.dataprotection.ie/docs/EU-Directive-95-46-EC/89.htm

[8] See the following for the full text of the e-privacy directive:
http://eur-lex.europa.eu/LexUriServ/LexUriServ.do?uri=CELEX:32002L0058:en:HTML

[9] See the following for overview material on the EU General Data Protection Regulation:
http://ec.europa.eu/justice/newsroom/data-protection/news/120125_en.htm

[10] See the following for NIST SP800-145:
http://nvlpubs.nist.gov/nistpubs/Legacy/SP/nistspecialpublication800-145.pdf

[11] See the following for the full text of the opinion:
http://www.cil.cnrs.fr/CIL/IMG/pdf/wp196_en.pdf

[12] See the following for the Basel Accords: http://www.bis.org/bcbs/
See the following PCI DSS:
https://www.pcisecuritystandards.org/documents/PCI_DSS_v3-1.pdf

[13] E-discovery refers to any process in which electronic data is sought, located, secured, and searched with the intent of using it as evidence.

[14] See the following for the OWASP logging cheat sheet: https://www.owasp.org/index.php/Logging_Cheat_Sheet

[15] https://www.owasp.org/index.php/Logging_Cheat_Sheet

[16] See the following for more information on SCAP: http://scap.nist.gov/

See the following for more information on CAPEC: https://capec.mitre.org/

[17] https://www.iso.org/obp/ui/#iso:std:iso-iec:27037:ed-1:v1:en

CLOUD DATA SECURITY

DOMAIN 3

Cloud Platform and Infrastructure Security

THE GOAL OF THE Cloud Platform and Infrastructure Security domain is to provide you with knowledge regarding both the physical and the virtual components of the cloud infrastructure.

You will gain knowledge of risk-management analysis, including tools and techniques necessary for maintaining a secure cloud infrastructure. In addition to risk analysis, you will learn how to prepare and maintain business continuity and disaster recovery (BCDR) plans, including techniques and concepts for identifying critical systems and lost data recovery.

DOMAIN OBJECTIVES

After completing this domain, you will be able to do the following:

❑ Describe both the physical and the virtual infrastructure components as they pertain to a cloud environment

❑ Define the process for analyzing risk in a cloud infrastructure

❑ Develop a plan for mitigating risk in a cloud infrastructure based on the risk-assessment plan, including countermeasure strategies

❑ Create a security control plan that includes the physical environment, virtual environment, system communications, access management, and mechanisms necessary for auditing

❑ Describe disaster recovery (DR) and business continuity management for cloud systems with regard to the environment, business requirements, risk management, and developing and implementing the plan

INTRODUCTION

The cloud infrastructure consists of data centers and the hardware that runs in them, including compute, storage, and networking hardware; virtualization software; and a management layer (*Figure 3.1*).

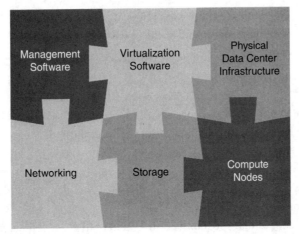

FIGURE 3.1 **The cloud infrastructure.**

The Physical Environment of the Cloud Infrastructure

Just like traditional or onsite computing, cloud computing runs on real hardware that runs in real buildings. At the contemporary scale of operations, data center design and operation are unlike anything else.

The following characteristics provide a backdrop to this topic:

- There is a high volume of expensive hardware—up to hundreds of thousands of servers in a single facility.

- Per square meter, power densities can be found up to 10kW (kilowatts).

- There is an enormous and immediate impact of downtime on all dependent business.

- Data center owners can provide multiple levels of service. The basic level is often summarized as "power, pipe, and ping."

- There is electrical power and cooling pipe—that is, air conditioning. "Power" and "pipe" limit the density with which servers can be stacked in the data center.

- Power density is expressed in kW per rack, where a data center can house up to 25 racks per 100 square meters. Power densities of 100W per rack were once the norm, but these days 10kW or more per rack is seen and often required to ensure adequate supply can satisfy operational and functional requirements. These densities require advanced cooling engineering.

- Network connectivity is provided to the data center networks to access storage, and external connectivity is provided to access wide area network (WAN) resources.
- Data center providers (colocation) can provide floor space, rack space, and cages (lockable floor space) on any level of aggregation. The smallest unit can range from a 1U slot in a rack to a full room.

Given the low tolerance for failure, the physical environment of the data center should be evaluated for geographic and political risks (seismic activity, floods, availability of power, and accessibility).

Data Center Design

A large part of data center design revolves around the redundancy in the design (*Figure 3.2*). Anything that can break down should be replicated. No single point of failure should remain. This means backup power, multiple independent cooling units, multiple power lines to individual racks and servers, multiple power distribution units (PDUs), multiple entrances to the building, multiple external entry points for power and network, and so on. *Figure 3.3* illustrates what a redundant data center design might look like, taking into account that geographic distribution of the data centers themselves is not addressed as part of the design redundancy in this particular figure.

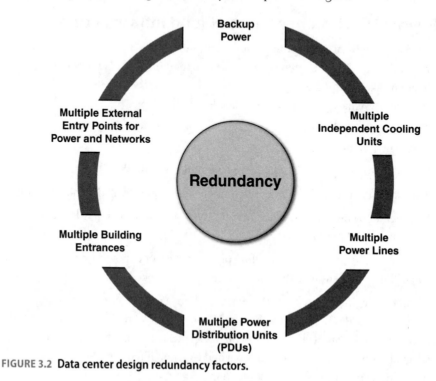

FIGURE 3.2 Data center design redundancy factors.

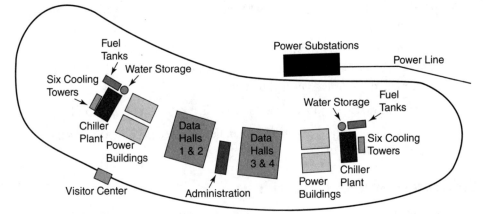

FIGURE 3.3 **Sample redundant data center design.**

NETWORK AND COMMUNICATIONS IN THE CLOUD

The purpose of the network is to provide for and control communication between computers—that is, servers and clients.

According to National Institute of Standards and Technology's (NIST's) "Cloud Computing Synopsis and Recommendations," the following first-level terms are important to define:[1]

- **Cloud service consumer:** Person or organization that maintains a business relationship with and uses service from the cloud service providers (CSPs)

- **CSP:** Person, organization, or entity responsible for making a service available to service consumers

- **Cloud carrier:** The intermediary that provides connectivity and transport of cloud services between the CSPs and the cloud service consumers

In the NIST cloud computing reference model, the network and communication function is provided as part of the cloud carrier role. In practice, this is an Internet protocol (IP) service, increasingly delivered through both IPv4 and IPv6. This IP network may or may not be part of the public Internet.

Network Functionality

Functionality in the network includes the following:

- **Address allocation:** The ability to be able to provide one or more IP addresses to a cloud resource via either a static or a dynamic assignment.

- **Access control:** The mechanisms used to grant or deny access to a resource.

- **Bandwidth allocation:** A specified amount of bandwidth provided for system access or use.
- **Rate limiting:** The ability to control the amount of traffic sent or received. Can be used to control the number of application programming interface (API) requests made within a specified period.
- **Filtering:** The ability to selectively allow or deny content or access to resources.
- **Routing:** The ability to direct the flow of traffic between endpoints based on selecting the best path.

Software-Defined Networking

Software-defined networking's (SDN's) objective is to provide a clearly defined and separate network control plane to manage network traffic that is separated from the forwarding plane. This approach allows for network control to become directly programmable and distinct from forwarding, allowing for dynamic adjustment of traffic flows to address changing patterns of consumption. SDN enables you to execute the control plane software on general-purpose hardware, allowing for the decoupling from specific network hardware configurations and allowing for the use of commodity servers.

Further, the use of software-based controllers permits a view of the network that presents a logical switch to the applications running above, allowing for access via APIs that can be used to configure, manage, and secure network resources. For example, an SDN service might allow Internet access to a certain server with a single command, which the SDN layer can map to configuration changes on multiple intermediate network components.

Take a look at the sample SDN architecture (*Figure 3.4*).

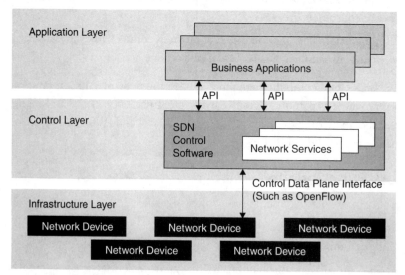

FIGURE 3.4 Sample SDN architecture.

THE COMPUTE PARAMETERS OF A CLOUD SERVER

The compute parameters of a cloud server follow:

- The number of CPUs
- The amount of RAM memory

What becomes important about the compute resources of a host is the ability to manage and allocate these resources effectively, either on a per-guest operating-system (OS) basis or on a per-host basis within a resource cluster.

The use of reservations, limits, and shares offers the contextual ability for an administrator to allocate the compute resources of a host.

A reservation creates a guaranteed minimum resource allocation that the host must meet with physical compute resources to allow for a guest to power on and operate. This reservation is traditionally available for either central processing unit (CPU) or random access memory (RAM), or both, as needed.

A limit creates a maximum ceiling for a resource allocation. This ceiling may be fixed, or it may be expandable, allowing for the acquisition of more compute resources through a borrowing scheme from the root resource provider (the host).

The concept of shares is used to arbitrate the issues associated with compute resource contention situations. Resource contention implies the existence of too many requests for resources based on the actual available resources currently in the system. If resource contention takes place, share values are used to prioritize compute resource access for all guests assigned a certain number of shares. The shares are weighed and used as a percentage against all outstanding shares assigned and in use by all powered-on guests to calculate the resources each guest is given access to. The higher the share value assigned to the guest, the larger the percentage of the remaining resources they are given access to during the contention period.

Virtualization

Virtualization is the foundational technology that underlies and makes cloud computing possible. Virtualization is based on the use of powerful host computers to provide a shared resource pool that can be managed to maximize the number of guest operating systems (OSs) running on each host. Following are the key drivers and business cases for using virtualization:

- Sharing underlying resources to enable a more efficient and agile use of hardware
- Easier management through reduced personnel resourcing and maintenance

Scalability

With virtualization, there is the ability to run multiple guest OSs (virtual machines, or VMs) and their associated applications on a single host. The guest is an isolated software instance that is capable of running side by side with other guests on the host, taking advantage of the resource abstraction capabilities provided by the hypervisor to dynamically utilize resources from the host as needed.

The Hypervisor

A hypervisor can be a piece of software, firmware, or hardware that gives the impression to the guest OSs that they are operating directly on the physical hardware of the host. It allows multiple guest OSs to share a single host and its hardware. The hypervisor manages requests by VMs to access the physical hardware resources of the host, abstracting it, and allowing the VM to behave as if it were an independent machine (*Figure* 3.5). The hypervisor will use a virtual machine manager (VMM) instance to create a one-to-one association with each VM being managed, allowing the hypervisor to securely manage the VM. There are two types of hypervisors.

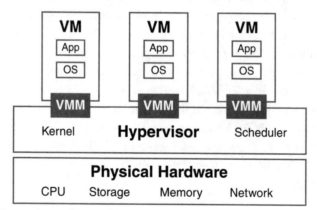

FIGURE 3.5 **The hypervisor architecture.**

The Type 1 hypervisor has the following characteristics:

- Is commonly known as a bare metal, embedded, or native hypervisor
- Works directly on the hardware of the host and can monitor OSs that run above the hypervisor
- Is small because its main task is sharing and managing hardware resources between different guest OSs

The Type 2 hypervisor has these characteristics:

- Is installed on top of the host's OS and supports other guest OSs running above it as VMs
- Is completely dependent on the host OS for its operations

Using this architecture has risks and challenges:

- Security flaws in the hypervisor can lead to malicious software targeting individual VMs running on it or other components in the infrastructure.
- A flawed hypervisor can facilitate inter-VM attacks (also known as VM hopping) when isolation between VMs or trust levels have not been configured appropriately; that is, one tenant's VM can peek into the data of another tenant's VM on the same underlying host.
- Network traffic between VMs is not necessarily visible to physical network security controls, which means additional security controls may be necessary.
- Resource availability for VMs can be flawed. Individual VMs can be starved of resources. Conversely, some servers are managed on the assumption that there are tasks that can run in idle time, such as virus scanning. In a virtualized environment, one virtual server's idle time is another server's production time, so those assumptions need to be revisited.
- VMs and their disk images are simply files residing somewhere. This means that, for example, a stopped VM is potentially accessible on a file system by third parties if no controls are applied. Inspection of this file can circumvent any controls that the guest OS applies.

STORAGE ISSUES IN THE CLOUD

On a technical level, persistent mass storage in cloud computing typically consists of spinning hard disk drives or solid-state drives (SSDs).

For reliability purposes, disk drives are often grouped to provide redundancy. The typical approach is Redundant Array of Inexpensive Disks (RAID), which is actually a group of techniques. RAID groups have redundant disks configured so that the disk controller can still retrieve the data when one of the disks fails. An average disk drive has a 3–5% failure rate per year. Roughly speaking, on 5,000 installed disks, you can expect one failure every day. RAID techniques differ in the percentage of redundant disks and in the aggregate performance they can deliver.

Part of the storage functionality is to slice and group disks into logical volumes of arbitrary sizes (alternatively called logical unit numbers [LUNs], virtual hard disks, volume storage, elastic block storage, Amazon EBS, and Rackspace Cloud Block Storage).

These storage volumes have no file system. The file system structure is applied by the OS on the VM instance to which they are provisioned.

Object Storage

The CSP can provide a file system–like scheme to its customers. This is traditionally called object storage, where objects (files) are stored with additional metadata (content type, redundancy required, creation date, and so on). These objects are accessible through APIs and potentially through a web user interface. Instead of organizing files in a directory hierarchy, object storage systems store files in a flat organization of containers (called buckets in Amazon S3) and use unique IDs (called keys in S3) to retrieve them.

Commercial examples include Amazon S3 and Rackspace cloud files.

Object storage is typically the way to store OS images, which the hypervisor boots into running instances.

Technically, object storage can implement redundancy as a way to improve resilience by dispersing data via fragmenting and duplicating it across multiple object storage servers. This can increase resilience and performance and may reduce data loss risks.

The features you get in an object storage system are typically minimal. You can store, retrieve, copy, and delete files, as well as control which users can undertake these actions. If you want to be able to search or to have a central repository of object metadata that other applications can draw on, you generally have to implement it yourself. Amazon S3 and other object storage systems provide Representational State Transfer (REST) APIs that allow programmers to work with the containers and objects.

The key issue that the CCSP has to be aware of with object storage systems is that data consistency is achieved only eventually. Whenever you update a file, you may have to wait until the change is propagated to all the replicas before requests return the latest version. This makes object storage unsuitable for data that changes frequently. However, it provides a good solution for data that does not change much, such as backups, archives, video and audio files, and VM images.

Management Plane

The management plane allows the administrator to remotely manage any or all of the hosts, as opposed to having to visit each server physically to turn it on or install software on it (*Figure 3.6*).

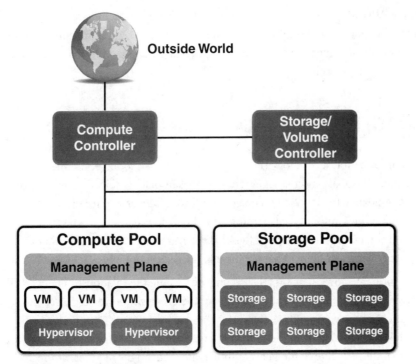

FIGURE 3.6 **The management plane.**

The key functionality of the management plane is to create, start, and stop VM instances and provision them with the proper virtual resources such as CPU, memory, permanent storage, and network connectivity. When the hypervisor supports it, the management plane also controls live migration of VM instances. The management plane, thus, can manage all these resources across an entire farm of equipment.

The management plane software typically runs on its own set of servers and has dedicated connectivity to the physical machines under management.

Because the management plane is the most powerful tool in the entire cloud infrastructure, it also integrates authentication, access control, and logging and monitoring of resources used.

The management plane is used by the most privileged users: those who install and remove hardware, system software, firmware, and so on. The management plane is also the pathway for individual tenants who have limited and controlled access to the cloud's resources.

The management plane's primary interface is the API, both toward the resources managed as well as toward the users. A graphical user interface (GUI, or web page) is typically built on top of those APIs.

These APIs allow automation of control tasks. Examples include scripting and orchestrating the setup of complex application architectures, populating the configuration management database, allocating resources over physical assets, and provisioning and rotation of user access credentials.

MANAGEMENT OF CLOUD COMPUTING RISKS

Because information technology (IT) is typically deployed to serve the interests of the organization, the goals and management practices in that organization are an important source of guidance to cloud risk management. From the perspective of the enterprise, cloud computing represents outsourcing, and it becomes part of the IT supply chain.

Cloud risk management should therefore be linked to corporate governance and enterprise risk management. That means that the same principles should be applied.

- Corporate governance is a broad area describing the relationship between the shareholders and other stakeholders in the organization versus the senior management of the corporation. These stakeholders need to see that their interests are taken care of and that the management has a structure and a process to ensure that they execute to the goals of the organization. This requires, among other things, transparency on costs and risks.

  In the end, risks relating to cloud computing should be judged in relation to the corporate goals. It makes sense to develop any IT governance processes in alignment with existing corporate governance processes.

  For example, corporate governance pays attention to supply chains, management structure, compliance, financial transparency, and ownership. All these are relevant for any cloud computing consumer provider relationship that is significant to the corporation.

- Enterprise risk management is the set of processes and structure to systematically manage all risks to the enterprise. This explicitly covers supply chain risks and third-party risks, the biggest of which is typically the failure of an external provider to deliver the services that are contracted.

Risk Assessment and Analysis

There are several lists of risks maintained and published by industry organizations. These lists can be a source of valuable insight and information, but in the end, every cloud-consuming or cloud-providing organization remains responsible for its own risk assessment.

Several general categories of risks have been identified (*Figure* 3.7).

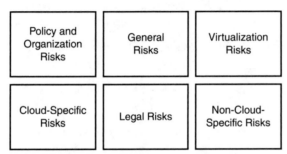

FIGURE 3.7 **General categories of risk related to the cloud infrastructure.**

Policy and Organization Risks

Policy and organization risks are related to the choices that the cloud service consumer makes about the CSP. To some extent, they are the natural consequence of outsourcing IT services. Outside the IT industry, these are often called third-party risks.

A few of the most noteworthy are provider lock-in, loss of governance, compliance challenges, and provider exit.

- **Provider lock-in:** This refers to the situation in which the consumer has made significant vendor-specific investments. These can include adaptation to data formats, procedures, and feature sets. These investments can lead to high costs of switching between providers.

- **Loss of governance:** This refers to the consumer not being able to implement all required controls. This can lead to the consumer not realizing her required level of security and potential compliance risks.

- **Compliance risks:** Consumers often have significant compliance obligations, such as when handling payment card information, health data, or other PII. A specific cloud vendor and solution may not be able to fulfill all those obligations, for example, when the location of stored data is insufficiently under control.

- **Provider exit:** In this situation, the provider is no longer willing or capable of providing the required service. This could be triggered by bankruptcy or a need to restructure the business.

General Risks

A risk exists if there is the potential failure to meet any requirement that can be expressed in technical terms, such as performance, operability, integration, and protection. Generally speaking, CSPs have a larger technology scale than cloud customers and traditional IT departments. This has three effects on risk, the net result of which depends on the actual situation:

- The consolidation of IT infrastructure leads to consolidation risks, where a single point of failure can have a bigger impact.

- A larger-scale platform requires the CSP to bring to bear more technical skills to manage and maintain the infrastructure.

- Control over technical risks shifts toward the provider.

Virtualization Risks

Virtualization risks include but are not limited to the following:

- **Guest breakout:** This occurs when there is a breakout of a guest OS so that it can access the hypervisor or other guests. This is presumably facilitated by a hypervisor flaw.

- **Snapshot and image security:** The portability of images and snapshots makes people forget that images and snapshots can contain sensitive information and need protecting.

- **Sprawl:** This occurs when you lose control of the amount of content on your image store.

Cloud-Specific Risks

Cloud-specific risks include but are not limited to the following:

- **Management plane breach:** Arguably, the most important risk is a management plane (management interface) breach. Malicious users, whether internal or external, can affect the entire infrastructure that the management interface controls.

- **Resource exhaustion:** Because cloud resources are shared by definition, resource exhaustion represents a risk to customers. This can play out as being denied access to resources already provisioned or as the inability to increase resource consumption. Examples include sudden lack of CPU or network bandwidth, which can be the result of overprovisioning to tenants by the CSP. Related to resource exhaustion are the following:

  - Denial-of-service (DoS) attacks, where a common network or other resource is saturated, leading to starvation of users

  - Traffic analysis

  - Manipulation or interception of data in transit

- **Isolation control failure:** Resource sharing across tenants typically requires the CSP to realize isolation controls. Isolation failure refers to the failure or nonexistence of these controls. Examples include one tenant's VM instance accessing or affecting instances of another tenant, failure to limit one user's access to the data of another user (in a software as a service [SaaS] solution), and entire IP address blocks being blacklisted as the result of one tenant's activity.

- **Insecure or incomplete data deletion:** Data erasure in most OSs is implemented by just removing directory entries rather than by reformatting the storage used. This places sensitive data at risk when that storage is reused due to the potential for recovery and exposure of that data.

- **Control conflict risk:** In a shared environment, controls that lead to more security for one stakeholder (blocking traffic) may make it less secure for another (loss of visibility).

- **Software-related risks:** Every CSP runs software, not just the SaaS providers. All software has potential vulnerabilities. From the customer's perspective, control is transferred to the CSP, which can mean an enhanced security and risk awareness, but the ultimate accountability for compliance still falls to the customer.

Legal Risks

Cloud computing brings several new risks from a legal perspective. These risks can be grouped broadly into data protection, jurisdiction, law enforcement, and licensing.

- **Data protection:** Cloud customers may have legal requirements about the way that they protect data—in particular, PII. The controls and actions of the CSP may not be sufficient for the customer.

- **Jurisdiction:** CSPs may have data storage locations in multiple jurisdictions, which can affect other risks and their controls.

- **Law enforcement:** As a result of law enforcement or civil legal activity, it may be required to hand over data to authorities. The essential cloud characteristic of shared resources may make this process hard to do and may result in exposure risks to other tenants. For example, seizure and examination of a physical disk may expose the data of multiple customers.

- **Licensing:** Finally, when customers want to move existing software into a cloud environment, any licensing agreements on that software might make this legally impossible or prohibitively expensive. An example could be licensing fees that are tied to the deployment of software based on a per-CPU licensing model.

Non-Cloud-Specific Risks

Of course, most IT risks still play out in the cloud environment as well: natural disasters, unauthorized facility access, social engineering, network attacks on the consumer and on the provider side, default passwords, and other malicious or nonmalicious actions.

Cloud Attack Vectors

Cloud computing brings additional attack vectors that need to be considered in addition to new technical and governance risks.

- Cloud computing uses new technology such as virtualization, federated identity management, and automation through a management interface.

- Cloud computing introduces external service providers.

Hence, following are some of the main new attack vectors:

- Guest breakout

- Identity compromise, either technical or social (for example, through employees of the provider)

- API compromise, such as by leaking API credentials

- Attacks on the provider's infrastructure and facilities (for example, from a third-party administrator that may be hosting with the provider)

- Attacks on the connecting infrastructure (cloud carrier)

COUNTERMEASURE STRATEGIES ACROSS THE CLOUD

Although the next section explains in more detail the controls that can be applied on various levels of the cloud infrastructure, this section is about countermeasure strategies that span those levels.

First, it is highly recommended that you implement multiple layers of defense against any risk. For example, in physical protection there should not be reliance on a single lock; there should be multiple layers of access control, including locks, guards, barriers, and video surveillance.

Equally, for a control that directly addresses a risk, there should be an additional control to catch the failure of the first control. These controls are referred to as compensating controls. Every compensating control must meet four criteria: have the intent and rigor of the original requirement, provide a similar level of defense as the original requirement, be above and beyond other requirements, and be commensurate with the additional risk imposed by not adhering to the requirement.

As an example, consider disk space monitoring. There should be a basic control in place that monitors available disk space in a system and that alerts you when a certain threshold has been reached. A compensating control would be used to create an additional layer of monitoring "above and beyond" the initial control, to ensure that if the initial control were to fail or experience difficulty due to some sort of attack, that the amount of disk free space could still be accurately monitored and reported on.

Continuous Uptime

Cloud infrastructure needs to be designed and maintained for continuous uptime. This implies that every component is redundant. This serves two purposes:

- It makes the infrastructure resilient against component failure.
- It allows individual components to be updated without affecting the cloud infrastructure uptime.

Automation of Controls

On the technical level, controls should be automated as much as possible, thus ensuring their immediate and comprehensive implementation. One way to do this is to integrate software into the build process of VM images that detects malware, encrypts data, configures log files, and registers new machines into configuration management databases.

Automating the configuration of operational resources enables additional drastic changes to traditional practices. Rather than updating resources—such as OS instances— at runtime with security patches, an automated system for configuration and resilience makes it possible to replace the running instance with a fresh, updated one. This is often referred to as the baseline image.

Access Controls

Because new technology as well as new service models are introduced by cloud computing, access controls need to be revisited. Depending on the service and deployment models, the responsibility and actual execution of the control can lie with the cloud service consumer, with the CSP, or both.

Cloud computing allows enterprises to scale resources up and down as their needs require. The pay-as-you-go model of computing has made it popular among businesses. However, one of the biggest hurdles in the widespread adoption of cloud computing is security. The multitenant nature of the cloud is vulnerable to data loss, threats, and malicious attacks. Therefore, enterprises need strong access control policies in place to maintain the privacy and confidentiality of data in the cloud.

Following is a nonexhaustive listing of access controls:

- Building access
- Computer floor access
- Cage or rack access
- Access to physical servers (hosts)
- Hypervisor access (API or management plane)
- Guest OS access (VMs)
- Developer access
- Customer access
- Database access rights
- Vendor access
- Remote access
- Application and software access to data (SaaS)

Cloud services should deploy a user-centric approach for effective access control, in which every user request is bundled with the user identity. In addition, there should be strong authentication and identity management for both CSPs and their clients.

Particular attention is required for enabling adequate access to external auditors without jeopardizing the infrastructure.

PHYSICAL AND ENVIRONMENTAL PROTECTIONS

The physical infrastructure and its environment consist of the data center, its buildings, and surroundings. These facilities and its staff are most relevant, not just for the security of the IT assets but because they are the focus of a lot of security controls on other components.

There is, of course, infrastructure outside the data center that needs protecting. This includes network and communication facilities and endpoints such as PCs, laptops, mobile phones, and other smart devices. A number of controls on the infrastructure described here can be applied outside the data center as well.

There are well-established bodies of knowledge around physical security, such as NIST's SP 800-14 and SP 800-123, and that knowledge is consolidated in a number of regulations.[2]

Key Regulations

Some of the regulations that may be applicable to the CSP facility include the Healthcare Insurance Portability and Accountability Act (HIPAA) and the Payment Card Industry Data Security Standard (PCI DSS). In addition, many countries have critical infrastructure protection plans and legislation, such as the North American Electric Reliability Corporation Critical Infrastructure Protection (NERC CIP) in the United States.

Examples of Controls

Based on one or more regulations, the following control examples may be relevant:

- Policies and procedures shall be established for maintaining a safe and secure working environment in offices, rooms, facilities, and secure areas.

- Physical access to information assets and functions by users and support personnel shall be restricted.

- Physical security perimeters (fences, walls, barriers, guards, gates, electronic surveillance, physical authentication mechanisms, reception desks, and security patrols) shall be implemented to safeguard sensitive data and information systems.

Protecting Data Center Facilities

Data center facilities are typically required to have multiple layers of access controls. Between these zones, controls are implemented that deter, detect, delay, and deny unauthorized access.

At the facilities level, key resources and assets should be made redundant, preferably in independent ways such as multiple electricity feeds, network cables, cooling systems, and uninterruptable power supplies (UPSs).

On the computer floor, as it is often called, redundancy continues in power and network cabling to racks.

Finally, the data center and facility staff represent a risk. Controls on staff include extensive background checks and screening, but also adequate and continuous training in security awareness and incident response capability.

SYSTEM AND COMMUNICATION PROTECTIONS

To protect systems, components, and communication, we can take a number of complementary analysis approaches. It generally makes sense to analyze the important data assets, trace their flow across various processing components and actors, and use those to map out the relevant controls.

Cloud computing still runs on real hardware, so it inherits all the risks associated with that. Infrastructure as a service (IaaS) requires a great number of individual services working in harmony.

Here's a nonexhaustive list of services:

- Hypervisor
- Storage controllers
- Volume management
- IP address management (dynamic host configuration protocol [DHCP])
- Security group management
- VM image service
- Identity service
- Message queue
- Management databases
- Guest OS protection

All these components run software that needs to be properly configured, maintained, and analyzed for risk. When these components have security functions, such as virus scanners and network intrusion detection systems (IDSs) and network intrusion prevention systems (IPSs), these need to be virtualization aware.

Automation of Configuration

Manually configuring all the infrastructure components in a system can be a tedious, expensive, error-prone, and insecure process. As indicated earlier, automation of configuration and deployment is essential to make sure that components implement all relevant controls. This automation also allows for a more granular proliferation of controls.

For example, an IDS, an IPS, and firewalls can be deployed as components of OSs and their configuration adapted to the actual state of the infrastructure through the use of automation technology.

Responsibilities of Protecting the Cloud System

Implementation of controls requires cooperation and a clear demarcation of responsibility between the CSP and the cloud service consumer. Without that, there is a real risk for certain important controls to be absent. For example, IaaS providers typically do not consider guest OS hardening their responsibility.

Figure 3.8 presents a visual responsibility matrix across the cloud environment.

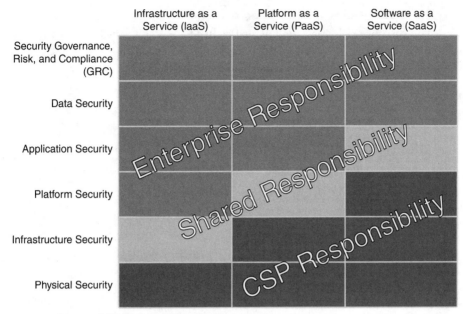

	Infrastructure as a Service (IaaS)	Platform as a Service (PaaS)	Software as a Service (SaaS)
Security Governance, Risk, and Compliance (GRC)			
Data Security			
Application Security			
Platform Security			
Infrastructure Security			
Physical Security			

Enterprise Responsibility
Shared Responsibility
CSP Responsibility

FIGURE 3.8 **Responsibility matrix across the cloud environment.**

It is incumbent upon the CCSP to understand where responsibility is placed and what level of responsibility the organization is expected to undertake regarding the use and consumption of cloud services.

Following the Data Lifecycle

Monitoring and logging events plays an important role in detecting security events, demonstrating compliance, and responding adequately to incidents.

As discussed earlier, following the data across its lifecycle is an important approach in ensuring sufficient coverage of controls. The main grouping of that data lifecycle is in three broad categories: data at rest (DAR), data in motion (DIM), and data in use (DIU).

- **DAR:** In storage, the primary control against unauthorized access is encryption, which helps to ensure confidentiality. Availability and integrity are controlled through the use of redundant storage across multiple locations.

- **DIM:** Data center networking can be segregated into multiple zones physically and logically through the use of technology such as VLANs. The resulting traffic separation acts as a control to improve DIM confidentiality and integrity. It is also a countermeasure against availability and capacity risks caused by resource contention. Traffic separation is often mandated from a compliance perspective.

Encryption is also a relevant control to consider on networks for DIM. This control provides for data confidentiality. In addition, the network components are a potential area for controls. The concept of a firewall acting as the gatekeeper on the single perimeter is an outdated thought process in cloud architectures. Nevertheless, between demarcated network zones, control is possible by utilizing technology such as data loss prevention (DLP), data activity monitoring, and egress filtering.

- **DIU:** This requires access control with granularity that is relevant for the data at risk. APIs should be protected through the use of digital signatures and encryption where necessary, and access rights should be restricted to the roles of the consumer.

VIRTUALIZATION SYSTEMS CONTROLS

The virtualization components include compute, storage, and network, all governed by the management plane. These components merit specific attention. Because they are used to implement cloud multitenancy, they are a prime source of both cloud-specific risks and compensating controls.

Because the management plane controls the entire infrastructure and parts of it are exposed to customers independently of network location, it is a prime resource to protect. Its GUI, command-line interface (CLI, if any), and APIs all need to have stringent and role-based access controls (RBACs) applied. In addition, logging all the relevant actions in a logging system is highly recommended. This includes machine image changes, configuration changes, and management access logging. Proper alerting and auditing of these actions needs to be considered and governed.

The management plane components are among the highest risk components with respect to software vulnerabilities because these vulnerabilities can also affect tenant isolation. For example, a hypervisor flaw might allow a guest OS to "break out" and access other tenants' information or even take over the hypervisor. These components therefore need to be hardened to the highest relevant standards by following vendor hardening and security guides, including malware detection and patch management.

The isolation of the management network with respect to other networks (storage, tenant, and so on) needs to be considered. This might need to be a separate physical network to meet regulatory and compliance requirements.

Network security includes proper design and operation of firewalls, IDS, IPS, honeypots, and so on.

The virtualization system components implement controls that isolate tenants. This includes availability, integrity, and confidentiality (AIC). Fair, policy-based resource allocation over tenants is also a function of the virtualization system components. For this, capacity monitoring of all relevant physical and virtual resources should be considered. This includes network, disk, memory, and CPU.

When controls implemented by the virtualization components are deemed to be not strong enough, trust zones can be used to segregate the physical infrastructure. This control can address confidentiality risks as well as control availability and capacity risks. It is often required by certain regulations.

A trust zone can be defined as a network segment within which data flows relatively freely, whereas data flowing in and out of the trust zone is subject to stronger restrictions. Following are some examples of trust zones:

- Demilitarized zones (DMZs)

- Site-specific zones, such as segmentation according to department or function

- Application-defined zones, such as the three tiers of a web application

Let's explore the concept of trust zones from the perspective of a private cloud deployment to illustrate how they may be used.

Imagine for a moment that you are the CCSP for ABC Corp. ABC has decided to utilize a private cloud to host data that certain vendors need access to. You have been asked to recommend the steps ABC Corp should consider to ensure the integrity and confidentiality of the data stored while vendors are accessing it.

After some consideration, you settle on the idea of using trust zones as an administrative control based on application use. To allow vendor access, you propose creating a jump server for the vendor, which is placed in its own trust zone and allowed only to access the application trust zone you create.

This approach allows the vendor to utilize the application necessary to access the data but do so in a controlled manner, as prescribed by the architecture of the trust zone. This limits the application's ability to access data outside the trust zone. It also ensures that the application can be opened and accessed only from within a computer operating inside the trust zone. Thus, confidentiality and availability can be addressed in a meaningful way.

The virtualization layer is a potential residence for other controls (traffic analysis, DLP, virus scanning), as indicated earlier.

Procedures for snapshotting live images should be incorporated into incident response procedures to facilitate cloud forensics.

The virtualization infrastructure should also enable the tenants to implement the appropriate security controls:

- Traffic isolation by using specific security group and transmission encryption.

- Guest security. This can be out of the scope of the IaaS provider, but it certainly is in the scope of the IaaS consumer.

- File and volume encryption.
- Control of image provenance: image creation, distribution, storage, use, retirement, and destruction.

MANAGING IDENTIFICATION, AUTHENTICATION, AND AUTHORIZATION IN THE CLOUD INFRASTRUCTURE

Entities that have an identity in cloud computing include users, devices, code, organizations, and agents. As a principle, anything that needs to be trusted has an identity.

The distinguishing characteristic of an identity in cloud computing is that it can be federated across multiple collaborating parties. This implies a split between "identity providers" and "relying parties," who rely on identities to be issued by the providers. This leads to a model whereby an identity provider can service multiple relying parties and a relying party can federate multiple identity providers (*Figure* 3.9).

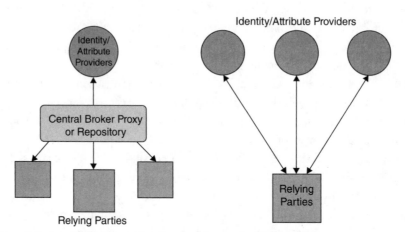

FIGURE 3.9 **Relationship between identity providers and relying parties.**

Managing Identification

In the public cloud world, identity providers are increasingly adopting OpenID and OAuth as standard protocols.[3] In a corporate environment, corporate identity repositories can be used. Microsoft Active Directory is a dominant example. Relevant standard protocols in the corporate world are Security Assertion Markup Language (SAML) and WS-Federation.[4]

Managing Authentication

Authentication is the process of establishing with adequate certainty the identity of an entity. Authentication is a function of the identity provider that is done through factors such as passwords, key generators, and biometrics. Multifactor authentication is often advised for high-risk roles such as administrative functions.

Managing Authorization

Authorization is the process of granting access to resources. This can be based on identities, attributes of identities such as roles, and contextual information such as location and time of day. Authorization is enforced near the relevant resource, at the policy enforcement point. In a federated identity model, this is typically at the relying party.

Accounting for Resources

Accounting measures the resources a user consumes during access. This can include the amount of system time or the amount of data a user has sent or received during a session. Accounting is carried out by logging session statistics and usage information and is used for authorization control, billing, trend analysis, resource utilization, and capacity planning activities.

Managing Identity and Access Management

Identity management is the entire process of registering, provisioning, and deprovisioning identities for all relevant entities and their attributes, while making that information available to the proper audit.

Access management includes managing the identities' access rights. Access management is where the real risk decisions are made. It is more important to control access rights than it is to control the number of identities.

Making Access Decisions

Examples of access decisions include questions such as these:

- Can a device be allowed to receive an IP address on the local network?
- Can a webserver communicate with a particular database server?
- Can a user access a certain application, a function within an application, or data within an application?
- Can an application access data from another application?

These access rights might be very detailed, down to the individual row of a database.

What is clear from these examples is that access decisions can be enforced at various points with various technologies. These are called policy enforcement points (PEPs). The individual policies are controlled at the policy decision point (PDP) and communicated via standard protocols.

The Entitlement Process

The entitlement process starts with business and security requirements and translates these into a set of rules. An example could be a Human Resource (HR) employee who is allowed read/write access to records in the HR database only when working on a trusted device with a trusted connection.

This rule represents a risk decision; it's a balance between enabling users to be productive while reducing abuse potential. This rule refers to a number of attributes of entities (user account, user role, user device, and device network connection). These rules are then translated into component authorization decisions to be enforced at the PEPs.

Figure 3.10 provides a high-level, generic view of the overall entitlement process.[5]

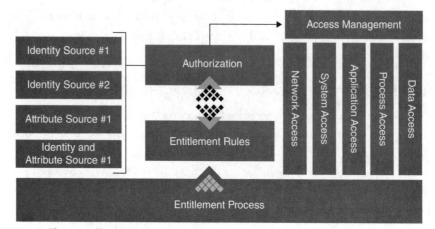

FIGURE 3.10 The overall entitlement process.

Now that you have a basic idea of how an entitlement process works, you'll look at a specific example of what an access control decision in an application may look like.

The Access Control Decision-Making Process

Table 3.1 illustrates how an access control decision in an application is based on a number of identifiers and attributes. Keep in mind the generic view of the entitlement process discussed previously as you explore the specific details of this example.

TABLE 3.1 The Access Control Decision-Making Process

CLAIM/ATTRIBUTE	CORPORATE HR MANAGER ACCESS	CORPORATE USER ACCESS	CORPORATE HR MANAGER HOME ACCESS USING CORPORATE LAPTOP	CORPORATE USER HOME ACCESS USING PERSONAL LAPTOP
ID: Organization ID	Valid	Valid	Valid	No
ID: User Identifier	Valid	Valid	Valid	Valid
ID: Device	Valid	Valid	Valid	No
Attribute: Device is clean	Valid	Valid	Valid	Unknown
Attribute: Device is patched	Valid	Valid	Valid	Unknown
Attribute: Device IP (is on corporate network?)	Valid	Valid	No	No
Attribute: User is HR manager	Valid	No	Valid	No
Access Result	Read/write access to all HR accounts	Read/write access to user's HR account only	Read/write access to user's HR account only	Read-only access to user's HR account only

You can see the identity sources and attributes of Table 3.1 in the first column. The entitlement rules are represented by the column headers along the top of the table for the rest of the columns. Authorization and access management are represented by the entries listed in the appropriate column as referred to by the appropriate Claim/Attribute row entry. The Access Result entry listed at the bottom of each column represents the outcome of the enablement process for that entitlement rule.

Ultimately, it is the combination of where the users are presenting from, as well as what they are using to identify themselves that drives the outcome of what access they are authorized to have.

RISK AUDIT MECHANISMS

The purpose of a risk audit is to provide reasonable assurance that adequate risk controls exist and are operationally effective.

There are a number of reasons for conducting audits. The obvious reasons are regulatory or compliance related. But more and more, (internal) audits are employed as part of a quality system. Cloud customers are also demanding more demonstration of quality.

It is wise to embed audits in existing structures for corporate governance and enterprise risk management. In these frameworks, all requirements for risk controls can be aggregated, including technical, legal, contractual, jurisdictional, and compliance requirements.

The Cloud Security Alliance Cloud Controls Matrix

In the cloud computing world, the Cloud Security Alliance's Cloud Controls Matrix serves as a framework to enable cooperation between cloud service consumers and CSPs on demonstrating adequate risk management.[6]

An essential component of audits is evidence that controls are actually operational. This evidence includes management structures, configurations, configuration files and policies, activity reports, log files, and so on. The downside is that gathering evidence can be a costly effort. Cloud computing, however, can give a new angle to the audit process.

Cloud Computing Audit Characteristics

The characteristics of cloud computing affect audit requirements and the audit process in a number of ways.

Cloud computing raises the level of attention that the entire supply chain should have. The cloud service consumer is typically dependent on multiple CSPs, who in turn are dependent on other providers.

Cloud infrastructure, for example, is often located at a hosting facility, which is a dependency: issues at that facility can affect the cloud infrastructure. From the perspective of the cloud service consumer, the required controls are now under the scope of a supplier. This poses a compliance challenge because the cloud service consumers may experience restrictions on the audit activity they conduct on their provider.

Individual tenants may not be in a position to physically inspect and audit data centers. This would overburden CSPs, and it could reduce security. Customers should require the provider to offer independent audit results and should review these for scope and relevance to their own requirements. Contract clauses should require transparency that is adequate for the validation of the controls that are important to the consumer.

The good news is that cloud computing can improve transparency and assurance if the essential cloud characteristics are being exploited properly. Management of cloud infrastructure involves high degrees of self-service and service automation. Applying these principles on audit requirements and incorporating these requirements in the development of the cloud infrastructure can make it possible to reach new levels of assurance.

The CSP should always bear in mind that the use of contractual agreements such as hosting agreements and service-level agreements (SLAs) distributes responsibility and risk among both CSPs and cloud service consumers. In this way, all parties can properly document and understand the liability for the failure of one or more controls and the corresponding realization of risk.

Using a VM

Service automation can be instrumental in automatically generating evidence. For example, a VM image can be built according to a specified configuration. This configuration baseline and the logs of the build process then provide evidence that all instances of this VM will implement adequate controls.

Controls that can be built in a VM image include an automated vulnerability scan on system start, an automatic registration in a configuration management database, and an asset management system. The configuration might imply any number of management and control agents, such as VM-level firewalls, DLP agents, and automated log file generation. All this can lead to the automatic generation of evidence.

Cloud computing's automation and self-service provisioning can be progressed to lead to continuous auditing, where the existence and effectiveness of controls are tested and demonstrated on a continuous and near real-time basis. The evidence can then be accessible to authorized consumers in a dashboard style. This allows the consumer self-service in collecting the evidence from his CSP and potentially from his upstream CSPs in the delivery chain.

UNDERSTANDING THE CLOUD ENVIRONMENT RELATED TO BCDR

There are a number of characteristics of the cloud environment that you need to consider for your BCDR plan. They represent opportunities as well as challenges. First, though, it pays to have a more detailed look at some different scenarios in which you might want to consider BCDR. The following sections discuss these scenarios, BCDR planning factors, and relevant cloud infrastructure characteristics.

Before proceeding, two definitions need to be presented to help ensure the appropriate understanding of what BCDR is in the mind of the CCSP. The business continuity plan (BCP) allows a business to plan what it needs to do to ensure that its key products and services continue to be delivered in case of a disaster, whereas the disaster recovery plan (DRP) allows a business to plan what needs to be done immediately after a disaster to recover from the event.

On-Premises, Cloud as BCDR

The first scenario is focused on an existing on-premises infrastructure, which may or may not have a BCDR plan in place already. In this scenario, a CSP is considered the provider of alternative facilities should a disaster strike the on-premises infrastructure. This is essentially the "traditional" failover conversation that IT has been engaged in for the enterprise since before the advent of cloud. The only difference is that the cloud is now being introduced as the endpoint for failover services and BCDR activities (*Figure 3.11*).

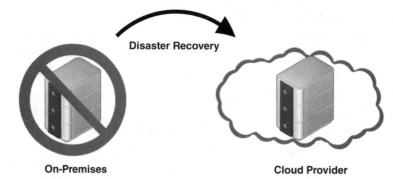

Disaster Recovery

On-Premises   **Cloud Provider**

FIGURE 3.11 **The cloud serves as the endpoint for failover services and BCDR activities.**

Cloud Service Consumer, Primary Provider BCDR

In the second scenario, the infrastructure under consideration is already located at a CSP. The risk being considered is potential failure of part of the CSP's infrastructure, for example one of its regions or availability zones. The business continuity strategy then focuses on restoration of service or failover to another part of that same CSP infrastructure (*Figure 3.12*).

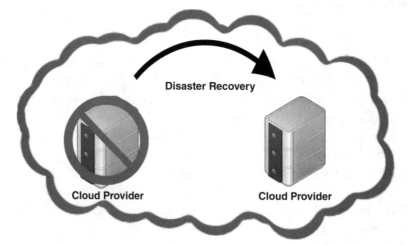

Disaster Recovery

Cloud Provider   **Cloud Provider**

FIGURE 3.12 **When one region or availability zone fails, the service is restored to another part of that same cloud.**

Cloud Service Consumer, Alternative Provider BCDR

The third scenario is somewhat like the second scenario, but instead of restoration of service to the same provider, the service has to be restored to a different provider. This also addresses the risk of complete CSP failure.

DR almost by definition requires replication. The key difference between these scenarios is where the replication happens (*Figure 3.13*).

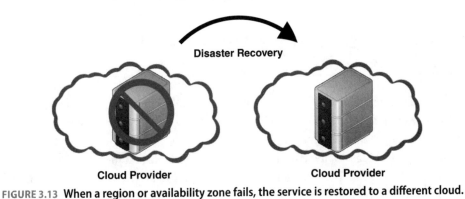

Disaster Recovery

Cloud Provider   **Cloud Provider**

FIGURE 3.13 **When a region or availability zone fails, the service is restored to a different cloud.**

BCDR Planning Factors

Information relevant in BCDR planning includes the following:

- The important assets: data and processing
- The current locations of these assets
- The networks between the assets and the sites of their processing
- Actual and potential location of workforce and business partners in relation to the disaster event

Relevant Cloud Infrastructure Characteristics

Cloud infrastructure has a number of characteristics that can be distinct advantages in realizing BCDR, depending on the scenario:

- Rapid elasticity and on-demand self-service lead to flexible infrastructure that can be quickly deployed to execute an actual DR without hitting unexpected ceilings.
- Broad network connectivity, which reduces operational risk.
- Cloud infrastructure providers have resilient infrastructure, and an external BCDR provider has the potential for being experienced and capable because the provider's technical and people resources are being shared across a number of tenants.

- Pay-per-use can mean that the total BCDR strategy can be a lot cheaper than alternative solutions. During normal operation, the BCDR solution is likely to have a low cost.

Of course, as part of due diligence in your BCDR plan, you should validate all assumptions with the candidate service provider and ensure that they are documented in your SLAs.

UNDERSTANDING THE BUSINESS REQUIREMENTS RELATED TO BCDR

When considering the use of CSPs in establishing BCDR, there are general concerns and business requirements that hold for other cloud services as well, and there are business requirements that are specific to BCDR.

BCDR protects against the risk of data not being available and the risk that the business processes that it supports are not functional, leading to adverse consequences for the organization. The analysis of this risk leads to the business requirements for BCDR.

✔ Vocabulary Review

It is important for the CCSP to remember two of the terms defined in Domain 1: RPO and RTO. What follows is a quick review of those definitions:

- The **recovery point objective** (RPO) helps determine how much information must be recovered and restored. Another way of looking at RPO is to ask yourself, "how much data can the company afford to lose?"

- The **recovery time objective** (RTO) is a time measure of how fast you need each system to be up and running in the event of a disaster or critical failure.

The following graphic illustrates these two concepts.

In addition, you need to be aware of the recovery service level (RSL). RSL is a percentage measurement (0–100%) of how much computing power is necessary based on the percentage of the production system needed during a disaster.

Now that you understand RPO, RTO, and RSL, the following questions can be framed within the appropriate context.

A more modern, cloud-centric view of BCDR is, perhaps, that it is not an activity to be performed after the application and systems architecture are developed. Instead, it should lead to requirements that are to be used as inputs to the design and selection of the information system.

As in any IT system deployment, requirements should always include considerations on regulatory and legal requirements, SLA commitments, protection against relevant risks, and so on.

Here are some of the questions that need to be answered before an optimal cloud BCDR strategy can be developed:

- Is the data sufficiently valuable for additional BCDR strategies?
- What is the required RPO; that is, what data loss would be tolerable?
- What is the required RTO; that is, what unavailability of business functionality is tolerable?
- What kinds of "disasters" are included in the analysis?
- Does that include provider failure?
- What is the necessary RSL for the systems covered by the plan?

This is part of an overall threat model that the BCDR aims to mitigate.

In the extreme case, both the RPO and the RTO requirements are zero. In practice, some iteration from requirements to proposed solutions is likely to occur to find an optimal balance between loss prevention and its cost.

Some additional concerns can be created when BCDR across geographic boundaries is considered. Geographically separating resources for the purpose of BCDR can result in a reduction of, say, flooding or earthquake risk. Counter balancing this is the fact that every CSP is subject to local laws and regulations based on geographic location.

The key for the CCSP is to understand how BCDR can differ in a cloud environment from the traditional approaches that exist in noncloud environments. For instance, in a virtualized environment, the use of snapshots can offer a bare-metal restoration option that can be deployed extremely quickly, whereas improvements to backup technology such as the ability to examine data sets in variable segment widths and change block tracking have enabled the handling of large and complex data and systems in compressed timeframes. These can affect the RTO specified for a system. In addition, as data becomes both larger and more valuable as the result of being able to be better quantified, the RPO window will only continue to widen with regard to more historical data being considered important enough to include in RPO policy and the initial RPO point continuing to move closer to the disaster event.

UNDERSTANDING THE BCDR RISKS

There are a number of categories of risks to consider in the context of BCDR. First, there are risks threatening the assets and support infrastructure that the BCDR plan is protecting against. Second, there are risks that threaten the successful execution of a BCDR plan invocation; that is, what can go wrong if and when you need to fail over?

BCDR Risks Requiring Protection

A nonexhaustive list of risks that BCDR may be tasked to protect against is the following:

- Damage from natural causes and disasters as well as deliberate attacks, including fire, flood, atmospheric electrical discharge, solar-induced geomagnetic storm, wind, earthquake, tsunami, explosion, nuclear accident, volcanic activity, biological hazard, civil unrest, mudslide, tectonic activity, and other forms of natural or manmade disaster

- Wear and tear of equipment

- Availability of qualified staff

- Utility service outages (such as power failures and network disruptions)

- Failure of a provider to deliver services, perhaps because of a result of bankruptcy, a change of business plan, or a lack of adequate resources

BCDR Strategy Risks

The risks that are intrinsic to the BCDR strategy itself need to be considered, too. Here is a list of some of the relevant risks:

- A BCDR strategy typically involves a redundant architecture, or failover tactic. Such architectures intrinsically add complication to the existing solution. Because of that, it has new failure modes and requires additional skills. These represent a new risk that needs to be managed.

- Most BCDR strategies still have common failure modes. For example, the mitigation of VM failure by introducing a failover cluster still has a residual risk of failure of the zone in which the cluster is located. Likewise, multizone architectures are still vulnerable to region failures.

- The DR site is likely to be geographically remote from any primary sites. This may affect performance because of network bandwidth and latency considerations. In addition, there could be regulatory compliance concerns if the DR site is in a different jurisdiction.

Potential Concerns About the BCDR Scenarios

For each of the three scenarios described earlier, some concerns stand out as being specific to the particular scenario.

- **Existing on-premise solution, using cloud as BCDR:** This case includes the selection of a (new) CSP. Especially noteworthy here are the capabilities that need to be available for speedy DR. These consist of functional and resource capabilities.

  For example, workloads on physical machines may need to be converted to workloads in a virtual environment. It is also important to review the speed with which the required resources can be made available.

- **Existing cloud service consumer, evaluating their cloud service provider's BCDR:** Even though this scenario relies heavily on the resources and capabilities of the existing CSP, a reevaluation of the provider's capabilities is necessary because the BCDR strategy is likely to require new resources and functionality.

  As examples, consider load-balancing functionality and available bandwidth between the redundant facilities of the CSP.

- **Existing cloud service consumer, evaluating alternative CSP as BCDR:** An additional provider's capability to execute is a risk that needs to be managed. Again, this is similar to the selection of a new provider. It might be helpful to reconsider the selection process that was done for the primary provider.

  Again, the speediness with which the move to the new provider can be made should be a primary additional concern. In the case of protecting against the failure of a SaaS provider, it is likely that there will be an impact on the business users because the functionality that these are used to is unlikely to be totally equivalent to the functionality of the failing SaaS provider.

  It may prove worthwhile to involve the business users as soon as possible so that they can make an assessment of the residual risks directly to the business.

In all cases, a proper assessment and enumeration of the risks that BCDR protects against, risks inherent in BCDR, and potential remaining risks are important for designing adequate BCDR strategies and making balanced business decisions on them.

BCDR STRATEGIES

The previous topics discussed BCDR scenarios. Although the departing positions are different and each situation requires a tailored approach, there are a number of common components to these scenarios. A logical sequence to discuss these components is location, data replication, functionality replication, event anticipation, failover event, and return to normal.

As always in risk management, it is important to take the business requirements into account when developing and evaluating alternatives. These alternatives should strike an acceptable balance between mitigation and cost. It may be necessary to iterate a few times.

Consider the main components of a sample failover architecture (*Figure 3.14*). Keep this in mind as you explore the components of BCDR strategies in the following sections.

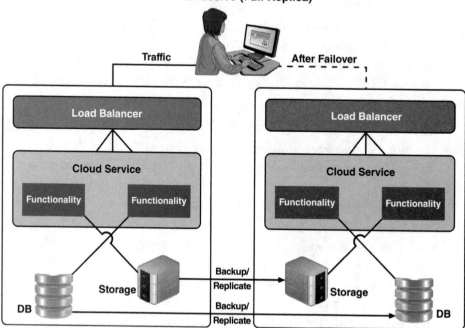

FIGURE 3.14 **Main components of a sample failover architecture.**

Location

As each BCDR strategy addresses the loss of important assets, replication of those assets across multiple locations is more or less assumed. The relevant locations to be considered depend on the geographic scale of the calamity anticipated. Power or network failure may be mitigated in a different zone in the same data center. Flooding, fire, and earthquakes likely require locations that are more remote.

Switching to a different CSP will also likely affect the sites of operations. This is unique to the cloud model because traditional IT solutions do not readily lend themselves to contemplating a switch to a different provider. Unless some sort of outsourcing scenario were to be contemplated and executed on, a switch in IT providers would not be possible. It's important for the CCSP to understand this difference because they have to account for the possibility of a switch in CSPs as part of their due diligence planning to address risk. The use of a memo of understanding, along with SLAs to regulate and guide a switch, if necessary, should be thought out ahead of time and put in place prior to a switch taking place.

Data Replication

Data replication is about maintaining an up-to-date copy of the required data on a different location. It can be done on a number of technical levels and with different granularity. For example, data can be replicated at the block level, the file level, and the database level. Replication can be in bulk, on the byte level, by file synchronization, database mirroring, daily copies, and so on. These alternatives can differ in their RPOs, recovery options, bandwidth requirements, and failover strategies.

Each of these levels allows the mitigation of certain risks, but not all risks. For example, block-level data replication protects against physical data loss but not against database corruption. Also, it does not necessarily permit recovery to a different software solution that requires different data formats.

Furthermore, backup and archive are traditionally used for snapshot functionality, which can mitigate risks related to accidental file deletion and database corruption.

Beyond replication, there may exist an opportunity to rearchitect the application so that relevant data sets are moved to a different provider. This modularizes the application and makes the data more resilient in the face of a power failure. Examples of components to split off include database as a service (DBaaS) and remote storage of log files.

In contrast with IaaS services, PaaS and SaaS service models often have data replication implicit in their services. However, that does not protect against failure of the service provider, and exports of the important data to external locations may still be necessary.

In all cases, selecting the proper data replication strategy requires consideration of storage and bandwidth requirements.

CLOUD PLATFORM AND
INFRASTRUCTURE SECURITY

Functionality Replication

Functionality replication is about re-creating the processing capacity on a different location. Depending on the risk to be mitigated and the scenario chosen, this could be as simple as selecting an additional deployment zone or as involved as performing an extensive rearchitecting. In the SaaS case, this replication of functionality might even involve selecting a new provider with a different offering, implying a substantial impact on the users of the service.

Examples of simple cases are a business that already has a heavily virtualized workload. The relevant VM images can then simply be copied to the CSP, where they would be ready for service restoration on demand.

A modern infrastructure cloud service consumer is likely to have the application architecture described and managed in an orchestration tool or other cloud infrastructure management system. With these, replicating the functionality can be a simple activity.

Functionality replication timing can be across a wide spectrum. The worst recovery elapsed time is probably when functionality is replicated only when disaster strikes. A little better is the active passive form, where resources are held standby. In active mode, the replicated resources are participating in production. The latter approach is likely to demonstrate the most resilience.

Rearchitecting a monolithic application in anticipation of a BCDR may be necessary to enable the type of data replication and functionality replication that are required for the desired BCDR strategy.

Finally, many applications have extensive connections to other providers and consumers acting as data feeds. These should be included in any BCDR planning.

Planning, Preparing, and Provisioning

Planning, preparing, and provisioning are about the tooling, functionality, and processes that lead up to the actual DR failover response. The most important component here is adequate monitoring, where more time is often available ahead of the required failover event. In any case, the sooner anomalies are detected, the easier it is to attain an RTO.

Failover Capability

The failover capability itself requires some form of load balancer to redirect user service requests to the appropriate services.

This capability can take the technical form of cluster managers, load balancer devices, or domain name system (DNS) manipulation. It is important to consider the risks that these components introduce because they might become a new single point of failure.

Returning to Normal

Return to normal is where DR ends. In case of a temporary failover, the return to normal would be back to the original provider (or in-house infrastructure, as the case may be). Alternatively, the original provider may no longer be a viable option, in which case the DR provider becomes the "new normal." In all cases, it is wise to adequately document any lessons learned and clean up any resources that are no longer needed, including sensitive data.

The whole BCDR process, and in particular the failover event, represents a risk mitigation strategy. Practicing it in whole or part strengthens the confidence in this strategy. At the same time, such a trial run can result in a risk to production. These opposing outcomes should be carefully balanced when developing the BCDR strategy.

CREATING THE BCDR PLAN

The creation and implementation of a fully tested BCDR plan that is ready for the failover event has a great structural resemblance to any other IT implementation plan as well as other disaster response plans. It is wise to consult or even adapt existing IT project planning and risk management methodologies. In this section, some activities and concerns are highlighted that are relevant for cloud BCDR.

When organizations are incorporating IT systems and cloud solutions on an ongoing basis, creating and reevaluating BCDR plans should be a defined and documented process.

The Scope of the BCDR Plan

The BCDR plan and its implementation are embedded in an information security strategy, which encompasses clearly defined roles, risk assessment, classification, policy, awareness, and training.

It makes sense to consider BCDR as an intrinsic part of the IT service that is regularly invoked, if only for testing purposes.

Gathering Requirements and Context

The requirements that are input for BCDR planning include identification of critical business processes and their dependence on specific data and services. The characteristics, descriptions, and service agreements (if any) of these services and systems are required in the analysis.

Input to the analysis and design of BCDR solutions also includes a list of risks and threats that can negatively affect any important business processes. This threat model should include failure of any CSPs.

Business strategy influences the acceptable RTO and RPO values.

Finally, requirements for BCDR may derive from company internal policies and procedures as well as from applicable legal, statutory, or regulatory compliance obligations.

Analysis of the Plan

The purpose of the analysis phase is to translate BCDR requirements into input to be used in the design phase. The most important inputs for the design phase are scope, requirements, budget, and performance objectives.

Business requirements and the threat model should be analyzed for completeness and consistency and then translated into an identification of the assets at risk.

With that, requirements on resources needs for mitigating those risks can be made. This includes the identification of all dependencies, including processes, applications, business partners, and third-party service providers.

For example, what are the technical components and underlying services of an application operated in house that would need to be replicated in a BCDR facility?

Analysis should identify any opportunities for decoupling systems and services and breaking any common failure modes. Capabilities of the current providers in delivering resources to the BCDR solution should be investigated.

Performance requirements such as bandwidth and offsite storage needs derive from the assets at risk. Careful analysis and assessment should be undertaken with the objective of minimizing these performance requirements.

Risk Assessment

In the same way as any IT solution should be assessed for residual risk, BCDR solutions should be assessed for residual risks. Some risks have been elaborated in earlier topics.

All scenarios involve evaluation of the CSP's capability to deliver. The typical challenges include the following:

- Elasticity of the CSP: Can the CSP provide all the resources if BCDR is invoked?
- Contractual issues: Will any new CSP address all contractual issues and SLA requirements?
- Available network bandwidth for timely replication of data.
- Available bandwidth between the impacted user base and the BCDR locations.
- Legal and licensing risks: There may be legal or licensing constraints that prohibit the data or functionality to be present in the backup location.

Plan Design

The objective of the design phase is to establish and evaluate candidate architecture solutions. The approaches and their components have been illustrated in earlier topics.

This design phase should not just result in technical alternatives but also flesh out procedures and workflow.

As with any IT service or system, the BCDR solution should have a clear owner—with a clear role and mandate in the organization—who is accountable for the correct setup and maintenance of the BCDR capability.

Following are additional BCDR-specific questions that should be addressed in the design phase:

- How will the BCDR solution be invoked?
- What is the manual or automated procedure for invoking the failover services?
- How will the business use of the service be affected during the failover, if at all?
- How will the BCDR be tested?

NOTE   Testability requirements can potentially be addressed by compartmentalizing the infrastructure in multiple independent resilient components.

Other Plan Considerations

Once the design of the BCDR solution is ready, work will start on implementing the solution. This is likely to require work both on the primary solution platform and on the DR platform.

On the primary platform, these activities are likely to include the implementation of functionality for enabling data replication on a regular or continuous schedule and functionality to automatically monitor for any contingency that might arise and raise a failover event.

On the DR platform, the required infrastructure and services need to be built up and brought into trial production mode.

Care must be taken so that not only the required infrastructure and services are made available but the DR platform tracks any relevant changes and functional updates that are being made on the primary platform.

Additionally, it is advisable to include all DR-related infrastructure and services in the regular IT services management.

Planning, Exercising, Assessing, and Maintaining the Plan

Once the plan has been completed and the recovery strategies have been fully implemented, it is important to test all parts of the plan to validate that it would work in a real event. The testing policy should include enterprise-wide testing strategies that establish expectations for individual business lines. Business lines include all internal and external supporting functions, such as IT and facilities management. The testing strategy should include the following:

- Expectations for business lines and support functions to demonstrate the achievement of business continuity test objectives consistent with the business impact analysis (BIA) and risk assessment
- A description of the depth and breadth of testing to be accomplished
- The involvement of staff, technology, and facilities
- Expectations for testing internal and external interdependencies
- An evaluation of the reasonableness of assumptions used in developing the testing strategy

Testing strategies should include the testing scope and objectives, which clearly define which functions, systems, or processes are going to be tested and what will constitute a successful test. The objective of a testing program is to ensure that the business continuity planning (BCP) process is accurate, relevant, and viable under adverse conditions. Therefore, the BCP process should be tested at least annually, with more frequent testing required when significant changes have occurred in business operations. Testing should include applications and business functions that were identified during the BIA. The BIA determines the recovery point objectives and recovery time objectives, which then help determine the appropriate recovery strategy. Validation of the RPOs and RTOs is important to ensure that they are attainable.

Testing objectives should start simply and gradually increase in complexity and scope. The scope of individual tests can be continually expanded to eventually encompass enterprise-wide testing and testing with vendors and key market participants. Achieving the following objectives provides progressive levels of assurance and confidence in the plan. At a minimum, the testing scope and objectives should do the following:

- Ensure support for normal business operations
- Gradually increase the complexity, level of participation, functions, and physical locations involved
- Demonstrate a variety of management and response proficiencies under simulated crisis conditions, progressively involving more resources and participants
- Uncover inadequacies so that testing procedures can be revised
- Consider deviating from the test script to interject unplanned events, such as the loss of key individuals or services
- Involve a sufficient volume of all types of transactions to ensure adequate capacity and functionality of the recovery facility

The testing policy should also include test planning, which is based on the predefined testing scope and objectives established as part of management's testing strategies. Test planning includes test plan review procedures and the development of various testing scenarios and methods. Management should evaluate the risks and merits of various types of testing scenarios and develop test plans based on identified recovery needs. Test plans should identify quantifiable measurements of each test objective and should be reviewed prior to the test to ensure they can be implemented as designed. Test scenarios should include a variety of threats, event types, and crisis management situations and should vary from isolated system failures to wide-scale disruptions. Scenarios should also promote testing alternate facilities with the primary and alternate facilities of key counterparties and third-party service providers.

Comprehensive test scenarios focus attention on dependencies, both internal and external, between critical business functions, information systems, and networks. Integrated testing moves beyond the testing of individual components to include testing with internal and external parties and the supporting systems, processes, and resources. As such, test plans should include scenarios addressing local and wide-scale disruptions, as appropriate. Business line management should develop scenarios to effectively test internal and external interdependencies, with the assistance of IT staff members who are knowledgeable of application data flows and other areas of vulnerability. Organizations should periodically reassess and update their test scenarios to reflect changes in the organization's business and operating environments.

Test plans should clearly communicate the predefined test scope and objectives and give participants relevant information, such as the following:

- A master test schedule that encompasses all test objectives
- Specific descriptions of test objectives and methods
- Roles and responsibilities for all test participants, including support staff
- Designation of test participants
- Test decision makers and succession plans
- Test locations
- Test escalation conditions and test contact information

Test Plan Review

Management should prepare and review a script for each test prior to testing to identify weaknesses that could lead to unsatisfactory or invalid tests. As part of the review process, the testing plan should be revised to account for any changes to key personnel, policies, procedures, facilities, equipment, outsourcing relationships, vendors, or other components that affect a critical business function. In addition, as a preliminary step to the testing process, management should perform a thorough review of the BCP. This is a checklist review. A checklist review involves distributing copies of the BCP to the managers of each critical business unit and requesting that they review portions of the plan applicable to their department to ensure that the procedures are comprehensive and complete.

It is often wise to stop using the word *test* for this and begin to use the word *exercise*. The reason to call them exercises is that when the word *test* is used, people think pass or fail. In fact, there is no way to fail a contingency test. If the security professionals knew that it worked, they would not bother to test it. The reason to test is to find out what does not work so issues can be fixed before a disaster happens for real.

Testing methods can vary from simple to complex depending on the preparation and resources required. Each bears its own characteristics, objectives, and benefits. The type or combination of testing methods employed by an organization should be determined by, among other things, the organization's age and experience with BCP, size, complexity, and the nature of its business.

Testing methods include both business recovery and DR exercises. Business recovery exercises primarily focus on testing business line operations, whereas DR exercises focus on testing the continuity of technology components, including systems, networks, applications, and data. To test split processing configurations, in which two or more sites support part of a business line's workload, tests should include the transfer of work among processing sites to demonstrate that alternate sites can effectively support customer-specific requirements and work volumes and site-specific business processes. A comprehensive test should involve processing a full day's work at peak volumes to ensure that equipment capacity is available and that RTOs and RPOs can be achieved.

More rigorous testing methods and greater frequency of testing provide greater confidence in the continuity of business functions. Although comprehensive tests do require greater investments of time, resources, and coordination to implement, detailed testing more accurately depicts a true disaster and assists management in assessing the actual responsiveness of the individuals involved in the recovery process. Furthermore, comprehensive testing of all critical functions and applications allows management to identify potential problems; therefore, management should use one of the more thorough testing methods discussed in this section to ensure the viability of the BCP before a disaster occurs.

The security professional can conduct many different types of exercises. Some take minutes, whereas others take hours or days. The amount of exercise planning needed is entirely dependent on the exercise type, the exercise length, and the exercise scope the security professional will plan to conduct. The most common types of exercises are call exercises, walk-through exercises, simulated or actual exercises, and compact exercises.

Tabletop Exercise/Structured Walk-Through Test

A tabletop exercise/structured walk-through test is considered a preliminary one in the overall testing process and may be used as an effective training tool; however, it is not a preferred testing method. Its primary objective is to ensure that critical personnel from all areas are familiar with the BCP and that the plan accurately reflects the organization's ability to recover from a disaster. This exercise/test is characterized by the following:

- Attendance of business unit management representatives and employees who play a critical role in the BCP process

- Discussion about each person's responsibilities as defined by the BCP

- Individual and team training, which includes a walk-through of the step-by-step procedures outlined in the BCP

- Clarification and highlighting of critical plan elements, as well as problems noted during testing

Walk-Through Drill/Simulation Test

A walk-through drill/simulation test is somewhat more involved than a tabletop exercise/structured walk-through test because the participants choose a specific event scenario and apply the BCP to it. It includes the following:

- Attendance by all operational and support personnel who are responsible for implementing the BCP procedures

- Practice and validation of specific functional response capabilities

- Focus on the demonstration of knowledge and skills, as well as team interaction and decision-making capabilities

- Role playing with simulated response at alternate locations to act out critical steps, recognize difficulties, and resolve problems in a nonthreatening environment

- Mobilization of all or some of the crisis management and response team to practice proper coordination without performing actual recovery processing

- Varying degrees of actual, as opposed to simulated, notification and resource mobilization to reinforce the content and logic of the plan

Functional Drill/Parallel Test

A functional drill/parallel test is the first type that involves the actual mobilization of personnel to other sites in an attempt to establish communications and perform actual recovery processing as set forth in the BCP. The goal is to determine whether critical systems can be recovered at the alternate processing site and if employees can actually deploy the procedures defined in the BCP. A functional drill/parallel test encompasses the following:

- A full test of the BCP, which involves all employees
- Demonstration of emergency management capabilities of several groups practicing a series of interactive functions, such as direction, control, assessment, operations, and planning
- Testing medical response and warning procedures
- Response(s) to alternate locations or facilities using actual communications capabilities
- Mobilization of personnel and resources at varied geographical sites, including evacuation drills in which employees test the evacuation route and procedures for personnel accountability
- Varying degrees of actual, as opposed to simulated, notification and resource mobilization in which parallel processing is performed and transactions are compared to production results

Full-Interruption/Full-Scale Test

Full-interruption/full-scale test is the most comprehensive type of test. In a full-scale test, a real-life emergency is simulated as closely as possible. Therefore, comprehensive planning should be a prerequisite to this type of test to ensure that business operations are not negatively affected. The organization implements all or portions of its BCP by processing data and transactions using backup media at the recovery site. This test involves the following:

- Enterprise-wide participation and interaction of internal and external management response teams with full involvement of external organizations
- Validation of crisis response functions
- Demonstration of knowledge and skills as well as management response and decision-making capability
- On-the-scene execution of coordination and decision-making roles
- Actual, as opposed to simulated, notifications, mobilization of resources, and communication of decisions
- Activities conducted at actual response locations or facilities
- Actual processing of data using backup media
- Exercises generally extending over a longer period of time to allow issues to fully evolve as they would in a crisis and to allow realistic role-playing of all the involved groups

After every exercise the security professional conducts, the results need to be published and action items identified to address the issues that were uncovered. Action items should be tracked until they have been resolved and, where appropriate, the plan should be updated. It is unfortunate when an organization has the same issue in subsequent tests simply because someone did not update the plan.

Testing and Acceptance to Production

The BCP, as any other security incident response plan, is subject to testing at planned intervals or upon significant organizational or environmental changes, as discussed previously.

Ideally, a test realizes a full switchover to the DR platform. At the same time, it should be recognized that this test does represent a risk to the production user population.

Just to provide an idea of the realism level that organizations can aspire to, consider the architecture of a well-known online video distribution service. Its infrastructure is designed to operate without a single point of failure being allowed to affect production. To test and ensure that this is and remains so, the video distribution service employs a so-called chaos monkey, which is a process that continuously triggers component failures in the production service. For each of these components, an automatic failover mechanism is in place.[7]

SUMMARY

As discussed, cloud platform and infrastructure security covers a range of topics focused on both physical and virtual components as they pertain to cloud environments. CCSPs focused on cloud security must use and apply standards to ensure that the systems under their protection are maintained and supported properly. As part of the use of standards, CCSPs must be in the vanguard of the identification, analysis, and management of risk in the enterprise as it pertains to the cloud. The ability to develop a plan to mitigate risk in cloud infrastructures based on the outcome of a risk assessment and focused on the appropriate countermeasures is a vital set of skills for CCSPs. When CCSPs examine the security landscape of the cloud, they have to ensure that they have put in place security control plans that include the physical environment, virtual environment, system communications, access management, and all mechanisms necessary for auditing. In addition, they have to ensure that DR and business continuity management for cloud-based systems are documented within the enterprise with regard to the environment, business requirements, and risk management.

REVIEW QUESTIONS

1. What is a cloud carrier?

   A. A person, organization, or entity responsible for making a service available to service consumers

   B. The intermediary that provides connectivity and transport of cloud services between CSPs and cloud service consumers

   C. A person or organization that maintains a business relationship with, and uses service from, CSPs

   D. The intermediary that provides business continuity of cloud services between cloud service consumers

2. Which of the following statements about SDN is correct? (Choose two.)

   A. SDN enables you to execute the control plane software on general-purpose hardware, allowing for the decoupling from specific network hardware configurations and allowing for the use of commodity servers. Further, the use of software-based controllers permits a view of the network that presents a logical switch to the applications running above, allowing for access via APIs that can be used to configure, manage, and secure network resources.

   B. SDN's objective is to provide a clearly defined network control plane to manage network traffic that is not separated from the forwarding plane. This approach allows for network control to become directly programmable and for dynamic adjustment of traffic flows to address changing patterns of consumption.

   C. SDN enables you to execute the control plane software on specific hardware, allowing for the binding of specific network hardware configurations. Further, the use of software-based controllers permits a view of the network that presents a logical switch to the applications running above, allowing for access via APIs that can be used to configure, manage, and secure network resources.

   D. SDN's objective is to offer a clearly defined and separate network control plane to manage network traffic that is separated from the forwarding plane. This approach permits network control to become directly programmable and distinct from forwarding, allowing for dynamic adjustment of traffic flows to address changing patterns of consumption.

3. With regards to management of the compute resources of a host in a cloud environment, what does a reservation provide?

   A. The ability to arbitrate the issues associated with compute resource contention situations. Resource contention implies that there are too many requests for resources based on the actual available resources currently in the system.

   B. A guaranteed minimum resource allocation that must be met by the host with physical compute resources to allow a guest to power on and operate.

   C. A maximum ceiling for a resource allocation. This ceiling may be fixed, or it may be expandable, allowing for the acquisition of more compute resources through a borrowing scheme from the root resource provider (the host).

   D. A guaranteed maximum resource allocation that must be met by the host with physical compute resources to allow a guest to power on and operate.

4. What is the key issue associated with the object storage type that the CCSP has to be aware of?

   A. Data consistency, which is achieved only after change propagation to all replica instances has taken place

   B. Access control

   C. Data consistency, which is achieved only after change propagation to a specified percentage of replica instances has taken place

   D. Continuous monitoring

5. What types of risks are typically associated with virtualization?

   A. Loss of governance, snapshot and image security, and sprawl

   B. Guest breakout, snapshot and image availability, and compliance

   C. Guest breakout, snapshot and image security, and sprawl

   D. Guest breakout, knowledge level required to manage, and sprawl

6. When using a SaaS solution, who is responsible for application security?

   A. Both the cloud service consumer and the enterprise

   B. The enterprise only

   C. The CSP only

   D. Both CSP and the enterprise

7. Which of the following are examples of trust zones? (Choose two.)

   A. A specific application being used to carry out a general function such as printing

   B. Segmentation according to department

   C. A web application with a two-tiered architecture

   D. Storage of a baseline configuration on a workstation

8. What are the relevant cloud infrastructure characteristics that can be considered distinct advantages in realizing a BCDR plan objective with regards to cloud computing environments?

   A. Rapid elasticity, provider-specific network connectivity, and a pay-per-use model

   B. Rapid elasticity, broad network connectivity, and a multitenancy model

   C. Rapid elasticity, broad network connectivity, and a pay-per-use model

   D. Continuous monitoring, broad network connectivity, and a pay-per-use model

NOTES

[1] http://nvlpubs.nist.gov/nistpubs/Legacy/SP/nistspecialpublication800-146.pdf

[2] See the following:

http://csrc.nist.gov/publications/nistpubs/800-14/800-14.pdf

http://csrc.nist.gov/publications/nistpubs/800-123/SP800-123.pdf

[3] See the following for more information:

OpenID: http://openid.net/

OAuth2: http://oauth.net/2/

[4] See the following for more information:

SAML: https://www.oasis-open.org/committees/tc_home.php?wg_abbrev=security

WS-Federation: http://docs.oasis-open.org/wsfed/federation/v1.2/os/ws-federation-1.2-spec-os.html

[5] https://cloudsecurityalliance.org/guidance/csaguide.v3.0.pdf (p. 140)

[6] https://cloudsecurityalliance.org/group/cloud-controls-matrix/

[7] See the following: http://techblog.netflix.com/2012/07/chaos-monkey-released-into-wild.html

DOMAIN 4

Cloud Application Security

THE GOAL OF THE Cloud Application Security domain is to provide you with knowledge as it relates to cloud application security. Through an exploration of the software development lifecycle, you will gain an understanding in utilizing secure software and understand the controls necessary for developing secure cloud environments and program interfaces.

You will gain knowledge in identity and access management solutions for the cloud and the cloud application architecture. You'll also learn how to ensure data and application availability, integrity, and confidentiality (AIC) through cloud software assurance and validation.

DOMAIN OBJECTIVES

After completing this domain, you will be able to do the following:

- ❑ Identify the necessary training and awareness required for successful cloud application security deployment, including common pitfalls and vulnerabilities

- ❑ Describe the software development lifecycle process for a cloud environment

- ❑ Demonstrate the use and application of the software development lifecycle as it applies to secure software in a cloud environment

- ❑ Identify the requirements for creating secure identity and access management solutions

- ❑ Describe specific cloud application architecture

- ❑ Describe the steps necessary to ensure and validate cloud software

- ❑ Identify the necessary functional and security testing for software assurance

- ❑ Summarize the process for verifying secure software, including application programming interface (API) and supply chain management

INTRODUCTION

As cloud-based application development continues to gain popularity and widespread adoption, it is important to recognize the benefits and efficiencies, along with the challenges and complexities. Cloud development typically includes integrated development environments (IDEs), application lifecycle management components, and application security testing (*Figure 4.1*).

FIGURE 4.1 **Benefits and efficiencies tend to conflict with challenges and complexities.**

Inherent to the continued and expanded use of technology to deliver services, organizations are presented with quantitative and qualitative risks and challenges. The failure to address these risks directly affects the organization, its software supply chain (extended enterprise API management), and its customers. For the appropriate steps and controls to be implemented, these organizations must understand application security in a cloud environment, along with the differences from traditional information technology (IT) computing.

Just as traditional deployments within a data center or even a hosted solution where network controls are ubiquitous and compensating perimeter controls are sometimes depended upon to offer application security, cloud applications can be secure as long as the same security evaluation for cloud environments is performed.

Organizations and practitioners alike need to understand and appreciate that cloud-based development and applications can vary from traditional or on-premises development. When considering an application for cloud deployment, you must remember that applications can be broken down to the following subcomponents:

- Data
- Functions
- Processes

The components can be broken up so that the portions that have sensitive data can be processed or stored in specified locations to comply with enterprise policies, standards, and applicable laws and regulations.

This domain highlights some of the key security differences that must be addressed in a cloud-operating environment.

DETERMINING DATA SENSITIVITY AND IMPORTANCE

To begin, applications should undergo an assessment of the sensitivity and importance of an application that may be implemented in a cloud environment. The following six key questions can be used to open a discussion of the application to determine its cloud-friendliness.

What would the impact be in the following situations:

- The data became widely public and widely distributed (including crossing geographic boundaries)
- An employee of the cloud service provider (CSP) accessed the application
- The process or function was manipulated by an outsider
- The process or function failed to provide expected results
- The data was unexpectedly changed
- The application was unavailable for a period of time

These questions form the basis of an information-gathering exercise to identify and understand the requirements for AIC of an application and its associated information assets. These questions can be discussed with a system owner to begin a collaborative security discussion. Further assessments will be discussed in later sections of this domain.

Note that this exercise should be performed by an independent resource or function without bias or preference within the organization. Independence and the ability to present a true and accurate account of information types along with the requirements for AIC may be the difference between a successful project and a failure.

UNDERSTANDING THE API FORMATS

In many cloud environments, access is acquired through the means of an API. These APIs consume tokens rather than traditional usernames and passwords. This topic is discussed in greater detail in the "Identity and Access Management" section later in this domain.

APIs can be broken into multiple formats, two of which follow:

- **Representational State Transfer (REST):** A software architecture style consisting of guidelines and best practices for creating scalable web services[1]
- **Simple object access protocol (SOAP):** A protocol specification for exchanging structured information in the implementation of web services in computer networks[2]

Table 4.1 provides a high-level comparison of the two common API formats.

TABLE 4.1 **High-Level Comparison of REST and SOAP**

REST	SOAP
Representational State Transfer	Simple object access protocol
Uses simple hypertext transfer protocol (HTTP)	Uses SOAP envelope and then HTTP (or file transfer protocol [FTP]/simple mail transfer protocol [SMTP] to transfer the data
Supports many different data formats like JavaScript Object Notation (JSON), eXtensible Markup Language (XML), and Yet Another Multicolumn Layout (YAML)	Only supports XML format
Performance and scalability are good and uses caching	Slower performance, scalability can be complex, and caching is not possible
Widely used	Used where REST is not possible, provides WS-* features

CCSPs should familiarize themselves with API formats as they relate to cloud services.

COMMON PITFALLS OF CLOUD SECURITY APPLICATION DEPLOYMENT

The ability to identify, communicate, and plan for potential cloud-based application challenges proves an invaluable skill for developers and project teams. Failure to do so can result in additional costs, failed projects, and duplication of efforts along with loss of efficiencies and executive sponsorship. Although many projects and cloud journeys may have an element of unique or nonstandard approaches, the pitfalls discussed in this section should always be followed and understood (*Figure 4.2*).

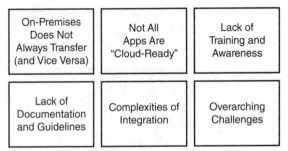

FIGURE 4.2 **Common pitfalls related to cloud security.**

On-Premises Does Not Always Transfer (and Vice Versa)

Present performance and functionality may not be transferable. Current configurations and applications may be hard to replicate on or through cloud services. The rationale for this is twofold.

- First, they were not developed with cloud-based services in mind. The continued evolution and expansion of cloud-based service offerings looks to enhance previous technologies and development, not always maintaining support for more historical development and systems. Where cloud-based development has occurred, this may need to be tested against on-premises or legacy-based systems.

- Second, not all applications can be forklifted to the cloud. Forklifting an application is the process of migrating an entire application the way it runs in a traditional infrastructure with minimal code changes. Generally, these applications are self-contained and have few dependencies; however, transferring or utilizing cloud-based environments may introduce additional change requirements and additional interdependencies.

Not All Apps Are Cloud Ready

Where high-value data and hardened security controls are applied, cloud development and testing can be more challenging. The reason for this is typically compounded by the requirement for such systems to be developed, tested, and assessed in on-premises or traditional environments to a level where confidentiality and integrity have been verified and assured. Many high-end applications come with distinct security and regulatory restrictions or rely on legacy coding projects, many of which may have been developed using COBOL, along with other more historical development languages. These reasons, along with whatever control frameworks may have to be observed and adhered to, can cause one or more applications to fail at being cloud ready.

Lack of Training and Awareness

New development techniques and approaches require training and a willingness to utilize new services. Typically, developers have become accustomed to working with Microsoft .NET, SQL Server, Java, and other traditional development techniques. When cloud-based environments are required or are requested by the organization, this may introduce challenges (particularly if it is a platform or system with which developers are unfamiliar).

Lack of Documentation and Guidelines

Best practice requires developers to follow relevant documentation, guidelines, methodologies, processes, and lifecycles to reduce opportunities for unnecessary or heightened risk to be introduced.

Given the rapid adoption of evolving cloud services, this has led to a disconnect between some providers and developers on how to utilize, integrate, or meet vendor requirements for development. Although many providers are continuing to enhance levels of available documentation, the most up-to-date guidance may not always be available, particularly for new releases and updates.

For these reasons, the CCSP needs to understand the basic concept of a cloud software development lifecycle and what it can do for the organization. A software development lifecycle is essentially a series of steps, or phases, that provide a model for the development and lifecycle management of an application or piece of software. The methodology within the software development lifecycle process can vary across industries and organizations, but standards such as ISO/IEC 12207 represent processes that establish a lifecycle for software and provide a mode for the development, acquisition, and configuration of software systems.[3]

The intent of a software development lifecycle process is to help produce a product that is cost-efficient, effective, and high quality. The software development lifecycle methodology usually contains the following stages: analysis (requirements and design), construction, testing, release, and maintenance (response).

Complexities of Integration

Integrating new applications with existing ones can be a key part of the development process. When developers and operational resources do not have open or unrestricted access to supporting components and services, integration can be complicated, particularly where the CSP manages infrastructure, applications, and integration platforms.

From a troubleshooting perspective, it can prove difficult to track or collect events and transactions across interdependent or underlying components.

In an effort to reduce these complexities, where possible (and available), the CSP's API should be used.

Overarching Challenges

At all times, developers must keep in mind two key risks associated with applications that run in the cloud:

- Multitenancy
- Third-party administrators

It is also critical that developers understand the security requirements based on the following:

- Deployment model (public, private, community, hybrid) that the application will run in

- Service model (infrastructure as a service [IaaS], platform as a service [PaaS], or software as a service [SaaS])

These two models will assist in determining what security your provider will offer and what your organization is responsible for implementing and maintaining.

It is critical to evaluate who is responsible for security controls across the deployment and services models. Consider creating a sample responsibility matrix (*Figure 4.3*).

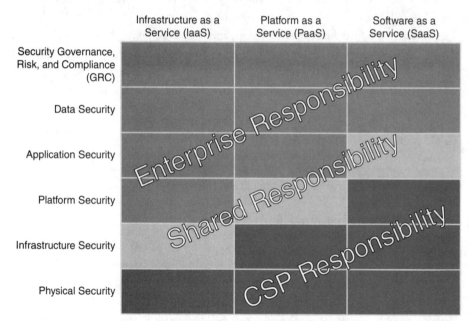

FIGURE 4.3 **Sample security responsibility matrix for cloud service models.**

Additionally, developers must be aware that metrics will always be required and cloud-based applications may have a higher reliance on metrics than internal applications to supply visibility into who is accessing the application and the actions they are performing. This may require substantial development time to integrate said functionality and may eliminate a forklift approach.

AWARENESS OF ENCRYPTION DEPENDENCIES

Development staff must take into account the environment their applications will be running in and the possible encryption dependencies in the following modes:

- **Encryption of data at rest:** Addresses encrypting data as it is stored within the CSP network (such as hard disc drive [HDD], storage area network [SAN], network attached storage [NAS], and solid-state drive [SSD])

- **Encryption of data in transit:** Addresses security of data while it traverses the network (such as CSP network or Internet)

Additionally, the following method may be applied to data to prevent unauthorized viewing or accessing of sensitive information:

- **Data masking (or data obfuscation):** The process of hiding original data with random characters or data

When encryption will be provided or supported by the CSP, an understanding of the encryption types, strength, algorithms, key management, and any associated responsibilities of other parties should be documented and understood. Additionally, depending on the industry type, relevant certifications or criteria may be required for the relevant encryption being used.

Beyond encryption aspects of security, threat modeling (discussed later in this domain) must address attacks from either other cloud tenants or attacks from one organization application being used as a mechanism to perform attacks on other corporate applications in the same or other systems.

UNDERSTANDING THE SOFTWARE DEVELOPMENT LIFECYCLE PROCESS FOR A CLOUD ENVIRONMENT

The cloud further heightens the need for applications to go through a software development lifecycle process. Following are the phases in all software development lifecycle process models:

1. **Planning and requirements analysis:** Business and security requirements and standards are being determined. This phase is the main focus of the project managers and stakeholders. Meetings with managers, stakeholders, and users are held to determine requirements. The software development lifecycle calls for all

business requirements (functional and nonfunctional) to be defined even before initial design begins. Planning for the quality-assurance requirements and identification of the risks associated with the project are also conducted in the planning stage. The requirements are then analyzed for their validity and the possibility of incorporating them into the system to be developed.

2. **Defining:** The defining phase is meant to clearly define and document the product requirements to place them in front of the customers and get them approved. This is done through a requirement specification document, which consists of all the product requirements to be designed and developed during the project lifecycle.

3. **Designing:** System design helps in specifying hardware and system requirements and helps in defining overall system architecture. The system design specifications serve as input for the next phase of the model. Threat modeling and secure design elements should be undertaken and discussed here.

4. **Developing:** Upon receiving the system design documents, work is divided into modules or units and actual coding starts. This is typically the longest phase of the software development lifecycle. Activities include code review, unit testing, and static analysis.

5. **Testing:** After the code is developed, it is tested against the requirements to make sure that the product is actually solving the needs gathered during the requirements phase. During this phase, unit testing, integration testing, system testing, and acceptance testing are conducted.

Most software development lifecycle models include a maintenance phase as their endpoint. Operations and disposal are included in some models as a way of further subdividing the activities that traditionally take place in the maintenance phase, as noted in the next sections.

Secure Operations Phase

From a security perspective, once the application has been implemented using software development lifecycle principles, the application enters a secure operations phase. Proper software configuration management and versioning are essential to application security. There are some tools that can be used to ensure that the software is configured according to specified requirements. Following are two such tools:

- **Puppet:** According to Puppet Labs, Puppet is a configuration management system that allows you to define the state of your IT infrastructure and then automatically enforces the correct state.[4]

- **Chef:** With Chef, you can automate how you build, deploy, and manage your infrastructure. The Chef server stores your recipes as well as other configuration data. The Chef client is installed on each server, virtual machine, container, or networking device you manage (called nodes). The client periodically polls the Chef server for the latest policy and the state of your network. If anything on the node is out of date, the client brings it up to date.[5]

The goal of these applications is to ensure that configurations are updated as needed and there is consistency in versioning. This phase calls for the following activities to take place:

- Dynamic analysis
- Vulnerability assessments and penetration testing (as part of a continuous monitoring plan)
- Activity monitoring
- Layer-7 firewalls (such as web application firewalls)

Disposal Phase

When an application has run its course and is no longer required, it is disposed of. From a cloud perspective, it is challenging to ensure that data is properly disposed of because you have no way to physically remove the drives. To this end, there is the notion of crypto-shredding. Crypto-shredding is effectively summed up as the deletion of the key used to encrypt data that's stored in the cloud.

ASSESSING COMMON VULNERABILITIES

Applications run in the cloud should conform to best practice guidance and guidelines for the assessment and ongoing management of vulnerabilities. As mentioned earlier, implementation of an application risk-management program addresses not only vulnerabilities but also all risks associated with applications.

The most common software vulnerabilities are found in the Open Web Application Security Project (OWASP) Top 10. Here are the OWASP Top 10 entries for 2013 as well as a description of each entry:

- "**Injection:** Includes injection flaws such as SQL, OS, LDAP, and other injections. These occur when untrusted data is sent to an interpreter as part of a command or query. If the interpreter is successfully tricked, it will execute the unintended commands or access data without proper authorization.

- **"Broken authentication and session management:** Application functions related to authentication and session in management are often not implemented correctly, allowing attackers to compromise passwords, keys, or session tokens or to exploit other implementation flaws to assume other users' identities.

- **"Cross-site scripting (XSS):** XSS flaws occur whenever an application takes untrusted data and sends it to a web browser without proper validation or escaping. XSS allows attackers to execute scripts in the victim's browser, which can hijack user sessions, deface websites, or redirect the user to malicious sites.

- **"Insecure direct object references:** A direct object reference occurs when a developer exposes a reference to an internal implementation object, such as a file, directory, or database key. Without an access control check or other protection, attackers can manipulate these references to access unauthorized data.

- **"Security misconfiguration:** Good security requires having a secure configuration defined and deployed for the application, frameworks, application server, web server, database server, and platform. Secure settings should be defined, implemented, and maintained, as defaults are often insecure. Additionally, software should be kept up to date.

- **"Sensitive data exposure:** Many web applications do not properly protect sensitive data, such as credit cards, tax IDs, and authentication credentials. Attackers may steal or modify such weakly protected data to conduct credit card fraud, identity theft, or other crimes. Sensitive data deserves extra protection, such as encryption at rest or in transit, as well as special precautions when exchanged with the browser.

- **"Missing function-level access control:** Most web applications verify function-level access rights before making that functionality visible in the UI. However, applications need to perform the same access control checks on the server when each function is accessed. If requests are not verified, attackers will be able to forge requests in order to access functionality without proper authorization.

- **"Cross-site request forgery (CSRF):** A CSRF attack forces a logged-on victim's browser to send a forged HTTP request, including the victim's session cookie and any other automatically included authentication information, to a vulnerable web application. This allows the attacker to force the victim's browser to generate requests that the vulnerable application thinks are legitimate requests from the victim.

- **"Using components with known vulnerabilities:** Components, such as libraries, frameworks, and other software modules, almost always run with full privileges. If a vulnerable component is exploited, such an attack can facilitate serious data loss or server takeover. Applications using components with known vulnerabilities may undermine application defenses and enable a range of possible attacks and impacts.

- **"Invalidated redirects and forwards:** Web applications frequently redirect and forward users to other pages and websites, and use untrusted data to determine the destination pages. Without proper validation, attackers can redirect victims to phishing or malware sites or use forwards to access unauthorized pages."[6]

To address these vulnerabilities, organizations must have an application risk-management program in place, which should be part of an ongoing managed process. One possible approach to building such a risk-management process can be derived from the NIST "Framework for Improving Critical Infrastructure Cybersecurity."[7] Initially released in February 2014 as version 1.0, the framework started out as Executive Order 13636, issued in February 2013.[8]

The framework is composed of three parts:

- **Framework Core:** Cybersecurity activities and outcomes divided into five functions: identify, protect, detect, respond, and recover

- **Framework Profile:** To help the company align activities with business requirements, risk tolerance, and resources

- **Framework Implementation Tiers:** To help organizations categorize where they are with their approach

Building from those standards, guidelines, and practices, the framework provides a common taxonomy and mechanism for organizations to do the following:

- Describe their current cybersecurity posture

- Describe their target state for cybersecurity

- Identify and prioritize opportunities for improvement within the context of a continuous and repeatable process

- Assess progress toward the target state

- Communicate among internal and external stakeholders about cybersecurity risk

A good first step in understanding how the framework can help inform and improve your existing application security program is to go through it with an application security–focused lens.

You will now examine the first function in the Framework Core, Identify (ID), and its categories—Asset Management (ID.AM) and Risk Assessment (ID.RA).

ID.AM contains the following subcategories:

- **ID.AM-2:** Software platforms and applications within the organization are inventoried.
- **ID.AM-3:** Organizational communication and data flows are mapped.
- **ID.AM-5:** Resources (such as hardware, devices, data, and software) are prioritized based on their classification, criticality, and business value.

ID.RA contains the following subcategories:

- **ID.RA-1:** Asset vulnerabilities are identified and documented.
- **ID.RA-5:** Threats, vulnerabilities, likelihoods, and impacts are used to determine risk.

According to Diana Kelley, executive security advisor at IBM Security, "There is a lot in the Framework that would map nicely to a risk-based software security program. Classifying applications on criticality and business value can be brought to a deeper and more precise level when the threat model and vulnerability profile of that application is understood and validated with testing."[9]

CLOUD-SPECIFIC RISKS

Whether run in platform as a service (PaaS) or infrastructure as a service (IaaS) deployment model, applications running in a cloud environment may enjoy the same security controls surrounding them as applications that run in a traditional data center environment. This makes the need for an application risk management program more critical than ever.

Applications that run in a PaaS environment may need security controls baked into them. For example, encryption may need to be programmed into applications, and logging may be difficult depending on what the cloud service provider can offer your organization.

Application isolation is another component that must be addressed in a cloud environment. You must take steps to ensure that one application cannot access other applications on the platform unless it's allowed access through a control.

The Cloud Security Alliance's Top Threats Working Group has published *The Notorious Nine: Cloud Computing Top Threats in 2013*.[10] Following are the nine top threats listed in the report:

- **Data breaches:** If a multitenant cloud service database is not properly designed, a flaw in one client's application can allow an attacker access not only to that client's data but to every other client's data as well.

- **Data loss:** Any accidental deletion by the CSP, or worse, a physical catastrophe such as a fire or earthquake, can lead to the permanent loss of customers' data unless the provider takes adequate measures to back it up. Furthermore, the burden of avoiding data loss does not fall solely on the provider's shoulders. If a customer encrypts his data before uploading it to the cloud but loses the encryption key, the data is still lost.

- **Account hijacking:** If attackers gain access to your credentials, they can eavesdrop on your activities and transactions, manipulate data, return falsified information, and redirect your clients to illegitimate sites. Your account or service instances may become a new base for the attacker.

- **Insecure APIs:** Cloud computing providers expose a set of software interfaces or APIs that customers use to manage and interact with cloud services. Provisioning, management, orchestration, and monitoring are all performed using these interfaces. The security and availability of general cloud services is dependent on the security of these basic APIs. From authentication and access control to encryption and activity monitoring, these interfaces must be designed to protect against both accidental and malicious attempts to circumvent policy.

- **Denial of service (DoS):** By forcing the victim cloud service to consume inordinate amounts of finite system resources such as processor power, memory, disk space, and network bandwidth, the attacker causes an intolerable system slowdown.

- **Malicious insiders:** European Organization for Nuclear Research (CERN) defines an insider threat as "A current or former employee, contractor, or other business partner who has or had authorized access to an organization's network, system, or data and intentionally exceeded or misused that access in a manner that negatively affected the confidentiality, integrity, or availability of the organization's information or information systems."[11]

- **Abuse of cloud services:** It might take an attacker years to crack an encryption key using his own limited hardware, but using an array of cloud servers, he might be able to crack it in minutes. Alternatively, he might use that array of cloud servers to stage a distributed denial-of-service (DDoS) attack, serve malware, or distribute pirated software.

- **Insufficient due diligence:** Too many enterprises jump into the cloud without understanding the full scope of the undertaking. Without a complete understanding of the CSP environment, applications, or services being pushed to the cloud, and operational responsibilities such as incident response, encryption, and security monitoring, organizations are taking on unknown levels of risk in ways they may not even comprehend but that are a far departure from their current risks.

- **Shared technology issues:** Whether it's the underlying components that make up this infrastructure (central processing unit [CPU] caches, graphics processing units [GPUs], and so on) that were not designed to offer strong isolation properties for a multitenant architecture (IaaS), redeployable platforms (PaaS), or multicustomer applications (SaaS), the threat of shared vulnerabilities exists in all delivery models. A defensive in-depth strategy is recommended and should include compute, storage, network, application and user security enforcement, and monitoring, whether the service model is IaaS, PaaS, or SaaS. The key is that a single vulnerability or misconfiguration can lead to a compromise across an entire provider's cloud.

THREAT MODELING

Threat modeling is performed once an application design is created. The goal of threat modeling is to determine any weaknesses in the application and the potential ingress, egress, and actors involved before the weakness is introduced to production. It is the overall attack surface that is amplified by the cloud, and the threat model has to take that into account. Quite often, this involves a security professional determining various ways to attack the system or connections or even performing social engineering against staff with access to the system. The CCSP should always remember that the nature of threats faced by a system changes over time. Because of the dynamic nature of a changing threat landscape, constant vigilance and monitoring are important aspects of overall system security in the cloud.

STRIDE Threat Model

STRIDE[12] is a system for classifying known threats according to the kinds of exploits that are used or the motivation of the attacker. In the STRIDE threat model, the following six threats are considered, and controls are used to address the threats:

- **Spoofing:** Attacker assumes identity of subject
- **Tampering:** Data or messages altered by an attacker
- **Repudiation:** Illegitimate denial of an event
- **Information disclosure:** Information obtained without authorization
- **Denial of service:** Attacker overloads system to deny legitimate access
- **Elevation of privilege:** Attacker gains a privilege level above what is permitted

Today's software applications are built by leveraging other software components as building blocks to create a unique software offering. The software that is leveraged is often seen as a "black box" by developers who might not have the ability or thought to ensure the security of the applications and code. However, it remains the responsibility of the organization to assess code for proper, secure function no matter where the code is sourced.

This section discusses some of the security aspects involved with the selection of software components that are leveraged by your organization's developers.

Approved Application Programming Interfaces

Application programming interfaces (APIs) are a means for a company to expose functionality to applications. Following are three benefits of APIs:

- Programmatic control and access

- Automation

- Integration with third-party tools

Consumption of APIs can lead to your firm leveraging insecure products. As discussed in the next section, organizations must also consider the security of software (and APIs) outside of their corporate boundaries. Consumption of external APIs should go through the same approval process that's used for all other software being consumed by the organization. The CCSP needs to ensure that there is a formal approval process in place for all APIs. If there is a change in an API or an issue due to an unforeseen threat, a vendor update, or any other reason, the API in question should not be allowed until a thorough review has been undertaken to assess the integrity of the API in light of the new information.

When leveraging APIs, the CCSP should take steps to ensure that API access is secured. This requires the use of secure sockets layer, or SSL (REST), or message-level crypto-access (SOAP) authentication and logging of API usage. In addition, the use of a tool such as OWASP's Dependency-Check—which is a utility that identifies project dependencies and checks whether there are any known, publicly disclosed, vulnerabilities—would be valuable.[13] This tool currently supports Java and .NET dependencies.[14]

Software Supply Chain (API) Management

It is critical for organizations to consider the implications of nonsecure software beyond their corporate boundaries. The ease with which software components with unknown pedigrees or with uncertain development processes can be combined to produce new applications has created a complex and highly dynamic software supply chain (API management). In effect, people are consuming more and more software that is being developed by a third party or accessed with or through third-party libraries to create or enable functionality, without having a clear understanding of the origins of the software and code in question. This often leads to a situation in which a complex and highly dynamic software interaction is taking place between and among one or more services and systems within the organization and between organizations via the cloud.

This supply chain supplies agility in the rapid development of applications to meet consumer demand. However, software components produced without secure software development guidance similar to that defined by ISO/IEC 27034-1 can create security risks throughout the supply chain.[15] Therefore, it is important to assess all code and services for proper and secure functioning no matter where they are sourced.

Securing Open Source Software

Software that the community at large has openly tested and reviewed is considered by many security professionals to be more secure than software that has not undergone such a process. This can include open source software.

By moving toward leveraging standards such as ISO 27034-1, companies can be confident that partners have the same understanding of application security. This increases security as organizations, regulatory bodies, and the IT audit community learn the importance of embedding security throughout the processes required to build and consume security.

IDENTITY AND ACCESS MANAGEMENT

Identity and access management (IAM) includes people, processes, and systems that manage access to enterprise resources by ensuring that the identity of an entity is verified and then granting the correct level of access based on the protected resource, this assured identity, and other contextual information (*Figure 4.4*).

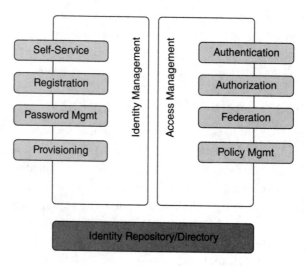

FIGURE 4.4 **IAM.**

IAM capabilities include the following:

- Identity management
- Access management
- Identity repository and directory services

Identity Management

Identity management is a broad administrative area that deals with identifying individuals in a system and controlling their access to resources within that system by associating user rights and restrictions with the established identity.

Access Management

Access management deals with managing an individual's access to resources and is based on the answers to "Who are you?" and "What do you have access to?"

- **Authentication** identifies the individual and ensures that he is who he claims to be. It establishes identity by asking, "Who are you?" and "How do I know I can trust you?"
- **Authorization** evaluates "What do you have access to?" after authentication occurs.
- **Policy management** establishes the security and access policies based on business needs and the degree of acceptable risk.
- **Federation** is an association of organizations that come together to exchange information as appropriate about their users and resources to enable collaborations and transactions.[16]
- **Identity repository** includes the directory services for the administration of user account attributes.

Identity Repository and Directory Services

Identity repositories provide directory services for the administration of user accounts and their attributes. Directory services are customizable information stores that offer a single point of administration and user access to resources and services used to manage, locate, and organize objects. Common directory services include these:

- x.500 and LDAP
- Microsoft Active Directory
- Novell eDirectory
- Metadata replication and synchronization
- Directory as a service

FEDERATED IDENTITY MANAGEMENT

Federated identity management (FIM) provides the policies, processes, and mechanisms that manage identity and trusted access to systems across organizations.

The technology of federation is much like that of Kerberos within an Active Directory domain: a user logs on once to a domain controller, is ultimately granted an access token, and uses that token to gain access to systems for which the user has authorization. The difference is that whereas Kerberos works well in a single domain, federated identities allow for the generation of tokens (authentication) in one domain and the consumption of these tokens (authorization) in another domain.

Federation Standards

Although many federation standards exist, Security Assertion Markup Language (SAML) 2.0 is by far the most commonly accepted standard used in the industry today. According to Oasis, SAML 2.0 is an "XML-based framework for communicating user authentication, entitlement, and attribute information. As its name suggests, SAML allows business entities to make assertions regarding the identity, attributes, and entitlements of a subject (an entity that is often a human user) to other entities, such as a partner company or another enterprise application."[17]

Other standards in the federation space exist:

- **WS-Federation:** According to the WS-Federation Version 1.2 OASIS standard, "this specification defines mechanisms to allow different security realms to federate, such that authorized access to resources managed in one realm can be provided to security principals whose identities are managed in other realms."[18]

- **OpenID Connect:** According to the OpenID Connect FAQ, this is an interoperable authentication protocol based on the OAuth 2.0 family of specifications. According to OpenID, "Connect lets developers authenticate their users across websites and apps without having to own and manage password files. For the app builder, it provides a secure verifiable answer to the question: 'What is the identity of the person currently using the browser or native app that is connected to me?'"[19]

- **OAuth:** OAuth is widely used for authorization services in web and mobile applications. According to RFC 6749, "The OAuth 2.0 authorization framework enables a third-party application to obtain limited access to an HTTP service, either on behalf of a resource owner by orchestrating an approval interaction between the resource owner and the HTTP service, or by allowing the third-party application to obtain access on its own behalf."[20]

In some cases, the standard that is used may be dictated based on the use cases to be supported. Take, for example, the Shibboleth standard. This federation standard is heavily used in the education space. If your organization is in this space, you may very well have a requirement to support the Shibboleth standard in addition to SAML. According to the Shibboleth Consortium, "A user authenticates with his or her organizational credentials, and the organization (or identity provider) passes the minimal identity information necessary to the service provider to enable an authorization decision. Shibboleth also provides extended privacy functionality allowing a user and their home site to control the attributes released to each application."[21]

Federated Identity Providers

In a federated environment, there is an identity provider and a relying party. The identity provider holds all the identities and generates a token for known users. The relying party is the service provider and consumes these tokens.

In a cloud environment, it is desirable that the organization itself continues to maintain all identities and act as the identity provider.

Federated SSO

Federated SSO is typically used for facilitating interorganizational and intersecurity domain access to resources leveraging federated identity management.

SSO should not be confused with reduced sign-on (RSO). RSO generally operates through some form of credential synchronization. Implementation of an RSO solution introduces security issues not experienced by SSO because the nature of SSO eliminates usernames and other sensitive data from traversing the network. The foundation of federation relies on the existence of an identity provider; therefore, RSO has no place in a federated identity system.

MULTIFACTOR AUTHENTICATION

Multifactor authentication goes by many names, including two-factor authentication and strong authentication. The general principle behind multifactor authentication is to add an extra level of protection to verify the legitimacy of a transaction. To be a multifactor system, users must be able to provide at least two of the following requirements:

- **What they know** (such as password)
- **What they have** (such as display token with random numbers displayed)
- **What they are** (such as biometrics)

One-time passwords also fall under the banner of multifactor authentication. The use of one-time passwords is strongly encouraged during provisioning and communicating of first-login passwords to users.

Step-up authentication is an additional factor or procedure that validates a user's identity, normally prompted by high-risk transactions or violations according to policy rules. Three methods are commonly used:

- Challenge questions
- Out-of-band authentication (a call or Short Message Service [SMS] text message to the end user)
- Dynamic knowledge-based authentication (questions unique to the end user)

SUPPLEMENTAL SECURITY DEVICES

Supplemental security devices add additional elements and layers to a defense-in-depth architecture. The general approach for a defense-in-depth architecture is to design using multiple overlapping and mutually reinforcing elements and controls that allow for the establishment of a robust security architecture. By using a selection of the supplemental security devices discussed next, the CCSP can augment the security architecture of the organization by strengthening the border defenses.

Supplemental security devices include the following:

- Web application firewall (WAF)
  - A WAF is a layer-7 firewall that can understand HTTP traffic.
  - A cloud WAF can be extremely effective in the case of a DoS attack; in several cases, a cloud WAF was used to successfully thwart DoS attacks of 350 Gbps and 450 Gbps.
- Database activity monitoring (DAM)
  - DAM is a layer-7 monitoring device that understands SQL commands.
  - DAM can be agent-based (ADAM) or network-based (NDAM).
  - A DAM can detect and stop malicious commands from executing on an SQL server.
- XML
  - XML gateways transform the way services and sensitive data are exposed as APIs to developers, mobile users, and cloud users.
  - XML gateways can be either hardware or software.

- XML gateways can implement security controls such as data loss prevention (DLP), antivirus, and antimalware services.
- Firewalls
  - Firewalls can be distributed or configured across the SaaS, PaaS, and IaaS landscapes; these can be owned and operated by the provider or can be outsourced to a third party for ongoing management and maintenance.
  - Firewalls in the cloud need to be installed as software components (such as host-based firewalls).
- API gateway
  - An API gateway is a device that filters API traffic; it can be installed as a proxy or as a specific part of your application stack before data is processed.
  - An API gateway can implement access control, rate limiting, logging, metrics, and security filtering.

CRYPTOGRAPHY

When working with cloud-based systems, it is important to remember they are operating within and across trusted and untrusted networks. These can also be referred to as semi-hostile and hostile environments. As such, data held within and communicated to and between systems and services operating in the cloud should be encrypted.

Following are some examples of data in transit encryption options:

- **Transport layer security (TLS):** A protocol that ensures privacy between communicating applications and their users on the Internet. When a server and client communicate, TLS ensures that no third party may eavesdrop or tamper with a message. TLS is the successor to SSL.
- **SSL:** The standard security technology for establishing an encrypted link between a web server and a browser. This link ensures that all data passed between the web server and browsers remains private and integral.
- **Virtual private network (VPN, such as IPSec gateway):** A network that is constructed by using public wires—usually the Internet—to connect to a private network, such as a company's internal network. A number of systems enable you to create networks using the Internet as the medium for transporting data.

All these technologies encrypt data to and from your data center and system communications within the cloud environment.

Here are examples of data-at-rest encryption used in cloud systems:

- **Whole instance encryption:** A method for encrypting all the data associated with the operation and use of a virtual machine, such as the data stored at rest on the volume, disk input/output (I/O), all snapshots created from the volume, as well as all data in transit moving between the virtual machine and the storage volume.

- **Volume encryption:** A method for encrypting a single volume on a drive. Parts of the hard drive are left unencrypted when using this method. (Full disk encryption should be used to encrypt the entire contents of the drive, if that is what is desired.)

- **File or directory encryption:** A method for encrypting a single file or directory on a drive.

Technologies and approaches such as tokenization, data masking, and sandboxing are valuable to augment the implementation of a cryptographic solution. The main goal of the application of cryptography to data is to ensure that confidentiality of data is maintained. Traditional cryptographic protections are applied using encryption based on the use of an algorithm of varying strength to generate either a single key (symmetric) or dual-key pair (asymmetric) solution. Sometimes the use of encryption is not the most appropriate or functional choice for a system protection element due to design, usage, and performance concerns. As a result, additional technologies and approaches become necessary for the CCSP to be aware of if needed.

TOKENIZATION

Tokenization generates a token (often a string of characters) that is used to substitute sensitive data, which is itself stored in a secured location such as a database. When accessed by a nonauthorized entity, only the token string is shown, not the actual data. Tokenization is often implemented to satisfy the Payment Card Industry Data Security Standard (PCI DSS) requirements for firms that process credit cards.

DATA MASKING

Data masking is a technology that keeps the format of a data string but alters the content. For instance, if you are storing development data for a system that is meant to parse Social Security numbers (a 3-2-4 number format), it is important that the format remain intact. Using traditional encryption, the format is altered to a long string of random characters. Data masking ensures that data retains its original format without being actionable by anyone who manages to intercept the data.

SANDBOXING

A sandbox isolates and utilizes only the intended components, while having appropriate separation from the remaining components (that is, the ability to store personal information in one sandbox, with corporate information in another sandbox). Within cloud environments, sandboxing is typically used to run untested or untrusted code in a tightly controlled environment. Several vendors have begun to offer cloud-based sandbox environments that can be leveraged by organizations to fully test applications.

Organizations can use a sandbox environment to better understand how an application actually works and fully test applications by executing them and observing the file behavior for indications of malicious activity.

APPLICATION VIRTUALIZATION

Application virtualization is a technology that creates a virtual environment for an application to run. This virtualization essentially creates an encapsulation from the underlying OS. Application virtualization can be used to isolate or sandbox an application to see the processes the application performs.

There are several examples of application virtualization available:

- Wine, which allows for some Microsoft applications to run on a Linux platform
- Microsoft App-V
- XenApp

The main goal of application virtualization is to be able to test applications while protecting the OS and other applications on a particular system.

Due to significant differences between running applications in the cloud compared with traditional infrastructure, it is of critical importance to address the security of applications through the use of assurance and validation techniques:

- **Software assurance:** Software assurance encompasses the development and implementation of methods and processes for ensuring that software functions as intended while mitigating the risks of vulnerabilities, malicious code, or defects that could bring harm to the end user.

Software assurance is vital to ensuring the security of critical information technology resources. Information and communications technology vendors have a responsibility to address assurance through every stage of application development.

- **Verification and validation:** For project and development teams to have confidence and to follow best practice guidelines, verification and validation of coding at each stage of the development process are required. Coupled with relevant segregation of duties and appropriate independent review, verification and validation look to ensure that the initial concept and delivered product are complete. As part of the process, you should verify that requirements are specified and measurable and that test plans and documentation are comprehensive and consistently applied to all modules and subsystems and integrated with the final product. Verification and validation occurs at each stage of development to ensure consistency of the application. Verification and validation should be performed at each stage of the software development lifecycle and in line with change management components.

Both concepts can be applied to code developed by the enterprise and to APIs and services sourced externally.

CLOUD-BASED FUNCTIONAL DATA

It is important to remember that cloud services are not an all-or-nothing approach. Data sets are not created equal; some have legal implications, and others do not. Functional data refers to specific services you may offer that have some form of legal implication. Put another way, the data collected, processed, and transferred by the separate functions of the application can have separate legal implications depending on how that data is used, presented, and stored.

When considering cloud-friendly systems and data sets, you must break down the legal implications of the data. Does the specific service being considered for the cloud have any contract associated with it that expressly forbids third-party processing or handling? Are there any regulatory requirements associated with the function?

Breaking down systems to the functions and services that have legal implications from those that don't is essential to the overall security posture of your cloud-based systems and overall enterprise need to meet contractual, legal, and regulatory requirements. See Domain 2, "Cloud Data Security," for a detailed look at the impact of contractual, legal, and regulatory requirements.

CLOUD-SECURE DEVELOPMENT LIFECYCLE

Although some view a single point-in-time vulnerability scan as an indicator of trustworthiness, much more important is a holistic evaluation of the people, processes, and technology that delivered the software and will continue to maintain it. Several software development lifecycles have been published, and most of them contain similar phases. One software development lifecycle is structured like this:

1. Requirements
2. Design
3. Implementation
4. Verification
5. Release

As mentioned earlier in this domain, another software development lifecycle is arranged like this:

1. Planning and requirements analysis
2. Defining
3. Designing
4. Developing
5. Testing
6. Maintenance

You can see the similarities between the two. There is a series of fairly intuitive phases in any lifecycle for developing software.

With the move to cloud-based applications, there has never been a greater importance of ensuring the security of applications that are being run in environments that may enjoy the same security controls available in a traditional data center environment.

It is well understood that security issues discovered once an application is deployed are exponentially more expensive to remediate. Understanding that security must be "baked in" from the onset of an application being created or consumed by an organization leads to a higher reasonable assurance that applications are properly secured prior to an organization using them. This is the purpose of a cloud-secure development lifecycle.

ISO/IEC 27034-1

Security of applications must be viewed as a holistic approach in a broad context that includes not just software development considerations but also the business and regulatory context and other external factors that can affect the overall security posture of the applications being consumed by an organization.

To this end, the International Organization for Standardization (ISO) has developed and published ISO/IEC 27034-1, "Information Technology—Security Techniques—Application Security." ISO/IEC 27034-1 defines concepts, frameworks, and processes to help organizations integrate security within their software development lifecycle.

Standards are also required to increase the trust that companies place in particular software development companies. Service-oriented architecture (SOA) views software as a combination of interoperable services, the components of which can be substituted at will. As SOA becomes more commonplace, the demand for proven adherence to secure software development practices will only gain in importance.

Organizational Normative Framework

ISO 27034-1 lays out an organizational normative framework (ONF) for all components of application security best practices (*Figure 4.5*).

FIGURE 4.5 **The ONF.**

The containers include the following:

- **Business context:** Includes all application security policies, standards, and best practices adopted by the organization
- **Regulatory context:** Includes all standards, laws, and regulations that affect application security

- **Technical context:** Includes required and available technologies that are applicable to application security

- **Specifications:** Documents the organization's IT functional requirements and the solutions that are appropriate to address these requirements

- **Roles, responsibilities, and qualifications:** Documents the actors within an organization who are related to IT applications

- **Processes:** Relates to application security

- **Application security control library:** Contains the approved controls that are required to protect an application based on the identified threats, the context, and the targeted level of trust

ISO 27034-1 defines an ONF management process. This bidirectional process is meant to create a continuous improvement loop. Innovations that result from securing a single application are returned to the ONF to strengthen all organization application security in the future.

Application Normative Framework

The application normative framework (ANF) is used in conjunction with the ONF and is created for a specific application. The ANF maintains the applicable portions of the ONF that are needed to enable a specific application to achieve a required level of security or the targeted level of trust. The ONF to ANF is a one-to-many relationship, where one ONF is used as the basis to create multiple ANFs.

Application Security Management Process

ISO/IEC 27034-1 defines an application security management process (ASMP) to manage and maintain each ANF (*Figure 4.6*). The ASMP is created in five steps:

1. Specifying the application requirements and environment
2. Assessing application security risks
3. Creating and maintaining the ANF
4. Provisioning and operating the application
5. Auditing the security of the application

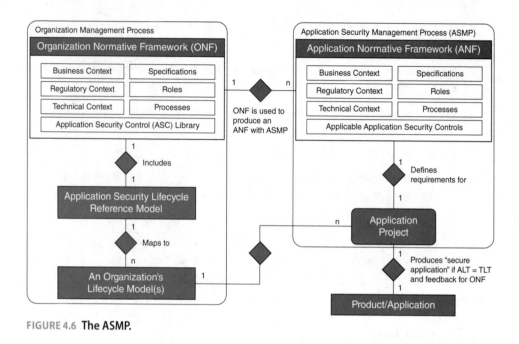

FIGURE 4.6 **The ASMP.**

APPLICATION SECURITY TESTING

Security testing of web applications through the use of testing software is generally broken into two distinct types of automated testing tools. This section looks at these tools and discusses the importance of penetration testing, which generally includes the use of human expertise and automated tools. The section also looks at secure code reviews and OWASP recommendations for security testing.

Static Application Security Testing

Static application security testing (SAST) is generally considered a white-box test, where the application test performs an analysis of the application source code, byte code, and binaries without executing the application code. SAST is used to determine coding errors and omissions that are indicative of security vulnerabilities. SAST is often used as a test method while the tool is under development (early in the development lifecycle).

SAST can be used to find XSS errors, SQL injection, buffer overflows, unhandled error conditions, and potential backdoors.

Because SAST is a white-box test tool, it typically delivers more comprehensive results than those found using the test described in the next section.

Dynamic Application Security Testing

Dynamic application security testing (DAST) is generally considered a black-box test, where the tool must discover individual execution paths in the application being analyzed. Unlike SAST, which analyzes code offline (when the code is not running), DAST is used against applications in their running state. DAST is mainly considered effective when testing exposed HTTP and HTML interfaces of web applications.

It is important to understand that SAST and DAST play different roles and that one is not better than the other. Static and dynamic application tests work together to enhance the reliability of organizations creating and using secure applications.

Runtime Application Self-Protection

Runtime application self-protection (RASP) is generally considered to focus on applications that possess self-protection capabilities built into their runtime environments, which have full insight into application logic, configuration, and data and event flows. RASP prevents attacks by self-protecting or reconfiguring automatically without human intervention in response to certain conditions (threats, faults, and so on).

Vulnerability Assessments and Penetration Testing

Both vulnerability assessment and penetration testing play a significant role and support security of applications and systems prior to an application going into and while in a production environment.

Vulnerability assessments or vulnerability scanning look to identify and report on known vulnerabilities in a system. Depending on the approach you take, such as automated scanning or a combination of techniques, the identification and reporting of a vulnerability should be accompanied by a risk rating, along with potential exposures.

Most often, vulnerability assessments are performed as white-box tests, where the assessor knows that application and the environment the application runs in.

Penetration testing is a process used to collect information related to system vulnerabilities and exposures, with the view to actively exploit the vulnerabilities in the system. Penetration testing is often a black-box test, in which the tester carries out the test as an attacker, has no knowledge of the application, and must discover any security issues within the application or system being tested. To assist with targeting and focusing the scope of testing, independent parties also often perform gray-box testing with some level of information provided.

NOTE   As with any form of security testing, permission must always be obtained prior to testing. This is to ensure that all parties have consented to testing, as well as to ensure that no malicious activity is performed without the acknowledgment and consent of the system owners.

Within cloud environments, most vendors allow for vulnerability assessments or penetration tests to be executed. Quite often, this depends on the service model (SaaS, PaaS, IaaS) and the target of the scan (application versus platform). Given the nature of SaaS, where the service consists of an application consumed by all consumers, SaaS providers are most likely not to grant permission for penetration tests to occur by clients. Generally, only a SaaS provider's resources are permitted to perform penetration tests on the SaaS application.

Secure Code Reviews

Conducting a secure code review, whether informally or formally, is another approach to assessing code for appropriate security controls. An informal code review may involve one or more individuals examining sections of the code, looking for vulnerabilities. A formal code review may involve the use of trained teams of reviewers that are assigned specific roles as part of the review process, as well as the use of a tracking system to report on vulnerabilities found. The integration of a code review process into the system development lifecycle can improve the quality and security of the code being developed.[22]

OWASP Recommendations

OWASP has created a testing guide (presently v4.0) that recommends nine types of active security testing categories as follows:[23]

- Identity management testing
- Authentication testing
- Authorization testing
- Session management testing
- Input validation testing
- Testing for error handling
- Testing for weak cryptography
- Business logic testing
- Client-side testing

These OWASP categories play as well in a cloud environment as they do in a traditional infrastructure. However, additional threat models associated with the deployment model you choose (such as public versus private) may introduce new threat vectors that require analysis.

SUMMARY

Cloud application security focuses the CCSP on identifying the necessary training and awareness activities required to ensure that cloud applications are deployed only when they are as secure as possible. This means that the CCSP has to run vulnerability assessments and use an software development lifecycle to ensure that secure development and coding practices are used at every stage of software development. In addition, the CCSP has to be involved in identifying the requirements necessary for creating secure identity and access management solutions for the cloud. The CCSP should be able to describe cloud application architecture as well as the steps that provide assurance and validation for cloud applications used in the enterprise. The CCSP must also be able to identify the functional and security testing needed to provide software assurance. Finally, the CCSP should be able to summarize the processes for verifying that secure software is being deployed. This includes the use of APIs and any supply chain management considerations.

4

CLOUD APPLICATION SECURITY

REVIEW QUESTIONS

1. What is REST?

   A. A protocol specification for exchanging structured information in the implementation of web services in computer networks

   B. A software architecture style consisting of guidelines and best practices for creating scalable web services

   C. The name of the process that an organization or person who moves data between CSPs uses to document what he is doing

   D. The intermediary process that provides business continuity of cloud services between cloud consumers and CSPs

2. What are the phases of a software development lifecycle process model?

   A. Planning and requirements analysis, defining, designing, developing, testing, and maintenance

   B. Defining, planning and requirements analysis, designing, developing, testing, and maintenance

   C. Planning and requirements analysis, defining, designing, testing, developing, and maintenance

   D. Planning and requirements analysis, designing, defining, developing, testing, and maintenance

3. When does an XSS flaw occur?

   A. Whenever an application takes trusted data and sends it to a web browser without proper validation or escaping

   B. Whenever an application takes untrusted data and sends it to a web browser without proper validation or escaping

   C. Whenever an application takes trusted data and sends it to a web browser with proper validation or escaping

   D. Whenever an application takes untrusted data and sends it to a web browser with proper validation or escaping

4. What are the six components that make up the STRIDE threat model?

   A. Spoofing, tampering, repudiation, information disclosure, DoS, and elevation of privilege

   B. Spoofing, tampering, nonrepudiation, information disclosure, DoS, and elevation of privilege

C. Spoofing, tampering, repudiation, information disclosure, DDoS, and elevation of privilege

D. Spoofing, tampering, repudiation, information disclosure, DoS, and social engineering

5. In a federated environment, who is the relying party, and what does it do?

   A. The relying party is the identity provider; it consumes the tokens that the service provider generates.

   B. The relying party is the service provider; it consumes the tokens that the customer generates.

   C. The relying party is the service provider; it consumes the tokens that the identity provider generates.

   D. The relying party is the customer; he consumes the tokens that the identity provider generates.

6. What are the five steps used to create an ASMP?

   A. Specifying the application requirements and environment, creating and maintaining the ANF, assessing application security risks, provisioning and operating the application, and auditing the security of the application

   B. Assessing application security risks, specifying the application requirements and environment, creating and maintaining the ANF, provisioning and operating the application, and auditing the security of the application

   C. Specifying the application requirements and environment, assessing application security risks, provisioning and operating the application, auditing the security of the application, and creating and maintaining the ANF

   D. Specifying the application requirements and environment, assessing application security risks, creating and maintaining the ANF, provisioning and operating the application, and auditing the security of the application

NOTES

[1] http://en.wikipedia.org/wiki/Representational_state_transfer

[2] http://en.wikipedia.org/wiki/SOAP

[3] See the following: https://www.iso.org/obp/ui/#iso:std:iso-iec:12207:ed-2:v1:en

[4] See the following: https://puppetlabs.com/puppet/what-is-puppet

[5] See the following: https://www.chef.io/chef/

CLOUD APPLICATION SECURITY

[6] https://www.owasp.org/index.php/Top10#OWASP_Top_10_for_2013 (p. 6)

[7] See the following:
http://www.nist.gov/cyberframework/upload/cybersecurity-framework-021214.pdf

[8] See the following: http://www.gpo.gov/fdsys/pkg/FR-2013-02-19/pdf/2013-03915.pdf

[9] See the following: http://securityintelligence.com/nist-cybersecurity-framework-application-security-risk-management/#.VSR1apgtHIU

[10] See the following: https://downloads.cloudsecurityalliance.org/initiatives/top_threats/The_Notorious_Nine_Cloud_Computing_Top_Threats_in_2013.pdf

[11] http://www.cert.org/insider-threat/index.cfm

[12] https://www.owasp.org/index.php/Threat_Risk_Modeling#STRIDE

[13] See the following: https://www.owasp.org/index.php/OWASP_Dependency_Check

[14] The OWASP Top 10 for 2013, A9 item—Using Components with Known Vulnerabilities—is one example of where a tool such as Dependency-Check could be used to offer a mitigating control element to combat the risk(s) associated with this item.

[15] See the following: https://www.iso.org/obp/ui/#iso:std:iso-iec:27034:-1:ed-1:v1:en

[16] The goal of federation is to allow user identities and attributes to be shared between trusting organizations through the use of policies that dictate under what circumstances trust can be established. When federation is applied to web service environments, the goal is to seek automation of the credential sharing and trust establishment processes, removing the user from the process as much as possible, unless user participation is required by one or more governing policies.

[17] https://www.oasis-open.org/committees/tc_home.php?wg_abbrev=security

[18] See the following:
http://docs.oasis-open.org/wsfed/federation/v1.2/os/ws-federation-1.2-spec-os.html

[19] See the following: http://openid.net/connect/faq/

[20] See the following: http://tools.ietf.org/html/rfc6749

[21] See the following: http://shibboleth.net/about/

[22] See the following:
https://www.owasp.org/index.php/Security_Code_Review_in_the_SDLC

[23] See the following: https://www.owasp.org/images/5/52/OWASP_Testing_Guide_v4.pdf

Operations

THE GOAL OF THE Operations domain is to explain the requirements needed to develop, plan, implement, run, and manage the physical and logical cloud infrastructure.

You will gain an understanding of the necessary controls and resources, the best practices in monitoring and auditing, and the importance of risk assessment in both the physical and the logical cloud infrastructures. With an understanding of specific industry compliance and regulations, you will know how to protect resources, restrict access, and apply appropriate controls in the cloud environment.

DOMAIN OBJECTIVES

After completing this domain, you will be able to do the following:

❏ Describe the specifications necessary for the physical, logical, and environmental design of the data center

❏ Identify the requirements to build and implement the physical cloud infrastructure

❏ Define the process for running the physical infrastructure based on access, security, and availability configurations

❏ Define the process for managing the physical infrastructure with regard to access, monitoring, security controls, analysis, and maintenance

❏ Identify the requirements to build and implement the logical cloud infrastructure

❏ Define the process for running the logical infrastructure based on access, security, and availability configurations

❏ Define the process for managing the logical infrastructure with regard to access, monitoring, security controls, analysis, and maintenance

❏ Identify the necessary regulations and controls to ensure compliance for the operation and management of the cloud infrastructure

❏ Describe the process of conducting a risk assessment of the physical and logical infrastructure

❏ Describe the process for the collection, acquisition, and preservation of digital evidence

INTRODUCTION

Data center design, planning, and architecture have long formed an integral part of the information technology (IT) services for providers of computing services. Over time, these have typically evolved and grown in line with computing developments and enhanced capabilities. Data centers continue to be refined, enhanced, and improved upon globally; however, they still rely heavily on the same essential components to support their activities (power, water, structures, connectivity, security, and more).

Implementing a secure design when creating a data center involves many considerations. Prior to making any design decisions, work with senior management and other key stakeholders to identify all compliance requirements for the data center. If you're designing a data center for public cloud services, consider the different levels of security that will be offered to your customers.

MODERN DATA CENTERS AND CLOUD SERVICE OFFERINGS

Until recently, data centers were built with the mind-set of supplying hosting, compute, storage, or other services with typical or standard organization types in mind. The same cannot (and should not!) be said for modern-day data centers and cloud service offerings. A fundamental shift in consumer use of cloud-based services has thrust the users into the same data centers as the enterprises, thereby forcing providers to take into account the challenges and complexities associated with differing outlooks, drivers, requirements, and services.

For example, if customers will host Payment Card Industry data or a payments platform, these need to be identified and addressed in the relevant design process to ensure a fit-for-purpose design that meets and satisfies all current Payment Card Industry Data Security Standard (PCI DSS) requirements.

FACTORS THAT AFFECT DATA CENTER DESIGN

The location of the data center and the users of the cloud affect compliance decisions and can further complicate the organization's ability to meet legal and regulatory requirements because the geographic location of the data center impacts its jurisdiction. Prior to selecting a location for the data center, an organization should have a clear understanding of requirements at the national, state, and local levels. Contingency, failover, and redundancy involving other data centers in different locations are important to understand.

The type of service models (platform as a service [PaaS], infrastructure as a service [IaaS], and software as a service [SaaS]) the cloud provides also influence design decisions. Once the compliance requirements have been identified, they should be included in the data center design.

Additional data center considerations and operating standards should be included in the design. Some examples include ISO 27001:2013 and Information Technology Infrastructure Library (ITIL) IT service management (ITSM).

There is a close relationship between the physical and the environmental design of a data center. Poor design choices in either area can affect the other and cause a significant cost increase, delay completion, or impinge upon operations if not done properly. The early adoption of a data center design standard that meets organizational requirements is a critical factor when creating a cloud-based data center.

Additional areas to consider as they pertain to data center design include the following:

- Automating service enablement
- Consolidating monitoring capabilities
- Reducing mean time to repair (MTTR)
- Reducing mean time between failure (MTBF)

Logical Design

The characteristics of cloud computing can affect the logical design of a data center.

Multitenancy

As enterprises transition from traditional dedicated server deployments to virtualized environments that leverage cloud services, the cloud computing networks they are building must provide security and segregate sensitive data and applications. In some cases, multitenant networks are a solution.

Multitenant networks, in a nutshell, are data center networks that are logically divided into smaller, isolated networks. They share the physical networking gear but operate on their own network without visibility into the other logical networks.

The multitenant nature of a cloud deployment requires a logical design that partitions and segregates client and customer data. Failure to do so can result in the unauthorized access, viewing, or modification of tenant data.

Cloud Management Plane

Additionally, the cloud management plane needs to be logically isolated, although physical isolation may offer a more secure solution. The cloud management plane provides monitoring and administration of the cloud network platform to keep the whole cloud operating normally, including the following:

- Configuration management and services lifecycle management
- Services registry and discovery
- Monitoring, logging, accounting, and auditing
- Service-level agreement (SLA) management
- Security services and infrastructure management

Virtualization Technology

Virtualization technology offers many of the capabilities needed to meet the requirements for partitioning and data. The logical design should incorporate a hypervisor that meets the system requirements. Following are key areas that need to be incorporated in the logical design of the data center:

- Communications access (permitted and not permitted), user access profiles, and permissions, including application programming interface (API) access
- Secure communication within and across the management plane
- Secure storage (encryption, partitioning, and key management)
- Backup and disaster recovery (DR) along with failover and replication

Other Logical Design Considerations

Other logical design considerations include these:

- Design for segregation of duties so data center staff can access only the data needed to do their job.
- Design for monitoring of network traffic. The management plane should also be monitored for compromise and abuse. Hypervisor and virtualization technology need to be considered when designing the monitoring capability. Some hypervisors may not allow enough visibility for adequate monitoring. The level of monitoring depends on the type of cloud deployment.
- Automation and the use of APIs, which are essential for a successful cloud deployment. The logical design should include the secure use of APIs and a method to log API use.
- Logical design decisions that are enforceable and monitored. For example, access control should be implemented with an identity and access management (IAM) system that can be audited.
- The use of software-defined networking tools to support logical isolation.

Logical Design Levels

Logical design for data separation needs to be incorporated at the following levels:

- Compute nodes
- Management plane
- Storage nodes
- Control plane
- Network

Service Model

The service model influences the logical design. Here are examples:

- For IaaS, many of the hypervisor features can be used to design and implement security.
- For PaaS, logical design features of the underlying platform and database can be leveraged to implement security.
- For SaaS, the same as above applies, and additional measures in the application can be used to enhance security.

All logical design decisions should be mapped to specific compliance requirements, such as logging, retention periods, and reporting capabilities for auditing. There also needs to be ongoing monitoring systems designed to enhance effectiveness.

Physical Design

No two data centers are alike, and they should not be, for it is the business that drives the requirements for IT and the data centers. IT infrastructure in today's data center is designed to provide specific business services and can affect the physical design of the data center.

For example, thin blade rack-mounted web servers are required for high-speed user interaction, whereas data-mining applications require larger mainframe-style servers. The physical infrastructure to support these different servers can vary greatly. Given their criticality, data center design becomes an issue of paramount importance in terms of technical architecture, business requirements, energy efficiency, and environmental requirements.

Over the past decade, data center design has been standardized as a collection of standard components that are plugged together. Each component has been designed to optimize its efficiency, with the expectation that, taken as a whole, optimum efficiency would be achieved. That view is shifting to one in which an entire data center is viewed as an integrated combination designed to run at the highest possible efficiency level, which requires custom-designed subcomponents to ensure they contribute to the overall efficiency goal.

One example of this trend can be seen in the design of the chicken coop data center, which is designed to host racks of physical infrastructure within long rectangles with a long side facing the prevailing wind, thereby allowing natural cooling.[1] Facebook, in its open compute design, places air intakes and outputs on the second floor of its data centers so that cool air can enter the building and drop on the machines, while hot air rises and is evacuated by large fans.

The physical design should also account for possible expansion and upgrading of both computing and environmental equipment. For example, is there enough room to add cooling or access points that are large enough to support equipment changes?

The physical design of a data center is closely related to the environmental design. Physical design decisions can shape the environmental design of the data center. For example, the choice to use raised floors affects the heating, ventilation, and air conditioning (HVAC) design.

When designing a cloud data center, consider the following areas:

- Does the physical design protect against environmental threats such as flooding, earthquakes, and storms?

- Does the physical design include provisions for access to resources during disasters to ensure the data center and its personnel can continue to operate safely? Examples include the following:

    - Clean water

    - Clean power

    - Food

    - Telecommunications

    - Accessibility during and after a disaster

- Are there physical security design features that limit access to authorized personnel? Some examples include these:

    - Perimeter protections such as walls, fences, gates, and electronic surveillance

    - Access points to control ingress and egress and verify identity and access authorization with an audit trail; this includes egress monitoring to prevent theft

Building or Buying

Organizations can build a data center, buy one, or lease space in a data center. Regardless of the decision made by the organization, certain standards and issues need to be considered and addressed through planning, such as data center tier certification, physical security level, and usage profile (multitenant hosting versus dedicated hosting).

As a certified cloud security professional (CCSP), both you and the enterprise architect play a role in ensuring these issues are identified and addressed as part of the decision process.

If you build the data center, the organization has the most control over its design and security. However, a significant investment is required to build a robust data center.

Buying a data center or leasing space in a data center may be a cheaper alternative, but either one of these options may include limitations on design inputs. The leasing organization needs to include all security requirements in the request for proposal (RFP) and contract.

When using a shared data center, physical separation of servers and equipment needs to be included in the design.

Data Center Design Standards

Any organization building or using a data center should design the data based on the standard or standards that meet its organizational requirements. An organization has many standards available to choose from:

- **Building Industry Consulting Service International Inc. (BICSI):** The ANSI/BICSI 002-2014 standard covers cabling design and installation. `http://www.bicsi.org`

- **The International Data Center Authority (IDCA):** The Infinity Paradigm covers data center location, facility structure, and infrastructure and applications. `http://www.idc-a.org/`

- **The National Fire Protection Association (NFPA):** NFPA 75 and 76 standards specify how hot or cold aisle containment is to be carried out, and NFPA standard 70 requires the implementation of an emergency power-off button to protect first responders in the data center in case of emergency. `http://www.nfpa.org/`

This section briefly examines the Uptime Institute's Data Center Site Infrastructure Tier Standard Topology. The Uptime Institute is a leader in data center design and management. Its "Data Center Site Infrastructure Tier Standard: Topology" document provides the baseline that many enterprises use to rate their data center designs.[2]

The document describes a four-tiered architecture for data center design, with each tier progressively more secure, reliable, and redundant in its design and operational elements (*Figure 5.1*). The four tiers are named as follows:

- Tier I: Basic Data Center Site Infrastructure

- Tier II: Redundant Site Infrastructure Capacity Components

- Tier III: Concurrently Maintainable Site Infrastructure

- Tier IV: Fault-Tolerant Site Infrastructure

The document also addresses the supporting infrastructure systems that these designs rely on, such as power generation systems, ambient temperature control, and makeup (backup) water systems. The CCSP may want to familiarize herself with the detailed requirements laid out for each of the four tiers of the architecture to be better prepared for the demands and issues associated with designing a data center to be compliant with a certain tier if required by the organization. "The Data Center Site Infrastructure Tier Standard: Topology" document may be accessed at http://www.gpxglobal.net/wp-content/uploads/2012/08/tierstandardtopology.pdf. Pages 5–7 are where the technical specifications by tier are to be found.

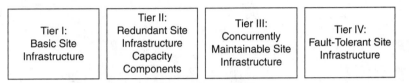

FIGURE 5.1 **The four-tiered architecture for data center design.**

The CCSP may use the tiered model summary in Table 5.1 as a reference for the key design elements and requirements by tier level.

TABLE 5.1 **The Tiered Model**

FEATURE	TIER I	TIER II	TIER III	TIER IV
Active capacity components to support the IT load	N	N+1	N+1	N after any failure
Distribution paths	1	1	1 active and 1 alternate	2 simultaneously active
Concurrently maintainable	No	No	Yes	Yes
Fault tolerance	No	No	No	Yes
Compartmentalization	No	No	No	Yes
Continuous cooling	No	No	No	Yes

Environmental Design Considerations

The environmental design must account for adequate heating, ventilation, air conditioning, power with adequate conditioning, and backup. Network connectivity should come from multiple vendors and include multiple paths into the facility.

Temperature and Humidity Guidelines

The American Society of Heating, Refrigeration, and Air Conditioning Engineers (ASHRAE) Technical Committee 9.9 has created a set of guidelines for temperature and humidity ranges in the data center. The guidelines are available as the *2011 Thermal Guidelines for Data Processing Environments — Expanded Data Center Classes and Usage Guidance.*[3] These guidelines specify the recommended operating range for temperature and humidity, as shown in Table 5.2.

TABLE 5.2 Recommended Operating Range for Temperature and Humidity

Low-end temperature	64.4° F (18° C)
High-end temperature	80.6° F (27° C)
Low-end moisture	40% relative humidity and 41.9° F (5.5° C) dew point
High-end moisture	60% relative humidity and 59° F (15° C) dew point

These ranges refer to the IT equipment intake temperature. Temperature can be controlled in several ways at locations in the data center including the following:

- Server inlet
- Server exhaust
- Floor tile supply temperature
- HVAC unit return air temperature
- Computer room air conditioning unit supply temperature

HVAC Considerations

Normally, data center HVAC units are turned on and off based on return air temperature. When used, the ASHRAE temperature recommendations specified in Table 5.2 produce lower inlet temperatures. The CCSP should be aware that the lower the temperature in the data center is, the greater the cooling costs per month. Essentially, the air conditioning system moves heat generated by equipment in the data center outside, allowing the data center to maintain a stable temperature range for the operating equipment. The power requirements for cooling a data center depend on the amount of heat being removed as well as the temperature difference between the inside of the data center and the outside air.

Air Management for Data Centers

Air management for data centers entails that all the design and configuration details minimize or eliminate mixing between the cooling air supplied to the equipment and the hot air rejected from the equipment. Effective air management implementation minimizes the bypass of cooling air around rack intakes and the recirculation of heat exhaust back into rack intakes. When designed correctly, an air management system can reduce operating costs, reduce first cost equipment investment, increase the data center's power density (watts/square foot), and reduce heat-related processing interruptions or failures.

A few key design issues include the configuration of equipment's air intake and heat exhaust ports, the location of supply and returns, the large-scale airflow patterns in the room, and the temperature set points of the airflow.

Cable Management

A data center should have a cable management strategy to minimize airflow obstructions caused by cables and wiring. This strategy should target the entire cooling airflow path, including the rack-level IT equipment air intake and discharge areas, as well as under-floor areas.

The development of hot spots can be promoted through these two methods:

- Under-floor and over-head obstructions, which often interfere with the distribution of cooling air. Such interferences can significantly reduce the air handlers' airflow and negatively distress the air distribution.

- Cable congestion in raised-floor plenums, which can sharply reduce the total airflow as well as degrade the airflow distribution through the perforated floor tiles.

A minimum effective (clear) height of 24 inches should be provided for raised-floor installations. Greater under-floor clearance can help achieve a more uniform pressure distribution in some cases.

Persistent cable management is a key component of effective air management. Instituting a cable mining program (that is, a program to remove abandoned or inoperable cables) as part of an ongoing cable management plan optimizes the air delivery performance of data center cooling systems.

Aisle Separation and Containment

A basic hot aisle or cold aisle configuration is created when the equipment racks and the cooling system's air supply and return are designed to prevent mixing of the hot rack exhaust air and the cool supply air drawn into the racks. As the name implies, the data center equipment is laid out in rows of racks with alternating cold (rack air intake side) and hot (rack air heat exhaust side) aisles between them. Strict hot aisle and cold aisle configurations can significantly increase the air-side cooling capacity of a data center's cooling system (*Figure 5.2*).

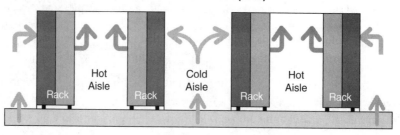

Hot Aisle Containment (HAC)

Side View

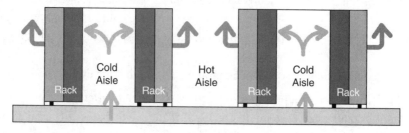

Cold Aisle Containment (CAC)

Side View

FIGURE 5.2 Separating the hot and cold aisles can significantly increase the air-side cooling capacity of the system.

All equipment should be installed into the racks to achieve a front-to-back airflow pattern that draws conditioned air in from cold aisles, located in front of the equipment, and rejects heat through the hot aisles behind the racks. Equipment with nonstandard exhaust directions must be addressed (shrouds, ducts, and so on) to achieve a front-to-back airflow. The racks are placed back to back, and holes through the rack (vacant equipment slots) are blocked off on the intake side to create barriers that reduce recirculation. Additionally, cable openings in raised floors and ceilings should be sealed as tightly as possible.

With proper isolation, the temperature of the hot aisle no longer influences the temperature of the racks or the reliable operation of the data center; the hot aisle becomes a heat exhaust. The air-side cooling system is configured to supply cold air exclusively to the cold aisles and pull return air only from the hot aisles.

One recommended design configuration supplies cool air via an under-floor plenum to the racks. The air then passes through the equipment in the rack and enters a separated, semisealed area for return to an overhead plenum. This approach uses a baffle panel or barrier above the top of the rack and at the ends of the hot aisles to mitigate short-circuiting (the mixing of hot and cold air).

HVAC Design Considerations

Industry guidance should be followed to provide adequate HVAC to protect the server equipment. Include the following considerations in your design:

- The local climate will affect the HVAC design requirements.
- Redundant HVAC systems should be part of the overall design.
- The HVAC system should provide air management that separates the cool air from the heat exhaust of the servers. Various methods provide air management, including racks with built-in ventilation or alternating cold and hot aisles. The best design choices depend on space and building design constraints.
- Consideration should be given to energy-efficient systems.
- Backup power supplies should be provided to run the HVAC system for the time required for the system to stay up.
- The HVAC system should filter contaminants and dust.

Multivendor Pathway Connectivity

Uninterrupted service and continuous access are critical to the daily operation and productivity of your business. With downtime translating directly to loss of income, data centers must be designed for redundant, fail-safe reliability and availability.

Data center reliability is also defined by the performance of the infrastructure. Cabling and connectivity backed by a reputable vendor with guaranteed error-free performance help avoid poor transmission in the data center.

There should be redundant connectivity from multiple providers into the data center. This helps prevent a single point of failure for network connectivity. The redundant path should offer the minimum expected connection speed for data center operations.

Implementing Physical Infrastructure for Cloud Environments

Many components make up the design of the data center, including logical components such as general service types and physical components such as the hardware used to host the logical service types envisioned. The hardware has to be connected to allow networking to take place and information to be exchanged. To do so securely, follow the standards for data center design, where applicable, as well as best practices and common sense.

Cloud computing removes the traditional silos within the data center and introduces a new level of flexibility and scalability to the IT organization. This flexibility addresses challenges facing enterprises and IT service providers, including rapidly changing IT landscapes, cost reduction pressures, and focus on time-to-market.

ENTERPRISE OPERATIONS

As enterprise IT environments have dramatically grown in scale, complexity, and diversity of services, they have typically deployed application and customer environments in silos of dedicated infrastructure. These silos are built around specific applications, customer environments, business organizations, operational requirements, and regulatory compliance (Sarbanes-Oxley, Health Insurance Portability and Accountability Act [HIPAA], and PCI DSS) or to address specific proprietary data confidentiality. For example:

- Large enterprises need to isolate HR records, finance, customer credit card details, and so on.

- Resources externally exposed for outsourced projects require separation from internal corporate environments.

- Healthcare organizations must ensure patient record confidentiality.

- Universities need to partition student user services from business operations, student administrative systems, and commercial or sensitive research projects.

- Service providers must separate billing, customer relationship management (CRM), payment systems, reseller portals, and hosted environments.

- Financial organizations need to securely isolate client records and investment, wholesale, and retail banking services.

- Government agencies must partition revenue records, judicial data, social services, operational systems, and so on.

Enabling enterprises to migrate such environments to cloud architecture demands the capability to provide secure isolation while still delivering the management and flexibility benefits of shared resources.

Private and public cloud service providers (CSPs) must enable all customer data, communication, and application environments to be securely separated, protected, and isolated from other tenants. The separation must be so complete and secure that the tenants have no visibility of each other. Private CSPs must deliver the secure separation required by their organizational structure, application requirements, or regulatory compliance.

To accomplish these goals, all hardware inside the data center need to be securely configured. This includes servers, network devices, storage controllers, and any other peripheral equipment. Automation of these functions supports large-scale deployments.

SECURE CONFIGURATION OF HARDWARE: SPECIFIC REQUIREMENTS

The actual settings for the hardware depend on the chosen operating system (OS) and virtualization platform. In some cases, the virtualization platform may have its own OS.

Best Practices for Servers

Implement the following best practice recommendations to secure host servers within cloud environments:

- **Secure build:** To implement fully, follow the specific recommendations of the OS vendor to securely deploy their operating system.
- **Secure initial configuration:** This may mean many different things depending on a number of variables, such OS vendor, operating environment, business requirements, regulatory requirements, risk assessment, risk appetite, and workloads to be hosted on the system.

Following is the common list of best practices:

- **Host hardening:** Achieve this by removing all nonessential services and software from the host.
- **Host patching:** To achieve this, install all required patches provided by the vendors whose hardware and software are being used to create the host server. These may include basic input/output system (BIOS)/firmware updates, driver updates for specific hardware components, and OS security patches.
- **Host lockdown:** Implement host-specific security measures, which vary by vendor. These may include the following:
  - Blocking of nonroot access to the host under most circumstances (that is, local console access only via a root account)
  - Only allowing the use of secure communication protocols and tools to access the host remotely, such as PuTTY with secure shell (SSH)
  - Configuration and use of host-based firewall to examine and monitor all communications to and from the host and all guest OSs and workloads running on the host

- Use of role-based access controls (RBACs) to limit which users can access a host and what permissions they have

- **Secure ongoing configuration maintenance:** Achieved through a variety of mechanisms, some vendor specific and some not. Engage in the following types of activities:

  - Patch management of hosts, guest OSs, and application workloads running on them

  - Periodic vulnerability assessment scanning of hosts, guest OSs, and application workloads running on hosts

  - Periodic penetration testing of hosts and guest OSs running on them

Best Practices for Storage Controllers

Storage controllers may be in use for Internet small computer system interface (iSCSI), Fiber Channel (FC), or Fibre Channel over Ethernet (FCoE). Regardless of the storage protocols being used, they should be secured in accordance with vendor guidance plus any required additional measures. For example, some storage controllers offer a built-in encryption capability that may be used to ensure confidentiality of the data transiting the controller. In addition, close attention to configuration settings and options for the controller are important because unnecessary services should be disabled, and insecure settings should be addressed.

A detailed discussion of each storage protocol and its associated controller types is beyond the scope of this section. This section focuses on iSCSI as an example of the types of issues and considerations you may encounter in the field while working with cloud-based storage solutions.

iSCSI is a protocol that uses transmission control protocol (TCP) to transport small computer system interface (SCSI) commands, enabling the use of the existing transmission control protocol/Internet protocol (TCP/IP) networking infrastructure as a storage area network (SAN). iSCSI presents SCSI targets and devices to iSCSI initiators (requesters). Unlike network-attached storage (NAS), which presents devices at the file level, iSCSI makes block devices available via the network.

Initiators and Targets

A storage network consists of two types of equipment:

- **Initiator:** The consumer of storage, typically a server with an adapter card in it called a host bus adapter (HBA). The initiator commences a connection over the fabric to one or more ports on your storage system, which are called target ports.

- **Target:** The ports on your storage system that deliver storage volumes (called target devices or logical unit numbers [LUNs]) to the initiators.

iSCSI should be considered a local-area technology, not a wide-area technology, because of latency issues and security concerns. You should also segregate iSCSI traffic from general traffic. Layer 2 virtual local area networks (VLANs) are a particularly good way to implement this segregation.

Oversubscription

Beware of oversubscription. It occurs when more users are connected to a system than can be fully supported at the same time. Networks and servers are almost always designed with some amount of oversubscription with the assumption that users do not all need the service simultaneously. If they do, delays are certain and outages are possible. Oversubscription is permissible on general-purpose LANs, but you should not use an oversubscribed configuration for iSCSI.

Here's best practice:

- To have a dedicated local area network (LAN) for iSCSI traffic

- Not to share the storage network with other network traffic such as management, fault tolerance, or vMotion/Live Migration

iSCSI Implementation Considerations

The following items are the security considerations when implementing iSCSI:

- **Private network:** iSCSI storage traffic is transmitted in an unencrypted format across the LAN. Therefore, it is considered a best practice to use iSCSI on trusted networks only and to isolate the traffic on separate physical switches or to leverage a private VLAN. All iSCSI-array vendors agree that it is good practice to isolate iSCSI traffic for security reasons. This means isolating the iSCSI traffic on its own separate physical switches or leveraging a dedicated VLAN (IEEE 802.1Q).[4]

- **Encryption:** iSCSI supports several types of security. IP Security (IPSec) is used for security at the network or packet-processing layer of network communication. Internet Key Exchange (IKE) is an IPSec standard protocol used to ensure security for virtual private networks (VPNs).

- **Authentication:** Numerous authentication methods are supported with iSCSI:

  - **Kerberos:** A network authentication protocol. It is designed to provide strong authentication for client/server applications by using secret-key cryptography. The Kerberos protocol uses strong cryptography so that a client can prove its identity to a server (and vice versa) across an insecure network connection. After a client and server have used Kerberos to prove their identities, they can encrypt all their communications to ensure privacy and data integrity as they go about their business.[5]

- **Secure remote password (SRP):** SRP is a secure password-based authentication and key-exchange protocol. SRP exchanges a cryptographically strong secret as a by-product of successful authentication, which enables the two parties to communicate securely.

- **Simple public-key mechanism (SPKM1/2):** Provides authentication, key establishment, data integrity, and data confidentiality in an online distributed application environment using a public-key infrastructure. SPKM can be used as a drop-in replacement by any application that uses security services through Generic Security Service Application Program Interface (GSSAPI) calls. The use of a public-key infrastructure allows digital signatures supporting nonrepudiation to be employed for message exchanges.[6]

- **Challenge handshake authentication protocol (CHAP):** Used to periodically verify the identity of the peer using a three-way handshake. This is done upon initial link establishment and may be repeated anytime after the link has been established. The following are the steps involved in using CHAP:[7]

  1. After the link establishment phase is complete, the authenticator sends a challenge message to the peer.

  2. The peer responds with a value calculated using a one-way hash function.

  3. The authenticator checks the response against its own calculation of the expected hash value. If the values match, the authentication is acknowledged; otherwise the connection should be terminated.

  4. At random intervals, the authenticator sends a new challenge to the peer and repeats steps 1 to 3.

Network Controllers Best Practices

As an increasing number of servers in the data center become virtualized, network administrators and engineers are pressed to find ways to better manage traffic running between these machines. Virtual switches aim to manage and route traffic in a virtual environment, but often network engineers do not have direct access to these switches. When they do, they often find that virtual switches living inside hypervisors do not offer the type of visibility and granular traffic management they need.

Traditional physical switches determine where to send message frames based on MAC addresses on physical devices. Virtual switches act similarly in that each virtual host must connect to a virtual switch the same way a physical host must connect to a physical switch.

But a closer look reveals major differences between physical and virtual switches. With a physical switch, when a dedicated network cable or switch port goes bad, only one server goes down. Yet with virtualization, one cable can offer connectivity to 10 or more virtual machines (VMs), causing a loss in connectivity to multiple VMs. In addition, connecting multiple VMs requires more bandwidth, which the virtual switch must handle.

These differences are especially apparent in larger networks with more intricate designs, such as those that support VM infrastructure across data centers or DR sites.

Virtual Switches Best Practices

Virtual switches are the core networking component on a host, connecting the physical network interface cards (NICs) in the host server to the virtual NICs in VMs.

In planning virtual switch architecture, engineers must decide how they will use physical NICs to assign virtual switch port groups to ensure redundancy, segmentation, and security.

All these switches support 802.1Q tagging, which allows multiple VLANs to be used on a single physical switch port to reduce the number of physical NICs needed in a host. This works by applying tags to all network frames to identify them as belonging to a certain VLAN.[8]

Security is also an important consideration when using virtual switches. Utilizing several types of ports and port groups separately rather than all together on a single virtual switch offers higher security and better management.

Virtual switch redundancy is another important consideration. Redundancy is achieved by assigning at least two physical NICs to a virtual switch, with each NIC connecting to a different physical switch. Redundancy can also be achieved through the use of port channeling, which does the following:

- Increases the available bandwidth between two devices
- Creates one logical path out of multiple physical paths

Network Isolation

The key to virtual network security is isolation. Every host has a management network through which it communicates with other hosts and management systems. In a virtual infrastructure, the management network should be isolated physically and virtually. Connect all hosts, clients, and management systems to a separate physical network to secure the traffic. You should also create isolated virtual switches for your host management network and never mix virtual-switch traffic with normal VM network traffic. Although this does not address all problems that virtual switches introduce, it's an important start.

Other Virtual Network Security Best Practices

In addition to isolation, there are other virtual network security best practices to keep in mind.

- Note that the network that is used to move live VMs from one host to another does so in clear text. That means it may be possible to "sniff" the data or perform a man-in-the-middle attack when a live migration occurs.

- When dealing with internal and external networks, always create a separate isolated virtual switch with its own physical network interface cards and never mix internal and external traffic on a virtual switch.

- Lock down access to your virtual switches so that an attacker cannot move VMs from one network to another and so that VMs do not straddle an internal and external network.

In virtual infrastructures where a physical network has been extended to the host as a virtual network, physical network security devices and applications are often ineffective. Often, these devices cannot see network traffic that never leaves the host (because they are, by nature, physical devices). Plus, physical intrusion detection and prevention systems may not be able to protect VMs from threats.

- For a better virtual network security strategy, use security applications that are designed specifically for virtual infrastructure and integrate them directly into the virtual networking layer. This includes network intrusion detection and prevention systems, monitoring and reporting systems, and virtual firewalls that are designed to secure virtual switches and isolate VMs. You can integrate physical and virtual network security to provide complete data center protection.

- If you use network-based storage such as iSCSI or Network File System (NFS), use proper authentication. For iSCSI, bidirectional CHAP authentication is best. Be sure to physically isolate storage network traffic because the traffic is often sent as clear text. Anyone with access to the same network can listen and reconstruct files, alter traffic, and possibly corrupt the network.

INSTALLATION AND CONFIGURATION OF VIRTUALIZATION MANAGEMENT TOOLS FOR THE HOST

Securely configuring the virtualization management toolset is one of the most important steps when building a cloud environment. Compromising on the management tools may allow an attacker unlimited access to the VM, the host, and the enterprise network.

Therefore, you must securely install and configure the management tools and then adequately monitor them.

All management should take place on an isolated management network.

The virtualization platform determines what management tools need to be installed on the host. The latest tools should be installed on each host, and the configuration management plan should include rules on updating these tools. Updating these tools may require server downtime, so sufficient server resources should be deployed to allow for the movement of VMs when updating the virtualization platform. You should also conduct external vulnerability testing of the tools.

Follow the vendor security guidance when configuring and deploying these tools. Access to these management tools should be role based. You should audit and log the management tools as well.

You need to understand what management tools are available by vendor platform, as well as how to securely install and configure them appropriately based on the configuration of the systems involved.

Leading Practices

Regardless of the toolset used to manage the host, ensure that the following best practices are used to secure the tools and ensure that only authorized users are given access when necessary to perform their jobs.

- **Defense in depth:** Implement the tools used to manage the host as part of a larger architectural design that mutually reinforces security at every level of the enterprise. The tools should be seen as a tactical element of host management, one that is linked to operational elements such as procedures and strategic elements such as policies.

- **Access control:** Secure the tools and tightly control and monitor access to them.

- **Auditing and monitoring:** Monitor and track the use of the tools throughout the enterprise to ensure proper usage is taking place.

- **Maintenance:** Update and patch the tools as required to ensure compliance with all vendor recommendations and security bulletins.

Running a Physical Infrastructure for Cloud Environments

Although virtualization and cloud computing can help companies accomplish more by breaking the physical bonds between an IT infrastructure and its users, security threats must be overcome to benefit fully from this paradigm. This is particularly true for the SaaS provider. In some respects, you lose control of certain assets in the cloud, and your security model must account for that. Enterprise security is only as good as the least reliable partner, department, or vendor. Can you trust your data to your service provider?

In a public cloud, you are sharing computing resources with other companies. In a shared pool outside the enterprise, you will not have knowledge of or control over where the resources run.

Following are some important considerations when sharing resources:

- **Legal:** Simply by sharing the environment in the cloud, you may put your data at risk of seizure. Exposing your data in an environment shared with other companies can give the government "reasonable cause" to seize your assets because another company has violated the law.

- **Compatibility:** Storage services provided by one cloud vendor may be incompatible with another vendor's services should you decide to move from one to the other.

- **Control:** If information is encrypted while passing through the cloud, does the customer or cloud vendor control the encryption and decryption keys? Most customers probably want their data encrypted both ways across the Internet using the secure sockets layer (SSL) protocol. They also most likely want their data encrypted while it is at rest in the cloud vendor's storage pool. Make sure you control the encryption and decryption keys, just as if the data were still resident in the enterprise's own servers.

- **Log data:** As more and more mission-critical processes are moved to the cloud, SaaS suppliers have to provide log data in a real-time, straightforward manner, probably for their administrators as well as their customers' personnel. Will customers trust the CSP enough to push their mission-critical applications out to the cloud? Because the SaaS provider's logs are internal and not necessarily accessible externally or by clients or investigators, monitoring is difficult.

- **PCI DSS access:** Because access to logs is required for PCI DSS compliance and may be requested by auditors and regulators, security managers need to make sure to negotiate access to the provider's logs as part of any service agreement.

- **Upgrades and changes:** Cloud applications undergo constant feature additions. Users must keep up to date with application improvements to be sure they are protected. The speed at which applications change in the cloud affects both the software development lifecycle and security. A secure software development lifecycle may not be able to provide a security cycle that keeps up with changes that occur so quickly. This means that users must constantly upgrade because an older version may not function or protect the data.

- **Failover technology:** Having proper failover technology is a component of securing the cloud that is often overlooked. The company can survive if a non-mission-critical application goes offline, but this may not be true for mission-critical applications. Security needs to move to the data level so that enterprises can be sure their data is protected wherever it goes. Sensitive data is the domain of the enterprise, not of the cloud computing provider. One of the key challenges in cloud computing is data-level security.

- **Compliance:** SaaS makes the process of compliance more complicated because it may be difficult for a customer to discern where his data resides on a network controlled by the SaaS provider, or a partner of that provider, which raises all sorts of compliance issues of data privacy, segregation, and security. Many compliance regulations require that data not be intermixed with other data, such as on shared servers or databases. Some countries have strict limits on what data about its citizens can be stored and for how long, and some banking regulators require that customers' financial data remain in their home country.

- **Regulations:** Compliance with government regulations, such as the Sarbanes-Oxley Act (SOX), the Gramm-Leach-Bliley Act (GLBA), and the Health Insurance Portability and Accountability Act (HIPAA), and industry standards such as the PCI DSS are much more challenging in the SaaS environment. There is a perception that cloud computing removes data compliance responsibility; however, the data owner is still fully responsible for compliance. Those who adopt cloud computing must remember that it is the responsibility of the data owner, not the service provider, to secure valuable data.

- **Outsourcing:** Outsourcing means losing significant control over data. Although this is not a good idea from a security perspective, the business ease and financial savings continue to increase the usage of these services. You need to work with your company's legal staff to ensure that appropriate contract terms are in place to protect corporate data and provide for acceptable SLAs.

- **Placement of security:** Cloud-based services result in many mobile IT users accessing business data and services without traversing the corporate network. This increases the need for enterprises to place security controls between mobile users and cloud-based services. Placing large amounts of sensitive data in a globally accessible cloud leaves organizations open to large, distributed threats. Attackers no longer have to come onto the premises to steal data; they can find it all in the one virtual location.

- **Virtualization:** Virtualization efficiencies in the cloud require VMs from multiple organizations to be colocated on the same physical resources. Although traditional data center security still applies in the cloud environment, physical segregation and hardware-based security cannot protect against attacks between VMs on the same server. Administrative access is through the Internet rather than the controlled and restricted direct or on-premises connection that is adhered to in the traditional data center model. This increases risk and exposure and requires stringent monitoring for changes in system control and access control restriction.

- **VM:** The dynamic and fluid nature of VMs makes it difficult to maintain the consistency of security and ensure that records can be audited. The ease of cloning and distribution between physical servers can result in the propagation of configuration errors and other vulnerabilities. Proving the security state of a system and identifying the location of an insecure VM is challenging. The colocation of multiple VMs increases the attack surface and risk of VM-to-VM compromise.

Localized VMs and physical servers use the same OSs as well as enterprise and web applications in a cloud server environment, increasing the threat of an attacker or malware exploiting vulnerabilities in these systems and applications remotely. VMs are vulnerable as they move between the private cloud and the public cloud. A fully or partially shared cloud environment is expected to have a greater attack surface and therefore can be considered to be at greater risk than a dedicated resources environment.

- **Operating system and application files:** Operating system and application files are on a shared physical infrastructure in a virtualized cloud environment and require system, file, and activity monitoring to provide confidence and auditable proof to enterprise customers that their resources have not been compromised or tampered with. In the cloud computing environment, the enterprise subscribes to cloud computing resources, and the responsibility for patching is the subscriber's rather than the cloud computing vendor's. The need for patch maintenance vigilance is imperative. Lack of due diligence in this regard can rapidly make the task unmanageable or impossible.

- **Data fluidity:** Enterprises are often required to prove that their security compliance is in accord with regulations, standards, and auditing practices, regardless of the location of the systems at which the data resides. Data is fluid in cloud computing and may reside in on-premises physical servers, on-premises VMs, or off-premises VMs running on cloud computing resources. This requires some rethinking on the part of auditors and practitioners alike.

In the rush to take advantage of the benefits of cloud computing, many corporations are likely rushing into cloud computing without a serious consideration of the security implications. To establish zones of trust in the cloud, the VMs must be self-defending, effectively moving the perimeter to the VM itself. Enterprise perimeter security (that is, demilitarized zones [DMZs], network segmentation, intrusion detection systems [IDSs] and intrusion prevention systems [IPSs], monitoring tools, and the associated security policies) only controls the data that resides and transits behind the perimeter. In the cloud computing world, the cloud computing provider is in charge of customer data security and privacy.

Configuring Access Control and Secure Kernel-Based Virtual Machine

You need to have a plan to address access control to the cloud-hosting environment.

Physical access to servers should be limited to users who require access for a specific purpose. Personnel who administer the physical hardware should not have other types of administrative access.

Access to hosts should be done by secure kernel-based virtual machine (KVM); for added security, access to KVM devices should require a checkout process. A secure KVM prevents data loss from the server to the connected computer. It also prevents unsecure emanations. The Common Criteria (CC) provides guidance on different security levels and a list of KVM products that meet those security levels. Two-factor authentication should be considered for remote console access. All access should be logged and routine audits conducted.

A secure KVM meets the following design criteria:

- **Isolated data channels:** Located in each KVM port, these make it impossible for data to be transferred between connected computers through the KVM.

- **Tamper-warning labels on each side of the KVM:** These provide clear visual evidence if the enclosure has been compromised.

- **Housing intrusion detection:** This causes the KVM to become inoperable and the LEDs to flash repeatedly if the housing has been opened.

- **Fixed firmware:** It cannot be reprogrammed, preventing attempts to alter the logic of the KVM.

- **Tamper-proof circuit board:** It's soldered to prevent component removal or alteration.

- **Safe buffer design:** It does not incorporate a memory buffer, and the keyboard buffer is automatically cleared after data transmission, preventing transfer of keystrokes or other data when switching between computers.

- **Selective universal serial bus (USB) access:** It only recognizes human interface device USB devices (such as keyboards and mice) to prevent inadvertent and insecure data transfer.

- **Push-button control:** It requires physical access to KVM when switching between connected computers.

Console-based access to VMs is also important. Regardless of vendor platform, all VM management software offers a "manage by console" option. The use of these consoles to access, configure, and manage VMs offers an administrator the opportunity to easily control almost every aspect of the VMs' configuration and usage. As a result, a malicious hacker, or bad actor, can achieve the same level of access and control by using these consoles if they are not properly secured and managed. The use of access controls for console access is available in every vendor platform and should be implemented and regularly audited for compliance as a best practice.

SECURING THE NETWORK CONFIGURATION

When it comes to securing the network configuration, there is a lot to be concerned with. Several technologies, protocols, and services are necessary to ensure a secure and reliable network is provided to the end user of the cloud-based services (*Figure 5.3*). For example, Transport layer security (TLS) and IPSec can be used for securing communications to prevent eavesdropping. Domain name system security extensions (DNSSEC) should be used to prevent domain name system (DNS) poisoning. DNSSEC is a suite of Internet Engineering Task Force (IETF) specifications for securing certain kinds of information provided by DNS as used on Internet protocol (IP) networks.

FIGURE 5.3 **A secure network configuration involves all these protocols and services.**

Network Isolation

Before discussing the services, it's important to understand the role of isolation. Isolation is a critical design concept for a secure network configuration in a cloud environment. All management of the data center systems should be done on isolated networks. These management networks should be monitored and audited regularly to ensure that confidentiality and integrity are maintained.

Access to the storage controllers should also be granted over isolated network components that are nonroutable to prevent the direct download of stored data and to restrict the likelihood of unauthorized access or accidental discovery. Customer access should be provisioned on isolated networks. This isolation can be implemented through the use of physically separate networks or via VLANs.

All networks should be monitored and audited to validate separation. Access to the management network should be strictly limited to those that require access. Strong authentication methods should be used on the management network to validate identity and authorize usage.

Protecting VLANs

The network can be one of the most vulnerable parts of any system.

The VM network requires as much protection as the physical one. Using VLANs can improve networking security in your environment. In simple terms, a VLAN is a set of workstations within a LAN that can communicate with each other as though they were on a single, isolated LAN. They are an Institute of Electrical and Electronics Engineers (IEEE) standard networking scheme with specific tagging methods that allow routing of packets to only those ports that are part of the VLAN.

When properly configured, VLANs provide a dependable means to protect a set of machines from accidental or malicious intrusions. VLANs let you segment a physical network so that two machines in the network can transmit packets back and forth unless they are part of the same VLAN.

VLAN Communication

What does it mean to say that the VLAN workstations "communicate with each other as though they were on a single, isolated LAN"? Among other things, it means the following:

- Broadcast packets sent by one of the workstations can reach all the others in the VLAN.

- Broadcasts sent by one of the workstations in the VLAN cannot reach any workstations that are not in the VLAN.

- Broadcasts sent by workstations that are not in the VLAN can never reach workstations that are in the VLAN.

- All the workstations can communicate with each other without needing to go through a gateway.

VLAN Advantages

The ability to isolate network traffic to certain machines or groups of machines via association with the VLAN allows for the opportunity to create secured pathing of data between endpoints.

Although the use of VLANs by themselves does not guarantee that data will be transmitted securely and that it will not be tampered with or intercepted while on the wire, it is a building block that, when combined with other protection mechanisms, allows for data confidentiality to be achieved.

5

OPERATIONS

Using TLS

TLS[9] is a cryptographic protocol designed to provide communication security over a network. It uses X.509 certificates to authenticate a connection and to exchange a symmetric key. This key is then used to encrypt any data sent over the connection. The TLS protocol allows client/server applications to communicate across a network in a way designed to ensure confidentiality.

TLS is made up of two layers:

- **TLS record protocol:** Provides connection security and ensures that the connection is private and reliable. Used to encapsulate higher-level protocols, among them the TLS handshake protocol.

- **TLS handshake protocol:** Allows the client and the server to authenticate each other and to negotiate an encryption algorithm and cryptographic keys before data is sent or received.

Using DNS

DNS[10] is a hierarchical, distributed database that contains mappings of the DNS domain names to various types of data, such as Internet protocol (IP) addresses. DNS allows you to use friendly names, such as `www.isc2.org`, to easily locate computers and other resources on a TCP/IP-based network.

DNSSEC

DNSSEC[11] is a suite of extensions that adds security to the domain name system (DNS) protocol by enabling DNS responses to be validated. Specifically, DNSSEC provides origin authority, data integrity, and authenticated denial of existence. With DNSSEC, the DNS protocol is much less susceptible to certain types of attacks—particularly DNS spoofing attacks.

If it's supported by an authoritative DNS server, a DNS zone can be secured with DNS-SEC using a process called zone signing. Signing a zone with DNSSEC adds validation support to a zone without changing the basic mechanism of a DNS query and response.

Validation of DNS responses occurs through the use of digital signatures that are included with DNS responses. These digital signatures are contained in new, DNSSEC-related resource records that are generated and added to the zone during zone signing.

When a DNSSEC-aware recursive or forwarding DNS server receives a query from a DNS client for a DNSSEC-signed zone, it requests that the authoritative DNS server also send DNSSEC records and then attempt to validate the DNS response using these records. A recursive or forwarding DNS server recognizes that the zone supports DNS-SEC if it has a DNSKEY, also called a trust anchor, for that zone.

Threats to the DNS Infrastructure

Following are the typical ways in which attackers can threaten the DNS infrastructure:

- **Footprinting:** The process by which an attacker obtains DNS zone data, including DNS domain names, computer names, and IP addresses for sensitive network resources.

- **Denial-of-service attack:** When an attacker attempts to deny the availability of network services by flooding one or more DNS servers in the network with queries.

- **Data modification:** An attempt by an attacker to spoof valid IP addresses in IP packets that the attacker has created. This gives these packets the appearance of coming from a valid IP address in the network. With a valid IP address, the attacker can gain access to the network and destroy data or conduct other attacks.

- **Redirection:** When an attacker can redirect queries for DNS names to servers that are under the control of the attacker.

- **Spoofing:** When a DNS server accepts and uses incorrect information from a host that has no authority giving that information. DNS spoofing is in fact malicious cache poisoning where forged data is placed in the cache of the name servers.

Using IPSec

IPSec uses cryptographic security to protect communications over IP networks. IPSec includes protocols for establishing mutual authentication at the beginning of the session and negotiating cryptographic keys to be used during the session. IPSec supports network-level peer authentication, data origin authentication, data integrity, encryption, and replay protection.

You may find IPSec to be a valuable addition to the network configuration that requires end-to-end security for data while transiting a network.

The deployment and use of IPSec has two key challenges:

- **Configuration management:** The use of IPSec is optional. As such, many endpoint devices connecting to the cloud infrastructure do not have IPSec support enabled and configured. If IPSec is not enabled on the endpoint, then depending on the configuration choices made on the server side of the IPSec solution, the endpoint may not be able to connect and complete a transaction if it does not support IPSec. CSPs may not have the proper visibility on the customer endpoints or the server infrastructure to understand IPSec configurations. As a result, the ability to ensure the use of IPSec to secure network traffic may be limited.

- **Performance:** The use of IPSec imposes a performance penalty on the systems deploying the technology. Although the impact on the performance of an average system is small, it is the cumulative effect of IPSec across an enterprise architecture, end to end, that must be evaluated prior to implementation.

IDENTIFYING AND UNDERSTANDING SERVER THREATS

To secure a server, it is essential to first define the threats that must be mitigated.

Organizations should conduct risk assessments to identify the specific threats against their servers and determine the effectiveness of existing security controls in counteracting the threats. They then should perform risk mitigation to decide what additional measures, if any, should be implemented, as discussed in National Institute of Standards and Technology (NIST) Special Publication 800-30 Revision 1, "Risk Assessment Guide for Information Technology Systems."[12]

Performing risk assessments and mitigation helps organizations better understand their security posture and decide how their servers should be secured.

There are several types of threats to be aware of:

- Many threats against data and resources exist as a result of mistakes, either bugs in OS and server software that create exploitable vulnerabilities or errors made by end users and administrators.

- Threats may involve intentional actors (such as attackers who want to access information on a server) or unintentional actors (such as administrators who forget to disable user accounts of former employees).

- Threats can be local, such as a disgruntled employee, or remote, such as an attacker in another geographical area.

The following general guidelines should be addressed when identifying and understanding threats:

- Use an asset management system that has configuration management capabilities to enable documentation of all system configuration items (CIs) authoritatively.

- Use system baselines to enforce configuration management throughout the enterprise. Note the following in configuration management:

  - A baseline is an agreed-upon description of the attributes of a product, at a point in time that serves as a basis for defining change.

  - A change is a movement from this baseline state to a next state.

- Consider automation technologies that help with the creation, application, management, updating, tracking, and compliance checking for system baselines.

- Develop and use a robust change management system to authorize the required changes that need to be made to systems over time. In addition, enforce a requirement that no changes can be made to production systems unless the change has been properly vetted and approved through the change management system in place. This forces all changes to be clearly articulated, examined, documented, and weighed against the organization's priorities and objectives. Forcing the examination of all changes in the context of the business allows you to ensure that risk is minimized whenever possible and that all changes are seen as being acceptable to the business based on the potential risk that they pose.

- Use an exception reporting system to force the capture and documentation of any activities undertaken that are contrary to the expected norm with regard to the lifecycle of a system under management.

- Use vendor-specified configuration guidance and best practices as appropriate based on the specific platform(s) under management.

USING STANDALONE HOSTS

As a Certified Cloud Security Professional (CCSP), you may be called upon to help the business decide on the best way to safely host a virtualized infrastructure. The needs and requirements of the business need to be clearly identified and documented before a decision can be made as to which hosting models are the best to deploy.

In general, the business seeks to do the following:

- Create isolated, secured, dedicated hosting of individual cloud resources; the use of a standalone host would be an appropriate choice.

- Make the cloud resources available to end users so they appear as if they are independent of any other resources and are isolated; either a standalone host or a shared host configuration that offers multitenant secured hosting capabilities is appropriate.

The CCSP needs to understand the business requirements because they drive the choice of hosting model and the architecture for the cloud security framework. For instance, consider the following scenario:

ABC Corp. has decided that it wants to move its CRM system to a cloud-based platform. The company currently has a "homegrown" CRM offering that it hosts in its data center and that is maintained by its own internal development and IT infrastructure teams.

ABC Corp. has to make its decision along the following lines:

- It could continue as is and effectively become a private CSP for its internal CRM application.

- It could look to a managed service provider to partner with and effectively hand over the CRM application to be managed and maintained according to the provider's requirements and specifications.

- It could decide to engage in an RFP process and look for a third-party CRM vendor that would provide cloud-based functionality through a SaaS model that could replace its current application.

As the CCSP, you would have to help ABC Corp. figure out which of these three options would be the most appropriate one to choose. Although on the surface that may seem to be a simple and fairly straightforward decision to make, it requires consideration of many factors.

Aside from the business requirements already touched on, you would need to understand, to the best of your abilities, the following issues:

- What are the current market conditions in the industry vertical that ABC Corp. is part of?

- Have ABC Corp.'s major competitors made a similar transition to cloud-based services recently? If so, what paths have they chosen?

- Is there an industry vendor that specializes in migrating or implementing CRM systems in this vertical for the cloud?

- Are there regulatory issues or concerns that would have to be noted and addressed as part of this project?

- What are the risks associated with each of the three options outlined as possible solutions? What are the benefits?

- Does ABC Corp. have the required skills available in house to manage the move to becoming a private CSP of CRM services to the business? To manage and maintain the private cloud platform once it's up and running?

As you can see, the path to making a clear and concise recommendation is long, and it's often obscured by many issues that may not be apparent at the outset of the conversation. The CCSP's responsibilities will vary based on need and situation, but at its core, the CCSP must always be able to examine the parameters of the situation at hand and frame the conversation with the business regarding risk and benefit to ensure that the best possible decision can be made.

Be sure to address the following standalone host availability considerations:

- Regulatory issues
- Current security policies in force
- Any contractual requirements that may be in force for one or more systems or areas of the business
- The needs of a certain application or business process that may be using the system in question
- The classification of the data contained in the system

USING CLUSTERED HOSTS

You should understand the basic concept of host clustering as well as the specifics of the technology and implementation requirements that are unique to the vendor platforms they support.

A clustered host is logically and physically connected to other hosts within a management framework. This is done to allow central management of resources for the collection of hosts, applications, and VMs running on a member of the cluster to fail over, or move, between host members as needed for continued operation of those resources, with a focus on minimizing the downtime that host failures can cause.

Resource Sharing

Within a host cluster, resources are allocated and managed as if they were pooled or jointly available to all members of the cluster. The use of resource-sharing concepts such as reservations limits and shares may be used to further refine and orchestrate the allocation of resources according to requirements that the cluster administrator imposes.

- Reservations guarantee a minimum amount of the cluster's pooled resources be made available to a specified VM.
- Limits guarantee a maximum amount of the cluster's pooled resources be made available to a specified VM.
- Shares provision the remaining resources left in a cluster when there is resource contention. Specifically, shares allow the cluster's reservations to be allocated and then to address any remaining resources that may be available for use by members of the cluster through a prioritized percentage-based allocation mechanism.

Clusters are available for the traditional "compute" resources of the hosts that make up the cluster: random access memory (RAM) and central processing unit (CPU). In addition, storage clusters can be created and deployed to allow back-end storage to be managed in the same way that the traditional compute resources are. The management of the cluster involves a cluster manager or some kind of management toolset. The chosen virtualization platform determines the clustering capability of the cloud hosts. Many virtualization platforms utilize clustering for HA and DR.

Distributed Resource Scheduling/Compute Resource Scheduling

All virtualization vendors use distributed resource scheduling (DRS) in one form or another to allow for a cluster of hosts to do the following:[13]

- Provide highly available resources to your workloads

- Balance workloads for optimal performance

- Scale and manage computing resources without service disruption

Using the initial workload placement across the cluster as a VM is powered on is the beginning point for all load-balancing operations. This initial placement function can be fully automated or manually implemented based on a series of recommendations made by the DRS service, depending on the chosen configuration for DRS. Some DRS implementations offer the ability to engage in ongoing load balancing once a VM has been placed and is running in the cluster. This load balancing is achieved through a movement of the VM between hosts in the cluster to achieve or maintain the desired compute resource allocation thresholds specified for the DRS service.

These movements of VMs between hosts in the DRS cluster are policy driven and are controlled through the application of affinity and anti-affinity rules. These rules allow for the separation (anti-affinity) of VMs across multiple hosts in the cluster or the grouping (affinity) of VMs on a single host. The need to separate or group VMs can be driven by architectural, policy and compliance, or performance and security concerns.

ACCOUNTING FOR DYNAMIC OPERATION

A cloud environment is dynamic in nature. The cloud controller dynamically allocates resources to maximize their use. In cloud computing, elasticity is defined as the degree to which a system can adapt to workload changes by provisioning and deprovisioning resources automatically, such that at each point in time the available resources match the current demand as closely as possible.

In outsourced and public deployment models, cloud computing also can provide elasticity. This refers to the ability for customers to quickly request, receive, and later release as many resources as needed.

By using an elastic cloud, customers can avoid excessive costs from overprovisioning—that is, building enough capacity for peak demand and then not using the capacity in nonpeak periods.

With rapid elasticity, capabilities can be rapidly and elastically provisioned, in some cases automatically, to scale rapidly outward and inward, commensurate with demand. To the consumer, the capabilities available for provisioning often appear to be unlimited and can be appropriated in any quantity at any time.

For a cloud to provide elasticity, it must be flexible and scalable. An onsite private cloud, at any specific time, has a fixed computing and storage capacity that has been sized to correspond to anticipated workloads and cost restrictions. If an organization is large enough and supports a sufficient diversity of workloads, an onsite private cloud may be able to provide elasticity to clients within the consumer organization. Smaller onsite private clouds, however, exhibit maximum capacity limits similar to those of traditional data centers.

USING STORAGE CLUSTERS

Clustered storage is the use of two or more storage servers working together to increase performance, capacity, or reliability. Clustering distributes workloads to each server, manages the transfer of workloads between servers, and provides access to all files from any server regardless of the physical location of the file.

Clustered Storage Architectures

Two basic clustered storage architectures exist, known as tightly coupled and loosely coupled:

- A tightly coupled cluster has a physical backplane into which controller nodes connect. While this backplane fixes the maximum size of the cluster, it delivers a high-performance interconnect between servers for load-balanced performance and maximum scalability as the cluster grows. Additional array controllers, input/output (I/O) ports, and capacity can connect into the cluster as demand dictates.

- A loosely coupled cluster offers cost-effective building blocks that can start small and grow as applications demand. A loose cluster offers performance, I/O, and storage capacity within the same node. As a result, performance scales with capacity and vice versa.

Storage Cluster Goals

Storage clusters should be designed to do the following:

- Meet the required service levels as specified in the SLA

- Provide for the ability to separate customer data in multitenant hosting environments

- Securely store and protect data through the use of availability, integrity, and confidentiality (AIC) mechanisms, such as encryption, hashing, masking, and multipathing

USING MAINTENANCE MODE

Maintenance mode is utilized when updating or configuring different components of the cloud environment. While in maintenance mode, customer access is blocked, and alerts are disabled (although logging is still enabled).

Any data or hosted VMs should be migrated prior to entering maintenance mode if they still need to be available for use while the system undergoes maintenance. This may be automated in some virtualization platforms.

Maintenance mode can apply to both data stores and hosts. Although the procedure to enter and use maintenance mode varies by vendor, the traditional service mechanism that maintenance mode is tied to is the SLA. The SLA describes the IT service, documents the service-level targets, and specifies the responsibilities of the IT service provider and the customer.

You should enter maintenance mode, operate within it, and exit it successfully using the vendor-specific guidance and best practices.

PROVIDING HA ON THE CLOUD

In the enterprise data center, systems are managed with an expectation of uptime, or availability. This expectation is usually formally documented with an SLA and is communicated to all the users so that they understand the system's availability.

Measuring System Availability

The traditional way that system availability is measured and documented in SLAs is using a measurement matrix such as the one outlined in Table 5.3.

TABLE 5.3 **System Availability Measurement Matrix**

AVAILABILITY PERCENTAGE	DOWNTIME PER YEAR	DOWNTIME PER MONTH	DOWNTIME PER WEEK
90% ("one nine")	36.5 days	72 hours	16.8 hours
99% ("two nines")	3.65 days	7.20 hours	1.68 hours
99.9% ("three nines")	8.76 hours	43.8 minutes	10.1 minutes
99.99% ("four nines")	52.56 minutes	4.32 minutes	1.01 minutes
99.999% ("five nines")	5.26 minutes	25.9 seconds	6.05 seconds
99.9999% ("six nines")	31.5 seconds	2.59 seconds	0.605 seconds
99.99999% ("seven nines")	3.15 seconds	0.259 seconds	0.0605 seconds

Note that uptime and availability are not synonymous; a system can be up but not available, as in the case of a network outage. To ensure system availability, the focus needs to be on ensuring that all required systems are available as stipulated in their SLAs.

Achieving HA

You can take many approaches to achieve HA.

- One example is the use of redundant architectural elements to safeguard data in case of failure, such as a drive-mirroring solution. This system design, commonly called Redundant Array of Independent Disks (RAID), would allow for a hard drive containing data to fail. Then, depending on the design of the system (hardware versus software implementation of the RAID functionality), it would allow for a small window of downtime while the secondary, or redundant, hard drive was brought online in the system and made available.

- Another example specific to cloud environments is the use of multiple vendors within the cloud architecture to provide the same services. This allows you to build certain systems that need a specified level of availability to be able to switch, or fail over, to an alternate provider's system within the specified period defined in the SLA that is used to define and manage the availability window for the system.

Cloud vendors provide differing mechanisms and technologies to achieve HA within their systems. Always consult with the business stakeholders to understand the HA requirements that need to be identified, documented, and addressed. The CCSP needs to ensure that these requirements are accurately captured and represented in the SLAs that are in place to manage these systems. The CCSP must also periodically revisit the requirements by validating them with the stakeholder and then ensuring that, if necessary, the SLAs are updated to reflect any changes.

THE PHYSICAL INFRASTRUCTURE FOR CLOUD ENVIRONMENTS

Mid-to-large corporations and government entities, independent system vendors (ISVs), and service providers use cloud infrastructure to build private and public clouds and deliver cloud computing services.

Virtualization provides the foundation for cloud computing, enabling rapid deployment of IT resources from a shared pool and economies of scale. Integration reduces complexity and administrative overhead and facilitates automation to enable end user resource provisioning, allocation and reallocation of physical capacity, and information security and protection, without IT staff intervention.

Fully capturing and effectively delivering the benefits of cloud computing requires a tightly integrated infrastructure that is optimized for virtualization, but an infrastructure built for cloud computing provides numerous benefits:

- Flexible and efficient utilization of infrastructure investments

- Faster deployment of physical and virtual resources

- Higher application service levels

- Less administrative overhead

- Lower infrastructure, energy, and facility costs

- Increased security

Cloud infrastructure encompasses the computers, storage, network, components, and facilities required for cloud computing and IT as a service (ITaaS). Cloud computing infrastructure includes the following:

- **Servers:** Physical servers provide host machines for multiple VMs or guests. A hypervisor running on the physical server allocates host resources (CPU and memory) dynamically to each VM.

- **Virtualization:** Virtualization technologies abstract physical elements and location. IT resources—servers, applications, desktops, storage, and networking—are uncoupled from physical devices and presented as logical resources. Examples include virtual switches and virtual NICs, as well as the use of software definition for networking and storage.

- **Storage:** SAN, NAS, and unified systems provide storage for primary block and file data, data archiving, backup, and business continuance. Advanced storage software components are utilized for big data, data replication, cloud-to-cloud data movement, and HA.

- **Network:** Switches interconnect physical servers and storage. Routers provide LAN and wide area network (WAN) connectivity. Additional network components provide firewall protection and traffic load balancing.

- **Management:** Cloud infrastructure management includes server, network, and storage orchestration, configuration management, performance monitoring, storage resource management, and usage metering.

- **Security:** Components ensure information security and data integrity, fulfill compliance and confidentiality needs, manage risk, and provide governance.

- **Backup and recovery:** Virtual servers and virtual desktops are backed up automatically to disk or tape. Advanced elements provide continuous protection, multiple restore points, data deduplication, and DR.

- **Infrastructure systems:** Preintegrated software and hardware, such as complete backup systems with deduplication and preracked platforms containing servers, hypervisor, network, and storage, streamline cloud infrastructure deployment, and further reduce complexity.

CONFIGURING ACCESS CONTROL FOR REMOTE ACCESS

Cloud-based systems provide resources to users across many different deployment methods and service models, as has been discussed throughout this book. According to NIST SP 800-145, "The NIST Definition of Cloud Computing," the three service models for cloud computing are software as a service (SaaS), platform as a service (PaaS), and infrastructure as a service (IaaS). The four cloud deployment methods are private cloud, public cloud, community cloud, and hybrid cloud.[14]

The scope of deployment methods is shown in Table 5.4.

TABLE 5.4 **Scope of the Deployment Methods**

SCOPE NAME	APPLICABILITY
General	Applies to all cloud deployment models
Onsite private	Applies to private clouds implemented at a customer's premises
Outsourced private	Applies to private clouds where the server side is outsourced to a hosting company
Onsite community	Applies to community clouds implemented on the premises of the customers composing a community cloud
Outsourced community	Applies to community clouds where the server side is outsourced to a hosting company
Public	Applies to public clouds

Regardless of the model, deployment method, and scope of the cloud system in use, the need to allow customers to securely access data and resources is consistent. Your job as a CCSP is to ensure that all authenticated and authorized users of a cloud resource can access that resource securely, ensuring that confidentiality and integrity are maintained, if necessary, and that availability is maintained at the documented and agreed-upon levels for the resource based on the SLA in force.

Some of the threats that the CCSP needs to consider regarding remote access are as follows:

- Lack of physical security controls

- Unsecured networks

- Infected endpoints accessing the internal network

- External access to internal resources

Given the nature of cloud resources, all customer access is remote. Several methods are available for controlling remote access, including these:

- Tunneling via a VPN—IPSec or SSL[15]

- Remote desktop protocol (RDP), which allows for desktop access to remote systems

- Access via a secure terminal

- Deployment of a DMZ

There are several cloud environment access requirements. The cloud environment should provide each of the following:

- Encrypted transmission of all communications between the remote user and the host

- Secure login with complex passwords or certificate-based login

- Two-factor authentication providing enhanced security

- A log and audit of all connections

It is important to establish OS baseline compliance monitoring and remediation. In doing so, determine who is responsible for the secure configuration of the underlying OSs installed in the cloud environment based on the deployment method and service model being used.

Regardless of who is responsible, a secure baseline should be established, and all deployments and updates should be made from a change- and version-controlled master image.

Conduct automated and ad hoc vulnerability scanning and monitoring activities on the underlying infrastructure to validate compliance with all baseline requirements. This ensures that any regulatory-based compliance issues and risks are discovered and documented. Resolve or remediate any deviation in a timely manner.

Sufficient supporting infrastructure and tools should be in place to allow for the patching and maintenance of relevant infrastructure without impact on the end user or customer. Patch management and other remediation activities typically require entry into maintenance mode. Many virtualization vendors offer OS image baselining features as part of their platforms.

The specific activities and technology that will be used to create, document, manage, and deploy OS image baselines vary by vendor. Follow the best practice recommendations and guidance provided by the vendor.

PERFORMING PATCH MANAGEMENT

All organizations must perform patch management, which is a crucial task. Regularly patch OSs, middleware, and applications to guard against newly found vulnerabilities or to provide additional functionality.

Patch management is the process of identifying, acquiring, installing, and verifying patches for products and systems. Patches correct security and functionality problems in software and firmware.

From a security perspective, patches are most often of interest because they are mitigating software flaw vulnerabilities. Applying patches to eliminate these vulnerabilities significantly reduces the opportunities for exploitation. Patches serve other purposes than just fixing software flaws; they can also add new features to software and firmware, including security capabilities.

New features can also be added through upgrades, which bring software or firmware to a newer version in a much broader change than just applying a patch. Upgrades may also fix security and functionality problems in previous versions of software and firmware. Also, vendors often stop supporting older versions of their products, which includes no longer releasing patches to address new vulnerabilities, thus making older unsupported versions less secure over time. Upgrades are necessary to get such products to a supported version that is patched and that has ongoing support for patching newly discovered vulnerabilities.

You should develop a patch management plan for the implementation of system patches. The plan should be part of the configuration-management process and allow you to test patches prior to deployment. Live migration of VMs should take place prior to patching through the use of maintenance mode for all hosts that need to be patched.

You need to understand the vendor-specific requirements of patch management based on the technology platforms under management.

The NIST SP 800-40 Revision 3, "Guide to Enterprise Patch Management Technologies," is a good point of reference.[16]

The Patch Management Process

A patch management process should address the following items:

- Vulnerability detection and evaluation by the vendor
- Subscription mechanism to vendor patch notifications
- Severity assessment of the patch by the receiving enterprise using that software
- Applicability assessment of the patch on target systems
- Opening of tracking records in case of patch applicability
- Customer notification of applicable patches, if required
- Change management
- Successful patch application verification
- Issue and risk management in case of unexpected troubles or conflicting actions
- Closure of tracking records with all auditable artifacts

Some of the steps in the outlined process are well suited for automation in cloud and traditional IT environment implementations, but others require human interaction to be successfully carried out.

Examples of Automation

Automation starts with notifications. Several things happen when a vulnerability is detected:

- Its severity is assessed.
- A security patch or an interim solution is provided.
- This information is entered into a system.
- Automated email notifications are sent to predefined accounts in a straightforward process.

Following are other areas for automation:

- Security patch applicability. If there is an up-to-date software inventory available for reference that includes all software versions, releases, and maintenance levels in production, automatic matching of incoming security vulnerability information can be easily performed against the software inventory.

- The creation of tracking records and their assignment to predefined resolver groups, in case of matching.

- Change record creation, change approval, and change implementation (if agreed-upon maintenance windows have been established and are being managed via SLAs).

- Verification of the successful implementation of security patches.

- Creation of documentation to support that patching has been successfully accomplished.

Challenges of Patch Management

The cloud presents unique opportunities and challenges for patch management. Although the cloud offers highly standardized solutions for customers, it also offers unique challenges because cloud deployments can range from small, single tenant to the extremely large, multitenant environments, with a deep vertical stack due to virtualization.

The following are major hurdles for patch management automation in existing managed environments:

- There's a lack of service standardization. For enterprises transitioning to the cloud, lack of standardization is the main issue. For example, a patch management solution tailored to one customer often cannot be used or easily adopted by another customer.

- Patch management is not simply using a patch tool to apply patches to endpoint systems, but rather a collaboration of multiple management tools and teams, such as change management and patch advisory tools.

- In a large enterprise environment, patch tools need to be able to interact with a large number of managed entities in a scalable way and handle the heterogeneity that is unavoidable in such environments.

- To avoid problems associated with automatically applying patches to endpoints, thorough testing of patches beforehand is absolutely mandatory.

Beyond those issues, two additional key challenges include VMs running in multiple time zones and VMs that have been suspended and snapshotted. These concerns are addressed in the following sections.

Multiple Time Zones

In a cloud environment, VMs that are physically located in the same time zone can be configured to operate in different time zones. When a customer's VMs span multiple time zones, patches need to be scheduled carefully so the correct behavior is implemented.

For some patches, the correct behavior is to apply the patches at the same local time of each VM, such as applying MS98-021 from Microsoft to all Windows machines at 11:00 p.m. of their respective local time.

For other patches, the correct behavior is to apply at the same absolute time to avoid a mixed-mode problem where multiple versions of software are concurrently running, resulting in data corruption.

Here are some of the challenges that the CCSP may face in this area:

- How can a patch be applied to 1,000 VMs at the same time across multiple time zones?

- How do we coordinate maintenance mode windows for such a deployment activity?

- Is the change-management function aware of the need to patch across multiple time zones?

- If it is, has a rolling window been stipulated and approved for the application of the patches?

VM Suspension and Snapshot

In a virtualized environment, additional modes of operations are available to system administrators and users, such as VM suspension and resume, snapshot, and revert back. The management console that allows use of these operations needs to be tightly integrated with the patch management and compliance processes. Otherwise, a VM can become noncompliant unexpectedly.

For example, before a VM is suspended, it is patched to the latest deployed patch level using the automated patch management process. When it resumes after an extended amount of time, it is most likely in a noncompliant state with missing patches. Therefore, it is important that the patch management system catches it up to the latest patch level before handing the VM to the user's control. Likewise, when a VM is reverted to an earlier snapshot, baselining the VM to the latest patch level is most likely required.

Following are some of the challenges that the CCSP may face in this area:

- Have *all* VMs that require the update been patched?

- Can that be validated for compliance reporting or auditing?

- Does the technology platform allow for patching of a suspended VM? A snapshotted instance of a VM?

- Can these activities be automated using the technology platform?

PERFORMANCE MONITORING

Performance monitoring is essential for the secure and reliable operation of a cloud environment. Data on the performance of the underlying components may provide early indications of hardware failure. Traditionally, four key subsystems are recommended for monitoring in cloud environments:

- **Network:** Excessive dropped packets
- **Disk:** Full disk or slow reads and writes to the disks (input/output operations per second [IOPS])
- **Memory:** Excessive memory usage or full utilization of available memory allocation
- **CPU:** Excessive CPU utilization

Familiarize yourself with these four subsystems and learn about the vendor-specific monitoring recommendations, best practice guidelines, and thresholds for performance as required. Although each vendor has specific thresholds and ranges for acceptable operation identified by area for their products and platforms, generally, for each of the four subareas identified, a lower value based on measurement over time indicates better performance. However, this obviously is directly dependent on the specific parameters of the monitored item in question.

Outsourcing Monitoring

Adequate staffing should be allocated for the 24/7 monitoring of the cloud environment. One option is to outsource the monitoring function to a trusted third party. Exercise due care and due diligence if you're pursing an outsourcing option. The need to assess risk and manage a vendor relationship in such a critical area for the enterprise means that you must take your time vetting potential cloud monitoring partners.

Use common-sense approaches such as these:

- Having HR check references
- Examining the terms of any SLA or contract being used to govern service terms
- Executing some form of trial of the managed service in question before implementing into production

Hardware Monitoring

In cloud environments, regardless of how much virtualized infrastructure you deploy, there is always physical infrastructure underlying it that has to be managed, monitored, and maintained.

Extend your monitoring of the four key subsystems discussed in the previous section to include the physical hosts and infrastructure that the virtualization layer rides on top of. The same monitoring concepts and thought processes apply, as have already been discussed. The only difference to account for is the need to add some additional items that exist in the physical plane of these systems, such as CPU temperature, fan speed, and ambient temperature within the data center hosting the physical hosts.

Many of the monitoring systems to be deployed to observe virtualized infrastructure can be used to monitor the physical performance aspects of the hosts as well. These systems can also be used to alert on thresholds established for performance based on several methods, whether activity or task based, metric based, or time based. Each vendor has its own specific methodologies and tools to be deployed to monitor their infrastructure according to their requirements and recommendations.

Ensure that you are aware of the vendor recommendations and best practices pertinent to their environments and they are implemented and followed as required to ensure compliance.

Redundant System Architecture

The use of redundant system architecture is an acceptable and standard practice in cloud environments to accomplish the following:

- Allow for additional hardware items to be incorporated directly into the system as an online real-time component
- Share the load of the running system or in a hot standby mode
- Allow for a controlled failover to minimize downtime

Work with the vendors that supply the data center infrastructure to fully understand what the available options are for designing and implementing system resiliency through redundancy.

Monitoring Functions

Many hardware systems offer built-in monitoring functions specific to the hardware itself, separate from any centralized monitoring that the enterprise may engage in. Be aware of what vendor-specific hardware system monitoring capabilities are already bundled or included in the platforms that they are asked to be responsible for.

The use of any vendor-supplied monitoring capabilities to their fullest extent is necessary to maximize system reliability and performance. Hardware data should be collected along with the data from any external performance monitoring undertaken.

Monitoring hardware may provide early indications of hardware failure and should be treated as a requirement to ensure stability and availability of all systems being managed.

Some virtualization platforms offer the capability to disable hardware and migrate live data from the failing hardware if certain thresholds are met.

You may need to work with other professionals in the organization on the networking and administration teams to fully understand and plan for the proper usage of these kinds of technology options.

BACKING UP AND RESTORING THE HOST CONFIGURATION

Configuration data for hosts in the cloud environment should be part of the backup plan.

You should conduct routine tests and restore hosts as part of the disaster recovery plan (DRP) to validate proper functioning of the backup system. This thought process is the same regardless of the vendor equipment being used to supply hosts to the organization and the vendor software or hardware being used to create and manage backups across the enterprise.

You need to understand what the critical configuration information is for all the infrastructure you manage and ensure that this information is being backed up consistently in line with the organization's existing backup policies. Further, ensure that this information is being integrated into, and accounted for within, the businesses continuity and disaster recovery (BCDR) plans of the enterprise.

The biggest challenge in this area is understanding the extent of your access to the hosts and the configuration management they are allowed to do as a result. This discussion is typically framed with two important capabilities:

- **Control:** The ability to decide, with high confidence, who and what is allowed to access consumer data and programs and the ability to perform actions (such as erasing data or disconnecting a network) with high confidence both that the actions have been taken and that no additional actions were taken that would subvert the consumer's intent. (For example, a consumer request to erase a data object should not be subverted by the silent generation of a copy.)

- **Visibility:** The ability to monitor, with high confidence, the status of a consumer's data and programs and how consumer data and programs are being accessed by others.

The extent, however, to which consumers may need to relinquish control or visibility depends on a number of factors, including physical possession and the ability to configure (with high confidence) protective access boundary mechanisms around a consumer's computing resources. This is driven by the choice of both deployment model and service model, as has been discussed previously.

IMPLEMENTING NETWORK SECURITY CONTROLS: DEFENSE IN DEPTH

The traditional model of defense in depth, which requires a design thought process that seeks to build mutually reinforcing layers of protective systems and policies to manage them, should be considered as a baseline. Using a defense-in-depth strategy to drive design for the security architecture of cloud-based systems makes it necessary to examine each layer's objectives and to understand the impact of the choices being made as the model is assembled.

Firewalls

A firewall is a software- or hardware-based network security system that controls the incoming and outgoing network traffic based on an applied rule set. A firewall establishes a barrier between a trusted, secure internal network and another network (such as the Internet) that is not assumed to be secure and trusted. The ability to use a host-based firewall is not unique to a cloud environment. Every major OS ships with some form of host-based firewall natively available or with the capability to add one if needed. The issue is not if to use, but rather where to use.

Host-Based Software Firewalls

Traditional host-based software firewalls exist for all the major virtualization platforms. These firewalls can be configured through either a command line or a graphical interface and are designed to be used to protect the host directly and the VMs running on the hosts indirectly. This approach may work well for a small network with few hosts and VMs configured to run in a private cloud, but it is not as effective for a large enterprise network with hundreds of hosts and thousands of VMs running in a hybrid cloud. The use of additional hardware-based firewalls, external to the cloud infrastructure but designed to provide protection for it, needs to be considered for deployment in this case. The use of cloud-based firewalls to provide enterprise-grade protection may also be considered.

Configuration of Ports Through the Firewall

In addition to the standard TCP and user datagram protocol (UDP) ports typically opened on a firewall, you can configure other ports depending on your needs. Supported services and management agents that are required to operate the host are described in a rule set configuration file. The file contains firewall rules and lists each rule's relationship with ports and protocols.

Layered Security

Layered security is the key to protecting any size network, and for most companies that means deploying IDSs and IPSs. When it comes to IPS and IDS, it's not a question of which technology to add to your security infrastructure; both are required for maximum protection against malicious traffic.

IDS

An IDS device is passive, watching packets of data traverse the network from a monitoring port, comparing the traffic to configured rules, and setting off an alarm if it detects anything suspicious. An IDS can detect several types of malicious traffic that would slip by a typical firewall, including network attacks against services, data-driven attacks on applications, host-based attacks such as unauthorized logins, and malware such as viruses, Trojan horses, and worms. Most IDS products use several methods to detect threats, usually signature-based detection, anomaly-based detection, and stateful protocol analysis.

The IDS engine records the incidents that are logged by the IDS sensors in a database and generates alerts to send to the network administrator. Because the IDS gives deep visibility into network activity, it can also be used to pinpoint problems with an organization's security policy, document existing threats, and discourage users from violating an organization's security policy.

The primary complaint with IDS is the number of false positives the technology is prone to spitting out—some legitimate traffic is inevitably tagged as bad. The trick is tuning the device to maximize its accuracy in recognizing true threats while minimizing the number of false positives. These devices should be regularly tuned as new threats are discovered and the network structure is altered. As the technology has matured in the past several years, it has gotten better at weeding out false positives.

An IDS can be host based or network based.

Network Intrusion Detection Systems

Network intrusion detection systems (NIDSs) are placed at a strategic point within the network to monitor traffic to and from all devices on the network. They perform analysis for traffic passing across the entire subnet, work in a promiscuous mode, and match the traffic that is passed on the subnets to the library of known attacks. Once the attack is identified or abnormal behavior is sensed, an alert can be sent to the administrator.

One example of the use of a NIDS would be installing it on the subnet where firewalls are located to see if someone is trying to break into the firewall (*Figure 5.4*). Ideally, you would scan all inbound and outbound traffic; however, doing so might create a bottleneck that impairs the overall speed of the network.

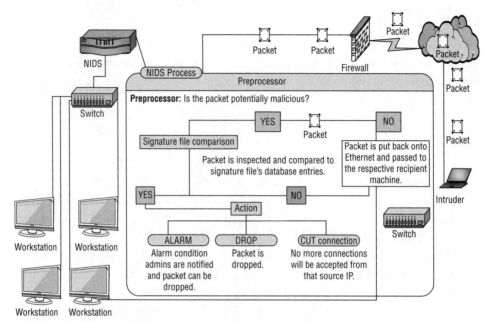

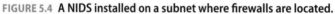

FIGURE 5.4 **A NIDS installed on a subnet where firewalls are located.**

Host Intrusion Detection Systems

Host intrusion detection systems (HIDSs) run on individual hosts or devices on the network. A HIDS monitors the inbound and outbound packets from the device only and alerts the user or administrator if suspicious activity is detected. It takes a snapshot of existing system files and matches it to the previous snapshot. If the critical system files were modified or deleted, the alert is sent to the administrator to investigate. An example of HIDS usage can be seen on mission-critical machines, which are not expected to change their configurations.

IPS

An IPS has all the features of a good IDS but can also stop malicious traffic from invading the enterprise. Unlike an IDS, an IPS sits inline with traffic flows on a network, actively shutting down attempted attacks as they are sent over the wire. It can stop the attack by terminating the network connection or user session originating the attack by blocking access to the target from the user account, IP address, or other attribute associated with that attacker or by blocking all access to the targeted host, service, or application (*Figure 5.5*).

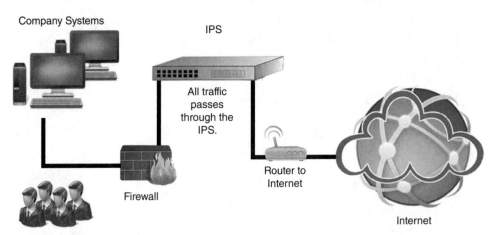

Company Systems

IPS

All traffic passes through the IPS.

Firewall

Company Employees

Router to Internet

Internet

FIGURE 5.5 **All traffic passes through the IPS.**

In addition, an IPS can respond to a detected threat in two other ways:

- It can reconfigure other security controls, such as a firewall or router, to block an attack; some IPS devices can even apply patches if the host has particular vulnerabilities.

- Some IPSs can remove the malicious contents of an attack to mitigate the packets, perhaps deleting an infected attachment from an email before forwarding the email to the user.

Combined IDS and IPS

You need to be familiar with IDSs and IPSs to ensure you use the best technology to secure the cloud environment. Be sure to consider combining the IDS and IPS into a single architecture (*Figure 5.6*).

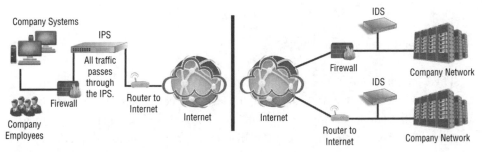

Company Systems

IPS

All traffic passes through the IPS.

Firewall

Company Employees

Router to Internet

Internet

Internet

Firewall

Company Network

IDS

IDS

Router to Internet

Company Network

FIGURE 5.6 **Combined IPS and IDS.**

Different virtualization platforms offer different levels of visibility of intra-VM communications. In some cases, there may be little or no visibility of the network communications of VMs on the same host.

You should fully understand the capabilities of the virtualization platform to validate that all monitoring requirements are met.

Virtual Machine Introspection

Virtual Machine Introspection (VMI) allows for agentless retrieval of the guest OS state, such as the list of running processes, active networking connections, and opening files. VMI can be used to perform external monitoring of the VM by security applications such as an IDS or an IPS. This monitoring is widely used for malware analysis, memory forensics, and process monitoring.

Utilizing Honeypots

A honeypot is used to detect, deflect, or in some manner counteract attempts at unauthorized use of information systems. Generally, a honeypot consists of a computer, data, or a network site that appears to be part of a network but is actually isolated and monitored and that seems to contain information or a resource of value to attackers (*Figure 5.7*).

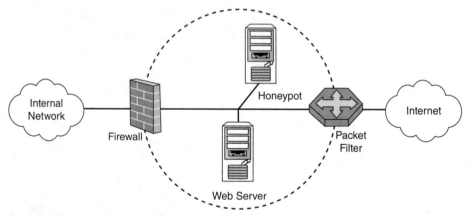

FIGURE 5.7 **Typical setup of a honeypot.**

There are some risks associated with deploying honeypots in the enterprise. The CCSP needs to ensure that he understands the legal and compliance issues that may be associated with the use of a honeypot. Honeypots should be segmented from the production network to ensure that any potential activity they generate cannot affect other systems. Honeynets are an extension of the honeypot, grouping multiple honeypot systems to form a network that is used in the same manner as the honeypot, but with more scalability and functionality.

Conducting Vulnerability Assessments

During a vulnerability assessment, the cloud environment is tested for known vulnerabilities. Detected vulnerabilities are not exploited during a vulnerability assessment (nondestructive testing) and may require further validation to detect false positives.

Conduct routine vulnerability assessments and have a process to track, resolve, or remediate detected vulnerabilities. The specifics of the processes should be governed by the nature of the regulatory requirements and compliance issues to be addressed.

Different levels of testing need to be conducted based on the type of data stored. For example, if medical information is stored, you should conduct checks for compliance with HIPAA.

All vulnerability data should be securely stored, with appropriate access controls applied and version and change control tracking turned on. The vulnerability data should be limited in circulation to only those authorized parties requiring access. Customers may request proof of vulnerability scanning and may also request the results. The CSP should define a clear policy on the disclosure of vulnerabilities, along with remediation stages or timelines. Work with the CSP to ensure that all relevant policies and agreements are in place and clearly documented as part of the decision to host with the provider.

You should also conduct external vulnerability assessments to validate internal assessments.

There are various vulnerability assessment tools, including cloud-based tools that require no additional software installation to deploy and use. CCSPs should ensure that they are familiar with whatever tools they are going to use and manage, as well as the tools that the CSP may be using. If a third-party vendor will be used to validate internal assessment findings through an independent assessment and audit, the CCSP needs to understand the tools used by the vendor as well.

Log Capture and Log Management

According to NIST SP 800-92, a log is a record of the events occurring within an organization's systems and networks. Logs are composed of log entries; each entry contains information related to a specific event that has occurred in a system or network. Many logs in an organization contain records related to computer security. These computer security logs are generated by many sources, including security software, such as antivirus software, firewalls, and intrusion detection and prevention systems; OSs on servers, workstations, and networking equipment; and applications.[17]

Log data should be protected, with consideration given to the external storage of log data. It should also be part of the backup recovery plan and DRP of the organization. As a CCSP, it is your responsibility to ensure that proper log management takes place.

The type of log data collected depends on the type of service provided. For example, with IaaS, the CCSP does not typically collect or have access to the log data of the VMs; the collection of log data is the customer's responsibility. In a PaaS or SaaS environment, the CCSP may collect application- or OS-level log data.

NIST SP 800-92 offers the following recommendations that should help you facilitate more efficient and effective log management for the enterprise:

- Organizations should establish policies and procedures for log management. To establish and maintain successful log management activities, an organization should take these actions:

  - Develop standard processes for performing log management.

  - Define its logging requirements and goals as part of the planning process.

  - Develop policies that clearly define mandatory requirements and suggested recommendations for log management activities, including log generation, transmission, storage, analysis, and disposal.

  - Ensure that related policies and procedures incorporate and support the log management requirements and recommendations.

  The organization's management should provide the necessary support for the efforts involving log management planning, policy, and procedures development.

  The organization's policies and procedures should also address the preservation of original logs. Many organizations send copies of network traffic logs to centralized devices. They also use tools that analyze and interpret network traffic. When logs may be needed as evidence, organizations may want to acquire copies of the original log files, the centralized log files, and interpreted log data in case there are questions about the fidelity of the copying and interpretation processes. Retaining logs for evidence may involve the use of different forms of storage and different processes, such as additional restrictions on access to the records.

- Organizations should prioritize log management appropriately throughout the organization. After an organization defines its requirements and goals for the log management process, it should prioritize the requirements and goals based on the perceived reduction of risk and the expected time and resources needed to perform log management functions.

- Organizations should create and maintain a log management infrastructure. A log management infrastructure consists of the hardware, software, networks, and media used to generate, transmit, store, analyze, and dispose of log data.

  After establishing an initial log management policy and identifying roles and responsibilities, an organization should develop one or more log management infrastructures that effectively support the policy and roles.

  Following are major factors to consider in the design:

  - Volume of log data to be processed

  - Network bandwidth

- Online and offline data storage
- Security requirements for the data
- Time and resources needed for staff to analyze the logs

- Organizations should provide proper support for all staff with log management responsibilities.
- Organizations should establish standard log management operational processes. The major log management operational processes typically include configuring log sources, performing log analysis, initiating responses to identified events, and managing long-term storage. Administrators have other responsibilities as well, such as the following:
  - Monitoring the logging status of all log sources
  - Monitoring log rotation and archival processes
  - Checking for upgrades and patches to logging software and acquiring, testing, and deploying them
  - Ensuring that each logging host's clock is synced to a common time source
  - Reconfiguring logging as needed based on policy changes, technology changes, and other factors
  - Documenting and reporting anomalies in log settings, configurations, and processes

Using Security Information and Event Management

Security information and event management (SIEM) is the centralized collection and monitoring of security and event logs from different systems. SIEM allows for the correlation of different events and early detection of attacks.

A SIEM system can be set up locally or hosted in an external cloud-based environment. A SIEM system can support early detection of these events.

- A locally hosted SIEM system offers easy access and lower risk of external disclosure.
- An external SIEM system may prevent tampering of data by an attacker.

SIEM systems are also beneficial because they map to and support the implementation of the Critical Controls for Effective Cyber-Defense. The Critical Controls for Effective Cyber-Defense (the Controls) are a recommended set of actions for cyber-defense that provide specific and actionable ways to stop today's most pervasive attacks. They were developed and are maintained by a consortium of hundreds of security experts from across the public and private sectors under the guidance of the Center for Internet Security (CIS) and SANS. An underlying theme of the controls is support for large-scale, standards-based security automation for the management of cyber defenses.[18] See Table 5.5.

TABLE 5.5 **Sample Controls and Effective Mapping to a SIEM Solution**

CRITICAL CONTROL	RELATIONSHIP TO SIEM TOOLS
Critical Control 1: Inventory of Authorized and Unauthorized Devices	SIEM should be used as the inventory database of authorized asset information. SIEMs can use the awareness of asset information (location, governing regulations, data criticality, and so on) to detect and prioritize threats.
Critical Control 2: Inventory of Authorized and Unauthorized Software	SIEM should be used as the inventory database of authorized software products for correlation with network and application activity.
Critical Control 3: Secure Configurations for Hardware and Software on Laptops, Workstations, and Servers	If an automated device-scanning tool discovers a misconfigured network system during a common configuration enumeration (CCE) scan, that misconfiguration should be reported to the SIEM as a central source for these alerts. This helps with troubleshooting incidents as well as improving the overall security posture.
Critical Control 10: Secure Configurations for Network Devices Such as Firewalls, Routers, and Switches	Any misconfiguration on network devices should be reported to the SIEM for consolidated analysis.
Critical Control 12: Controlled Use of Administrative Privileges	When the principles of this control are not met (such as an administrator running a web browser or unnecessary use of administrator accounts), SIEM can correlate access logs to detect the violation and generate an alert.
Critical Control 13: Boundary Defense	Network rule violations, such as CCE discoveries, should also be reported to one central source (a SIEM) for correlation with authorized inventory data stored in the SIEM solution.

DEVELOPING A MANAGEMENT PLAN

In partnership with the CSP, you need to have a detailed understanding of the management operation of the cloud environment. As complex networked systems, clouds face traditional computer and network security issues such as AIC. By imposing uniform management practices, clouds may be able to improve on some security update and response issues.

Clouds, however, also have the potential to aggregate an unprecedented quantity and variety of customer data in cloud data centers. This potential vulnerability requires a high degree of confidence and transparency that the CSP can keep customer data isolated and protected.

Also, cloud users and administrators rely heavily on web browsers, so browser security failures can lead to cloud security breaches. The privacy and security of cloud computing depend primarily on whether the CSP has implemented robust security controls and a sound privacy policy desired by their customers, the visibility that customers have into its performance, and how well it is managed.

Maintenance

When considering management-related activities and the need to control and organize them to ensure accuracy and impact, you need to think about the impact of change. It is important to schedule system repair and maintenance, as well as customer notifications, to ensure that they do not disrupt the organization's systems. When scheduling maintenance, the CSP needs to ensure adequate resources are available to meet expected demand and SLA requirements. You should make sure that appropriate change-management procedures are implemented and followed for all systems and that scheduling and notifications are communicated effectively to all parties that will potentially be affected by the work. Consider using automated system tools that send out messages.

Traditionally, a host system is placed into maintenance mode before starting any work on it that requires system downtime, rebooting, or disruption of services. For the host to be placed into maintenance mode, the VMs currently running on it have to be powered off or moved to another host. The use of automated solutions such as workflow or tasks to place a host into maintenance mode is supported by all virtualization vendors and is something that you should be aware of.

Regardless of whether the decision to enter maintenance mode is a manual or an automated one, ensure that all appropriate security protections and safeguards continue to apply to all hosts while in maintenance mode and to all VMs while they are being moved and managed on alternate hosts as a result of maintenance mode activities being performed on their primary host.

Orchestration

When considering management-related activities and the need to control and organize them to ensure accuracy and impact, you need to think about the effect of automation. Most virtualization platforms automate the orchestration of system resources, so little human intervention is required. The goal of cloud orchestration is to automate the configuration, coordination, and management of software and software interactions. The process involves automating the workflows required for service delivery. Tasks involved include managing server runtimes and directing the flow of processes among applications. The orchestration capabilities of the virtualization platforms should meet the SLA requirements of the CSP.

BUILDING A LOGICAL INFRASTRUCTURE FOR CLOUD ENVIRONMENTS

The logical design of the cloud environment should include redundant resources, meet the requirements for anticipated customer loading, and embrace the secure configuration of hardware and guest virtualization tools.

Logical Design

Logical design is the part of the design phase of the software development lifecycle in which all functional features of the system chosen for development in analysis are described independently of any computer platform.

The following is true about the logical design for a network:

- It lacks specific details such as technologies and standards while focusing on the needs at a general level.

- It communicates with abstract concepts, such as a network, router, or workstation, without specifying concrete details.

Abstractions for complex systems, such as network designs, are important because they simplify the problem space so humans can manage it. An example of a network abstraction is a WAN, which carries data between remote locations. To understand a WAN, you do not need to understand the physics behind fiber-optic data communication, although WAN traffic may be carried over optical fiber, satellite, or copper wire. Someone specifying the need for a WAN connection on a logical network diagram can understand the concept of a WAN connection without understanding the detailed technical specifics behind it.

Logical designs are often described using terms from the customer's business vocabulary. Locations, processes, and roles from the business domain can be included in a logical design. An important aspect of a logical network design is that it is part of the requirements set for a solution to a customer problem.

Physical Design

The basic idea of physical design is that it communicates decisions about the hardware used to deliver a system.

The following is true about a physical network design:

- It is created from a logical network design.
- It often expands elements found in a logical design.

For instance, a WAN connection on a logical design diagram can be shown as a line between two buildings. When transformed into a physical design, that single line can expand into the connection, routers, and other equipment at each end of the connection. The actual connection media might be shown on a physical design, along with manufacturers and other qualities of the network implementation.

Secure Configuration of Hardware-Specific Requirements

The support that different hardware provides for a variety of virtualization technologies varies. Use the hardware that best supports the chosen virtualization platform. Incorrect BIOS settings may degrade performance, so follow the vendor-recommended guidance for the configuration of settings.

For instance, if you are using VMware's distributed power management (DPM) technology, you would need to turn off any power management settings in the host BIOS because they could interfere with the proper operation of DPM. Be aware of the requirements for secure host configuration based on the vendor platforms being used in the enterprise.

Storage Controllers Configuration

The following should be considered when configuring storage controllers:

1. Turn off all unnecessary services, such as web interfaces and management services that will not be needed or used.
2. Validate that the controllers can meet the estimated traffic load based on vendor specifications and testing (1Gbps | 10Gbps | 16Gbps | 40Gbps).
3. Deploy a redundant failover configuration such as a NIC team.
4. Consider deploying a multipath solution.
5. Change default administrative passwords for configuration and management access to the controller.

Note that specific settings vary by vendor.

Networking Models

The two networking models that should be considered are traditional and converged.

Traditional Networking Model

The traditional model is a layered approach with physical switches at the top layer and logical separation at the hypervisor level. This model allows for the use of traditional network security tools. There may be some limitation on the visibility of network segments between VMs.

Converged Networking Model

The converged model is optimized for cloud deployments and utilizes standard perimeter protection measures. The underlying storage and IP networks are converged to maximize the benefits for a cloud workload. This method facilitates the use of virtualized security appliances for network protection. You can think of a converged network model as being a super network, one that is capable of carrying a combination of data, voice, and video traffic across a single network that is optimized for performance.

RUNNING A LOGICAL INFRASTRUCTURE FOR CLOUD ENVIRONMENTS

There are several considerations for the operation and management of a cloud infrastructure. A secure network configuration assists in isolating customer data and helps prevent or mitigate denial-of-service (DoS) attacks. Numerous key methods are widely used to implement network security controls in a cloud environment, including physical devices, converged appliances, and virtual appliances.

You need to be familiar with standard best practices for secure network design, such as defense in depth, as well as the design considerations specific to the network topologies you may be managing, such as single tenant versus multitenant hosting systems. Further, you need to be familiar with the vendor-specific recommendations and requirements of the hosting platforms they support.

Building a Secure Network Configuration

The information in this section is merely a high-level summary of the functionality of the technology being discussed. Please refer to the "Running a Physical Infrastructure for Cloud Environments" section of this domain, earlier in this chapter, for specific details as needed when reviewing this material.

- **VLANs:** Allow for the logical isolation of hosts on a network. In a cloud environment, VLANs can be utilized to isolate the management network, storage network, and customer networks. VLANs can also be used to separate customer data.

- **TLS:** Allows for the encryption of data in transit between hosts. Implementation of TLS for internal networks prevents the sniffing of traffic by a malicious user. A TLS VPN is one method to allow for remote access to the cloud environment.

- **DNS:** DNS servers should be locked down. They should only offer required services and utilize domain name system security extensions (DNSSEC) when feasible. DNSSEC is a set of DNS extensions that provide authentication, integrity, and authenticated DOS for DNS data. Zone transfers should be disabled. If an attacker comprises DNS, he may be able to hijack or reroute data.

- **IPSec:** IPSec VPN is one method to remotely access the cloud environment. If an IPSec VPN is utilized, IP whitelisting, only allowing approved IP addresses, is considered a best practice for access. Two-factor authentication can also be used to enhance security.

OS Hardening via Application Baseline

The concept of using a baseline, which is a preconfigured group of settings, to secure, or harden, a machine is a common practice. The baseline should be configured to allow only the minimum services and software that are required to ensure that the system is able to perform as needed. A baseline configuration should be established for each OS and the virtualization platform in use. The baseline should be designed to meet the most stringent customer requirement. There are numerous sources for recommended baselines. By establishing a baseline and continuously monitoring for compliance, the provider can detect any deviations from the baseline.

Capturing a Baseline

The CCSP should consider the items outlined next as the bare minimum required to establish a functional baseline for use in the enterprise. There may be other procedures that would be engaged in at various points, based on specific policy or regulatory requirements pertinent to a certain organization. If needed, the CCSP can refer to many sources of guidance on the methodology for creating a baseline.[19]

- A clean installation of the target OS must be performed (physical or virtual).

- All nonessential services should be stopped and set to disabled to ensure that they do not run.

- All nonessential software should be removed from the system.

- All required security patches should be downloaded and installed from the appropriate vendor repository.

- All required configuration of the host OS should be accomplished per the requirements of the baseline being created.

- The OS baseline should be audited to ensure that all required items have been configured properly.

- Full documentation should be created, captured, and stored for the baseline being created.

- An image of the OS baseline should be captured and stored for future deployment. This image should be placed under change management control and have appropriate access controls applied.

- The baseline OS image should also be placed under the configuration management (CM) system and cataloged as a CI.

- The baseline OS image should be updated on a documented schedule for security patches and any additional required configuration updates as needed.

Baseline Configuration by Platform

There are several differences between Windows, Linux, and VMware configurations. The following sections examine them.

Windows

Microsoft provides several tools to measure the security baseline of a Windows system.

- The use of a toolset such as the Windows Server Update Service (WSUS) makes it possible to perform patch management on a Windows host and monitor for compliance with a preconfigured baseline.

- The Microsoft Deployment Toolkit (MDT), either as a standalone toolset or integrated into the System Center Configuration Manager (SCCM) product, allows you to create, manage, and deploy one or more Microsoft Windows Server OS baseline images.

- One or more of the Best Practice Analyzers (BPAs) that Microsoft makes available should also be considered.

Linux

The actual Linux distribution in use plays a large part in helping to determine what the baseline deployment will look like. The security features of each Linux distribution should be considered, and the one that best meets the organization's security requirements should be used. However, you still should be familiar with the recommended best practices for Linux baseline security.

VMware

VMware vSphere has built-in tools that allow the user to build custom baselines for their specific deployments. These tools range from host and storage profiles, which force configuration of an ESXi host to mirror a set of preconfigured baseline options, to the VMware Update Manager (VUM) tool, which allows for the updating of one or more ESXi hosts with the latest VMware security patches to allow updates to the VMs running on the host. VUM can be used to monitor compliance with a preconfigured baseline.

Availability of a Guest OS

The mechanisms available to the CCSP to ensure the availability of the guest OSs running on a host are varied. Redundant system hardware can be used to avert system outages due to hardware failure. Backup power supplies and generators can be used to ensure that the hosts have power, even if the electricity is cut off for a period of time. In addition, technologies such as HA and fault tolerance are important to consider. HA should be used when the goal is to minimize the impact of system downtime. Fault tolerance should be used when the goal is to eliminate system downtime as a threat to system availability altogether.

HA

Different customers in the cloud environment have different availability requirements. These can include things such as live recovery and automatic migration if the underlying host goes down.

Every cloud vendor has its own specific toolsets available to provide for HA on its platform. It is your responsibility to understand the vendor's requirements and capabilities within the HA area and to ensure these are documented properly as part of the DRP/BCP processes within the organization.

Fault Tolerance

Network components, storage arrays, and servers with built-in fault-tolerance capabilities should be utilized. In addition, if there is a fault-tolerance solution that a vendor makes available via software implementation that is appropriately scaled for the level of fault tolerance required by the guest OS, consider it as well.

MANAGING THE LOGICAL INFRASTRUCTURE FOR CLOUD ENVIRONMENTS

The logical design of the cloud infrastructure should include measures to limit remote access to only those authorized to access resources, provide the capability to monitor the cloud infrastructure, and allow for the remediation of systems in the cloud environment, as well as the backup and restoring of a guest OS.

Access Control for Remote Access

To support globally distributed data centers and secure cloud computing environments, enterprises must provide remote access to employees and third-party personnel with whom they have contracted. This includes field technicians, IT and help desk support, and many others.

Following are key questions that enterprises should be asking themselves:

- Do you trust the person connecting to provide access into your core systems?

- Are you replacing credentials immediately after a remote vendor has logged in?

A cloud remote access solution should be capable of providing secure anywhere access and extranet capabilities for authorized remote users. The service should utilize SSL/TLS as a secure transport mechanism and require no software clients to be deployed on mobile and remote users' Internet-enabled devices.

One of the fundamental benefits of cloud is the reduction of the attack surface. There are no open ports. As an example, Citrix Online runs the popular GoToMyPC.com service, a remote-access service that uses frequent polling to the company's cloud servers as a means to pass data back to a host computer. There are no inbound connections to the host computer; instead, GoToMyPC pulls data from the cloud. The result is that the attackable parts of the service—any open ports—are eliminated, and the attack surface is reduced to a centrally managed hub that can be more easily secured and monitored.

Key benefits of a remote access solution for the cloud are many:

- Secure access without exposing the privileged credential to the end user, eliminating the risk of credential exploitation or key logging.

- Accountability of who is accessing the data center remotely with a tamper-proof audit trail.

- Session control over who can access, enforcement of workflows such as managerial approval, ticketing integration, session duration limitation, and automatic termination when idle.

- Real-time monitoring to view privileged activities as they are happening or as a recorded playback for forensic analysis. Sessions can be remotely terminated or intervened with when necessary for more efficient and secure IT compliance and cyber security operations.

- Secure isolation between the remote user's desktop and the target system they are connecting to so that any potential malware does not spread to the target systems.

OS Baseline Compliance Monitoring and Remediation

Tools should be in place to monitor the OS baselines of systems in the cloud environment. When differences are detected, there should be a process for root cause determination and remediation.

You need to understand the toolsets available for use based on the vendor platforms being managed. Both Microsoft and VMware have their own built-in OS baseline compliance monitoring and remediation solutions, as has been discussed previously. (VMware has host and storage profiles and VUM, and Microsoft has WSUS.) There are also third-party toolsets available for use that you may consider, depending on a variety of circumstances.

Regardless of product deployed, the ultimate goal should be to ensure that real-time or near real-time monitoring of OS configuration and baseline compliance is taking place within the cloud. In addition, the monitoring data needs to be centrally managed and stored for audit and change-management purposes.

Any changes made under remediation should be thoroughly documented and submitted to a change-management process for approval. Once approved, the changes being implemented need to be managed through a release- and deployment-management process that is tied directly into configuration and availability management processes to ensure that all changes are managed through a complete lifecycle within the enterprise.

Backing Up and Restoring the Guest OS Configuration

As a CCSP, you are responsible for ensuring that the appropriate backup and restore capabilities for hosts as well as for the guest OSs running on top of them are set up and maintained within the enterprise's cloud infrastructure. The choices available for built-in tools vary by vendor platform being supported, but all vendors provide some form of built-in toolsets for backup and restore of the host configurations and the guest OSs. This is typically achieved through a combination of profiles, as well as cloning or templates, in addition to some form of a backup solution.

Whether the use of a third-party tool is used to provide the backup and restoration capability or not will have to be decided based on referencing the SLAs that the customer has in place as well as the capabilities of the built-in tools that are available. In addition, it's important to reference the existing BCDR solutions in place and ensure coordination with the plans and systems.

IMPLEMENTATION OF NETWORK SECURITY CONTROLS

The implementation of network security controls was discussed extensively earlier in this book. You need to be able to follow and implement best practices for all security controls. With regard to network-based controls, consider the following general guidelines:

- Defense in depth
- VLANs
- Access controls
- Secure protocol usage (that is, IPSec and TLS)
- IDS/IPS system deployments
- Firewalls
- Honeypots/honeynets
- Separation of traffic flows within the host from the guests via use of separate virtual switches dedicated to specific traffic
- Zoning and masking of storage traffic
- Deployment of virtual security infrastructure specifically designed to secure and monitor virtual networks (that is, VMware's vCloud Networking and Security [vCNS] or NSX products)

Log Capture and Analysis

Log data needs to be collected and analyzed both for the hosts as well as for the guest running on top of the hosts. Various tools allow you to collect and consolidate log data.

Centralization and offsite storage of log data can prevent tampering provided the appropriate access controls and monitoring systems are put in place.

You are responsible for understanding the needs of the organization with regard to log capture and analysis. You are also responsible for ensuring that the necessary toolsets and solutions are implemented so that information can be managed using best practices and standards.

Management Plan Implementation Through the Management Plane

You must develop a detailed management plan for the cloud environment. You are ultimately accountable for the security architecture and resiliency of the systems you design, implement, and manage.

Ensure due diligence and due care are exercised in the design and implementation of all aspects of the enterprise cloud security architecture.

Further, keep abreast of changes in the vendor's offerings that can influence the choices being made or considered with regard to management capabilities and approaches for the cloud.

Stay informed about issues and threats that could impact the secure operation and management of the cloud infrastructure. Also be aware of mitigation techniques and vendor recommendations that may need to be applied or implemented within the cloud infrastructure.

Ensuring Compliance with Regulations and Controls

Effective contracting for cloud services reduces the risk of vendor lock-in, improves portability, and encourages competition. Establishing explicit, comprehensive SLAs for security, continuity of operations, and service quality is key for any organization.

There are a variety of compliance regimes, and the provider should clearly delineate which it supports and which it does not. Compliance responsibilities of the provider and the customer should be clearly delineated in contracts and SLAs. The Cloud Security Alliance Cloud Controls Matrix (CCA CCM) provides a good list of controls required by different compliance bodies. In many cases, controls from one carry over to those of another.

To ensure all compliance and regulatory requirements can be met, consider the provider and customers' geographic locations. Involving the organization's legal team from the beginning when designing the cloud environment keeps the project on track and focused on the necessary compliance concerns at the appropriate times in the project cycle.

Keep in mind that there is probably a long history of project-driven compliance in one form or another within the enterprise. The challenge is often not the need to create an awareness around the importance of compliance overall, or even compliance specific to a certain business need, customer segment, or service offering. Rather, the challenge is to translate that awareness and historical knowledge to the cloud with the appropriate context.

Often, certain agreements focusing on premise service provisioning may be in place but not structured appropriately to encompass a full cloud services solution. The same may be true with some of the existing outsource agreements that may be in place. In general, these agreements may be providing an acceptable level of service to internal customers or allow for the acquisition of a service from an external third party but may not be structured appropriately for a full-blown cloud service to be immediately spun up on top of them.

It is imperative that you clearly identify your customer's needs and ensure that IT and the business are aligned to support the provisioning of services and products that provide value to the customer in a secure and compliant manner.

USING AN ITSM SOLUTION

The use of an ITSM solution to drive and coordinate communication may be useful. ITSM is needed for the cloud because the cloud is a remote environment that requires management and oversight to ensure alignment between IT and business. An ITSM solution makes it possible to do the following:

- Ensure portfolio management, demand management, and financial management are all working together for efficient service delivery to customers and effective charging for services if appropriate

- Involve all the people and systems necessary to create alignment and ultimately success

Look to the organization's policies and procedures for specific guidance on the mechanisms and methodologies for communication that are acceptable. More broadly, there are many additional resources to leverage as needed, depending on circumstance.

CONSIDERATIONS FOR SHADOW IT

Shadow IT is often defined as money spent on technology to acquire services without the IT department's dollars or knowledge. On March 26, 2015, a survey based on research from Canopy, the Atos cloud, was released, revealing that 60 percent of chief information officers (CIOs) said that shadow IT spending was an estimated €13 million in their organizations in 2014, and that figure was expected to grow in subsequent years. This trend highlights the need for greater IT governance to be deployed in organizations to support digital transformation initiatives.

A review of organizations' shadow IT expenditures showed that backup needs were the primary driver, with 44 percent of respondents stating their department had invested in backup in the previous year. Other main areas of shadow IT spending included file sharing software (36 percent) and archiving data (33 percent).

"Surprisingly, shadow IT is being spent on back-office functions—areas which for most businesses should be centralized and carefully managed by the IT department," said Philippe Llorens, CEO of Canopy. "As businesses embrace digital, it is essential that the IT department not only provides the IT infrastructure and services to enable and support the digital transformation but also the governance model to maximize cost efficiencies, manage risk, and provide the business with secure IT services."[20]

According to the survey, the biggest shadow IT spenders were U.S. companies, outlaying a huge €26 million per company as a proportion of their 2014 global IT budget—more than double that of companies in the UK and France that admitted to spending €11 million and €10 million, respectively. Firms in Germany estimated spending over four times less on shadow IT than U.S. companies. The findings demonstrate international firms' challenge to manage employees' varied attitudes to shadow IT spending across countries.

OPERATIONS MANAGEMENT

There are many aspects and processes of operations that need to be managed, and they often relate to each other. Some of these include the following:

- Information security management
- Configuration management
- Change management
- Incident management
- Problem management
- Release and deployment management
- Service-level management
- Availability management
- Capacity management
- Business continuity management (BCM)
- Continual service improvement management

The following sections explore each of these types of management and then look more closely at how they relate to each other.

Information Security Management

Organizations should have a documented and operational information security management plan that generally covers the following areas:

- Security management
- Security policy
- Information security organization
- Asset management
- Human resources security
- Physical and environmental security
- Communications and operations management
- Access control
- Information systems acquisition, development, and maintenance
- Provider and customer responsibilities

Configuration Management

Configuration management aims to maintain information about CIs required to deliver an IT service, including their relationships. As mentioned in the "Release and Deployment Management" section, there are lateral ties between many of the management areas discussed in this section. All these lateral connections are extremely important because they form the basis for the mutually reinforcing web that is created to support the proper documentation and operation of the cloud infrastructure.

In the case of configuration management, the specific ties to change management and availability management are important to mention.

You should develop a configuration-management process for the cloud infrastructure. The process should include policies and procedures for each of the following:

- The development and implementation of new configurations that should apply to the hardware and software configurations of the cloud environment
- Quality evaluation of configuration changes and compliance with established security baselines
- Changing systems, including testing and deployment procedures, that should include adequate oversight of all configuration changes
- The prevention of any unauthorized changes in system configurations

Change Management

Change management is an approach that allows organizations to manage and control the impact of change through a structured process. The primary goal of change management within a project-management context is to create and implement a series of processes that allow changes to the scope of a project to be formally introduced and approved.

Change-Management Objectives

Change management has several objectives:

- Respond to a customer's changing business requirements while maximizing value and reducing incidents, disruption, and rework.

- Respond to business and IT requests for change that aligns services with business needs.

- Ensure that changes are recorded and evaluated.

- Ensure that authorized changes are prioritized, planned, tested, implemented, documented, and reviewed in a controlled manner.

- Ensure that all changes to CIs are recorded in the configuration management system.

- Optimize overall business risk. It is often correct to minimize business risk, but sometimes it is appropriate to knowingly accept a risk because of the potential benefit.

Change-Management Process

You should develop or augment a change-management process for the cloud infrastructure to address any cloud-specific components or components that may not have been captured under historical processes. You may not be a change-management expert, but you do still bear responsibility for change and its impact in the organization. To ensure the best possible use of change management within the organization, attempt to partner with the project management professionals (PMPs) who exist in the enterprise to incorporate the cloud infrastructure and service offerings into an existing change-management program if possible. The existence of a project management office (PMO) is usually a strong indication of an organization's commitment to a formal change-management process that is fully developed and broadly communicated and adopted.

A change-management process focused on the cloud should include policies and procedures for each of the following:

- The development and acquisition of new infrastructure and software

- Quality evaluation of new software and compliance with established security baselines

- Changing systems, including testing and deployment procedures; they should include adequate oversight of all changes
- Preventing the unauthorized installation of software and hardware

Preventing the Unauthorized Installation of Software: Critical Security Control Implementation Example

The CCSP should be focused on all the change-management activities outlined previously and how they will be implemented for the cloud within the framework of the enterprise architecture.

At this point, you may be asking yourself, "What exactly does that mean, and just how am I supposed to do that?"

Well, the topic of preventing the unauthorized installation of software will be used as an example of how to answer those questions.

Although there are many acceptable ways to effectively implement a system that prevents the unauthorized installation of software, the need to do so in a documented and auditable manner is important.

To that end, the use of the CIS/SANS Critical Security Controls provides a well-documented solution that allows the CCSP to actively manage (inventory, track, and correct) all software on the network so that only authorized software is installed and can execute and that unauthorized and unmanaged software is found and prevented from installation or execution.

CIS/SANS Critical Security Control 2: Inventory of Authorized and Unauthorized Software can be implemented using one or more of the methods explained in Table 5.6.[21]

TABLE 5.6 **CIS/SANS Critical Security Control 2**

ID #	DESCRIPTION
CSC 2-1	Application whitelisting technology that prevents execution of all software in the system not listed on the whitelist should be deployed. The whitelist may be tailored to the needs of the organization with regards to the amount of software to be allowed permission to run. When protecting systems with customized software that may be seen as difficult to whitelist, use item CSC 2-8 (isolating the custom software in a virtual OS that does not retain infections).
CSC 2-2	A list of authorized software required in the enterprise for each type of system should be created. File integrity checking tools should be used to monitor and validate that the authorized software has not been modified.
CSC 2-3	Alerts should be generated whenever regular scanning for unauthorized software discovers anything unusual on a system. Change control should be used to control any changes or installation of software to any systems on the network.

ID #	DESCRIPTION
CSC 2-4	Software inventory tools should be used throughout the organization, covering each of the OS types in use as well as the platform it is deployed onto. The version of the underlying OS as well as the applications installed on it and the version number and patch level should all be recorded.
CSC 2-5	The software and hardware asset/inventory systems must be integrated so that all devices and associated software are tracked centrally.
CSC 2-6	Dangerous file types should be closely monitored or blocked.
CSC 2-7	Systems that are evaluated as having a high risk potential associated with their deployment and use within a networked environment should be implemented as either VMs or air-gapped systems to isolate and run applications that are required for business operations.
CSC 2-8	Virtualized OSs that can be easily restored to a trusted state on a periodic basis should be used on client workstations.
CSC 2-9	Only use software that allows for the use of signed software ID tags. A software ID tag is an XML file that uniquely identifies the software, providing data for software inventory and asset management.

The CCSP needs to evaluate the nine mechanisms listed in Table 5.6 and decide which, if any, are relevant for use in the organization that she manages. Once the mechanisms have been selected, she must devise a plan to evaluate, acquire, implement, manage, monitor, and optimize the relevant technologies involved. The plan then must be submitted for approval to senior management to ensure that there is support for the recommended course of action, the allocated budget (if necessary), and the ability to ensure alignment with any relevant strategic objectives and business drivers that may be pertinent to this project.

Once senior management has approved the plan, the CCSP can engage in the various activities outlined, in the proper order, to ensure successful implementation of the plan according to the timeline specified and agreed to.

Once the plan has been successfully executed and the new systems are in place and operational, the CCSP must think about monitoring and validation to ensure that the system is compliant with any relevant security policies as well as regulatory requirements and that it is effective and operating as designed.

A critical element of this type of solution is the ability to highly automate many, if not all, of the monitoring and processes, as well as the resulting workflows that are generated when an unauthorized software installation is detected and blocked.

These objectives can be achieved as described in the following sections.

CSC 2 Effectiveness Metrics

When testing the effectiveness of the automated implementation of this control, organizations should determine the following:

- The amount of time it takes to detect new software installed on the organization's systems

- The amount of time it takes the scanning functions to alert the organization's administrators when an unauthorized application has been discovered on a system

- The amount of time it takes for an alert to be generated when a new application has been discovered on a system

- Whether the scanning function identifies the department, location, and other critical details about the unauthorized software that has been detected

CSC 2 Automation Metrics

Organizations should gather the following information to automate the collection of relevant data from these systems:

- The total number of unauthorized applications located on the organization's business systems

- The average amount of time it takes to remove unauthorized applications from the organization's business systems

- The total number of the organization's business systems that are not running whitelisting software

- The total number of applications that have been recently blocked from executing by the organization's whitelisting software

The CCSP also needs to create some sort of ongoing, periodic sampling system that allows for the testing of the effectiveness of the system deployed in its entirety. The specific approach to be used to achieve this is open to discussion, but the implemented solution should use a predetermined number of randomly sampled endpoints deployed in the production network and assess the responses generated by an unauthorized software deployment to them within a specified period of time. As a follow-up, the automated messaging and logging generated by the unauthorized deployment need to be monitored and evaluated as well. If failures are detected, these need to be logged and investigated. A failure in this case is defined as a successful deployment of the unauthorized software package to the targeted endpoint without notification being generated and sent, as well as logging of that activity taking place.

If blocking is not allowed or is unavailable, the CCSP must verify that unauthorized software is detected and results in a notification to alert the security team.

Incident Management

Incident management describes the activities of an organization to identify, analyze, and correct hazards to prevent a future reoccurrence. Within a structured organization, an incident response team (IRT) or an incident management team (IMT) typically addresses these types of incidents. These are often designated beforehand or during the event and are placed in control of the organization while the incident is dealt with to restore normal functions.

Events Versus Incidents

According to the ITIL framework, an event is defined as a change of state that has significance for the management of an IT service or other CI. The term can also be used to mean an alert or notification created by an IT service, CI, or monitoring tool. Events often require IT operations staff to take actions and lead to incidents being logged.

According to the ITIL framework, an incident is defined as an unplanned interruption to an IT service or a reduction in the quality of an IT service.

Purpose of Incident Management

Incident management has three purposes:

- Restore normal service operation as quickly as possible
- Minimize the adverse impact on business operations
- Ensure service quality and availability are maintained

Objectives of Incident Management

Incident management has five objectives:

- Ensure that standardized methods and procedures are used for efficient and prompt response, analysis, documentation of ongoing management, and reporting of incidents
- Increase visibility and communication of incidents to business and IT support staff
- Enhance business perception of IT by using a professional approach in quickly resolving and communicating incidents when they occur
- Align incident management activities with those of the business
- Maintain user satisfaction

Incident Management Plan

You should have a detailed incident management plan that includes the following:

- Definitions of an incident by service type or offering
- Customer and provider roles and responsibilities for an incident
- Incident management process from detection to resolution
- Response requirements
- Media coordination
- Legal and regulatory requirements such as data breach notification

You may also want to consider the use of an incident management tool. The incident management plan should be routinely tested and updated based on lessons learned from real and practice events.

Incident Classification

Incidents can be classified as either minor or major depending on several criteria. Work with the organization and customers to ensure that the correct criteria are used for incident identification and classification and that these criteria are well documented and understood by all parties to the system.

Incident prioritization is made up of the following items:

- Impact = Effect upon the business
- Urgency = Extent to which the resolution can bear delay
- Priority = Urgency × Impact

When these items are combined into a matrix, you have a powerful tool to help the business understand incidents and prioritize their management (*Figure 5.8*).

*Where 1 is the highest priority and 5 is the lowest

FIGURE 5.8 **The impact/urgency/priority matrix.**

Example of an Incident Management Process

Incident management should be focused on the identification, classification, investigation, and resolution of an incident, with the ultimate goal of returning the effected systems to normal as soon as possible. To manage incidents effectively, a formal incident management process should be defined and used. In *Figure 5.9*, a traditional incident management process is shown.

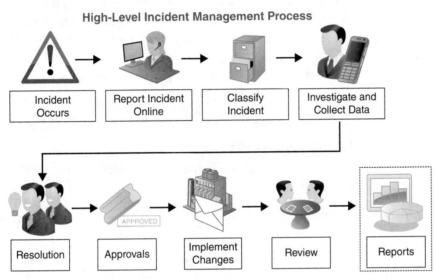

FIGURE 5.9 **Incident management process example.**

Problem Management

The objective of problem management is to minimize the impact of problems on the organization by identifying the root cause of the problem at hand. Problem management plays an important role in the detection of and providing of solutions to problems (workarounds and known errors) and prevents their reoccurrence.

- A problem is the unknown cause of one or more incidents, often identified as a result of multiple similar incidents.
- A known error is an identified root cause of a problem.
- A workaround is a temporary way of overcoming technical difficulties (that is, incidents or problems).

It's important to understand the linkage between incident and problem management. In addition, you need to ensure there is a tracking system established to track and monitor all system-related problems. The system should gather metrics to identify possible trends.

Problems can be classified as minor or major depending on several criteria. Work with the organization and the customers to ensure that the correct criteria are used for problem identification and classification and that these criteria are well documented and understood by parties to the system.

Release and Deployment Management

Release and deployment management aims to plan, schedule, and control the movement of releases to test and live environments. The primary goal of release and deployment management is to ensure that the integrity of the live environment is protected and that the correct components are released.

Following are the objectives of release and deployment management:

- Define and agree upon deployment plans
- Create and test release packages
- Ensure the integrity of release packages
- Record and track all release packages in the Definitive Media Library (DML)
- Manage stakeholders
- Check delivery of utility and warranty (utility + warranty = value in the mind of the customer)
  - Utility is the functionality offered by a product or service to meet a specific need; it's what the service does.
  - Warranty is the assurance that a product or service will meet agreed-upon requirements (SLA); it's how the service is delivered.
- Manage risks
- Ensure knowledge transfer

New software releases should be done in accordance with the configuration management plan. You should conduct security testing on all new releases prior to deployment. Release management is especially important for SaaS and PaaS providers.

You may not be directly responsible for release and deployment management and may be involved only tangentially in the process. Regardless of who is in charge, it is important that the process is tightly coupled to change management, incident and problem management, and configuration and availability management and the help desk.

Service-Level Management

Service-level management aims to negotiate agreements with various parties and to design services in accordance with the agreed-upon service-level targets. Typical negotiated agreements include the following:

- SLAs are negotiated with the customers.

- Operational-level agreements (OLAs) are SLAs negotiated between internal business units within the enterprise.

- Underpinning contracts (UCs) are external contracts negotiated between the organization and vendors or suppliers.

Ensure that policies, procedures, and tools are put in place so the organization meets all service levels as specified in their SLAs with their customers. Failure to meet SLAs can have a significant financial impact to the provider. The legal department should be involved in developing the SLA and associated policies to ensure that they are drafted correctly.

Availability Management

Availability management aims to define, analyze, plan, measure, and improve all aspects of the availability of IT services. Availability management is responsible for ensuring that all IT infrastructure, processes, tools, roles, and so on, are appropriate for the agreed-upon availability targets.

Systems should be designed to meet the availability requirements listed in all SLAs. Most virtualization platforms allow for the management of system availability and can act in the event of a system outage (that is, failover running guest OSs to a different host).

Capacity Management

Capacity management is focused on ensuring that the business IT infrastructure is adequately provisioned to deliver the agreed service-level targets in a timely and cost-effective manner. Capacity management considers all resources required to deliver IT services within the scope of the defined business requirements.

Capacity management is a critical function. The system capacity must be monitored and thresholds must be set to prevent systems from reaching an over-capacity situation.

Business Continuity Management

Business continuity management (BCM) is focused on the planning steps that businesses engage in to ensure that their mission-critical systems are able to be restored to service following a disaster or service interruption event. To focus the BCM activities correctly, a prioritized ranking or listing of systems and services must be created and maintained. This is accomplished through the use of a business impact analysis (BIA) process. The BIA is designed to identify and produce a prioritized listing of systems and services critical to the normal functioning of the business. Once the BIA has been completed, the CCSP can go about devising plans and strategies that will enable the continuation of business operations and the quick recovery from any type of disruption.

Comparing BC and BCM

It is important to understand the difference between BC and BCM:

- BC is defined as the capability of the organization to continue delivery of products or services at acceptable predefined levels following a disruptive incident. (Source: ISO 22301:2012)[22]

- BCM is defined as a holistic management process that identifies potential threats to an organization and the impacts to business operations those threats, if realized, might cause. It provides a framework for building organizational resilience with the capability of an effective response that safeguards the interests of its key stakeholders, reputation, brand, and value-creating activities. (Source: ISO 22301:2012)[23]

Continuity Management Plan

A detailed continuity management plan should include the following:

- Required capability and capacity of backup systems
- Trigger events to implement the plan
- Clearly defined roles and responsibilities by name and title
- Clearly defined continuity and recovery procedures
- Notification requirements

The plan should be tested at regular intervals.

Continual Service Improvement Management

Metrics on all services and processes should be collected and analyzed to find areas of improvement using a formal process. You can use various tools and standards to monitor performance. One example is the ITIL framework. The organization should adopt and utilize one or more of these tools.

How Management Processes Relate to Each Other

It is inevitable in operations that management processes will have an impact on each other and interrelate. The following sections explore some of the ways in which this happens.

Release and Deployment Management and Change Management

Release and deployment management need to be tied to change management because change management must approve any activities that release and deployment management will be engaging in prior to the release. In other words, change management must approve the request to carry out the release, and then deployment management can schedule and execute the release.

Release and Deployment Management Role and Incident and Problem Management

Release and deployment management is tied to incident and problem management because if anything were to go wrong with the release, incident and problem management would need to be involved to fix whatever went wrong. This is typically done by executing whatever rollback or back-out plan may have been created along with the release for just such an eventuality.

Release and Deployment Management and Configuration Management

Release and deployment management is tied to configuration management because once the release is officially live in the production environment, the existing configurations for all systems and infrastructure affected by the release have to be updated to accurately reflect their new running configurations and status within the configuration management database (CMDB).

Release and Deployment Management Is Related to Availability Management

Release and deployment management is tied to availability management because if the release were not to go as planned, any negative impacts on system availability would have to be identified, monitored, and remediated as per the existing SLAs for the services and systems affected. In addition, once the release were officially "live" in the production environment, the impact of it against the existing systems and infrastructure affected by the release would have to be monitored to accurately reflect their new running status to ensure compliance with all SLAs.

Release and Deployment Management and the Help Desk

Release and deployment management is tied to the help desk because the communication around the release and the status updates need to be centrally coordinated and managed.

Configuration Management and Availability Management

Configuration management is tied to availability management. If an existing configuration were to have negative impacts on system availability, they would have to be identified, monitored, and remediated as per the existing SLAs for the services and systems affected. In addition, any changes to existing system configurations would have to be monitored to accurately reflect their new running status to ensure compliance with all SLAs.

Configuration Management and Change Management

Configuration management must be tied to change management because change management has to approve modifications to all production systems prior to them taking place. In other words, there should never be a change that is allowed to take place to a CI in a production system unless change management has approved the change first.

Service-Level Management and Change Management

Service-level management has to be tied to change management because change management must approve changes to all SLAs as well as ensure that the legal function has a chance to review them and offer guidance and direction on the nature and language of the proposed changes prior to them taking place. In other words, there should never be a change that is allowed to take place to an SLA that governs a production system unless change management has approved the change first.

Incorporating Management Processes

There are traditional business cycles or rhythms that all businesses experience. Some are seasonal; some are cyclical based on a variety of variables. Whatever the case, be aware of these business cycles to work with capacity management as well as change, availability, incident and problem, service level and release, and deployment management to ensure that the appropriate infrastructure is always provisioned and available to meet customer demand.

An example of this is a seasonal or holiday-related spike in system capacity requirements for web-based retailers. Another example is a spike in bandwidth and capacity requirements for streaming media outlets during high-profile news or sporting events, such as the World Cup, the Olympics, and the NBA playoffs.

MANAGING RISK IN LOGICAL AND PHYSICAL INFRASTRUCTURES

Risk is a measure of the extent to which an entity is threatened by a potential circumstance or event and is typically a function of the following:

- The adverse impacts that would arise if the circumstance or event occurred
- The likelihood of occurrence

Information security risks arise from the loss of AIC of information or information systems. They reflect the potential adverse impacts to organizational operations (that is, mission, functions, image, or reputation), organizational assets, individuals, or other organizations.

THE RISK-MANAGEMENT PROCESS OVERVIEW

The risk-management process has four components:

- Framing risk
- Assessing risk
- Responding to risk
- Monitoring risk

Take a look at the four components in the risk-management process—including the risk-assessment step and the information and communications flows necessary to make the process work effectively (*Figure 5.10*).

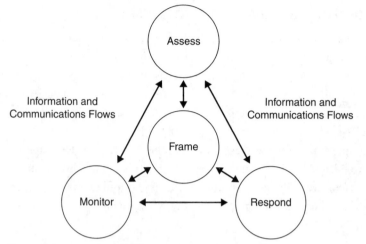

FIGURE 5.10 Four components in the risk-management process.
SOURCE: NIST Special Publication 800-39, "Managing Information Security Risk: Organization, Mission, and Information System View"

Framing Risk

Framing risk is the first step in the risk management process, which addresses how organizations describe the environment in which risk-based decisions are made. Risk framing is designed to produce a risk-management strategy intended to address how organizations assess, respond to, and monitor risk. This allows the organization to clearly articulate the risks that it needs to manage, and it establishes and delineates the boundaries for risk-based decisions within organizations.

Risk Assessment

Risk assessment is the process used to identify, estimate, and prioritize information security risks. Risk assessment is a key component of the risk management process as defined in NIST Special Publication 800-39, "Managing Information Security Risk: Organization, Mission, and Information System View."

According to NIST SP 800-39, the purpose of engaging in risk assessment is to identify the following:

- "Threats to organizations (i.e., operations, assets, or individuals) or threats directed through organizations against other organizations

- "Vulnerabilities internal and external to organizations

- "The harm (i.e., adverse impact) that may occur given the potential for threats exploiting vulnerabilities

- "The likelihood that harm will occur"[24]

Identifying these factors helps to determine risk, which includes the likelihood of harm occurring and the potential degree of harm.

Conducting a Risk Assessment

Assessing risk requires the careful analysis of threat and vulnerability information to determine the extent to which circumstances or events can adversely affect an organization and the likelihood that such circumstances or events will occur.

Organizations have the option of performing a risk assessment in one of two ways: qualitatively or quantitatively.

- **Qualitative assessments** typically employ a set of methods, principles, or rules for assessing risk based on non-numerical categories or levels (very low, low, moderate, high, or very high).

- **Quantitative assessments** typically employ a set of methods, principles, or rules for assessing risk based on the use of numbers. This type of assessment most effectively supports cost-benefit analyses of alternative risk responses or courses of action.

Qualitative Risk Assessment

Qualitative risk assessments produce valid results that are descriptive versus measurable. A qualitative risk assessment is typically conducted in the following cases:

- The risk assessors available for the organization have limited expertise in quantitative risk assessment; that is, assessors typically do not require as much experience in risk assessment when conducting a qualitative assessment.

- The timeframe to complete the risk assessment is short.

- Implementation is typically easier.

- The organization does not have a significant amount of data readily available that can assist with the risk assessment and, as a result, descriptions, estimates, and ordinal scales (such as high, medium, and low) must be used to express risk.

- The assessors and team available for the organization are long-term employees and have significant experience with the business and critical systems.

The following methods are typically used during a qualitative risk assessment:

- Management approval to conduct the assessment must be obtained prior to assigning a team and conducting the work. Management is kept apprised during the process to continue to promote support for the effort.

- Once management approval has been obtained, a risk-assessment team can be formed. Members may include staff from senior management, information security, legal or compliance, internal audit, HR, facilities and safety coordination, IT, and business unit owners, as appropriate.

The assessment team requests documentation, which may include, depending on the scope, any of these:

- Information security program strategy and documentation
- Information security policies, procedures, guidelines, and baselines
- Information security assessments and audits
- Technical documentation, including network diagrams, network device configurations and rule sets, hardening procedures, patching and configuration management plans and procedures, test plans, vulnerability assessment findings, change control and compliance information, and other documentation as needed
- Applications documentation, to include software development lifecycle, change control and compliance information, secure coding standards, code promotion procedures, test plans, and other documentation as needed
- BCDR and corresponding documents, such as business impact analysis surveys
- Security incident response plan and corresponding documentation
- Data classification schemes and information handling and disposal policies and procedures
- Business unit procedures, as appropriate
- Executive mandates, as appropriate
- Other documentation, as needed

The team sets up interviews with organizational members to identify vulnerabilities, threats, and countermeasures within the environment. All levels of staff should be represented, including these:

- Senior management
- Line management
- Business unit owners
- Temporary or casual staff (that is, interns)
- Business partners, as appropriate
- Remote workers, as appropriate
- Any other staff deemed appropriate to task

It is important to note that staff across all business units within scope for the risk assessment should be interviewed. It is not necessary to interview every staff person within a unit; a representative sample is usually sufficient.

Once interviews are completed, the analysis of the data gathered can be completed. This can include matching the threat to a vulnerability, matching threats to assets, determining how likely the threat is to exploit the vulnerability, and determining the impact to the organization in the event an exploit is successful. Analysis also includes matching of current and planned countermeasures (that is, protection) to the threat-vulnerability pair.

When the matching is completed, risk can be calculated. In a qualitative analysis, the product of likelihood and impact produces the level of risk. The higher the risk level, the more immediate is the need for the organization to address the issue to protect the organization from harm.

Once risk has been determined, additional countermeasures can be recommended to minimize, transfer, or avoid the risk. When this is completed, the risk that is left over—after countermeasures have been applied to protect against the risk—is also calculated. This is the residual risk, or risk left over after countermeasure application.

Qualitative risk assessment is sometimes used in combination with quantitative risk assessment, as is discussed in the following section.

Quantitative Risk Assessment

As an organization becomes more sophisticated in its data collection and retention and staff becomes more experienced in conducting risk assessments, an organization may find itself moving more toward quantitative risk assessment. The hallmark of a quantitative assessment is the numeric nature of the analysis. Frequency, probability, impact, countermeasure effectiveness, and other aspects of the risk assessment have a discrete mathematical value in a pure quantitative analysis.

Often, the risk assessment an organization conducts is a combination of qualitative and quantitative methods. Fully quantitative risk assessment may not be possible because there is always some subjective input present, such as the value of information. Value of information is often one of the most difficult factors to calculate.

It is clear to see the benefits and the pitfalls of performing a purely quantitative analysis. Quantitative analysis allows the assessor to determine whether the cost of the risk outweighs the cost of the countermeasure. Purely quantitative analysis, however, requires an enormous amount of time and must be performed by assessors with a significant amount of experience. Additionally, subjectivity is introduced because the metrics may need to be applied to qualitative measures. If the organization has the time and manpower to complete a lengthy and complex accounting evaluation, this data may be used to assist with a quantitative analysis; however, most organizations are not in a position to authorize this level of work.

Three steps are undertaken in a quantitative risk assessment: initial management approval, construction of a risk assessment team, and the review of information currently available within the organization. Single-loss expectancy (SLE) must be calculated to provide an estimate of loss. SLE is defined as the difference between the original value and the remaining value of an asset after a single exploit. The formula for calculating SLE follows:

$$SLE = \text{asset value (in \$)} \times \text{exposure factor (loss due to successful threat exploit, as a percent)}$$

Losses can include lack of availability of data assets due to data loss, theft, alteration, or DoS (perhaps due to business continuity or security issues).

Next, the organization calculates the annualized rate of occurrence (ARO). ARO is an estimate of how often a threat will be successful in exploiting a vulnerability over the period of a year.

When this is completed, the organization calculates the annualized loss expectancy (ALE). The ALE is a product of the yearly estimate for the exploit (ARO) and the loss in value of an asset after an SLE. The calculation follows:

$$ALE = SLE \times ARO$$

Given that there is now a value for SLE, it is possible to determine what the organization should spend, if anything, to apply a countermeasure for the risk in question. Remember that no countermeasure should be greater in cost than the risk it mitigates, transfers, or avoids. Countermeasure cost per year is easy and straightforward to calculate. It is simply the cost of the countermeasure divided by the years of its life (that is, use within the organization). Finally, the organization can compare the cost of the risk versus the cost of the countermeasure and make some objective decisions regarding its countermeasure selection.

For an example of how to implement the $ALE = SLE \times ARO$ formula against a potential situation that, as a CCSP, you are likely to encounter at some point, consider the following scenario:

ABC Corp. has been experiencing increased hacking activity as indicated by firewall and IPS logs gathered from its managed service provider. The logs also indicate that the company has experienced at least one successful breach in the past 30 days. Upon further analysis of the breach, the security team has reported to senior management that the dollar value impact of the breach appears to be $10,000.

Senior management has asked the security team to come up with a recommendation to fix the issues that led to the breach. The recommendation from the team is that the countermeasures required to address the root cause of the breach will cost $30,000.

Senior management has asked you, as the CCSP, to evaluate the recommendation of the security team and ensure that the $30,000 expense to implement the countermeasures is justified.

Taking the loss encountered of $10,000 per month, you can determine the annual loss expectancy as $120,000, assuming the frequency of attack and loss are consistent. Thus, the mitigation would pay for itself after three months ($30,000) and would provide a $10,000 loss prevention for each month after.

Therefore, this is a sound investment.

Identifying Vulnerabilities

NIST Special Publication 800–30 Rev. 1, page 9, defines a vulnerability as "an inherent weakness in an information system, security procedures, internal controls, or implementation that could be exploited by a threat source."[25]

In the field, it is common to identify vulnerabilities as they are related to people, processes, data, technology, and facilities. Examples of vulnerabilities can include these:

- Absence of a receptionist, mantrap, or other physical security mechanism upon entrance to a facility.

- Inadequate integrity checking in financial transaction software.

- Neglecting to require users to sign an acknowledgment of their responsibilities with regard to security, as well as an acknowledgment that they have read, understand, and agree to abide by the organization's security policies.

- Patching and configuration of an organization's information systems are done on an ad hoc basis. Therefore, they are neither documented nor up to date.

Unlike a risk assessment, vulnerability assessments tend to focus on the technology aspects of an organization, such as the network or applications. Data gathering for vulnerability assessments typically includes the use of software tools, which provide volumes of raw data for the organization and the assessor. This raw data includes information on the type of vulnerability, its location, its severity (typically based on an ordinal scale of high, medium, and low), and sometimes a discussion of the findings.

Assessors who conduct vulnerability assessments must be experts in properly reading, understanding, digesting, and presenting the information obtained from a vulnerability assessment to a multidisciplinary, sometimes nontechnical audience. Why? Data that's obtained from the scanning may not truly be a vulnerability. False positives are findings that are reported when no vulnerability truly exists in the organization (that is, something that is occurring in the environment has been flagged as an exposure when it really is not). Likewise, false negatives are vulnerabilities that should have been reported and are not. This sometimes occurs when tools are inadequately tuned to the task or the vulnerability in question exists outside the scope of the assessment.

Some findings are correct and appropriate but require significant interpretation for the organization to make sense of what has been discovered and how to proceed in remediation (that is, fixing the problem). This task is typically suited for an experienced assessor or a team whose members have real-world experience with the tool in question.

Identifying Threats

NIST, in Special Publication (SP) 800–30 Rev. 1, pages 7–8, defines threats as "any circumstance or event with the potential to adversely impact organizational operations and assets, individuals, other organizations, or the Nation through an information system via unauthorized access, destruction, disclosure, or modification of information, and/or denial-of-service." In the OCTAVE framework, threats are identified as the source from which assets in the organization are secured (or protected).

NIST, in Special Publication (SP) 800-30 Rev.1, page 8, defines a threat-source as "either (1) intent and method targeted at the intentional exploitation of a vulnerability or (2) a situation and method that may accidentally trigger a vulnerability."

Threat-sources can be grouped into a few categories. Each category can be expanded with specific threats, as follows:

- **Human:** Malicious outsider, malicious insider, (bio) terrorist, saboteur, spy political or competitive operative, loss of key personnel, errors made by human intervention, and cultural issues

- **Natural:** Fire, flood, tornado, hurricane, snowstorm, and earthquake

- **Technical:** Hardware failure, software failure, malicious code, unauthorized use, and use of emerging services, such as wireless or new technologies

- **Physical:** Closed-circuit TV failure due to faulty components or perimeter defense failure

- **Environmental:** Hazardous waste, biological agent, and utility failure

- **Operational:** A process (manual or automated) that affects AIC

Many specific threats exist within each category; the organization identifies those sources as the assessment progresses, utilizing information available from groups such as

(ISC)² and SANS and from government agencies such as NIST, the Federal Financial Institutions Examination Council (FFIEC), the Department of Health and Human Services (HHS), and others.

Selecting Tools and Techniques for Risk Assessment

It is expected that an organization will make a selection of the risk-assessment methodology, tools, and resources (including people) that best fit its culture, personnel capabilities, budget, and timeline. Many automated tools, including proprietary tools, exist in the field. Although automation can make the data analysis, dissemination, and storage of results easier, it is not a required part of risk assessment. If an organization is planning to purchase or build automated tools for this purpose, it is highly recommended that this decision be based on an appropriate timeline and resource skillsets for creation, implementation, maintenance, and monitoring of the tools and data stored within, long term.

Likelihood Determination

Likelihood is a component of a qualitative risk assessment. Likelihood, along with impact, determines risk. Likelihood can be measured by the capabilities of the threat and the presence or absence of countermeasures. Initially, organizations that do not have trending data available may use an ordinal scale, labeled high, medium, and low, to score likelihood rankings.

Once a value on the ordinal scale has been chosen, the selection can be mapped to a numeric value for computation of risk. For example, the selection of high can be mapped to the value of 1. Medium can likewise be mapped to 0.5, and low can be mapped to 0.1. As the scale expands, the numeric assignments will become more targeted.

Determination of Impact

Impact can be ranked much the same way as likelihood. The main difference is that the impact scale is expanded and depends on definitions rather than ordinal selections. Definitions of impact to an organization often include loss of life, loss of dollars, loss of prestige, loss of market share, and other facets. Organizations need to take sufficient time to define and assign impact definitions for high, medium, low, or any other scale terms that are chosen. Tables 5.7 and 5.8 show a typical likelihood and consequences rating system.

TABLE 5.7 Likelihood and Consequences Rating

LIKELIHOOD			CONSEQUENCE
Rare (Very Low)	E	Insignificant (Low—No business impact)	1
Unlikely (Low)	D	Minor (Low—Minor business impact, some loss of confidence)	2
Moderate (Medium)	C	Moderate (Medium—Business is interrupted, loss of confidence)	3
Likely (High)	B	Major (High—Business is disrupted, major loss of confidence)	4
Almost Certain (Very High)	A	Catastrophic (High—Business cannot continue)	5

TABLE 5.8 Likelihood Qualification: How to Arrive at a Likelihood Rating

HOW TO QUALIFY LIKELIHOOD	RATING
Skill (High Skill Level Required ➤ Low or No Skill Required)	1 = High Skill Required ➤ 5 = No Skill Required
Ease of Access (Very Difficult to Do ➤ Very Simple to Do)	1 = Very Difficult ➤ 5 = Simple
Incentive (High Incentive ➤ Low Incentive)	1 = Low or No Incentive ➤ 5 = High Incentive
Resource (Requires Expensive or Rare Equipment ➤ No Resources Required)	1 = Rare/Expensive ➤ 5 = No Resource Required
Total (Add Rating and Divide by 4)	1 = E, 2 = D, 3 = C, 4 = B, 5 = A

Once the terms are defined, you can calculate impact. If an exploit has the potential to result in the loss of life (such as a bombing or bioterrorist attack), the ranking will always be high. In general, groups such as the National Security Agency view loss of life as the highest-priority risk in any organization. As such, it may be assigned the top value in the impact scale. As an example, 51 to 100 = high; 11 to 50 = medium; 0 to 10 = low.

Determination of Risk

Risk is determined as the by-product of likelihood and impact. For example, if an exploit has a likelihood of 1 (high) and an impact of 100 (high), the risk would be 100.[26] As a result, 100 would be the highest exploit ranking available. These scenarios (high likelihood and high impact) should merit immediate attention from the organization.

As the risk calculations are completed, they can be prioritized for attention, as required. Note that not all risks receive the same level of attention based on the organization's risk tolerance and its strategy for mitigation, transfer, or avoidance of risk (*Figure 5.11*).

	Consequence				
Likelihood	*Insignificant*	*Minor*	*Moderate*	*Major*	*Catastrophic*
	1	*2*	*3*	*4*	*5*
A (almost certain)	H	H	E	E	E
B (likely)	M	H	H	E	E
C (possible)	L	M	H	E	E
D (unlikely)	L	L	M	H	E
E (rate)	L	L	M	H	H
E	*Extreme Risk:* Immediate action required to mitigate the risk or decide to not proceed				
H	*High Risk:* Action should be taken to compensate for the risk				
M	*Moderate Risk:* Action should be taken to monitor the risk				
L	*Low Risk:* Routine acceptance of the risk				

FIGURE 5.11 **Rating likelihood and consequences.**

Critical Aspects of Risk Assessment

At a minimum, the risk assessment should cover the following:

- Risk of service failure and associated impact
- Insider threat risk impact; for example, what happens if a CSP system administrator steals customer data?
- Risk of compromised customer to other tenants in the cloud environment
- Risk of DoS attacks
- Supply chain risk to the CSP

Controls should be in place to mitigate identified risks. Senior management should be involved in the risk assessment and be willing to accept any residual risk. You should conduct the risk assessment periodically.

Risk Response

Risk response provides a consistent, organization-wide response to risk in accordance with the organizational risk frame by taking these steps:

- Developing alternative courses of action for responding to risk
- Evaluating the alternative courses of action
- Determining appropriate courses of action consistent with organizational risk tolerance
- Implementing risk responses based on selected courses of action

Traditional Risk Responses

The four traditional ways to address risk are described in this section.

Risk can be accepted: In some cases, it may be prudent for an organization to simply accept the risk that is presented in certain scenarios. Risk acceptance is the practice of accepting certain risks, typically based on a business decision that may also weigh the cost versus the benefit of dealing with the risk in another way.

For example, an executive may be confronted with risks identified during the course of a risk assessment for her organization. These risks have been prioritized by high, medium, and low impact to the organization. The executive notes that to mitigate or transfer the low-level risks, significant costs could be involved. Mitigation might involve the hiring of additional highly skilled personnel and the purchase of new hardware, software, and office equipment, whereas transference of the risk to an insurance company would require premium payments. The executive then further notes that minimal impact to the organization would occur if any of the reported low-level threats were realized. Therefore, she rightly concludes that it is wiser for the organization to forego the costs and accept the risk.

The decision to accept risk should not be taken lightly, nor without appropriate information to justify the decision. The cost versus benefit, the organization's willingness to monitor the risk long term, and the impact it has on the outside world's view of the organization must be taken into account when deciding to accept risk. When accepting risk, the business decision to do so must be documented.

Some organizations may track containment of risk. Containment lessens the impact to an organization when an exposure is exploited through distribution of critical assets (that is, people, processes, data, technologies, and facilities).

Risk can be avoided: Risk avoidance is the practice of coming up with alternatives so that the risk in question is not realized.

Imagine a global retailer who, knowing the risks associated with doing business on the Internet, decides to avoid the practice. This decision will likely cost the company a significant amount of its revenue (if, indeed, the company has products or services that consumers want to purchase). In addition, the decision may require the company to build or lease a site in each of the locations, globally, for which it wants to continue business. This could have a catastrophic effect on the company's ability to continue business operations.

Risk can be transferred: Risk transfer is the practice of passing on the risk in question to another entity, such as an insurance company.

The transfer of risk may be accompanied by a cost. This can be seen in insurance instances, such as liability insurance for a vendor or the insurance taken out by companies to protect against hardware and software theft or destruction. This may also be true if an organization must purchase and implement security controls to make its organization less desirable to attack.

Not all risk can be transferred. Although financial risk is simple to transfer through insurance, reputational risk may almost never be fully transferred. If a banking system is breached, there may be a cost in the money lost, but what about the reputation of the bank as a secure place to store assets? How about the stock price of the bank and the customers the bank may lose due to the breach?

Risk can be mitigated: Risk mitigation is the practice of the elimination of, or the significant decrease in the level of, risk presented. Examples of risk mitigation can be seen in everyday life and are readily apparent in the information technology world.

For example, to lessen the risk of exposing personal and financial information that is highly sensitive and confidential, organizations put countermeasures in place, such as firewalls, IDSs and IPSs, and other mechanisms.

Residual Risk

Although elimination of risk is a goal of the holistic risk management process, it is an unrealistic goal to set that all risks will be eliminated from a system or environment. There will always be some amount of risk left in any system after all countermeasures and strategies have been applied. This is referred to as the residual risk.

Risk Assignment

"Who is assigned and responsible for risk?" is a serious question with an intriguing answer: it depends. Ultimately, the organization (that is, senior management or stakeholders) owns the risks that are present during operation of the company. Senior management, however, may rely on business unit (or data) owners or custodians to assist in identification of risks so that they can be mitigated, transferred, or avoided. The organization also likely expects that the owners and custodians will minimize or mitigate risk as they work, based on policies, procedures, and regulations present in the environment. If expectations are not met, a consequence such as disciplinary action, termination, or prosecution will usually result.

Here is an example. A claims processor is working with a medical healthcare claim submitted to his organization for completion. The claim contains electronic personally identifiable healthcare information for a person the claims processor knows. Although he has acknowledged his responsibilities for the protection of the data, he calls his mother, who is a good friend of the individual who filed the claim. His mother in turn calls multiple people, who in turn contact the person who filed the claim. The claimant contacts an attorney, and the employee and company are sued for the intentional breach of information.

Several things are immediately apparent from this example. The employee is held immediately accountable for his action in intentionally exploiting a vulnerability (that is, sensitive information was inappropriately released, according to the U.S. federal law HIPAA). Although the employee was a custodian of the data (and a co-owner of the risk), the court also determined that the company was co-owner of the risk and hence also bore the responsibility for compensating the victim (in this example, the claimant).

Once the findings from the assessment have been consolidated and the calculations have been completed, it is time to present a finalized report to senior management. This can be done in a written report or through a presentation. Any written reports should include an acknowledgment to the participants, a summary of the approach taken, findings in detail (in either tabulated or graphical form), recommendations for remediation of the findings, and a summary. Organizations are encouraged to develop their own formats to make the most of the activity as well as the information collected and analyzed.

Countermeasure Selection

One of the most important steps for the organization is to appropriately select countermeasures to apply to risks in the environment. Many aspects of the countermeasure must be considered to ensure that they are a proper fit to the task. Following are considerations for countermeasures or controls:

- Accountability (can be held responsible)
- Auditability (can be tested)
- Trusted source (source is known)
- Independence (self-determining)
- Consistent application

- Cost effectiveness
- Reliability
- Independence from other countermeasures (no overlap)
- Ease of use
- Automation
- Sustainability
- Security
- Protection of AIC of assets
- Ability to be backed out in event of an issue
- Creates no additional issues during operation
- Leaves no residual data from its function

From this list, it is clear that countermeasures must be above reproach when deployed to protect an organization's assets.

Once risk assessment is completed and there is a list of remediation activities to be undertaken, an organization must ensure that it has personnel with appropriate capabilities to implement the remediation activities as well as to maintain and support them. This may require the organization to provide additional training opportunities to personnel involved in the design, deployment, maintenance, and support of security mechanisms in the environment.

In addition, it is crucial that appropriate policies, with detailed procedures and standards that correspond to each policy item, be created, implemented, maintained, monitored, and enforced throughout the environment. The organization should assign resources that can be accountable to each task and track tasks over time, reporting progress to senior management and allowing time for appropriate approvals during this process.

Implementation of Risk Countermeasures

When the security architects sit down to start pondering how to design the enterprise security architecture, they should be thinking about many things. What frameworks should they use as points of reference? What business issues do they need to take into account? Who are the stakeholders? Why are they only addressing this and not that area of the business? How will they be able to integrate this system design into the overall architecture? Where will the single points of failure (SPOFs) be in this architecture? The challenge for the architect is to coordinate all those streams of thought and channel them into a process that will let them design a coherent and strong enterprise security architecture.

When security practitioners sit down to start deploying the enterprise security architecture, they should be thinking about many things. What tools should they use to set up and deploy these systems? Who are the end users of this system going to be? Why are they only being given "x" amount of time to get this done? How will they be able to integrate this system design into the existing network? Where will they manage this from? The challenge for the practitioner is to coordinate all those streams of thought and channel them into a process that will let them deploy a coherent and strong enterprise security architecture.

When security professionals sit down to start pondering how to manage the enterprise security architecture, they should be thinking about many things. What are the metrics that they have available to manage these systems? Who do they need to partner with to ensure successful operation of the system? Why are they not addressing this or that concern? How will they be able to communicate the appropriate level of information regarding the system to each of their user audiences? Where will they find the time to be able to do this? The challenge for the professional is to coordinate all those streams of thought and channel them into a process that lets them manage a coherent and strong enterprise security architecture.

All three security actors are vital, and each contributes to the success of the enterprise security architecture, or its failure, in its own ways. However, all three also share many things in common. They all need to be focused on doing their job so that the others can do theirs. They all need to ensure that the communication regarding their part of the puzzle is bidirectional, clear, and concise with regard to issues and concerns with the architecture. Most importantly, they all need to use common sense to assess and evaluate not just the portions of the architecture that they are responsible for but all the actions that are engaged in to interact with it. The use of common sense often is the difference between success and failure in anything; it is no different for security.

For all three security actors, common sense means several things—situational awareness, paying attention to details, not assuming, and so on. It also means that they must become experts at understanding and managing risk in their own area, but with an eye toward a common goal. That goal is to manage risk in such a way that it does not negatively influence the enterprise. That goal is shared by everyone who interacts with the architecture at any level for any reason.

The end users need to use systems in such a way that they do not expose them to threats and vulnerabilities due to their behavior. The system administrators need to ensure that the systems are kept up to date in terms of security patching to ensure that all known vulnerabilities are being mitigated within the system. Senior management needs to provide the appropriate resources to ensure that the systems can be maintained as needed to guarantee safe operating conditions for all users.

The identification and management of risk through the deployment of countermeasures is the common ground that all system users, regardless of role or function, share in the enterprise. Here are some examples:

- Mobile applications
    - **Risks:** Lost or stolen devices, malware, multicommunication channel exposure, and weak authentication
    - **Countermeasures:** Meeting mobile security standards, tailoring security audits to assess mobile application vulnerabilities, secure provisioning, and control and monitoring of application data on personal devices
- Web 2.0
    - **Risks:** Securing social media, content management, and security of third-party technologies and services
    - **Countermeasures:** Security API, CAPTCHA, unique security tokens, and transaction approval workflows
- Cloud-computing services
    - **Risks:** Multitenant deployments, security of cloud computing deployments, third-party risk, data breaches, DoS attacks, and malicious insiders
    - **Countermeasures:** Cloud-computing security assessment, compliance-audit assessment on cloud-computing providers, due diligence, encryption in transit and at rest, and monitoring

The security actors need to identify and understand the risks they face within their area of the enterprise and move to deploy countermeasures that are appropriate to address them. The most important thing to ensure the relative success of these individual efforts is the ability to document and communicate effectively all the efforts being undertaken by area and platform. In this way, as complete a picture as possible of the current state of risk within the enterprise is always available.

This risk inventory should be made available through some form of centrally managed enterprise content management platform that allows secure remote access when required. It should also deploy a strong version control and change-management functionality so that the information is accurate and up to date at all times. Access control needs to be integrated into this system as well to ensure that role- or job-based access can be granted as appropriate to users.

Risk Monitoring

Risk monitoring is the process of keeping track of identified risks. It should be treated as an ongoing process and implemented throughout the system life cycle. The mechanisms and approaches used to engage in risk monitoring can vary from system to system, based on a variety of variables. The most important elements of a risk monitoring system include the ability to clearly identify a risk, the ability to classify or categorize the risk, and the ability to track the risk over time.

There are three purposes of the risk-monitoring component:

- Determine the ongoing effectiveness of risk responses (consistent with the organizational risk frame)

- Identify risk-impacting changes to organizational information systems and the environments in which the systems operate

- Verify that planned risk responses are implemented and information security requirements derived from and traceable to organizational missions and business functions, federal legislation, directives, regulations, policies, standards, and guidelines are satisfied

UNDERSTANDING THE COLLECTION AND PRESERVATION OF DIGITAL EVIDENCE

Forensic science is generally defined as the application of science to the law. Digital forensics, also known as computer and network forensics, has many definitions. Generally, it is considered the application of science to the identification, collection, examination, and analysis of data while preserving the integrity of the information and maintaining a strict chain of custody for the data. Data refers to distinct pieces of digital information that have been formatted in a specific way.

Organizations have an ever-increasing amount of data from many sources. For example, data can be stored or transferred by standard computer systems, networking equipment, computing peripherals, smartphones, and various types of media, among other sources.

Because of the variety of data sources, digital forensic techniques can be used for many purposes, such as investigating crimes and internal policy violations, reconstructing computer security incidents, troubleshooting operational problems, and recovering from accidental system damage. Practically every organization needs to have the capability to perform digital forensics. Without such a capability, an organization will have difficulty determining what events have occurred within its systems and networks, such as exposures of protected, sensitive data.

Cloud Forensics Challenges

Working with the cloud has several forensics challenges:

- **Control over data:** In traditional computer forensics, investigators have full control over the evidence (such as router logs, process logs, and hard disks). In a cloud, the control over data varies by service model. Cloud users have the highest level of control in IaaS and the least level of control in SaaS. This physical inaccessibility of the evidence and lack of control over the system make evidence acquisition a challenging task in the cloud.

- **Multitenancy:** Cloud computing platforms can be a multitenant system, while traditional computing is a single-owner system. In a cloud, multiple VMs can share the same physical infrastructure; that is, data for multiple customers can be colocated. An alleged suspect may claim that the evidence contains information of other users, not just theirs. In this case, the investigator needs to prove to the court that the provided evidence actually belongs to the suspect. Conversely, in traditional computing systems, a suspect is solely responsible for all the digital evidence located in his computing system. Moreover, in the cloud, the forensics investigator may need to preserve the privacy of other tenants.

- **Data volatility:** Volatile data cannot be sustained without power. Data residing in a VM is volatile because once the VM is powered off, all the data is lost unless some form of image is used to capture the state data of the VM. To provide the on-demand computational and storage services required in the cloud, cloud service providers do not always supply persistent storage to VM instances.

  Chain of custody should clearly depict how the evidence was collected, analyzed, and preserved to be presented as admissible evidence in court. In traditional forensic procedures, it is easy to maintain an accurate history of time, location, and persons accessing the target computer, hard disk, and so on, of a potential suspect. On the other hand, in a cloud, it is not obvious where a VM is physically located.

  Investigators can acquire a VM image from any workstation connected to the Internet. The investigator's location and a VM's physical location can be in different time zones. Hence, maintaining a proper chain of custody is much more challenging in the cloud.

- **Evidence acquisition:** Currently, investigators are completely dependent on CSPs for acquiring cloud evidence. However, the employee of a CSP, who collects data on behalf of investigators, is most likely not a licensed forensics investigator, so it is not possible to guarantee this person's integrity in a court of law. A dishonest employee of a CSP can collude with a malicious user to hide important evidence or to inject invalid evidence into a system to prove the malicious user is innocent. On the other hand, a dishonest investigator can collude with an attacker. Even if CSPs provide valid evidence to investigators, a dishonest investigator can remove some crucial evidence before presenting it to the court or can provide some fake evidence to the court to frame an honest cloud user. In traditional storage systems, only the suspect and the investigator can collude. The potential for three-way collusion in the cloud certainly increases the attack surface and makes cloud forensics more challenging.

Data Access Within Service Models

Access to data will be decided by the following:

- The service model
- The legal system in the country where data is legally stored

When using various service models, the CCSP can access different types of information, as shown in Table 5.9. If the CCSP needs additional information from the service model that is being used, which is not specified in Table 5.9, she needs to have the CSP provide the required information. In Table 5.9, the first column contains different layers that you might have access to when using cloud services. The SaaS, PaaS, and IaaS columns show the access rights you have when using various service models, and the last column presents the information you have available when using a local computer that you have physical access to.

TABLE 5.9 **Accessing Information in Service Models**

INFORMATION	SAAS	PAAS	IAAS	LOCAL
Networking	N	N	N	Y
Storage	N	N	N	Y
Servers	N	N	N	Y
Virtualization	N	N	N	Y
OS	N	N	Y	Y
Middleware	N	N	Y	Y
Runtime	N	N	Y	Y
Data	N	Y	Y	Y
Application	N	Y	Y	Y
Access Control	Y	Y	Y	Y

Steps of digital forensics vary according to the service and deployment model of cloud computing that is being used. For example, the evidence collection procedure for SaaS and IaaS will be unique. For SaaS, you can depend on the cloud service provider to secure access to the application log. In contrast, in IaaS, you can acquire the VM image from customers and can initiate the examination and analysis phase. In the public deployment model, you rarely can get physical access to the evidence, but this is guaranteed in the private cloud deployment model.

Forensics Readiness

Many incidents can be handled more efficiently and effectively if forensic considerations have been incorporated into the information system lifecycle.

Examples of such considerations follow:

- Performing regular backups of systems and maintaining previous backups for a specific period of time

- Enabling auditing on workstations, servers, and network devices

- Forwarding audit records to secure centralized log servers

- Configuring mission-critical applications to perform auditing, including recording all authentication attempts

- Maintaining a database of file hashes for the files of common OS and application deployments and using file integrity–checking software on particularly important assets

- Maintaining records (such as baselines) of network and system configurations

- Establishing data-retention policies that support performing historical reviews of system and network activity, complying with requests or requirements to preserve data relating to ongoing litigation and investigations, and destroying data that is no longer needed

Proper Methodologies for Forensic Collection of Data

Take a look at the process flow of digital forensics (*Figure 5.12*). Cloud forensics can be defined as applying all the processes of digital forensics in the cloud environment.

FIGURE 5.12 Process flow of digital forensics.

In the cloud, forensic evidence can be collected from the host or guest OS. The dynamic nature and use of pooled resources in a cloud environment can affect the collection of digital evidence.

Once an incident is identified, the process for performing digital forensics includes the following phases:

- **Collection:** Identifying, labeling, recording, and acquiring data from the possible sources of relevant data, while following procedures that preserve the integrity of the data

- **Examination:** Forensically processing collected data using a combination of automated and manual methods, and assessing and extracting data of particular interest, while preserving the integrity of the data

- **Analysis:** Analyzing the results of the examination, using legally justifiable methods and techniques, to derive useful information that addresses the questions that were the impetus for performing the collection and examination

- **Reporting:** Reporting the results of the analysis, which may include describing the actions used, explaining how tools and procedures were selected, determining what other actions need to be performed (such as forensic examination of additional data sources, securing of identified vulnerabilities, improvement of existing security controls), and providing recommendations for improvement to policies, procedures, tools, and other aspects of the forensic process

The following sections examine these phases in more detail.

Data Acquisition and Collection

After identifying potential data sources, acquire the data from the sources. Data acquisition should be performed using a three-step process:

- **Develop a plan to acquire the data:** Developing a plan is an important first step in most cases because there are multiple potential data sources. Create a plan that prioritizes the sources, establishing the order in which the data should be acquired. Important factors for prioritization include the following:

  - **Likely value:** Based on your understanding of the situation and previous experience in similar situations, estimate the relative likely value of each potential data source.

  - **Volatility:** Volatile data refers to data on a live system that is lost after a computer is powered down or due to the passage of time. Volatile data may also be lost as a result of other actions performed on the system. In many cases, volatile data should be given priority over nonvolatile data. However, nonvolatile data may also be somewhat dynamic in nature (for example, log files that are overwritten as new events occur).

- **Amount of effort required:** The amount of effort required to acquire different data sources may vary widely. The effort involves not only the time spent by security professionals and others within the organization (including legal advisors) but also the cost of equipment and services (such as outside experts). For example, acquiring data from a network router probably requires much less effort than acquiring data from a cloud service provider.

- **Acquire the data:** If the data has not already been acquired by security tools, analysis tools, or other means, the general process for acquiring data involves using forensic tools to collect volatile data, duplicating nonvolatile data sources to collect their data, and securing the original nonvolatile data sources.

  Data acquisition can be performed either locally or over a network. Although it is generally preferable to acquire data locally because there is greater control over the system and data, local data collection is not always feasible (such as for a system in a locked room or a system in another location).

  When acquiring data over a network, decisions should be made regarding the type of data to be collected and the amount of effort to use. For instance, it might be necessary to acquire data from several systems through different network connections, or it might be sufficient to copy a logical volume from just one system.

- **Verify the integrity of the data:** After the data has been acquired, its integrity should be verified. It is particularly important to prove that the data has not been tampered with if it might be needed for legal reasons. Data integrity verification typically consists of using tools to compute the message digest of the original and copied data and then comparing the digests to make sure they are the same.

Note that before you begin to collect data, a decision should be made based on the need to collect and preserve evidence in a way that supports its use in future legal or internal disciplinary proceedings. In such situations, a clearly defined chain of custody should be followed to avoid allegations of mishandling or tampering of evidence. This involves keeping a log of every person who had physical custody of the evidence, documenting the actions that they performed on the evidence and at what time, storing the evidence in a secure location when it is not being used, making a copy of the evidence and performing examination and analysis using only the copied evidence, and verifying the integrity of the original and copied evidence. If it is unclear whether evidence needs to be preserved; by default it generally should be.

Challenges in Collecting Evidence

The CCSP faces several challenges in the collection of evidence due to the nature of the cloud environment. You have already read about many of these in the "Cloud Forensics Challenges" section earlier; however, they bear repeating here in the context of the collection phase to emphasize the issues and concerns that the CCSP must contend with. Following are the main challenges with collection of data in the cloud:

- The seizure of servers containing files from many users creates privacy issues among the multitenants homed within the servers.
- The trustworthiness of evidence is based on the CSP, with no ability to validate or guarantee on behalf of the CCSP.
- Investigators are dependent on CSPs to acquire evidence.
- Technicians collecting data may not be qualified for forensic acquisition.
- Unknown location of the physical data can hinder investigations.

One of the best ways for the CCSP to address these challenges is to turn to the area of network forensics for help and guidance.

Network forensics is defined as the capture, storage, and analysis of network events. The idea is to capture every packet of network traffic and make it available in a single searchable database so that the traffic can be examined and analyzed in detail.

Network forensics can uncover the low-level addresses of the systems communicating, which investigators can use to trace an action or conversation back to a physical device. The entire contents of emails, IM conversations, web-surfing activities, and file transfers can be recovered and reconstructed to reveal the original transaction. This is important because of the challenges with the cloud environment already noted, as well as some additional underlying issues. Networks are continuing to become faster in terms of transmission speed. As a result, they are handling larger and larger volumes of data. The increasing use of converged networks and the data streams that they make possible has led to data that is multifaceted and richer today than it has ever been. (Think voice over IP [VoIP] and streaming HD video, as well as the metadata that comes with the content.)

Network forensics has various use cases:

- Uncovering proof of an attack
- Troubleshooting performance issues
- Monitoring activity for compliance with policies
- Sourcing data leaks
- Creating audit trails for business transactions

Collecting Data from a Host OS

Physical access is required to collect forensic evidence from a host. Due to the nature of virtualization technology, a VM that was on one host may have been migrated to one or more hosts after the incident occurred. Additionally, the dynamic nature of storage may affect the collection of digital evidence from a host OS.

Collecting Data from a Guest OS

For guest OSs, a snapshot may be the best method for collecting a forensic image. Some type of write blocker should be in place when collecting digital evidence to prevent the inadvertent writing of data to the host or guest OS. You can use various tools for the collection of digital evidence. Consider prestaging and testing of forensics tools as part of their infrastructure design for the enterprise cloud architecture.

Collecting Metadata

Specifically, consider the issue of metadata needs carefully. Whether to allow metadata or not is not really a decision point any longer because metadata exists and is created by end users at every level of the cloud architecture. Be aware of the metadata that exists in the enterprise cloud, and have a plan and a policy for managing and acquiring it, if required.

This issue can become more complicated in multitenant clouds because the ability to isolate tenants from each other can influence the scope and reach of metadata. If tenant isolation is not done properly, one tenant's metadata may be exposed to others, allowing for "data bleed" to occur.

Examining the Data

After data has been collected, the next phase is to examine the data, which involves assessing and extracting the relevant pieces of information from the collected data.

This phase may also involve the following:

- Bypassing or mitigating OS or application features that obscure data and code, such as data compression, encryption, and access control mechanisms
- Using text and pattern searches to identify pertinent data, such as finding documents that mention a particular subject or person or identifying email log entries for a particular email address
- Using a tool that can determine the type of contents of each data file, such as text, graphics, music, or a compressed file archive

- Using knowledge of data file types to identify files that merit further study, as well as to exclude files that are of no interest to the examination

- Using any databases containing information about known files to include or exclude files from further consideration

Analyzing the Data

The analysis should include identifying people, places, items, and events and determining how these elements are related so that a conclusion can be reached. Often, this effort includes correlating data among multiple sources. For instance, a NIDS log may link an event to a host, the host audit logs may link the event to a specific user account, and the host IDS log may indicate what actions that user performed.

Tools such as centralized logging and security event management software can facilitate this process by automatically gathering and correlating the data. Comparing system characteristics to known baselines can identify various types of changes made to the system.

Reporting the Findings

The final phase is reporting, which is the process of preparing and presenting the information resulting from the analysis phase. Many factors affect reporting, including the following:

- **Alternative explanations:** When the information regarding an event is incomplete, it may not be possible to arrive at a definitive explanation of what happened. When an event has two or more plausible explanations, each should be given due consideration in the reporting process. Use a methodical approach to attempt to prove or disprove each possible explanation that is proposed.

- **Audience consideration:** Knowing the audience to which the data or information will be shown is important. An incident requiring law enforcement involvement requires highly detailed reports of all information gathered and may also require copies of all evidentiary data obtained. A system administrator might want to see network traffic and related statistics in great detail. Senior management might simply want a high-level overview of what happened, such as a simplified visual representation of how the attack occurred, and what should be done to prevent similar incidents.

- **Actionable information:** Reporting also includes identifying actionable information gained from data that may allow you to collect new sources of information. For example, a list of contacts may be developed from the data that can lead to additional information about an incident or crime. Also, information might be obtained that can prevent future events, such as a backdoor on a system that can be used for future attacks, a crime that is being planned, a worm scheduled to start spreading at a certain time, or a vulnerability that can be exploited.

The Chain of Custody

You must take care when gathering, handling, transporting, analyzing, reporting on, and managing evidence that the proper chain of custody or chain of evidence has been maintained.

Every jurisdiction has its own definitions as to what this may mean in detail; however, in general, chain of custody and chain of evidence can be taken to be mean something similar to these points:

- When an item is gathered as evidence, that item should be recorded in an evidence log with a description, the signature of the individual gathering the item, a signature of a second individual witnessing the item being gathered, and an accurate time and date.

- Whenever that item is stored, the location in which the item is stored should be recorded, as should the item's condition. The signatures of the individual placing the item in storage and of the individual responsible for that storage location should also be included, along with an accurate time and date.

- Whenever an item is removed from storage, it should be recorded, as should the item's condition, the signatures of the person removing the item, the person responsible for that storage location, and an accurate time and date.

- Whenever an item is transported, that item's point of origin, method of transport, and destination should be recorded, as should the item's condition at origination and destination. Also record the signatures of the people performing the transportation, a responsible party at the origin and destination witnessing its departure and arrival, and accurate times and dates for each.

- Whenever any action, process, test, or other handling of an item is to be performed, a description of all such actions to be taken and the persons who will perform such actions should be recorded. The signatures of the person taking the item to be tested and of the person responsible for the item's storage should be recorded, as should an accurate time and date.

- Whenever any action, process, test, or other handling of an item is performed, record a description of all such actions, along with accurate times and dates for each. Also record the person performing such actions, any results or findings of such actions, the signatures of at least one person of responsibility as witness that the actions were performed as described, and the resulting findings as described.

Ultimately, the chain of evidence is a series of events that, when viewed in sequence, account for the actions of a person during a particular period of time or the location of a piece of evidence during a specified time period. (It is usually associated with criminal cases.) In other words, it can be thought of as the details that are left behind to tell the story of what happened.

The chain of custody requirement is the same whether the digital evidence is collected from a guest or a host OS. Do the following when it comes to chain of custody:

- Be able to prove that evidence was secure and under the control of some particular party at all times.

- Take steps to ensure that evidence is not damaged in transit or storage:

  - Example: If stored for a long time, batteries may die, causing loss of information in complementary metal-oxide semiconductor (CMOS) memory (such as BIOS configuration).

  - Example: Transport digital evidence in static-free containers, such as in paper or special foil, not in plastic bags.

Digital evidence has two parts: the physical medium containing the information and the information (bits) itself. Chain of custody must be maintained for both parts.

Evidence Management

Maintaining evidence from collection to trial is a critical part of digital forensics. Have policies and procedures in place for the collection and management of evidence. In some cases, you may need to collect digital evidence on short notice. Take care not to collect data outside the scope of the requesting legal document. Certain legal discovery documents, or orders, specify that the CSP is not allowed to disclose any activities undertaken in support of the order.

Both the CSP and the CCSP need to be aware of the issues surrounding disclosure of data-gathering activities. Depending on the SLAs that the customer has in place, the data-gathering activities undertaken to support a forensics examination of a tenant's data may not have to be disclosed to the tenant or to any of the other tenants in a multitenant hosting solution.

MANAGING COMMUNICATIONS WITH RELEVANT PARTIES

Communication between the provider, its customers, and its suppliers is critical for any environment. When you add the cloud to the mix, communication becomes even more central as a success factor overall.

The Five Ws and One H

The need to clearly identify the five Ws and the one H with regard to communication is important because the ability to do so directly affects the level of success that will be achieved with aligning the cloud-based solution architecture and the needs of the enterprise. In addition, the ability to successfully drive and coordinate effective governance across the enterprise is influenced by the success or failure of these communication activities.

Here are the five Ws and the one H of communication:

Who: Who is the target of the communication?

What: What is the communication designed to achieve?

When: When is the communication best delivered or most likely to reach its intended target?

Where: Where is the communication pathway best managed from?

Why: Why is the communication being initiated in the first place?

How: How is the communication being transmitted, and how is it being received?

The ability to ensure clear and concise communication, and, as a result, alignment and successful achievement of goals, relies on the ability to manage the five Ws and the one H of communication.

As a CCSP, you must drive communication in the enterprise and through the ecosystem that it supports to ensure the long-term survivability of the enterprise architecture is constantly examined, discussed, and provided for.

Communicating with Vendors and Partners

Establish communication paths with all partners that will consume or support cloud services in the enterprise. Clearly identify and document all partner organizations, ensuring that the relationships between the partner and the enterprise are clearly understood.

For example, if a partner is engaged through a federated relationship with the enterprise, she will have a different level of access to cloud services and systems than a nonfederated partner.

Make sure that there is a clearly defined on-boarding process for all partners, allowing the partner to be thoroughly vetted prior to granting access to any systems (*Figure 5.13*).

FIGURE 5.13 A communication path.

While the partnership is in force, make sure the partner is managed under the existing security infrastructure as much as possible to ensure that access by exception is avoided at all costs. This ensures that the partner's access and activities are managed and examined according to the existing policies and procedures already in place for the organization's systems and infrastructure.

When the partnership is terminated, ensure that there is a clearly documented and well-understood and communicated off-boarding policy and procedure in place to effectively and efficiently terminate the partner's access to all enterprise systems, cloud and noncloud based, that the partner had been granted access to.

It's important to understand the capabilities and polices of your supporting vendors. Establish and test emergency communication paths with all vendors.

Categorizing, or ranking, a vendor/supplier on some sort of scale is critical when appropriately managing the relationship with that vendor/supplier (*Figure 5.14*).

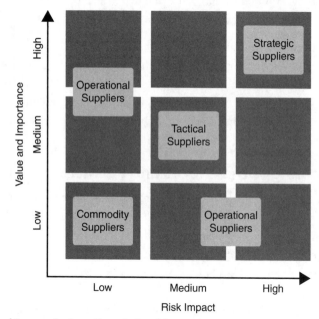

FIGURE 5.14 Ranking vendor/supplier relationships.

Strategic suppliers are deemed to be mission critical and cannot be easily replaced if they become unavailable. Although you will typically do business with very few of these types of partners, they are the most crucial to the success or failure of the enterprise cloud architecture.

Commodity suppliers, on the other hand, provide goods and services that can easily be replaced and sourced from a variety of suppliers if necessary.

Communicating with Customers

Organizations have internal customers and external customers. Both customer segments are important to the success of any cloud environment because both are typically involved in the consumption of cloud services in some way. Having a good understanding of the customer audience being addressed by the cloud is important because different audiences consume differently, with different needs, goals, and issues that have to be documented, understood, managed, and tracked over the lifecycle of the cloud environment.

If individual responsibilities are not clearly stated, the customer may assume the provider has responsibility for a specific area that may or may not be correct. This can lead to confusion and present legal and liability issues for both the customer and the provider if not addressed clearly and concisely.

✔ SLAs Recap

As we have mentioned in prior domains, SLAs are a form of communication that clarifies responsibilities. Appropriate SLAs should be in place to manage all services being consumed by each customer segment. These SLAs must define the service levels required by the customer as well as the customer's specific metrics, which vary by customer type and need. Some metrics that SLAs may specify include these:

- What percentage of the time services are available
- The number of users that can be served simultaneously
- Specific performance benchmarks to which actual performance is periodically compared
- The schedule for notification in advance of network changes that may affect users
- Help/service desk response time for various classes of problems
- Remote access availability
- Usage statistics that are provided

Communicating with Regulators

Early communication is essential with regulators when developing a cloud environment. As a CCSP, you are responsible for ensuring that all infrastructure is compliant with the regulatory requirements that may be applicable to the enterprise.

These requirements vary greatly based on several factors such as geography, business type, and services offered. However, if regulatory standards or laws have to be implemented or adhered to, you need to understand all the requirements and expectations of compliance to ensure the enterprise is able to prove compliance when asked to do so.

Communicating with Other Stakeholders

During the communication process, additional parties may be identified for inclusion in regular or periodic communications.

WRAP-UP: DATA BREACH EXAMPLE

Weak access control mechanisms in the cloud can lead to major data breaches. In early 2012, a large data breach took place on the servers of Utah's Department of Technology Services (DTS). A malicious hacker group from Eastern Europe succeeded in accessing the servers of DTS, compromising 780,000 Medicaid recipients and the Social Security numbers (SSNs) of 280,096 individual clients. The reason behind this breach is believed to be a configuration issue at the authentication level when DTS moved its claims to a new server.

The malicious hacker took advantage of this busy situation and managed to infiltrate the system, which contained sensitive user information such as client names, addresses, birth dates, SSNs, physician names, national provider identifiers, addresses, tax identification numbers, and procedure codes designed for billing purposes. The Utah DTS had proper access controls, policies, and procedures in place to secure sensitive data. However, in this particular case, a configuration error occurred while entering the password into the system. The malicious hacker accessed the password of the system administrator and gained the personal information of thousands of users.

The biggest lesson from this incident is that even if the data is encrypted, a flaw in the authentication system can render a system vulnerable.

The CCSP needs to consider approaches that can limit access through the use of access control policies, enforcing privileges and permissions for secure management of sensitive user data in the cloud.

SUMMARY

To operate a cloud environment securely, the CCSP needs to be able to focus on many different issues simultaneously. Understanding the physical and logical design elements of the cloud environment is the first step on the path toward operational stability and security. The CCSP should be able to describe the specifications necessary for the physical, logical, and environmental design of the data center as well as identify the necessary requirements to build and implement the physical and logical infrastructure of the cloud.

To be able to operate and manage the cloud, the CCSP needs to define policies and processes that are focused on providing secure access, availability, monitoring, analysis, and maintenance capabilities. The CCSP must also be able to demonstrate the ability to understand, identify, and manage risk within the organization, specifically as it relates to the cloud environment. Being able to identify the necessary regulations and controls to ensure compliance for the operation and management of cloud infrastructure within the organization, besides understand and manage the process of conducting a risk assessment of the physical and logical infrastructure, is important as well. The need to manage the process for the collection, acquisition, and preservation of digital evidence in a forensically sound manner with cloud environments should also be a focus for the CCSP.

REVIEW QUESTIONS

1. At which of the following levels should logical design for data separation be incorporated?

    A. Compute nodes and network

    B. Storage nodes and application

    C. Control plane and session

    D. Management plane and presentation

2. Which of the following is the correct name for Tier II of the Uptime Institute Data Center Site Infrastructure Tier Standard Topology?

    A. Concurrently Maintainable Site Infrastructure

    B. Fault-Tolerant Site Infrastructure

    C. Basic Site Infrastructure

    D. Redundant Site Infrastructure Capacity Components

3. Which of the following is the recommended operating range for temperature and humidity in a data center?

    A. Between 62° F and 81° F and 40 percent and 65 percent relative humidity

    B. Between 64° F and 81° F and 40 percent and 60 percent relative humidity

    C. Between 64° F and 84° F and 30 percent and 60 percent relative humidity

    D. Between 60° F and 85° F and 40 percent and 60 percent relative humidity

4. Which of the following are supported authentication methods for iSCSI? (Choose two.)

    A. Kerberos

    B. TLS

    C. SRP

    D. L2TP

5. What are the two biggest challenges associated with the use of IPSec in cloud computing environments?

    A. Access control and patch management

    B. Auditability and governance

    C. Configuration management and performance

    D. Training customers on how to use IPSec and documentation

6. When setting up resource sharing within a host cluster, which option would you choose to mediate resource contention?

   A. Reservations

   B. Limits

   C. Clusters

   D. Shares

7. When using maintenance mode, which two items are disabled and which item remains enabled?

   A. Customer access and alerts are disabled while logging remains enabled.

   B. Customer access and logging are disabled while alerts remain enabled.

   C. Logging and alerts are disabled while the ability to deploy new VMs remains enabled.

   D. Customer access and alerts are disabled while the ability to power on VMs remains enabled.

8. What are the three generally accepted service models of cloud computing?

   A. IaaS, DRaaS, and PaaS

   B. PaaS, SECaaS, and IaaS

   C. SaaS, PaaS, and IaaS

   D. Desktop as a service, PaaS, and IaaS

9. What is a key characteristic of a honeypot?

   A. Isolated, nonmonitored environment

   B. Isolated, monitored environment

   C. Composed of virtualized infrastructure

   D. Composed of physical infrastructure

10. What does the concept of nondestructive testing mean in the context of a vulnerability assessment?

   A. Detected vulnerabilities are not exploited during the vulnerability assessment.

   B. Known vulnerabilities are not exploited during the vulnerability assessment.

   C. Detected vulnerabilities are not exploited after the vulnerability assessment.

   D. Known vulnerabilities are not exploited before the vulnerability assessment.

11. Seeking to follow good design practices and principles, the CCSP should create the physical network design based on which of the following?

    A. A statement of work

    B. A series of interviews with stakeholders

    C. A design policy statement

    D. A logical network design

12. What should configuration management always be tied to?

    A. Financial management

    B. Change management

    C. IT service management

    D. Business relationship management

13. What are the objectives of change management? (Choose all that apply.)

    A. Respond to a customer's changing business requirements while maximizing value and reducing incidents, disruption, and rework.

    B. Ensure that changes are recorded and evaluated.

    C. Respond to business and IT requests for change that will disassociate services with business needs.

    D. Ensure that all changes are prioritized, planned, tested, implemented, documented, and reviewed in a controlled manner.

14. What is the definition of an incident according to the ITIL framework?

    A. An unplanned interruption to an IT service or a reduction in the quality of an IT service

    B. A planned interruption to an IT service or a reduction in the quality of an IT service

    C. The unknown cause of one or more problems

    D. The identified root cause of a problem

15. What is the difference between BC and BCM?

    A. BC is defined as the capability of the organization to continue delivery of products or services at acceptable predefined levels following a disruptive incident. BCM is defined as a holistic management process that identifies actual threats to an organization and the impacts to business operations that those threats, if realized, will cause. BCM provides a framework for building organizational resilience with the capability of an effective response that safeguards its key processes, reputation, brand, and value-creating activities.

B. BC is defined as a holistic process that identifies potential threats to an organization and the impacts to business operations that those threats, if realized, might cause. BC provides a framework for building organizational resilience with the capability of an effective response that safeguards the interests of its key stakeholders, reputation, brand, and value-creating activities. BCM is defined as the capability of the organization to continue delivery of products or services at acceptable predefined levels following a disruptive incident.

C. BC is defined as the capability of the first responder to continue delivery of products or services at acceptable predefined levels following a disruptive incident. BCM is defined as a holistic management process that identifies potential threats to an organization and the impacts to business operations that those threats, if realized, will cause. BCM provides a framework for building organizational resilience with the capability of an effective response that safeguards the interests of its key stakeholders, reputation, brand, and value-creating activities.

D. BC is defined as the capability of the organization to continue delivery of products or services at acceptable predefined levels following a disruptive incident. BCM is defined as a holistic management process that identifies potential threats to an organization and the impacts to business operations that those threats, if realized, might cause. BCM provides a framework for building organizational resilience with the capability of an effective response that safeguards the interests of its key stakeholders, reputation, brand, and value-creating activities.

16. What are the four steps in the risk-management process?

   A. Assessing, monitoring, transferring, and responding

   B. Framing, assessing, monitoring, and responding

   C. Framing, monitoring, documenting, and responding

   D. Monitoring, assessing, optimizing, and responding

17. An organization will conduct a risk assessment to evaluate which of the following?

   A. Threats to its assets, vulnerabilities not present in the environment, the likelihood that a threat will be realized by taking advantage of an exposure, the impact that the exposure being realized will have on the organization, and the residual risk

   B. Threats to its assets, vulnerabilities present in the environment, the likelihood that a threat will be realized by taking advantage of an exposure, the impact that the exposure being realized will have on another organization, and the residual risk

   C. Threats to its assets, vulnerabilities present in the environment, the likelihood that a threat will be realized by taking advantage of an exposure, the impact that the exposure being realized will have on the organization, and the residual risk

D. Threats to its assets, vulnerabilities present in the environment, the likelihood that a threat will be realized by taking advantage of an exposure, the impact that the exposure being realized will have on the organization, and the total risk

18. What is the minimum and customary practice of responsible protection of assets that affects a community or societal norm?

   A. Due diligence

   B. Risk mitigation

   C. Asset protection

   D. Due care

19. Within the realm of IT security, which of the following combinations best defines risk?

   A. Threat coupled with a breach

   B. Threat coupled with a vulnerability

   C. Vulnerability coupled with an attack

   D. Threat coupled with a breach of security

20. Qualitative risk assessment is earmarked by which of the following?

   A. Ease of implementation; it can be completed by personnel with a limited understanding of the risk assessment process

   B. Can be completed by personnel with a limited understanding of the risk assessment process and uses detailed metrics used for calculating risk

   C. Detailed metrics used for calculating risk and ease of implementation

   D. Can be completed by personnel with a limited understanding of the risk-assessment process and detailed metrics used for calculating risk

21. SLE is calculated by using which of the following?

   A. Asset value and ARO

   B. Asset value, LAFE, and SAFE

   C. Asset value and exposure factor

   D. LAFE and ARO

22. What is the process flow of digital forensics?

   A. Identification of incident and evidence, analysis, collection, examination, and presentation

   B. Identification of incident and evidence, examination, collection, analysis, and presentation

C. Identification of incident and evidence, collection, examination, analysis, and presentation

D. Identification of incident and evidence, collection, analysis, examination, and presentation

NOTES

[1] See the following for information on how Yahoo has been using the chicken coop design to drive its data center architecture: `http://www.datacenterknowledge.com/archives/2010/04/26/yahoo-computing-coop-the-shape-of-things-to-come/`

[2] See the following:
`http://www.gpxglobal.net/wp-content/uploads/2012/08/tierstandardtopology.pdf`

[3] See the following:
`http://ecoinfo.cnrs.fr/IMG/pdf/ashrae_2011_thermal_guidelines_data_center.pdf`

[4] See the following for more information on IEEE 802.1Q VLAN implementation:
`http://www.microhowto.info/tutorials/802.1q.html`

[5] See the following for the full RFC for Kerberos:
`http://www.ietf.org/rfc/rfc4120.txt` See the following for a good overview paper on Kerberos: *Kerberos: An Authentication Service for Computer Networks,*
`http://gost.isi.edu/publications/kerberos-neuman-tso.html`

[6] See the following for the full RFC for SPKM: `https://tools.ietf.org/html/rfc2025`

[7] See the following for the full RFC for CHAP: `http://tools.ietf.org/html/rfc1994`

[8] See the following for a detailed overview of the IEEE 802.1Q standard:
`https://www.ietf.org/meeting/86/tutorials/86-IEEE-8021-Thaler.pdf`

[9] See the following for the full RFC for TLS: `https://tools.ietf.org/html/rfc5246`

[10] See the following for the full RFCs for DNS:
`https://www.ietf.org/rfc/rfc1034.txt`
`https://www.ietf.org/rfc/rfc1035.txt`

[11] For more information on DNSSEC, see the following: `http://www.dnssec.net/`

[12] `http://csrc.nist.gov/publications/nistpubs/800-30-rev1/sp800_30_r1.pdf`

[13] VMware and Oracle both name their technology DRS, whereas OpenStack refers to its technology as Compute Resource Scheduling. Microsoft refers to its implementation under the feature name performance and resource optimization (PRO).

[14] `http://nvlpubs.nist.gov/nistpubs/Legacy/SP/nistspecialpublication800-145.pdf`
(pages 6–7)

[15] See the following for additional guidance on IPSec and SSL VPNs:
IPSec: `http://csrc.nist.gov/publications/nistpubs/800-77/sp800-77.pdf`
SSL: `http://csrc.nist.gov/publications/nistpubs/800-113/SP800-113.pdf`

[16] See the following:
http://nvlpubs.nist.gov/nistpubs/SpecialPublications/NIST.SP.800-40r3.pdf

[17] See the following:
http://csrc.nist.gov/publications/nistpubs/800-92/SP800-92.pdf

[18] See the following for more information on the Controls and to download the latest version: http://www.counciloncybersecurity.org/critical-controls/

[19] NIST SP 800-128, "Guide for Security-Focused Configuration Management of Information Systems":
http://csrc.nist.gov/publications/nistpubs/800-128/sp800-128.pdf

[20] http://atos.net/en-us/home/we-are/news/press-release/2015/pr-2015_03_26_01.html#

[21] Chart source: https://www.sans.org/critical-security-controls/control/2

[22] https://www.iso.org/obp/ui/#iso:std:iso:22301:ed-1:v2:en

[23] https://www.iso.org/obp/ui/#iso:std:iso:22301:ed-1:v2:en

[24] See the following:
http://csrc.nist.gov/publications/nistpubs/800-39/SP800-39-final.pdf

[25] http://csrc.nist.gov/publications/nistpubs/800-30-rev1/sp800_30_r1.pdf

[26] This can be represented by the following formula: Likelihood $\times$ Impact = Risk or L $\times$ I = R

DOMAIN 6

Legal and Compliance

THE GOAL OF THE Legal and Compliance domain is to offer you an understanding of how to approach the various legal and regulatory challenges unique to cloud environments. To achieve and maintain compliance, it is important to understand the audit processes utilized within a cloud environment, including auditing controls, assurance issues, and the specific reporting attributes.

You will gain an understanding of ethical behavior and required compliance within regulatory frameworks, which includes investigative techniques for crime analysis and evidence-gathering methods. Enterprise risk considerations and the impact of outsourcing for design and hosting are also explored.

DOMAIN OBJECTIVES

After completing this domain, you will be able to do the following:

❏ Understand how to identify the various legal requirements and unique risks associated with the cloud environment with regard to legislation and conflicting legislation, legal risks, controls, and forensic requirements

❏ Describe the potential personal and data privacy issues specific to personal identifiable information within the cloud environment

❏ Define the process, methods, and required adaptions necessary for an audit within the cloud environment

❏ Describe the different types of cloud-based audit reports

❏ Identify the impact of diverse geographical locations and legal jurisdictions

❏ Understand implications of cloud-to-enterprise risk management

❏ Explain the importance of cloud contract design and management for outsourcing a cloud environment

❏ Identify appropriate supply-chain management processes

INTRODUCTION

As the global nature of technology continues to evolve and essentially simplify and enable conveniences once thought impossible, the challenge and complexity of meeting internal legislations, regulations, and laws becomes greater all the time.

Ensuring adherence, compliance, or conformity with these can be challenging within traditional on-premises environments or even on third-party and hosted environments. Add cloud computing, and the complexity increases significantly (*Figure 6.1*).

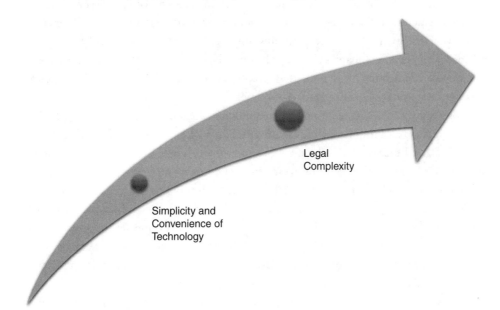

Legal
Complexity

Simplicity and
Convenience of
Technology

FIGURE 6.1 Cloud computing makes following regulations and laws more complicated.

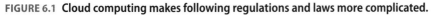

At all times, when dealing with legal, compliance, and regulatory issues, the first step should always be to consult with relevant professionals or teams specializing in those areas. As a security professional, your goal should be to establish a baseline understanding of the fluid and ever-changing legal and regulatory landscape with which you may need to interact.

INTERNATIONAL LEGISLATION CONFLICTS

Cloud computing provides wonderful opportunities for users related to ease of use, access, cost savings, automatic updates, scalable resourcing, and so on. From a legal perspective, the reality can be the exact opposite. Cloud computing introduces multiple legal challenges of which the security professional, architect, and practitioner all need to be aware. A primary challenge is created by the existence of conflicting legal requirements coupled with the inability to apply local laws to a global technology offering. This can result in uncertainty and a lack of clarity on the full scope of risks when operating globally.

In recent years, the increased use of technology and the rise in the number of businesses operating globally have resulted in the number of trans-border disputes increasing dramatically. In particular, these have included copyright law, intellectual property, and violation of patents. More recently, there have been breaches of data protection, legislative requirements, and other privacy-related components. Although these aren't new or exclusive to the Internet, they are becoming amplified and more widespread. How does it alter the stance of companies and organizations when state or national laws become stunted and limited due to technology? It complicates matters significantly. Some examples of recent areas of concern are discussed next.

In June 2011, Cloudfare, a web hosting and services company, became enmeshed in the middle of a multijurisdictional battle over the hacking activities of LulzSec. On June 15, 2011, LulzSec attacked the U.S. Central Intelligence Agency's (CIA's) websites and took them offline. LulzSec contracted to use Cloudfare for hosting services prior to launching the attacks, but it also used a total of seven hosting companies in Canada, the United States, and Europe. The ensuing hunt to find and take down LulzSec, involving various intelligence agencies and governments, as well as black-and-white-hat hackers from around the world, caused Cloudfare and other hosting companies to become the targets of distributed denial-of-service (DDoS) attacks that required the spreading of traffic across 14 data centers globally to successfully thwart.[1]

In a proceeding in 2014 before the U.S. Court, Microsoft was ordered to turn over an email belonging to a user of its hosted mail service. That email belonged to a user outside the United States. The email itself was located on a server in a data center in Ireland, which should be out of the reach of U.S. authorities and subject to the requirements of the EU privacy laws. Microsoft challenged the order and lost.[2]

LEGISLATIVE CONCEPTS

The following list is a general guide designed to help you focus on some of the areas and legislative items that might impact your cloud environments:

- **International law:** International law is the term given to the rules that govern relations between states or countries. It is made up of the following components:
  - International conventions, whether general or particular, establishing rules expressly recognized by contesting states

- International custom, as evidence of a general practice accepted as law
- The general principles of law recognized by civilized nations
- Judicial decisions and the teachings of the most highly qualified publicists of the various nations, as subsidiary means for the determination of rules of law

- **State law:** State law typically refers to the law of each U.S. state (50 states in total, each treated separately), with their own state constitutions, state governments, and state courts.

- **Copyright and piracy law:** Copyright infringement can be performed for financial or nonfinancial gain. It typically occurs when copyright material is infringed upon and made available to or shared with others by a party who is not the legal owner of the information.

- **Enforceable governmental request:** An enforceable governmental request is a request or order that is capable of being performed on the basis of the government's order.

- **Intellectual property right:** Intellectual property describes creations of the mind such as words, logos, symbols, other artistic creations, and literary works. Patents, trademarks, and copyright protection exist to protect a person's or a company's intellectual entitlements. Intellectual property rights give the individual who created an idea an exclusive right to that idea for a defined period of time.

- **Privacy law:** Privacy can be defined as the right of an individual to determine when, how, and to what extent she will release personal information. Privacy law also typically includes language indicating that personal information must be destroyed when its retention is no longer required.

- **The doctrine of the proper law:** When a conflict of laws occurs, this determines in which jurisdiction the dispute will be heard, based on contractual language professing an express selection or a clear intention through a choice-of-law clause. If there is not an express selection stipulated, implied selection may be used to infer the intention and meaning of the parties from the nature of the contract and the circumstances involved.

- **Criminal law:** Criminal law is a body of rules and statutes that defines conduct that is prohibited by the government and is set out to protect the safety and well being of the public. Besides defining prohibited conduct, criminal law defines the punishment when the law is breached. Crimes are categorized based on their seriousness with the categories carrying maximum punishments.

- **Tort law:** This is a body of rights, obligations, and remedies that sets out reliefs for persons suffering harm as a result of the wrongful acts of others. These laws set out that the individual liable for the costs and consequences of the wrongful act is the individual who committed the act as opposed to the individual who suffered the consequences. Tort actions are not dependent on an agreement between the parties to a lawsuit. Tort law serves four objectives:

- It seeks to compensate victims for injuries suffered by the culpable action or inaction of others.

- It seeks to shift the cost of such injuries to the person or persons who are legally responsible for inflicting them.

- It seeks to discourage injurious, careless, and risky behavior in the future.

- It seeks to vindicate legal rights and interests that have been compromised, diminished, or emasculated.

- **Restatement (second) conflict of laws:** A restatement is a collation of developments in the common law (that is, judge made law, not legislation) that inform judges and the legal world of updates in the area. Conflict of laws relates to a difference between the laws. In the United States, the existence of many states with legal rules often at variance makes the subject of conflict of laws especially urgent. The restatement (second) conflict of laws is the basis for deciding which laws are most appropriate when there are conflicting laws in the different states. The conflicting legal rules may come from U.S. federal law, the laws of U.S. states, or the laws of other countries.

FRAMEWORKS AND GUIDELINES RELEVANT TO CLOUD COMPUTING

Globally, a plethora of laws, regulations, and other legal requirements for organizations and entities exist to protect the security and privacy of digital and other information assets. This section examines guidelines and frameworks that are used in much of the world.

ISO/IEC 27017:2015 Information Technology—Security Techniques—Code of Practice for Information Security Controls Based on ISO/IEC 27002 for Cloud Services

ISO/IEC 27017:2015 offers guidelines for information security controls applicable to the provision and use of cloud services by providing additional implementation guidance for relevant controls specified in ISO/IEC 27002:2013 and additional controls with implementation guidance that specifically relate to cloud services.

Organization for Economic Cooperation and Development—Privacy and Security Guidelines

On September 9, 2013, the Organization for Economic Cooperation and Development (OECD) published a set of revised guidelines governing the protection of privacy and trans-border flows of personal data. This updated the OECD's original guidelines from 1980 that became the first set of accepted international privacy principles. These revised guidelines focused on the need to globally enhance privacy protection through improved interoperability and the need to protect privacy using a practical, risk-management-based approach.

According to the OECD, several new concepts have been introduced in the revised guidelines, including the following:[3]

- National privacy strategies
- Privacy management programs
- Data security breach notification

Asia-Pacific Economic Cooperation Privacy Framework[4]

Asia-Pacific Economic Cooperation (APEC) provides a regional standard to address privacy as it relates to the following:

- Privacy as an international issue
- Electronic trading environments and the effects of cross-border data flows

The goal of the framework is to promote a consistent approach to information privacy protection as a means of ensuring the free flow of information within the region. The APEC privacy framework is a principles-based privacy framework that is made up of four parts, as noted here:

- Part I: Preamble
- Part II: Scope
- Part III: Information Privacy Principles
- Part IV: Implementation

The nine principles that make up the framework are as follows:

- Preventing harm
- Notice
- Collection limitation
- Use of personal information

- Choice

- Integrity of personal information

- Security safeguards

- Access and correction

- Accountability

EU Data Protection Directive

The EU Directive[5] 95/46/EC provides for the regulation of the protection and free movement of personal data within the European Union. It is designed to protect the privacy and protection of all personal data collected for or about citizens of the European Union, especially as it relates to the processing, using, or exchanging of such data. The data protection directive encompasses the key elements from article 8 of the European Convention on Human Rights, which states its intention to respect the rights of privacy in personal and family life, as well as in the home and in personal correspondence. This directive applies to data processed by automated means and data contained in paper files. It does not apply to the processing of data in these instances:

- By a natural person in the course of purely personal or household activities

- In the course of an activity that falls outside the scope of community law, such as operations concerning public safety, defense, or state security

The directive aims to protect the rights and freedoms of persons with respect to the processing of personal data by laying down guidelines determining when this processing is lawful. The guidelines relate to the following:

- **The quality of the data:** Personal data must be processed fairly and lawfully and collected for specified, explicit, and legitimate purposes. It must also be accurate and, where necessary, kept up to date

- **The legitimacy of data processing:** Personal data may be processed only if the data subject has unambiguously given her consent or processing is necessary:

  - For the performance of a contract to which the data subject is party

  - For compliance with a legal obligation to which the controller is subject

  - To protect the vital interests of the data subject

  - For the performance of a task carried out in the public interest

  - For the purposes of the legitimate interests pursued by the controller

- **Special categories of processing:** It is forbidden to process personal data revealing racial or ethnic origin, political opinions, religious or philosophical beliefs, trade-union membership, and the processing of data concerning health or sex life. This provision comes with certain qualifications concerning, for example, cases where processing is necessary to protect the vital interests of the data subject or for the purposes of preventive medicine and medical diagnosis.

- **Information to be given to the data subject:** The controller must provide the data subject from whom data is collected with certain information relating to himself.

- **The data subject's right of access to data:** Every data subject should have the right to obtain from the controller the following:

  - Confirmation as to whether or not data relating to her is being processed and communication of the data undergoing processing

  - The rectification, erasure, or blocking of data for which the processing does not comply with the provisions of this directive either because of the incomplete or inaccurate nature of the data, and the notification of these changes to third parties to whom the data has been disclosed

- **Exemptions and restrictions:** The scope of the principles relating to the quality of the data, information to be given to the data subject, right of access, and publicizing of processing may be restricted to safeguard aspects such as national security, defense, public security, the prosecution of criminal offences, an important economic or financial interest of a member state or of the European Union, or the protection of the data subject.

- **The right to object to the processing of data:** The data subject should have the right to object, on legitimate grounds, to the processing of data relating to her. She should also have the right to object, on request and free of charge, to the processing of personal data that the controller anticipates being processed for the purposes of direct marketing. Finally, she should be informed before personal data is disclosed to third parties for the purposes of direct marketing and be expressly offered the right to object to such disclosures.

- **The confidentiality and security of processing:** Any person acting under the authority of the controller or of the processor, including the processor himself who has access to personal data, must not process the data except on instructions from the controller. In addition, the controller must implement appropriate measures to protect personal data against accidental or unlawful destruction or accidental loss, alteration, unauthorized disclosure, or access.

- **The notification of processing to a supervisory authority:** The controller must notify the national supervisory authority before carrying out any processing operation. Prior checks to determine specific risks to the rights and freedoms of data subjects are to be carried out by the supervisory authority following receipt of the notification. Measures are to be taken to ensure that processing operations are publicized, and the supervisory authorities must keep a register of the processing operations notified.

- **Scope:** Every person has the right to a judicial remedy for any breach of the rights guaranteed him by the national law applicable to the processing in question. In addition, any person who has suffered damage as a result of the unlawful processing of his personal data is entitled to receive compensation for the damage suffered. Transfers of personal data from a member state to a third country with an adequate level of protection are authorized. However, they may not be made to a third country that does not ensure this level of protection, except in the cases of the derogations listed. Each member state is obliged to provide one or more independent public authorities responsible for monitoring the application within its territory of the directive's provisions.

General Data Protection Regulation

On January 25, 2012, the European Commission unveiled a draft European General Data Protection Regulation to supersede the Data Protection Directive. The European Union is aiming to adopt the General Data Protection Regulation by 2016, and the regulation is planned to take effect after a transition period of two years. As of June 15, 2015, a common position on the EU data protection regulation was agreed to, allowing the first trialogue meeting to take place on June 24, 2015, to begin negotiations to finalize an agreement for implementation across the European Union.

ePrivacy Directive

The ePrivacy Directive,[6] Directive 2002/58/EC of the European Parliament and of the Council of July 12, 2002, is concerned with the processing of personal data and the protection of privacy in the electronic communications sector (as amended by Directives 2006/24/EC and 2009/136/EC).

Beyond Frameworks and Guidelines

Outside the wider frameworks and guidelines, a number of countries are currently adopting and aligning with data protection and privacy laws to enable swift and smoother business and trade relations, which include several Central and South American countries as well as Australia, New Zealand, and many Asian countries. For those operating within the United States (or having existing business relationships with U.S. entities), laws that take into account privacy and subsequent security requirements include Health Insurance Portability and Accountability Act (HIPAA) and Gramm-Leach-Bliley Act (GLBA).

There are additional privacy laws outlined by specific states, such as California and Colorado among others. Country-specific laws and regulations are discussed later in the section "Country-Specific Legislation and Regulations Related to PII, Data Privacy, and Data Protection."

COMMON LEGAL REQUIREMENTS

Because the cloud presents a dynamic environment, the necessity for the ongoing monitoring and review of legal requirements is essential. Following any contractual or signed acceptance of requirements by contractors, subcontractors, partners, and associated third parties, these should be subject to periodic review (in line with business reviews). The requirement to factor in any changes to third parties, to the supply chain, and to relevant laws and regulations should also form part of such reviews.

Table 6.1 examines legal requirements and issues that are often relevant when collecting, processing, storing, or transmitting personal data in cloud-based environments.

TABLE 6.1 **Legal Requirements**

REQUIREMENT	DESCRIPTION
U.S. Federal Laws	Federal laws and related regulations, such as GLBA, HIPAA, Children's Online Privacy Protection Act 1998 (COPPA), and additional Federal Trade Commission (FTC) orders that require organizations to implement specific controls and security measures when collecting, processing, storing, and transmitting data with partners, providers, or third parties.
U.S. State Laws	Requires processes and appropriate security controls to be implemented, along with providers and third parties. This typically includes a minimum requirement for a contract stipulating security controls and measures.
Standards	Standards look to capture requirements and guidelines such as International Organization for Standardization (ISO) 27001 and Payment Card Industry Data Security Standard (PCI DSS).
	Where applicable, the entities are required to stipulate and ensure that contractors, subcontractors, and third parties meet the requirements. Failure to do so can result in additional exposure from the supply chain as well as the company (that is, not the third party, or subcontractors) being liable for damages or being held fully accountable in the event of a breach.

(continues)

TABLE 6.1 *(continued)*

REQUIREMENT	DESCRIPTION
International Regulations and Regional Regulations	Many countries that are not bound to adhere to the EU data protection laws, OECD model, or APEC model are aligning themselves with such requirements and laws anyway. Under such laws, the entity who obtains consent from the data subject (the person providing the data to her) in turn is required to ensure any providers, partners, or third parties with any access to, or roles requiring the processing or storage of such information, satisfy data protection rules as the data processor, and so on. Additionally, the data owner requires verification and review of appropriate security controls being in place.
Contractual Obligations	Where specified activities and responsibilities are not listed or regulated by laws or acts, numerous contractual obligations may apply for the protection of personal information. Typically, these require that data is utilized or used only in accordance with the manner in which it was collected and to fulfill that function or task. Additionally, it is not permitted to share or distribute such information to entities or parties without the explicit consent of the data owner.
	The terms of permitted uses and requirements should be clearly specified as part of the contract. Where the individual (data subject) has access to his personal information, the individual owns the right to have the information amended, modified, or deleted in accordance with data protection and privacy laws.
Restrictions of Cross-Border Transfers	Multiple laws and regulations provide restrictions that do not allow for information to be transferred to locations where the level of privacy or data protection is deemed to be weaker than its current requirements. This is to ensure that wherever data transfers occur, they are afforded the same (or stronger) levels of protection and privacy.
	When information is being transferred to locations where laws or privacy/data protection controls are unknown, these should be clarified with the relevant data protection or privacy bodies prior to transfer or agreement to transfer.

LEGAL CONTROLS AND CLOUD SERVICE PROVIDERS

Depending on whether an organization is employing a hybrid, public, or community cloud, there are issues that the organization has to understand. The extra dynamic is the presence of a third party—the cloud service provider (CSP)—so the organization must understand how laws and regulations apply to the cloud. In other words, it becomes important to understand how laws apply to the different parties involved and how compliance will ultimately be addressed.

Regardless of which models you are using, you need to consider the legal issues that apply to how you collect, store, process, and, ultimately, destroy data. There are likely important national and international laws that you, with your legal functions, need to consider to ensure you are in legal compliance. There may be numerous compliance requirements, such as Safe Harbor, HIPAA, PCI DSS, and other technology and information privacy laws and regulations. Failure to comply may mean heavy punishments and liability issues.

Laws and regulations typically specify responsibility and accountability for the protection of information. For example, health information requires positions established for the security of that information. Sarbanes-Oxley Act (SOX), for example, makes the chief executive officer (CEO) and chief information officer (CIO) accountable for the protection of information, whereas GLBA specifies that the entire board of directors is accountable.

If you are using a cloud infrastructure that is sourced from a CSP, you must impose all legal and regulatory requirements that are inflicted on you to the CSP. Accountability remains with you, and making sure you are complying is your responsibility. Usually this can be addressed through clauses in the contract that specify that the CSP will use effective security controls and comply with any data privacy provisions. You are accountable for the actions of any of your subcontractors, including CSPs.

e-DISCOVERY

For those familiar with digital evidence's relevance and overall value in the event of an incident or suspected instance of cybercrime, e-discovery has long formed part of relevant investigations.

e-discovery refers to any process in which electronic data is sought, located, secured, and searched with the intent of using it as evidence in a civil or criminal legal case. e-discovery can be carried out online and offline (for static systems or within particular network segments). In the case of cloud computing, almost all e-discovery cases are done in online environments with resources remaining online.

e-Discovery Challenges

The challenges for the security professional here are complex and need to be fully understood. Picture this scene. You receive a call from your company's legal advisors or from a third party advising of potentially unlawful or illegal activities across the infrastructure and resources that employees access.

Given that your systems are no longer on-premises (or only a portion of your systems are), what are the first steps you are going to follow? Start acquiring local devices and obtaining portions or components from your data center? Surely, you can just get the data and information required from the CSP. This may or may not be the case, however. And if it is possible, it may be complicated to extract the relevant information required.

If you look at this from a U.S. perspective, under the Federal Rules of Civil Procedure, a party to litigation is expected to preserve and be able to produce electronically stored information that is in its possession, custody, or control. Sounds straightforward, right? Is the cloud under your control? Who is controlling or hosting the relevant data? Does this mean that it is under the provider's control?

Considerations and Responsibilities of e-Discovery

How good is your relationship with your cloud vendor? Good, bad, or fine? Have you ever spoken with your CSPs' technical teams? Imagine picking up the phone to speak with the CSP for the first time when trying to understand how to conduct an e-discovery investigation involving its systems.

At this point, do you know exactly where your data is housed within your CSP? If you do, you have a slight head start on many others. If you do not, it is time you find out. Imagine trying to collect and carry out e-discovery investigations in Europe, Asia, South America, the United States, or elsewhere when the location of your data is found to be in a different hemisphere or geography than you are.

Any seasoned investigator will tell you that carrying out investigations or acquisitions within locations or states that you are not familiar with in terms of laws, regulations, or other statutory requirements can be tricky and risky. Understanding and appreciating local laws and their implications is a must for the security professional prior to initiating or carrying out any such reviews or investigations.

Laws in one state may well clash with or contravene laws in another. It is the Certified Cloud Security Professional's (CCSP's) responsibility under due care and due diligence to validate that all the relevant laws and statutes that pertain to their investigation are documented and understood to the best of her ability prior to the start of the investigation.

Reducing Risk

Given that the cloud is an evolving technology, companies and security professionals can be caught short when dealing with e-discovery. There is a distinct danger that companies can lose control over access to their data due to investigations or legal actions being carried out against them. A key step to reducing the potential implications, costs, and business disruptions caused by loss of access to data is to ensure your cloud service contract takes into account such events. As a first requirement, your contract with the CSP should state that it is to inform you of any such events and enable you to control or make decisions in the event of a subpoena or other similar actions. These events should be factored into the organization's business continuity and incident response plans.

Conducting e-Discovery Investigations

There are various ways to conduct e-discovery investigations in cloud environments. A few examples include the following:

- **Software as a service (SaaS)-based e-discovery:** To some, "e-discovery in the cloud" means using the cloud to deliver tools used for e-discovery. These SaaS packages typically cover one of several e-discovery tasks, such as collection, preservation, and review.

- **Hosted e-discovery (provider):** e-discovery in the cloud can also mean hiring a hosted services provider to conduct e-discovery on data stored in the cloud. Typically, the customer stores data in the cloud with the understanding and mechanisms to support the cloud vendor doing the e-discovery. When the providers are not in a position to resource or provide the e-discovery, they may outsource to a credible or trusted provider.

- **Third-party e-discovery:** When no prior notifications or arrangements with the CSP for an e-discovery review exist, typically an organization needs a third party or specialized resources operating on its behalf.

Note that careful consideration and appreciation of the service-level agreement (SLA) and contract agreements must be undertaken to establish whether investigations of cloud-based assets are permitted or if prior notification and acceptance are required.

CLOUD FORENSICS AND ISO/IEC 27050-1

When incidents occur, it may be necessary to perform forensic investigations related to that incident. Depending on the cloud model that you are employing, it may not be easy to gather the required information to perform effective forensic investigations.

The industry refers to this as cloud forensics. Cloud computing forensic science is the application of scientific principles, technological practices, and derived and proven methods to reconstruct past cloud computing events through identification, collection, preservation, examination, interpretation, and reporting of digital evidence.

Conducting a forensic network analysis on the cloud is not as easy as conducting the same investigation across your own network and local computers. This is because you may not have access to the information that you require and, therefore, need to ask the service provider to provide the information.

Communication in this scenario becomes important, and all involved entities must work together to gather the important information related to the incident. In some cases, the cloud customer may not be able to obtain and review security incident logs because they are in the possession of the service provider. The service provider may be under no obligation to provide this information or may be unable to do so without violating the confidentiality of the other tenants sharing the cloud infrastructure.

ISO has provided a suite of standards specifically related to digital forensics, which include ISO/IEC 27037:2012, 27041:2014-01, 27042:2014-01, 27043, and 27050-1. The goal of such standards is to promote best practices for the acquisition and investigation of digital evidence.

Although some practitioners favor certain methods, processes, and controls, ISO 27050-1 looks to introduce and ensure standardization of approaches globally. The key thing for the CCSP to be aware of is that while doing cloud forensics, all relevant national and international standards must be adhered to.

PROTECTING PERSONAL INFORMATION IN THE CLOUD

This section describes the potential personal and data privacy issues specific to personally identifiable information (PII) within the cloud environment. Borderless computing is the fundamental concept that results in a globalized service, being widely accessible with no perceived borders.

With the cloud, the resources that are used for processing and storing user data and network infrastructure can be located anywhere on the globe, constrained only by where the capacities are available. The offering of listed availability zones by cloud service providers (CSPs) does not necessarily result in exclusivity within these zones, due to resilience, failover, redundancy, and other factors. Additionally, many other providers state that resources and information will be used within their primary location (that is, European Zone/North America, and so on); however, they will be backed up in at least two additional locations to enable recoverability and redundancy. In the absence of transparency related to exact data at rest locations, this leads to challenges from a customer perspective to ensure that relevant requirements for data security are being satisfied.

Regarding data protection and relevant privacy frameworks, standards, and legal requirements, cloud computing raises a number of interesting issues. In essence, data protection law is based on the premise that it is always clear where personal data is located, by whom it is processed, and who is responsible for data processing. At all times, the data subject (that is, the person to whom the information relates, such as John Smith) should have an understanding of these issues. Cloud computing appears to fundamentally conflict with these requirements and listed obligations.

The following sections explore the differences between contractual PII and regulated PII. Then they examine the laws of various countries that affect personal information.

Differentiating Between Contractual and Regulated PII

In cloud computing, the legal responsibility for data processing is borne by the user who enlists the services of a CSP. As in all other cases in which a third party is given the task of processing personal data, the user, or data controller, is responsible for ensuring that the relevant requirements for the protection and compliance with requirements for PII are satisfied or met.

The term *PII* is widely recognized across the area of information security and under U.S. privacy law. PII relates to information or data components that can be utilized by themselves or along with other information to identify, contact, or locate a living individual. PII is a legal term recognized under various laws and regulations across the United States.

National Institute of Standards and Technology (NIST), in Special Publication (SP) 800-122, defines PII as any information about an individual "that can be used to distinguish or trace an individual's identity, such as name, Social Security Number, date and place of birth, mother's maiden name, or biometric records; and any other information that is linked or linkable to an individual, such as medical, educational, financial, and employment information."[7]

Fundamentally, there are two main types of PII associated with cloud and noncloud environments.

Contractual PII

Where an organization or entity processes, transmits, or stores PII as part of its business or services, this information is required to be adequately protected in line with relevant local state, national, regional, federal, or other laws. Where any outsourcing of services, roles, or functions (involving cloud-based technologies, or manual processes such as call centers), the relevant contract should list the applicable rules and requirements from the organization that owns the data and the applicable laws to which the provider should adhere.

Additionally, the contractual elements related to PII should list requirements and appropriate levels of confidentiality, along with security provisions and requirements necessary. As part of the contract, the provider is bound by privacy, confidentiality, or information security requirements established by the organization or entity to which it provides services. The contracting body may be required to document adherence or compliance with the contract at set intervals and in line with any audit and governance requirements from its customers.

Failure to meet or satisfy contractual requirements may lead to penalties (financial or service compensation) through to termination of contract at the discretion of the organization to which services are provided.

Regulated PII

The key focus and distinct criteria to which the regulated PII must adhere is required under law and statutory requirements, as opposed to the contractual criteria that may be based on best practices or organizational security policies.

Key differentiators from a regulated perspective are the must-haves to satisfy regulatory requirements (such as HIPAA and GLBA). Failure to supply these can result in sizable and significant financial penalties and restrictions around processes, storing, and providing of services.

Regulations are put in place to reduce exposure and to ultimately protect entities and individuals from a number of risks. They also force providers and processers alike to take certain responsibilities and actions.

The reasons for regulations include but are not limited to the following:

- Take due care.

- Apply adequate protections.

- Protect customers and consumers.

- Ensure appropriate mechanisms and controls are implemented.

- Reduce likelihood of malformed or fractured practices.

- Establish a baseline level of controls and processes.

- Create a repeatable and measurable approach to regulated data and systems.

- Continue to align with statutory bodies and fulfill professional conduct requirements.

- Provide transparency among customers, partners, and related industries.

Mandatory Breach Reporting

Another key component and differentiator related to regulated PII is mandatory breach reporting requirements. At present, 47 states and territories within the United States, including the District of Columbia, Puerto Rico, and the Virgin Islands, have legislation in place that requires both private and government entities to notify and inform individuals of any security breaches involving PII.

Many affected organizations lack the understanding or find it a challenge to define what constitutes a breach, along with defining incidents versus events, and so on. More recently, the relevant security breach laws include clear and concise requirements related to who must comply with the law (businesses, information brokers, government entities, agencies, regulatory bodies, and so on) and defining what personally identifiable information means (name combined with Social Security number, driver's license, state identification documents, and relevant account numbers).

Finally, included in the laws are definitions and examples of what defines and constitutes a security or data breach (such as unauthorized access, acquisition, or sharing of data), how the affected parties and individuals are to be notified and informed of any breaches involving PII, and any exceptions (such as masked, scrambled, anonymized, or encrypted information).

The NIST Guide (SP 800-122) called "Protecting the Confidentiality of Personally Identifiable Information" should serve as a useful resource when identifying and ensuring requirements for contractual and regulated PII are established, understood, and enforced. A breakdown on incident response (IR) and its required stages is also captured in SP 800-122.

NIST Guide SP 800-122 was developed to assist agencies and state bodies in meeting PII requirements. Depending on your industry and geographic location, NIST guides may not ensure compliance. Always check if there are additional or differing controls that are applicable to your environment and based on local legislation.

Contractual Components

From a contractual, regulated, and PII perspective, the following should be reviewed and fully understood by the CCSP with regards to any hosting contracts (along with other overarching components within an SLA):

- **Scope of processing:** The CCSP needs a clear understanding of the permissible types of data processing. The specifications should also list the purpose for which the data can be processed or utilized.

- **Use of subcontractors:** The CCSP must understand where any processing, transmission, storage, or use of information will occur. A complete list should be drawn up, including the entity, location, rationale, and form of data use (processing, transmission, and storage), along with any limitations or nonpermitted uses. Contractually, the requirement for the procuring organization to be informed as to where data has been provided or will be utilized by a subcontractor is essential.

- **Deletion of data:** Where the business operations no longer require information to be retained for a specific purpose (that is, not retaining for convenience or potential future uses), the deletion of information should occur in line with the organization's data retention policies and standards. Data deletion is also of critical importance when contractors and subcontractors no longer provide services or when a contract is terminated.

- **Appropriate or required data security controls:** Where processing, transmission, or storage of data and resources is outsourced, the same level of security controls should be required for any entity's contracting or subcontracting services. Ideally, security controls should be of a higher level (which is the case for a large number of cloud computing services) than the existing levels of controls; however, this is never to be taken as a given in the absence of confirmation or verification. Additionally, technical security controls should be unequivocally called out and stipulated in the contract; they are applicable to subcontractors as well. Where such controls are unable to be met by either the contractor or the subcontractor, these need to be communicated, documented, understood, and have mitigating controls in place that enhance and satisfy the data owners' requirements. Common methods to ensure the ongoing confidentiality of the data include encryption of data during transmission or storage (ideally both), along with defense in depth and layered approaches to data and systems security.

- **Locations of data:** To ensure compliance with regulatory and legal requirements, the CCSP needs to understand the location of contractors and subcontractors. She must pay particular attention to where the organization is located and where operations, data centers, and headquarters are located. The CCSP needs to know where information is being stored, processed, and transmitted. (Many business units are outsourced or located in geographic locations where storage, resourcing, and skills may be more economically advantageous for the CSP, contractor, or subcontractor.) Finally, any contingency or continuity requirements may require failover to different geographic locations, which can affect or violate regulatory or contractual requirements. The CCSP should fully understand these and accept them prior to engagement of services with any contractor, subcontractor, or CSP.

- **Return or restitution of data:** For both contractors and subcontractors where a contract is terminated, the timely and orderly return of data has to be required both contractually and within the SLA. Appropriate notice should be provided, as well as the ongoing requirement to ensure the availability of the data is maintained between relevant parties, with an emphasis on live data being required. Format and structure of data should be clearly documented, with an emphasis on structured and agreed-upon formats being clearly understood by all parties. Data retention periods should be explicitly understood, with the return of data to the organization that owns the data resulting in the removal or secure deletion on any contractors' or subcontractors' systems or storage.

- **Right to audit subcontractors:** In line with the agreement between the organization utilizing services and the contracting entity where subcontractors are being utilized, the subcontracting entity should be in agreement and be bound by any right to audit clauses and requirements. Right to audit clauses should allow for the organization owning the data (not possessing) to audit or engage the services of an independent party to ensure that contractual and regulatory requirements are being satisfied by either the contractor or the subcontractor.

Country-Specific Legislation and Regulations Related to PII, Data Privacy, and Data Protection

It is important to understand the legislation and regulations of various countries as you deal with personal information, data privacy, and data protection. The varying data protection legislation among jurisdictions inevitably makes using global cloud computing challenging. This can be further complicated by the fact that sometimes regulations and laws can differ between a larger jurisdiction and its members, as in the case of the European Union and its member countries. Beyond laws, there are broader guidelines as discussed in the "Frameworks and Guidelines Relevant to Cloud Computing" section.

European Union

From an EU perspective, varying levels of data protection in different jurisdictions have resulted in the prohibition of EU data controllers transferring personal data outside their country to non–European Economic Area (EEA) jurisdictions that do not have an adequate level of protection (subject to some exceptions).

As a result, firms outsourcing to a cloud must have total certainty as to where in the cloud the data can be stored, or they must agree with the CSP about the specific jurisdictions in which the data can be processed. In reality, this can be difficult to do because many CSPs process data across multiple jurisdictions through federated clouds. This might include non-EEA countries where a different, and possibly lower, standard of data protection may apply.

Furthermore, this challenge is exacerbated by the fact that it is often difficult to know precisely where in the network a piece of data is being processed at any given time when there is a network of cloud servers and data stored on different servers in different jurisdictions.

These circumstances clearly raise specific issues and possible concerns relating to standards of data protection and the ability to adhere to obligations under data protection legislation.

Directive 95/46 EC

Directive 95/46/EC focuses on the protection of individuals with regard to the processing of personal data and on the free movement of such data; it also captures the human right to privacy, as referenced in the European Convention on Human Rights (ECHR).

EU General Data Protection Regulation 2012

In 2012, the European Commission proposed a major reform of the EU legal framework on the protection of personal data. The new proposals would strengthen individual rights and tackle the challenges of globalization and new technologies.

The proposed General Data Protection Regulation, expected to become effective by 2016, is intended to replace the 1995 directive. Because it is a regulation, member states will have no autonomy as to its application. The European Commission hopes this will address the inconsistency of application experienced with the 1995 directive.

The regulation introduces many significant changes for data processors and controllers. The following may be considered some of the more significant ones:

- The concept of consent
- Transfers abroad
- The right to be forgotten
- Establishment of the role of the data protection officer
- Access requests
- Home state regulation
- Increased sanctions

United Kingdom and Ireland

There is a common standard of protection at the EU level with respect to transferring personal data from Ireland and the UK to an EEA country. Challenges arise when data is being transferred from either country to a jurisdiction outside the EEA. Companies must meet special conditions to ensure that the country in question provides an adequate level of data protection.

There are, however, several means of getting such assurance. Some countries have been approved for this purpose by the EU commission on the basis of Article 25(6) of the Directive 95/46/EC by virtue of the country's domestic law or of the international commitment it has entered into. These countries include Switzerland, Australia, New Zealand, Argentina, and Israel.

U.S. companies that have subscribed to the Safe Harbor Principles are also approved for this purpose, albeit the framework is not available to all industries such as telecoms and financial services. Another means of ensuring adequacy of data protection is by using EU-approved "model contracts" or EU-approved "binding corporate rules" in the case of multinational companies that operate within and outside the European Union. It is possible to transfer personal data to a third country if the data subject's consent is given, but the Irish Data Protection Commissioner warns against this.

First, if you're transferring a database of individual records, you must obtain consent from each individual. Second, in practice, it's difficult to prove that the level of consent required was given because it must be established that clear, unambiguous, and specific consent was freely given.

Following are the key issues in transferring data from Ireland within the EEA enunciated by the Data Protection Guidance:

- **The security of the data:** Under Irish and UK law, it is clearly stated that the responsibility for data security lies with the data controller. Under the Irish Data Protection Acts, the data controller must be satisfied that if the personal data is outsourced to a CSP, the CSP has taken "…appropriate security measures against unauthorized access to, or unauthorized alteration, disclosure, or destruction of the data" (Section 2(1) (d) of the Acts). The data controller must also be satisfied that the CSP will only process data that it is instructed and permitted to.

- **The location of the data:** As noted, there is a common standard of protection at the EU level with respect to personal data held within the EEA. However, when data is transferred outside the EEA, you must take special measures to ensure that it continues to benefit from adequate protection.

- **The requirement for a written contract between the CSP and any subprocessors:** This is also a requirement under UK legislation (data protection authority [DPA], Schedule 1 Part II paragraph 12(a)(ii)). The contract must contain provisions that the CSP and any subprocessors it uses will only process the data as instructed. Also, the contract will detail assurance by the CSP on security measures—including measures to be taken to adequately guarantee the security of personal data processed outside the EEA.

Argentina

Argentina's legislative basis, over and above the constitutional right of privacy, is the Personal Data Protection Act 2000.[8] This act openly tracks the EU directive, resulting in the EU commission's approval of Argentina as a country offering an adequate level of data protection. This means personal data can be transferred between Europe and Argentina as freely as if Argentina were part of the EEA.

The Personal Data Protection Act, consistent with EU rules, prohibits transferring personal data to countries that do not have adequate protections, such as the United States. Argentina has also enacted a number of laws to supplement the 2000 act, such as a 2001 decree setting out regulations under the 2000 act, a 2003 disposition setting out privacy sanctions and classifying degrees of infractions, and a 2004 disposition that enacted a data code of ethics.

United States

Even though the United States has myriad laws that touch on various specific aspects of data privacy, there is no single federal law governing data protection. Interestingly, the word *privacy* is not mentioned in the United States Constitution; however, privacy is recognized differently in certain states and under different circumstances. The California and Montana constitutions both recognize privacy as an "inalienable right" that is "essential to the well-being of a free society."

There are few restrictions on the transfer of personal data out of the United States, making it relatively easy for firms to engage CSPs located outside the United States. The FTC and other associated U.S. regulators do, however, hold that the applicable U.S. laws and regulations apply to the data after it leaves its jurisdiction, and the U.S. regulated entities remain liable for the following:

- Data exported out of the United States
- Processing of data overseas by subcontractors
- Subcontractors using the same protections (such as security safeguards, protocols, audits, and contractual provisions) for the regulated data when it leaves the country

Most importantly, the Safe Harbor program deals with the international transfer of data. However, it is important to also understand about HIPAA, the GLBA, the Stored Communications Act (SCA), and SOX because each influences the way the United States handles privacy and data.

Safe Harbor Program

The Safe Harbor program was developed by the U.S. Department of Commerce and the EU Commission to address the Commission's determination that the United States does not have in place a regulatory framework that provides adequate protection for personal data transferred from the EEA. Any U.S. organization subject to the FTC's jurisdiction and some transportation organizations subject to the jurisdiction of the U.S. Department of Transportation can participate in the Safe Harbor program. Certain industries, such as telecommunication carriers, banks, and insurance companies, may not be eligible for this program.

Under the Safe Harbor program, U.S. companies have been able to voluntarily adhere to a set of seven principles:

- Notice
- Choice
- Transfers to third parties

- Access
- Security
- Data integrity
- Enforcement

Organizations must also be subject to enforcement and dispute resolution proceedings.

Safe Harbor Alternative

As an alternative to the Safe Harbor program, U.S. organizations can use standard contractual clauses (model contracts) in their agreements regulating the transfer of personal data from the EEA. The contractual clauses should establish adequate safeguards by creating obligations similar to those in the Safe Harbor program and incorporate the Data Protection Directive principles.

Under the U.S. Safe Harbor program and the standard contractual clauses framework, the relevant national regulator does not need to approve the data transfer agreement.

However, if a U.S. multinational wants to implement binding corporate rules, the rules must be approved separately in each member state where the multinational has an office.

EU View on U.S. Privacy

The European Commission believes that the United States fails to offer an adequate level of privacy protection; thus, there is a general prohibition on the transfer of personal data between the EEA and the United States. Although this causes considerable difficulties in practice, as mentioned, several methods have been developed to overcome this challenge. The Safe Harbor framework is one such way.

There is also a Switzerland Safe Harbor framework to bridge the differences between the two countries' approaches to privacy and provide a streamlined means for U.S. organizations to comply with Swiss data protection laws. If a company breaches the principles, enforcement action is taken by the U.S. FTC and not by EU bodies or national data protection authorities. (More information on the Swiss law is listed later in this domain.)

HIPAA

HIPAA (U.S. Act) sets out the requirements of the Department of Health and Human Services to adopt national standards for electronic healthcare transactions and national identifiers for providers, health plans, and employers. Protected health information can be stored via cloud computing under HIPAA.

GLBA

The GLBA (aka the Financial Modernization Act of 1999) is a federal law enacted in the United States to control the ways that financial institutions deal with the private information of individuals. The act consists of three sections:

- The Financial Privacy Rule regulates the collection and disclosure of private financial information.

- The Safeguards Rule stipulates that financial institutions must implement security programs to protect such information.

- The Pretexting Provisions prohibit the practice of pretexting (accessing private information using false pretenses).

The act also requires financial institutions to give customers written privacy notices that explain their information-sharing practices.

SCA

SCA was enacted in the United States in 1986 as part of the Electronic Communications Privacy Act. It provides privacy protections for certain electronic communication and computing services from unauthorized access or interception.

SOX

SOX is U.S. legislation enacted to protect shareholders and the general public from accounting errors and fraudulent practices in the enterprise. The act is administered by the Securities and Exchange Commission (SEC), which sets deadlines for compliance and publishes rules on requirements. SOX is not a set of business practices and does not specify how a business should store records; rather, it defines which records are to be stored and for how long.

Australia and New Zealand

Regulations in Australia and New Zealand make it extremely difficult for enterprises to move sensitive information to CSPs that store data outside of the Australian and New Zealand borders. The Office of the Australian Information Commissioner (OAIC) provides oversight and governance on data privacy regulations of sensitive personal information.

The Australian National Privacy Act of 1988 provides guidance and regulates how organizations collect, store, secure, process, and disclose personal information. Similar to many of the EU Privacy and Protection Acts, the National Privacy Principles (NPP) listed in the act were developed to ensure that organizations holding personal information handle and process it responsibly.

An emphasis is also placed on healthcare information and health service providers—similar to the U.S. equivalent HIPAA.

Within the privacy principles, the following components are addressed for personal information:

- Collection

- Use

- Disclosure

- Access

- Correction

- Identification

In addition to these requirements, the organization must take reasonable steps to protect the personal information it holds from misuse and loss and from unauthorized access, modification, or disclosure. Given the vagueness of "reasonable steps," this can allow for a large amount of ambiguity and challenge.

Since March 2014, the revised Privacy Amendment Act has introduced a set of new principles focusing on the handling of personal information, now called the Australian Privacy Principles (APPs). The Privacy Amendment Act requires organizations to put in place SLAs, with an emphasis on security. These SLAs must list the right to audit, reporting requirements, data locations permitted and not permitted, who can access the information, and cross-border disclosure of personal information (such as when personal data traverses Australian and New Zealand borders).

In the context of the cloud, agencies and businesses that deal with personal information need to be conscious of the following:

- **APP8 (cross-border disclosure of personal information):** Focuses on regulating the disclosure or transfer of personal information to a separate entity (including subsidiaries, third parties, partners, and parent companies) offshore or overseas. Prior to any sharing or disclosure of information offshore, companies must take reasonable steps to ensure the overseas recipients will comply with the APPs. (Documented evidence of this is strongly recommended.) The most effective manner to ensure this is performed is to include contractual requirements and associated provisions. Regardless of any provisions and agreement from the entity, the Australian entity will remain liable for the offshore recipient's actions (or lack thereof) and practices in respect of the personal information.

- **APP11.1 (security of personal information):** Requires that an organization take reasonable steps to protect the personal information it holds from misuse, interference, and loss and from unauthorized access, modification, or disclosure. In addition, a guidance document has been provided that highlights and outlines what steps would be deemed "reasonable." Although "reasonable" may be vague enough to ensure a number of approaches are reviewed, it does not ensure that appropriate or relevant steps will be taken.

Russia

On December 31, 2014, the Russian president signed into federal law No. 526-FZ a proposal to change the effective date of Russia's Data Localization Law, from September 1, 2016, to September 1, 2015. The State Duma (the lower chamber of the Russian Parliament) approved the legislation on December 17, 2014, after which it was approved by the Federation Council (the upper chamber) on December 25, 2014. Under the Data Localization Law, businesses collecting data of Russian citizens, including on the Internet, are obliged to record, systematize, accumulate, store, update, change, and retrieve the personal data of Russian citizens in databases located within the territory of the Russian Federation.

Switzerland

In accordance with Swiss data protection law, the basic principles of which are in line with EU law, three issues are important: the conditions under which the transfer of personal data processing to third parties is permissible, the conditions under which personal data may be sent abroad, and data security.

Data Processing by Third Parties

In systems of law with extended data protection, as is the case for the European Union and Switzerland, it is permissible to enlist the support of third parties for data processing. However, the data controller remains responsible for the processing of data, even if this is performed by one or more third parties on his instructions. According to Swiss data protection law, the data controller must ensure that an appointed third party (data processor) processes data only in a way as the data controller himself would be permitted to. Furthermore, the data controller has to make sure that the data processor meets the same requirements for data security that apply to the data collector.

Depending on the sector (e-health, utilities, retail, and so on) to which the data controller belongs, specific additional requirements may apply. For example, banks and stock traders have to conclude a written agreement with the data processor (an electronic, online closed contract is not sufficient) in which they oblige the data processor to observe Swiss banking confidentiality. In addition, the data processor must be incorporated into the internal monitoring system, and the internal and external audit and the bank supervisory authority must be able to conduct audits on the data processor at any time. In the contract with the data processor, the bank has to therefore agree to corresponding rights regarding inspection, rights of command, and rights of control.

Transferring Personal Data Abroad

Under Swiss law, as under EU law, special rules apply when sending personal data abroad. According to these, exporting data abroad is permissible if legislation that ensures adequate data protection in accordance with Swiss standards exists in the country in which the recipient of the data is located. The European Union and European Free Trade Association (EFTA) states in particular have such legislation. A list published by the Swiss Federal Data Protection Commissioner contains more details of whether adequate data protection legislation exists in a particular country. As mentioned, the United States does not have adequate data protection legislation.

However, if the data recipient is covered by the Safe Harbor Regime, which in addition to the European Union has also been applied to the relationship between Switzerland and the United States since the beginning of 2009, this guarantees the adequacy of the data protection and data transmission is permissible. Nevertheless, if no adequate data protection legislation exists in the recipient country, the transmission of data from Switzerland is permissible only under special circumstances.

In connection with the processing of personal data for business purposes, mention must be made of the following cases, in particular: conclusion of a contract with the data recipient in which they are obliged to observe adequate data protection, consent by the person(s) concerned, and transmission of data that concerns the contracting party in connection with the conclusion or implementation of a contract.

Data Security

Swiss data protection law requires—as do EU national laws—that data security is safeguarded when processing personal data. Availability, integrity, and confidentiality (AIC) of data must be ensured by means of appropriate organizational and technical measures.

These also include the protection of systems and data from the risks of unauthorized or arbitrary destruction, arbitrary loss, technical faults, forgery, theft and unlawful use, and unauthorized modification, copying, access, or other unauthorized processing. The data collector remains legally responsible for the observance of data security, even if he assigns data processing to a third party.

The small selection of different locations, jurisdictions, and legal requirements for data protection and privacy should serve as an insight into the sizeable challenge of global cloud computing, while trying to satisfy local and other relevant laws and regulations.

The CCSP should always engage with legal and other associated professionals across the areas of local and international laws prior to commencing the use of cloud-based services. The involvement of such professionals may restrict, shape, or remove the opportunity to utilize a certain set of services or providers and is a fundamental step that should not be overlooked or skipped for ease of convenience or to ensure timely adoption of services.

AUDITING IN THE CLOUD

This section defines the process, methods, and required adaptions necessary for an audit within the cloud environment.

As discussed throughout the book, the journey to cloud-based computing requires significant investments throughout the organization, with an emphasis on the business components such as finance, legal, compliance, technology, risk, strategy, executive sponsors, and so on.

Given the large number of elements and components to consider, it is safe to say that no small task of work is required before utilizing cloud services. The Cloud Security Alliance (CSA) has developed the Cloud Controls Matrix (CCM), which looks to list and categorize the domains and controls, along with which elements and components are relevant according to the controls. The CCM provides an invaluable resource when identifying and listing each action and what impacts these may have. Additionally, within the spreadsheet, a best practice guide is given for each control, along with mapping the CCM against frameworks and standards such as ISO 27001:2013, Federal Information Processing Standard (FIPS), NIST, Control Objectives for Information and Related Technology (COBIT), CSA Trusted Cloud Initiative, European Union Agency for Network and Information Security (ENISA), Federal Risk and Authorization Management Program (FedRAMP), Generally Accepted Privacy Principles (GAPP), HIPAA, North American Electric Reliability Corporation (NERC), Jericho Forum, and others. This should form the foundation for any cloud strategy, risk reviews, or provider-based risk assessments.

Internal and External Audits

As organizations begin to transition services to the cloud, there is a need for ongoing assurances from both cloud customers and providers that controls are put in place or are in the process of being identified.

An organization's internal audit acts as a third line of defense after the business or information technology (IT) functions and risk management functions through the following means:

- Independent verification of the cloud program's effectiveness
- Providing assurance to the board and risk management functions of the organization with regard to the cloud risk exposure

The internal audit function can also play a trusted advisor and proactively be involved by working with IT and the business in identifying and addressing the risk associated with the various cloud services and deployment models. In this capacity, the organization is actively taking a risk-based approach on its journey to the cloud. The internal audit function can engage with stakeholders, review the current risk framework with a cloud lens, assist with the risk-mitigation strategies, and perform a number of cloud audits such as these:

- The organization's current cloud governance program
- Data classification governance
- Shadow IT

CSPs should include an internal audit in their discussions about new services and deployment models to obtain feedback in the planned design of cloud controls their customers will need, as well as to mitigate the risk. The internal audit function will still require considering how to maintain independence from the overall process because, eventually, it must actually perform the audit on these controls.

The internal audit function will also continue to perform audits in the traditional sense. These are directly dependent on the outputs of the organization's risk-assessment process.

Cloud customers will want not only to engage in discussions with CSPs' security professionals but also to consider meeting with the organization's internal audit group.

Another potential source of independent verification on internal controls will be audits performed by external auditors. An external auditor's scope varies greatly from an internal audit, whereas the external audit usually focuses on the internal controls over financial reporting. Therefore, the scope of services is usually limited to the IT and business environments that support the financial health of an organization and in most cases doesn't provide specific assurance on cloud risks other than vendor risk considerations on the financial health of the CSP.

Types of Audit Reports

The internal and external audits assess cloud risks and relationships internally within the organization between IT and the business and externally between the organization and cloud vendors. These audits typically focus on the organization. In cloud relationships, where the ownership of the control that addresses the cloud risks resides within the CSP, organizations need to assess the CSP controls to understand if there are gaps within the

6

LEGAL AND COMPLIANCE

expected cloud control framework that is overlaid between the cloud customer and the CSP.

Cloud customers can utilize other reports, such as the American Institute of CPAs (AICPA) Service Organization Control (SOC) reports (the SOC 1, SOC 2, and SOC 3 reports—see Table 6.2). These examination reports can assist cloud customers in understanding the controls in place at a CSP.[9]

TABLE 6.2 AICPA SOC Reports

REPORT NUMBER	USERS	CONCERN	DETAIL REQUIRED
SOC 1	User entities and their financial statement auditors	Effect of service organization's control on user organization's financial statement assertions	Requires detail on the system, controls, tests performed by the service auditor, and results of those tests
SOC 2	User entities, regulators, business partners, and others with sufficient knowledge to appropriately use report	Effectiveness of controls at the service organization related to security, availability, processing integrity, confidentiality, or privacy	Requires detail on the system, controls, tests performed by the service auditor, and results of those tests
SOC 3	Any users with a need for confidence in the service organization's controls	Effectiveness of controls at the service organization related to security, availability, processing integrity, confidentiality, or privacy	Requires limited information focused on the boundaries of the system and the achievement of the applicable trust services criteria for security, availability, processing integrity, confidentiality, or privacy

- **SOC 1:** Reports on controls at service organizations relevant to user entities' internal control over financial reporting. This examination is conducted in accordance with the Statement on Standards for Attestation Engagements No. 16 (SSAE 16). This report is the replacement of the Statement on Auditing Standards No. 70 (SAS 70). The international equivalent to the AICPA SOC 1 is the International Auditing and Assurance Standards Board (IAASB) issued and approved ISAE 3402.

- **SOC 2:** Reports on controls at a service organization relevant to the Trust Services principles: security, availability, processing integrity, confidentiality, and privacy.

Similar to the SOC 1 in the evaluation of controls, the SOC 2 report is an examination that expands the evaluation of controls to the criteria set forth by the AICPA Trust Services principles and is a generally restricted report. The SOC 2 is an examination of the design and operating effectiveness of controls that meet the criteria for principles set forth in the AICPA's Trust Services principles. This report provides additional transparency into the enterprise's security based on a defined industry standard and further demonstrates the enterprise's commitment to protecting customer data. SOC 2 reports can be issued on one or more of the Trust Services principles.

There are two types of SOC 2 reports:

- **Type 1:** A report on management's description of the service organization's system and the suitability of the design of the controls

- **Type 2:** A report on management's description of the service organization's system and the suitability of the design and operating effectiveness of the controls

- **SOC 3:** Similar to the SOC 2, the SOC 3 report is an examination that expands the evaluation of controls to the criteria set forth by the AICPA Trust Services principles. The major difference between SOC 2 and SOC 3 reports is that SOC 3 reports are general use.

As the cloud matures, so do the varying types of accreditation reporting. As a provider or customer of cloud services, you need to stay in tune with the changing landscape. Other types of audit reports and accreditations you can consider are agreed-upon procedures (AUP) and cloud certifications.

AUP is another AICPA engagement based on the Statement on Standards for Attestation Engagement (SSAE).[10] AUP is one in which an auditor is engaged by an entity to carry out specific procedures agreed to by the entity and other third parties and to issue a report on findings based on the procedures performed on the subject matter. There is no opinion from the auditor. Instead, the entities or third parties form their own conclusions on the report. If a CSP cannot provide assurance over specific risks, you may engage an auditor to perform specific procedures over the CSP.

Shared Assessments (`https://sharedassessments.org`) is an organization that supplies firms a way to obtain a detailed report about a service provider's controls (people, processes, and procedures) and a procedure for verifying that the information in the report is accurate. It offers the tools to assess third-party risk, including cloud-based risks. You can use the Standard Information Gathering (SIG) or AUP tools to create specific procedures that address cloud risks against CSPs.

Other organizations are creating cloud assurance and certification programs to address concerns with providing assurance and certification stands, including these:

- CSA's Security, Trust and Assurance Registry (STAR) program[11]
- EuroCloud Star Audit (ESCA) program[12]

As with any of these newer organizations, a security professional needs to understand the types of certifications these and future organizations will bring to the market.

Impact of Requirement Programs by the Use of Cloud Services

CSPs and customers need to understand how cloud services will affect the audit requirements set forth by their organization. Due to the nature of the cloud, auditors need to rethink how they audit and obtain evidence to support their audit.

The CCSP needs to keep in mind that traditional auditing methods may not be applicable to cloud environments. The following questions help to frame the thought process of the cloud auditor:

- What is the universal population to sample from?
- What would be the sampling methods in a highly dynamic environment?
- How do you know that the virtualized server you are auditing was the same server over time?

Assuring Challenges of the Cloud and Virtualization

When you're using virtualization as an underlying component in the cloud, it's essential to be able to assess and obtain assurances relating to the security of virtual instances.

The task, however, is not a simple one, particularly from an auditing perspective and least of all using noninvasive systems that audit the hypervisor and associated components. How can the CCSP attest to the security relating to virtualization (sometimes spread across hundreds of devices) in the absence of testing and verification? Given the evolving technology landscape, the rate at which updates, version upgrades, additional components, and associated system changes are implemented presents the ultimate moving target for the CCSP.

At present, much of the focus is on the ongoing confidentiality and integrity of the virtual machine (VM) and its associated hypervisors (conscious that the availability will typically be covered extensively under the SLA). The thought process is that if the availability of the VM is affected, this fact will be captured as part of the general SLA, where confidentiality and integrity may not be explicitly covered under virtualization. Within the SLAs, items such as mean time between failures (MTBF) and mean time to repair (MTTR) may be called out; however, a failure to delve much deeper, or specifically focus on VMs or the hypervisor itself, is an issue.

To obtain assurance and conduct appropriate auditing on the VMs and hypervisor, the CCSP must do the following:

■ **Understand the virtualization management architecture:** From an external or independent perspective, this can be challenging. For the audit to be carried out effectively, all relevant documentation and diagrams illustrating the architecture within scope, including supporting systems and infrastructure, need to be available and up to date. This helps the auditor plan the assessment and associated testing.

■ **Verify systems are up to date and hardened according to best-practice standards:** Where systems updates, patches, and associated security changes have been made, these should be captured under change management as configuration items (CIs), along with corresponding details relating to patch versions, version release dates, and so on. All updates and patches should also have been tested prior to deployment into live environments.

■ **Verify configuration of hypervisor according to organizational policy:** Ensure that the security posture and management of the hypervisor defends against attacks or efforts to disrupt the hypervisor or hosted VMs. Given that hypervisors possess their own management tools allowing for remote access and administrations, particular focus should be placed here, along with other vulnerabilities within the hypervisor. All unnecessary services or nonessential services— including applications, application programming interfaces (APIs), and communications protocols—should be disabled in an effort to further strengthen the security of the hypervisor.

When any changes are made, they should be captured in log formats and where possible be tracked and alerted on, forming both an audit trail and a proactive alerting mechanism. This enables administrators and engineers to detect and respond in a timely fashion to any unauthorized changes or attempts to compromise systems security.

Information Gathering

Information gathering refers to the process of identifying, collecting, documenting, structuring, and communicating information from various sources to enable educated and swift decision making. From a cloud-computing perspective, information gathering is a necessary and essential component for selecting the appropriate services or providers.

Similar to other outsourcing or contracting of services and activities, the stages or variations may include the following:

- Initial scoping of requirements
- Market analysis
- Review of services
- Solutions assessment
- Feasibility study
- Supplementary evidence
- Competitor analysis
- Risk review and assessment
- Auditing
- Contract and SLA review

Additionally, information gathering forms part of a repeatable process as part of cloud computing (in line with plan, do, check, act [PDCA]), where the appropriate and effective governance relies heavily on the information gathered and reported.

Finally, as part of Federal Information Security Management Act (FISMA) and other regulations, the ability to illustrate and report on security activities is required. This relies strongly on information gathering, reporting, risk management (based on the information gathered), and verification of the information received. These processes should be captured as part of the overall information security management system (ISMS) and other risk-related activities.

Audit Scope

Auditing forms an integral part of effective governance and risk management. It provides both an independent and an objective review of overall adherence or effectiveness of processes and controls.

Although few organizations and their employees enjoy being subjected to audits, they are becoming far more commonplace both from a risk and compliance perspective and to ensure adequate risk management and security controls are in place.

For CSPs and their customers, auditing is fast becoming a distinct and fundamental component of any cloud program. Clients are continuing to expect more and ensure that their provider is satisfying requirements, whereas providers are keen to illustrate and preempt client requests and challenges around the overall security controls and their effectiveness.

Audit Scope Statements

An audit scope statement offers the required level of information for the client or organization subject to the audit to fully understand (and agree) with the scope, focus, and type of assessment being performed. Typically, an audit scope statement includes the following:

- General statement of focus and objectives
- Scope of audit (including exclusions)
- Type of audit (certification, attestation, and so on)
- Security assessment requirements
- Assessment criteria (including ratings)
- Acceptance criteria
- Deliverables
- Classification (confidential, highly confidential, secret, top secret, public, and so on)

The audit scope statement can also catalog the circulation list, along with the key individuals associated with the audit.

Audit Scope Restrictions

Parameters need to be set and enforced to focus an audit's efforts on relevancy and auditability. These parameters are commonly known as audit scope restrictions.

Audit scope restrictions ensure that the operational impact of the audit will be limited, effectively lowering any risk to production environments and high-priority or essential components required for the delivery of services.

Scope restrictions typically specify operational components, along with asset restrictions, which include acceptable times and time periods (such as time of day) and accepted and nonaccepted testing methods (such as no destructive testing). These limit the impact on production systems. Additionally, many organizations do not permit technical testing of systems and components on live systems because these can cause denial-of-service (DoS) issues or result in negative or degraded performance.

Because of the nature of audits, indemnification of any liability for systems performance degradation, along with any other adverse effects, is required where technical testing is being performed. For the majority of cloud-based audits, the focus does not include technical assessments (as part of contractual requirements); however, testing is focused on the ability to meet SLAs, contractual requirements, and industry best practice standards and frameworks.

Gap Analysis

Gap analysis benchmarks and identifies relevant gaps against specified frameworks or standards.

Typically, resources or personnel who are not engaged or functioning within the area of scope perform gap analysis. The use of independent or impartial resources is best served to ensure there are no conflicts or favoritism. You don't want existing relationships to dilute or in any way manipulate the findings (positively or negatively).

An auditor or subject matter expert performs the gap analysis against a number of listed requirements, which can range from a complete assessment to a random sample of controls (subset). This will result in a report highlighting the findings, including risks, recommendations, and conformity, or compliance against the specified standards (ISO 27001:2013, ISO 19011:2011, ISO 27017:2015, and so on).

Never underestimate the impact of an impartial resource or entity providing a report highlighting risks. The report will most likely be signed off on by a senior member of the organization, which will prompt risk treatment and a process of work to remediate or reduce the identified and reported risks.

Numerous stages are carried out prior to commencing a gap analysis review. Although they can vary depending on the review, common stages include the following:

- Obtain management support from the right managers.
- Define the scope and objectives.
- Plan an assessment schedule.
- Agree on a plan.
- Conduct information-gathering exercises.
- Interview key personnel.
- Review supporting documentation.
- Verify the information obtained.
- Identify any potential risks.
- Document the findings.
- Develop a report and recommendations.
- Present the report.
- Sign off and accept the report.

The objective of a gap analysis is to identify and report on any gaps or risks that may affect the AIC of key information assets. The value of such an assessment is often determined based on what you did not know or for an independent resource to communicate to relevant management or senior personnel such risks, as opposed to internal resources saying what you need or should be doing.

Cloud-Auditing Goals

Given that cloud computing represents many potential threats (along with a host of heightened and increased risks) for the enterprise, the requirement for auditing is a key component of the risk-management process.

Cloud auditing should result in the following key outcomes:

- Be able to understand, measure, and communicate the effectiveness of CSP controls and security to organizational stakeholders and executives
- Proactively identify any control weaknesses or deficiencies, while communicating these both internally and to the CSP
- Obtain levels of assurance and verification as to the CSP's ability to meet the SLA and contractual requirements, while not relying on reporting or CSP reports

Audit Planning

In line with financial, compliance, regulatory, and other risk-related audits, ensuring the appropriate focus and emphasis on components most relevant to cloud computing (and associated outsourcing) includes four phases (*Figure 6.2*).

| Define Audit Objectives | Define Audit Scope | Conduct Audit | Refine the Audit Process/ Lessons Learned |

FIGURE 6.2 **Audit planning's four phases.**

Defining Audit Objectives

These high-level objectives should interpret the goals and outputs from the audit:

- Document and define the audit objectives.
- Define the audit outputs and format.
- Define the frequency and the audit focus.
- Define the required number of auditors and subject matter experts.
- Ensure alignment with audit and risk management processes (internal).

Defining Audit Scope

There are several considerations when defining the audit scope:

- Ensure the core focus and boundaries to which the audit will operate.
- Document the list of current services and resources utilized from CSPs.

- Define the key components of services, including storage, utilization, and processing.
- Define the cloud services to be audited, such as infrastructure as a service (IaaS), platform as a service (PaaS), and SaaS.
- Define the geographic locations that are permitted and required.
- Define the locations for audits to be undertaken.
- Define the key stages to audit, including information gathering, workshops, gap analysis, and verification evidence.
- Document the key points of contact within the CSP as well as internally.
- Define the escalation and communication points.
- Define the criteria and metrics to which the CSP will be assessed.
- Ensure that criteria are consistent with the SLA and contract.
- Factor in busy periods or organizational periods, such as financial year-end, launches, and new services.
- Ensure that findings captured in previous reports or stated by the CSP are actioned and verified.
- Ensure that previous nonconformities and high-risk items are reassessed and verified as part of the audit process.
- Ensure that any operational or business changes internally have been captured as part of the audit plan, including reporting changes and governance.
- Agree on final reporting dates, being conscious of business operations and operational availability.
- Ensure that findings are captured and communicated back to relevant business stakeholders and executives.
- Confirm the report circulation and target audience.
- Document the risk management and risk treatment processes to be utilized as part of any remediation plans.
- Agree on a ticketing and auditable process for remediation actions, ensuring traceability and accountability.

Conducting the Audit

When conducting an audit, keep the following issues in mind:

- Adequate staff
- Adequate tools

- Schedule
- Supervision of audit
- Reassessment

Refining the Audit Process/Lessons Learned

Ensure that previous reviews are adequately analyzed and taken into account, with the view to streamline and obtain maximum value for future audits. To ensure that cloud services auditing is both effective and efficient, take each of these steps or phases either as a standalone activity or as part of a structured framework.

- Ensure that the approach and scope are still relevant.
- Factor in any provider changes that have occurred.
- Ensure that reporting details are sufficient to enable clear, concise, and appropriate business decisions to be made.
- Determine opportunities for reporting improvement and enhancement.
- Ensure that duplication of efforts is minimal (crossover or duplication with other audit and risk efforts).
- Make sure that audit criteria and scope are still accurate, factoring in business changes.
- Have a clear understanding of what levels of information and details can be collected using automated methods and mechanisms.
- Ensure that the right skillsets are available and utilized to provide accurate results and reporting.
- Ensure that the PDCA is also applied to the CSP auditing planning and processes.

These phases may coincide with other audit-related activities and be dependent on organizational structure. They may be structured (often influenced by compliance and regulatory requirements) or reside with a single individual (not recommended).

STANDARD PRIVACY REQUIREMENTS (ISO/IEC 27018)

ISO/IEC 27018 addresses the privacy aspects of cloud computing for consumers. ISO 27018 is the first international set of privacy controls in the cloud.[13] The ISO published ISO 27018 on July 30, 2014, as a new component of the ISO 27001 standard.

Both cloud security professionals and CSPs adopting ISO/IEC 27018 should be aware of the following five key principles:

- **Consent:** CSPs must not use the personal data they receive for advertising and marketing unless expressly instructed to do so by the customers. In addition, a customer should be able to employ the service without having to consent to the use of her personal data for advertising or marketing.

- **Control:** Customers have explicit control over how CSPs are to use their information.

- **Transparency:** CSPs must inform customers about items such as where their data resides. CSPs also need to disclose to customers the use of any subcontractors who will be used to process PII.

- **Communication:** CSPs should keep clear records about any incident and their response to it, and they should notify customers.

- **Independent and yearly audit:** To remain compliant, the CSP must subject itself to yearly third-party reviews. This allows the customer to rely upon the findings to support her own regulatory obligations.

Trust is key for consumers leveraging the cloud; therefore, vendors of cloud services are working toward adopting the stringent privacy principles outlined in ISO 27018.

GAPP

GAPP is the AICPA standard describing 74 detailed privacy principles. According to GAPP, following are the 10 main privacy principles:

- Management
- Notice
- Choice and consent
- Collection
- Use, retention, and disposal
- Access
- Disclosure to third parties
- Security for privacy
- Quality
- Monitoring and enforcement[14]

See the following for a full downloadable copy of GAPP:
`http://www.aicpa.org/InterestAreas/InformationTechnology/Resources/Privacy/`
`GenerallyAcceptedPrivacyPrinciples/DownloadableDocuments/GAPP_PRAC_%200909.pdf`.

INTERNAL ISMS

For the majority of medium- to large-scale entities, an ISMS (however formalized or structured) should exist with the goal of reducing risks related to the AIC of information and assets, while looking to strengthen the stakeholder confidence in the security posture of their organization in protecting such assets.

Although these systems may well vary in terms of the comprehensiveness, along with the manner in which the controls are applied, they should provide a formal structured mechanism and a number of approaches to protect business and information assets. The adequacy and completeness of such ISMSs tend to vary widely unless they are aligned and certified to standards such as ISO 27001:2013. ISO 27001:2013 does not mandate a specified level of comprehensiveness or effectiveness that controls are required to have (other than it is repeatable and part of a managed process to reduce risks in a proactive and measureable fashion), but it does look to ensure that these controls are continually reviewed and enhanced wherever possible.

Take, for example, a bank or highly regulated financial institution. The policies and standards will most likely be heavily influenced by regulatory and compliance requirements, whereas a technology company may not be as stringent in terms of what employees may be permitted to do. Although both the bank and the technology entity may be compliant, aligned, or have their ISMS independently certified, this is an example of how controls may vary across different entities and sectors.

The Value of an ISMS

Many are conscious of the role and value of an ISMS for an organization, but it is most prevalent when factoring cloud computing into a technology or business strategy. An ISMS typically ensures that a structured, measured, and ongoing view of security is taken across an organization, allowing security impacts and risk-based decisions to be taken. Of crucial importance is the top-down sponsorship and endorsement of information security across the business, highlighting its overall value and necessity. The use of an ISMS is even more critical within a cloud environment to ensure that changes being made to cloud infrastructure are being documented for reporting and auditability purposes.

But what is the effect of ISMS when outsourcing? How do internal security activities apply to third parties, CSPs, and other subcontractors?

This can go either way—it may or may not apply. The decision is yours and is based on what your organization is willing to accept in terms of risk, contracts, and SLAs.

Internal Information Security Controls System: ISO 27001:2013 Domains

The standard provides "established guidelines and general principles for initiating, implementing, maintaining, and improving information security management with an organization."[15] The controls are mapped to address requirements identified through a formal risk assessment.

The following domains make up ISO 27001:2013, the most widely used global standard for ISMS implementations. (NIST, FISMA, and so on will obviously influence the U.S. government and other industries as well.)

A.5—Security Policy Management
A.6—Corporate Security Management
A.7—Personnel Security Management
A.8—Organizational Asset Management
A.9—Information Access Management
A.10—Cryptography Policy Management
A.11—Physical Security Management
A.12—Operational Security Management
A.13—Network Security Management
A.14—System Security Management
A.15—Supplier Relationship Management
A.16—Security Incident Management
A.17—Security Continuity Management
A.18—Security Compliance Management

Repeatability and Standardization

Where an organization has implemented and is operating an ISMS, existing security policies, practices, and controls are implemented to take into account the requirements under the various domains. For example, supplier relationships ensure that appropriate mechanisms and requirements are put in place for the supply chain. These include appropriate due diligence, contingency, and the levels of security controls. The same can be true for compliance, which requires the organization to ensure that third parties are utilized for the delivery of services in accordance with relevant laws and regulations.

Looking across the remainder of the domains, it is easy to see how multiple components can provide a baseline or minimum levels of controls—particularly related to the confidentiality of information (communications security, cryptography, access controls, and so on). Related to the integrity of information system acquisition, development and maintenance are most relevant, but operations security and components of access control are also important factors.

Finally, the availability and resiliency components can be based on the components of incident management, business continuity management, and physical and environmental security.

Loosely grouped, these domains should also provide current levels of controls based on the internal ISMS and use these as a minimum acceptable level of control for the CSP. This mandates that the levels of security provided by the CSP be equal to or strengthen current controls, reemphasizing the benefit or driver for use of cloud services (using cloud security as an enabler).

In summary, the existence and continued use of an internal ISMS assists in standardizing and measuring security across the organization and beyond its perimeters. Given that cloud computing may be both an internal and an external solution for the organization, it is a strong recommendation that the ISMS has sight of and factors in reliance and dependencies on third parties for the delivery of business services.

IMPLEMENTING POLICIES

Policies are crucial to implementing an effective data security strategy. They typically act as the connectors that hold many aspects of data security together across both technical and nontechnical components. The failure to implement and utilize policies in cloud-based (or non-cloud-based) environments would likely result in disparate parts or isolation of activities, effectively operating as standalone or one-offs and leading to multiple duplication and limited standardization.

From an organizational perspective, policies are nothing new. In fact, they have long been providing guiding decisions and principles to ensure that actions and decisions achieve the desired and rational outcomes.

From a cloud computing angle, the use of policies can go a long way toward determining the security posture of cloud services, as can standardizing practices to guide implementation.

Organizational Policies

Organizational policies form the basis of functional policies that can reduce the likelihood of the following:

- Financial loss
- Irretrievable loss of data

- Reputational damage
- Regulatory and legal consequences
- Misuse and abuse of systems and resources

Functional Policies

As highlighted in prior sections of this book, particularly for organizations that have a well-engrained and fully operational ISMS, the following are typically utilized. (These are typical functional policies—this list is not all encompassing.)

- Information security policy
- Information technology policy
- Data classification policy
- Acceptable usage policy
- Network security policy
- Internet use policy
- Email use policy
- Password policy
- Virus and spam policy
- Software security policy
- Data backup policy
- Disaster recovery (DR) policy
- Remote access policy
- Segregation of duties policy
- Third-party access policy
- Incident response and management policy
- Human resources security policy
- Employee background checks
- Legal compliance guidelines

Cloud Computing Policies

The listed organizational policies define acceptable, desired, and required criteria for users to follow and adhere. Throughout a number of these, specified criteria or actions must be drawn out, with reference to any associated standards and processes, which typically list finite levels of information.

As part of the review of cloud services, either during the development of the cloud strategy or during vendor reviews and discussions, the details and requirements should be expanded to compare or assess the required criteria (as per existing policies). This also helps determine the provider's ability to meet or exceed relevant requirements.

Following are some policy examples:

- **Password policies:** If the organization's policy requires an eight-digit password comprised of numbers, uppercase and lowercase characters, and special characters, is this true for the CSP?

- **Remote access:** Where two-factor authentication may be required for access of network resources by users and third parties, is this true for the CSP?

- **Encryption:** If minimum encryption strength and relevant algorithms are required (such as minimum of AES 256-bit), is this met by the CSP or potential solution? Where keys are required to be changed every three months, is this true for the CSP?

- **Third-party access:** Can all third-party access (including the CSP) be logged and traced for the use of cloud-based services or resources?

- **Segregation of duties:** Where appropriate, are controls required for the segregation of key roles and functions, and can these be enforced and maintained on cloud-based environments?

- **Incident management:** Where required actions and steps are undertaken, particularly regarding communications and relevant decision makers, how can these be fulfilled when cloud-based services are in scope?

- **Data backup:** Is data backup included and in line with backup requirements listed in relevant policies? When data integrity is affected or becomes corrupt, will the information be available and in a position to be restored, particularly on shared platforms, storage, and infrastructure?

Bridging the Policy Gaps

When cloud-based services cannot fulfill the elements listed in the previous section, there needs to be an agreed-upon list or set of mitigation controls or techniques. You should not revise the policies to reduce or lower the requirements if at all possible. All changes and variations to policy should be explicitly listed and accepted by all relevant risk and business stakeholders.

IDENTIFYING AND INVOLVING THE RELEVANT STAKEHOLDERS

Identifying and involving the relevant stakeholders from the commencement of any cloud computing discussions are of utmost importance. Failure to do so can lead to a segregation or fractured approach to cloud decision making, as well as nonstandardization across the organization with regard to how cloud services are procured, reviewed, managed, and maintained.

To objectively assess within what areas of the business it may be appropriate to utilize cloud-based services, it is a key requirement to have visibility on what services are currently provided, how these are delivered, and on what platforms, systems, architectures, and interdependencies they are operating.

The determination of the key stakeholders should form the blueprint to identify potential impacts on current services, operations, and delivery models.

Note that where a business impact analysis (BIA) or related continuity and recovery plans exist, these should typically list or capture the technical components, related interdependencies, and order of restoration.

Depending on who is acting as the lead or primary driver behind potential cloud-computing services, an understanding of the current state and potential or desired future state is required. Once the information is collated, you need to consider the impact on the service, people, cost, infrastructure, and stakeholders.

Stakeholder Identification Challenges

This phase has several key challenges:

- Defining the enterprise architecture, which can be a sizeable task if it's not currently in place

- Independently and objectively viewing potential options and solutions, where individuals may be conflicted due to roles or functions

- Objectively selecting the appropriate service and provider

- Engaging with the users and IT personnel who will be impacted, particularly if their job is being altered or removed

- Identifying direct and indirect costs, such as training, up-skilling, reallocating, new tasks, and responsibilities

- Extending risk management and enterprise risk management

Governance Challenges

Following are the key challenges faced in this phase:

- Define audit requirements and extension of additional audit activities.

- Verify that all regulatory and legal obligations will be satisfied as part of the non-disclosure agreement (NDA) or contract.

- Establish reporting and communication lines both internal to the organization and for CSPs.

- Ensure that where operational procedures and processes are changed due to use of cloud services, all documentation and evidence are updated accordingly.

- Ensure that all business continuity, incident management and response, and disaster recovery plans (DRPs) are updated to reflect changes and interdependencies.

Communication Coordination

Conscious that these components may be handled by a number of individuals or teams across the organization, there needs to be a genuine desire to effect changes. Although many reference the finance departments as key supporters of cloud computing for the countless financial benefits, the operational, strategic, and enablement capabilities of the cloud can easily surpass and trump the financial savings if they are reviewed and communicated accordingly.

Communication and coordination with business units should include each of these areas:

- IT
- Information security
- Vendor management
- Compliance
- Audit
- Risk
- Legal
- Finance
- Operations
- Data protection and privacy
- Executive committee and directors

The levels of interest and appetite will vary significantly depending on the individuals and their roles, but given cloud computing's rising popularity and emergence as an established technology offering, it will continue to attract the discussion and thoughts of many executives and business professionals.

> ✔ **Specialized Compliance Requirements for Highly Regulated Industries**
>
> Organizations operating within highly regulated industries must be cognizant of any specific industry regulatory requirements (that is, HIPAA for healthcare, PCI for finance, and FedRAMP for the U.S. government). Although risk management in a cloud computing environment is a joint provider and customer activity, full accountability remains with the customer. Organizations need to consider current requirements, their current level of compliance, and any geographic- or jurisdiction-specific restrictions that will make leveraging true cloud scale difficult.

IMPACT OF DISTRIBUTED IT MODELS

Distributed IT and distributed information systems are becoming increasingly common in conjunction with and amplified by the adoption of cloud-computing services. The globalization of companies, along with collaboration and outsourcing, continues to allow organizations and users to avail themselves of distributed services.

The drivers for adopting such services are many but include increasing enterprise productivity and reducing development cost. The impact on organizations in terms of visibility and control over a distributed or effectively dispersed model can be wide ranging.

The CCSP must review and address the following components to ensure that the distributed IT model does not negatively influence the factors outlined in the rest of this topic.

Clear Communications

Traditional IT deployment and operations typically allow clear line of sight or understanding of the personnel, their roles, functions, and core areas of focus. This provides for far more access to individuals, either on a name basis or based on their roles. Communications allow for collaboration, information sharing, and the availability of relevant details and information when necessary. This can be from operations, engineering, controls, or development.

Distributed IT models challenge and essentially redefine the roles, functions, and ability for face-to-face communications or direct interactions, such as emails, phone calls, and messengers.

Although the convenience and speed at which operations or changes can be affected in such environments (such as asking an engineer or a developer to implement relevant changes), the potential for such swift amendments is typically replaced by more structured, regimented, and standardized requests. From a security perspective, this can be seen as an enhancement in many cases. It alleviates and removes the opportunity for untracked changes or for bypassing change management controls. It also reduces the risks associated with implementing changes or amendments without proper testing and risk management being taken into account.

Coordination and Management of Activities

Project management has long been an engrained and essential component to ensuring the smooth and successful delivery of technology projects, deployments, and solutions. Enter the complexity or benefit of distributed and outsourced IT models. Yes, there are benefits when outsourced models are involved in the delivery of services and solutions—particularly when it is their business to ensure such services and solutions are delivered to clients, and even more so when large-scale services and solutions are public offerings, such as Salesforce, Google, and Microsoft.

In short, bringing in an independent group of subject matter experts whose focus is on the delivery of such projects and functionality can make for a swift rollout or deployment. The lack of familiarity or an engrained working relationship with the provider can make for a refined and efficient process, versus multiple engagements, discussions, negotiations, and the need to provision resources and skills—not to mention ensuring the availability or willingness of internal or team resources to participate. Sign-off and acceptance typically allows the provider to deliver with accountability and independent oversight from the customer's perspective.

Governance of Processes and Activities

Effective governance allows for peace of mind and a level of confidence to be established in an organization. This is even more true with distributed IT and the use of IT services or solutions across dispersed organizational boundaries from a variety of users.

Where the IT department previously would provide details or facilitate reporting to a program management, risk management, audit, compliance, or legal function depending on the nature of the services, it may now need to pull information from numerous sources and providers, leading to the following:

- Increased number of sources for information
- Varying levels of cooperation
- Varying levels of information and completeness
- Varying response times and willingness to assist

- Multiple reporting formats and structures
- Lack of cohesion in terms of activities and focus
- Requirement for additional resources and interactions with providers
- Minimal evidence available to support claims and verify information
- Disruption or discontent from internal resources, where job function or role may have undergone change

Selecting the provider is the key to a smooth and repeatable mechanism around governance of services and processes. Governance can be automated to reduce ongoing requirements for continued interaction with providers or third parties, resulting in a streamlined audit and risk management engagement.

Coordination Is Key

Interacting with and collecting information from multiple sources requires coordination of efforts, including defining how these processes are to be managed.

The governance process should seek to establish how to achieve the common objective. For those familiar with third-party management—that is, organizing and maintaining communications and interactions between distributed people, processes, and technology across a number of locations (often involving different cultures, time zones, and operating environments)—the requirement should be integrated in the SLAs and contractual obligations. Clear assignment and identification of requirements (along with frequency, mechanisms, and resourcing) should be highlighted and agreed upon from the outset.

At this point, it will most likely become clear which components can be automated, along with who will be responsible for coordinating them between the customer and CSP. Once this is accepted and becomes operational, opportunities to improve this process may become clear. However, if these can be coordinated with ease across distributed IT environments and providers, it will be a key factor in having a clear view of performance versus SLAs and contracts, as well as the overall effectiveness and efficiency of outsourced activities and services.

Outsourced activities and services that are not explicitly meeting the agreed SLA or contract should be met with financial penalties.

Security Reporting

The previous stages should result in an independent report being provided as to the security posture of the virtualized machines. This should be reported in a format that illustrates any high, medium, or low risks (typical of audit reports). Alternatively, it should be based on industry ratings such as Common Vulnerabilities and Exposures (CVE) and Common Vulnerability Scoring System (CVSS). Common approaches also include reporting against the Open Web Application Security Project (OWASP) Top 10 and SANS Top 20 listings.

Many vendors do not make such reports available to customers or the public for obvious reasons. However, sanitized versions may be made available when a client requests such indications of vulnerabilities; any exposures to their information will be limited. In these cases, the provider may supply a statement from the auditors or assessors attesting to the fact that no high- or medium-level vulnerabilities were detected or the risk rating for the engagement was deemed to be low. These are not common; typically the organization does not want to share the findings or risks with customers or potential customers. The auditors or assessors usually make the report and findings available only for customers and not for public or external circulation.

UNDERSTANDING THE IMPLICATIONS OF THE CLOUD TO ENTERPRISE RISK MANAGEMENT

The cloud represents a fundamental shift in the way technology is offered. The shift is toward the consumerization of IT services and convenience. In addition to the countless benefits outlined in this book and those you may identify yourself, the cloud creates an organizational change (*Figure 6.3*).

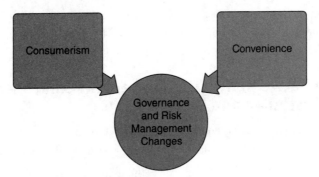

FIGURE 6.3 **How the cloud affects the enterprise.**

It is important for both the CSP and the cloud customer to be focused on risk. The manner in which typical risk management activities, behaviors, processes, and related procedures are performed may require significant revisions and redesign. After all, the way services are delivered changes delivery mechanisms, locations, and providers—all of which result in governance and risk-management changes.

These changes need to be identified from the scoping and strategy phases through the ongoing and recurring tasks, both ad hoc and periodically scheduled. Addressing these risks requires that the CSP and cloud customer's policies and procedures be aligned as closely as possible because risk management must be a shared activity to be implemented successfully.

Risk Profile

The risk profile is determined by an organization's willingness to take risks as well as the threats to which it is exposed. The risk profile should identify the level of risk to be accepted, the way risks are taken, and the way risk-based decision making is performed. Additionally, the risk profile should take into account potential costs and disruptions should one or more risks be exploited.

To this end, it is imperative that an organization fully engages in a risk-based assessment and review against cloud-computing services, service providers, and the overall effects on the organization should it utilize cloud-based services.

Risk Appetite

Swift decision making can lead to significant advantages for the organization, but when assessing and measuring the relevant risks in cloud-service offerings, it's best to have a systematic, measurable, and pragmatic approach. Undertaking these steps effectively enables the business to balance the risks and offset any excessive risk components, all while satisfying listed requirements and objectives for security and growth.

Emerging or rapid-growth companies will be more likely to take significant risks when utilizing cloud-computing services so they can be first to market.

Difference Between the Data Owner and Controller and the Data Custodian and Processor

Treating information as an asset requires a number of roles and distinctions to be clearly identified and defined. The following are key roles associated with data management:

- The data subject is an individual who is the focus of personal data.

- The data controller is a person who either alone or jointly with other persons determines the purposes for which and the manner in which any personal data is processed.

- The data processor in relation to personal data is any person other than an employee of the data controller who processes the data on behalf of the data controller.

- Data stewards are commonly responsible for data content, context, and associated business rules.

- Data custodians are responsible for the safe custody, transport, data storage, and implementation of business rules.

- Data owners hold the legal rights and complete control over a single piece or set of data elements. Data owners also possess the ability to define distribution and associated policies.

SLA

Similar to a contract signed between a customer and a CSP, the SLA forms the most crucial and fundamental component of how security and operations will be undertaken. The SLA should also capture requirements related to compliance, best practice, and general operational activities to satisfy each of these.

Within an SLA, the following contents and topics should be covered at a minimum:

- **Availability** (for example, 99.99 percent of services and data)

- **Performance** (for example, expected response times versus maximum response times)

- **Security and privacy of the data** (for example, encrypting all stored and transmitted data)

- **Logging and reporting** (for example, audit trails of all access and the ability to report on key requirements and indicators)

- **DR expectations** (for example, worse-case recovery commitment, recovery time objectives [RTOs], maximum period of tolerable disruption [MPTD])

- **Location of the data** (for example, ability to meet requirements or consistent with local legislation)

- **Data format and structure** (for example, data retrievable from provider in readable and intelligent format)

- **Portability of the data** (for example, ability to move data to a different provider or to multiple providers)

- **Identification and problem resolution** (for example, help desk/service desk, call center, or ticketing system)

- **Change-management process** (for example, updates or new services)

- **Dispute-mediation process** (for example, escalation process and consequences)

- **Exit strategy** with expectations on the provider to ensure a smooth transition

SLA Components

Although SLAs tend to vary significantly depending on the provider, more often than not they are structured in favor of the provider to ultimately expose them to the least amount of risk. Note the examples of how elements of the SLA can be weighed against the customer's requirements (*Figure 6.4*).

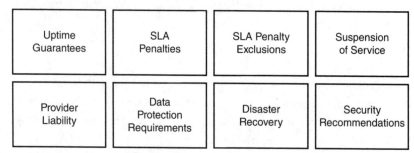

FIGURE 6.4 **SLA elements weighed against customer requirements.**

- **Uptime Guarantees**
  - Service levels regarding performance and uptime are usually featured in outsourcing contracts but not in software contracts, despite the significant business-criticality of certain cloud applications.
  - Numerous contracts have no uptime or performance service-level guarantees or are provided only as changeable URL links.
  - SLAs, if they are defined in the contract at all, are rarely guaranteed to stay the same upon renewal or not to significantly diminish.
  - A material diminishment of the SLA upon a renewal term may necessitate a rapid switch to another provider at significant cost and business risk.
- **SLA Penalties**
  - For SLAs to be used to steer the behavior of a cloud services provider, they need to be accompanied by financial penalties.
  - Contract penalties provide an economic incentive for providers to meet stated SLAs. This is an important risk-mitigation mechanism, but such penalties rarely, if ever, provide adequate compensation to a customer for related business losses.
  - Penalty clauses are not a form of risk transfer.

- Penalties, if they are offered, usually take the form of credits rather than refunds. But who wants an extension of a service that does not meet requirements for quality? Some contracts offer to give back penalties if the provider consistently exceeds the SLA for the remainder of the contract period.

- **SLA Penalty Exclusions**
  - **Limitation on when downtime calculations start:** Some CSPs require that the application is down for a period of time (for example, 5 to 15 minutes) before any counting toward SLA penalty will start.
  - **Scheduled downtime:** Several CSPs claim that if they give you warning, an interruption in service does not count as unplanned downtime but rather as scheduled downtime and, therefore, is not counted when calculating penalties. In some cases, the warning can be as little as eight hours.

- **Suspension of Service**
  - Some cloud contracts state that if payment is more than 30 days overdue (including any disputed payments), the provider can suspend the service. This gives the CSP considerable negotiation leverage in the event of any dispute over payment.

- **Provider Liability**
  - Most cloud contracts restrict liability apart from infringement claims relating to intellectual property to a maximum of the value of the fees over the past 12 months. Some contracts even state as little as six months.
  - If the CSP were to lose the customer's data, for example, the financial exposure would likely be much greater than 12 months of fees.

- **Data-Protection Requirements**
  - Most cloud contracts make the customer ultimately responsible for security, data protection, and compliance with local laws. If the CSP is complying with privacy regulations for personal data on your behalf, you need to be explicit about what the provider is doing and understand any gaps.

- **DR**
  - Cloud contracts rarely contain provisions about DR or provide financially backed RTOs. Some IaaS providers do not even take responsibility for backing up customer data.

- **Security Recommendations**
  - Gartner recommends negotiating SLAs for security, especially for security breaches, and has seen some CSPs agree to this. Immediate notification of any security or privacy breach as soon as the provider is aware is highly recommended.
  - Because the CSP is ultimately responsible for the organization's data and alerting its customers, partners, or employees of any breach, it is particularly critical for companies to determine what mechanisms are in place to alert customers if any security breaches do occur and to establish SLAs determining the time frame the CSP has to alert you of any breach.
  - The time frames you have to respond within will vary by jurisdiction but may be as little as 48 hours. Be aware that if law enforcement becomes involved in a provider security incident, it may supersede any contractual requirement to notify you or to keep you informed.

These examples highlight the dangers of not paying sufficient focus and due diligence when engaging with a CSP around the SLA. Because these controls list a general sample of potential pitfalls related to the SLA, the following documents can serve as useful reference points when ensuring that SLAs are in line with business requirements. They can also balance risks that may previously have been unforeseen.

Key SLA Elements

The following key elements should be assessed when reviewing and agreeing to the SLA:

- **Assessment of risk environment:** What types of risks does the organization face?
- **Risk profile:** What are the number of risks and potential effects of risks?
- **Risk appetite:** What level of risk is acceptable?
- **Responsibilities:** Who will do what?
- **Regulatory requirements:** Will these be met under the SLA?
- **Risk mitigation:** Which mitigation techniques and controls can reduce risks?
- **Risk frameworks:** What frameworks are to be used to assess the ongoing effectiveness? How will the provider manage risks?

Ensuring Quality of Service

A number of key indicators form the basis in determining the success or failure of a cloud offering.

The following should form a key component for metrics and appropriate monitoring requirements:

- **Availability:** This measures the uptime (availability) of the relevant services over a specified period as an overall percentage, that is, 99.99 percent.

- **Outage duration:** This captures and measures the loss of service time for each instance of an outage, such as 1/1/201X—09:20 start—10:50 restored—1 hour 30 minutes loss of service.

- **MTBF:** This captures the indicative or expected time between consecutive or recurring service failures—that is, 1.25 hours per day of 365 days.

- **Capacity metric:** This measures and reports on capacity capabilities and the ability to meet requirements.

- **Performance metrics:** This utilizes and actively identifies areas, factors, and reasons for bottlenecks or degradation of performance. Typically, performance is measured and expressed as requests or connections per minute.

- **Reliability Percentage metric:** This lists the success rate for responses and is based on agreed criteria—that is, 99 percent success rate in transactions completed to the database.

- **Storage Device Capacity metric:** This lists metrics and characteristics related to storage device capacity; it is typically provided in gigabytes.

- **Server Capacity metric:** These look to list the characteristics of server capacity, based and influenced by central processing units (CPUs), CPU frequency in GHz, random access memory (RAM), virtual storage, and other storage volumes.

- **Instance Startup Time metric:** This indicates or reports on the length of time required to initialize a new instance, calculated from the time of request by user or resource, and typically measured in seconds and minutes.

- **Response Time metric:** This reports on the time required to perform the requested operation or tasks, typically measured based on the number of requests and response times in milliseconds.

- **Completion Time metric:** This provides the time required to complete the initiated or requested task, typically measured by the total number of requests as averaged in seconds.

- **Mean-Time to Switchover metric:** This provides the expected time to switch over from a service failure to a replicated failover instance. This is typically measured in minutes and captured from commencement to completion.

- **Mean-Time System Recovery metric:** This highlights the expected time for a complete recovery to a resilient system in the event of or following a service failure or outage. This is typically measured in minutes, hours, and days.

- **Scalability Component metrics:** This is typically used to analyze customer use, behavior, and patterns that can allow for the auto-scaling and auto-shrinking of servers.

- **Storage Scalability metric:** This indicates the storage device capacity available if increased workloads and storage requirements are necessary.

- **Server Scalability metric:** This indicates the available server capacity that can be utilized when changes in increased workloads are required.

RISK MITIGATION

The approach and desired outcome when undertaking risk management and associated activities should always be to reduce and mitigate risks. Mitigation of risks reduces the exposure to a risk or the likelihood of it occurring. Risk mitigation to cloud-based assessments or environments is most often obtained by implementing additional controls, policies, processes, or procedures or utilizing enhanced technical security features. Additional access control, vulnerability management, and selection of a specified CSP are examples of risk mitigation or risk reduction.

NOTE Risk mitigation does not result in a zero or no-risk condition. Once risk mitigation steps have been performed, the risk that remains is known as the residual risk.

Risk-Management Metrics

Risks must be communicated in a way that is clear and easy to understand. It may also be important to communicate risk information outside the organization. To be successful in this, the organization must agree to a set of risk-management metrics.

Using a risk scorecard is recommended. The impact and probability of each risk are assessed separately, and then the results are combined to indicate exposure using a five-level scale in each of these quantities:

1. Minimal

2. Low

3. Moderate

4. High

5. Maximum (or Critical)

This enables a clear and direct graphical representation of project risks (*Figure 6.5*).

Consequence

Likelihood	Minimal	Low	Moderate	High	Critical
	1	2	3	4	5
A (almost certain)	H	H	E	E	E
B (likely)	M	H	H	E	E
C (possible)	L	M	H	E	E
D (unlikely)	L	L	M	H	E
E (rare)	L	L	M	H	H
E	**Extreme Risk:** Immediate action required to mitigate the risk or decide not to proceed				
H	**High Risk:** Action should be taken to compensate for the risk				
M	**Moderate Risk:** Action should be taken to monitor the risk				
L	**Low Risk:** Routine acceptance of the risk				

FIGURE 6.5 The risk scorecard provides a clear representation of potential risks.

Different Risk Frameworks

The challenge that having several risk frameworks poses is the significant effort and investment required to perform such risk reviews, along with the time and associated reporting. The risk frameworks include ISO 31000:2009, ENISA, and NIST—Cloud Computing Synopsis and Recommendations (*Figure 6.6*).

ISO 31000:2009	European Network and Information Security Agency (ENISA)	National Institute of Standards and Technology (NIST) - Cloud Computing Synopsis and Recommendations

FIGURE 6.6 The three main risk frameworks.

ISO 31000:2009

As ISO 31000:2009[16] is a guidance standard that is not intended for certification purposes; implementing it does not address specific or legal requirements related to risk assessments, risk reviews, and overall risk management. However, implementation and use of the ISO 31000:2009 standard sets out a risk-management framework and process that can assist in addressing organizational requirements and, most importantly, provide a structured and measurable risk-management approach to assist with the identification of cloud-related risks.

ISO 31000:2009 sets out terms and definitions, principles, a framework, and a process for managing risk. Similar to other ISO standards, it lists 11 key principles as a guiding set of rules to enable senior decision makers and organizations to manage risks, as noted:

- Risk management creates and protects value.

- Risk management is an integral part of the organizational procedure.

- Risk management is part of decision making.

- Risk management explicitly addresses uncertainty.

- Risk management is systematic, structured, and timely.

- Risk management is based on the best available information.

- Risk management is tailored.

- Risk management takes human and cultural factors into account.

- Risk management is transparent and inclusive.

- Risk management is dynamic, iterative, and responsive to change.

- Risk management facilitates continual improvement and enhancement of the organization.

The foundation components of ISO 31000:2009 focus on designing, implementing, and reviewing risk management. The overarching requirement and core component of ISO 31000:2009 is the management endorsement, support, and commitment to ensure overall accountability and support.

Similar to the PDCA lifecycle for continuous improvement in ISO 27001:2013, ISO 31000:2009 outlines the requirement for integration and implementation of risk management becoming an embedded component within organizational activities as opposed to a separated activity or function.

From a completeness perspective, ISO 31000:2009 focuses on risk identification, analysis, and evaluation through risk treatment. By performing the stages of the lifecycle, a proactive and measured approach to risk management should be the result, enabling management and business decision makers to make informed and educated decisions.

ENISA

ENISA produced "Cloud Computing: Benefits, Risks, and Recommendations for Information Security," which can be utilized as an effective foundation for risk management. The document identifies 35 types of risks for organizations to consider, coupled with the top 8 security risks based on likelihood and impact.[17]

NIST—Cloud Computing Synopsis and Recommendations

Following the release of the ENISA document, in May 2011 NIST released Special Publication 800-146, which focuses on risk components and the appropriate analysis of such risks. Although NIST serves as an international reference for many of the world's leading entities, it continues to be strongly adopted by the U.S. government and related agency sectors.[18]

UNDERSTANDING OUTSOURCING AND CONTRACT DESIGN

Understanding and appreciating outsourcing has long been the duty and focus of procurement and legal functions. Whether it is related to the single outsourcing of personnel, roles, functions, or entire business functions, these have been availed and utilized globally to maximize cost benefits, plug skills gaps, and ultimately ensure that entities run as smoothly and efficiently as possible.

What does all this entail? In short, it entails a complete understanding of the reasons, rationale, requirements, business drivers, and potential impacts that moving to cloud-based services will bring. It also entails the ability to coordinate, communicate, and interpret the challenges that lie ahead when moving toward cloud computing.

Historical outsourcing may have involved a set of key departments or practitioners, but the cloud amplifies that—significantly—even more than traditional IT outsourcing. Acting as the informed advisor coordinating this throughout the business leads to a far smoother and more efficient process, where risks and issues can be highlighted at the outset, as opposed to when you least expect them or as a result of an unforeseen event or incident.

BUSINESS REQUIREMENTS

Prior to entering into a contract with a cloud supplier, your enterprise should evaluate its specific needs and requirements that form the basis and foundation of the organizational cloud strategy. To develop a cloud strategy, the key organizational assets need to be agreed upon and assessed for adequacy or suitability for cloud environments. (Do not forget that not all systems and functions may be cloud ready.)

As part of this process, suitable and potential business units or functions should be defined as in scope, while outlining a phased or potential phased approach to your cloud journey. Any exceptions, restrictions, or potential risks should be highlighted and clearly documented. This process should also list regulatory and compliance components that need to be addressed and satisfied (whether that will be by the provider or a joint approach).

These stages enable you to shape and begin reviewing potential solutions or cloud services. Given the plethora of CSPs currently offering services, it is likely that more than one provider will be positioned to provide the services based on your cloud strategy and business requirements. Where an up-to-date business continuity and disaster recovery (BCDR) plan is available, this will more often speed up the process. Given that the plans and associated documents should capture the key assets and business function, list the business and system interdependencies.

VENDOR MANAGEMENT

With the continued growth and significant financial sums being posted quarterly by many of the leading CSPs, some are describing cloud computing as the digital gold rush. As with the gold rush, the arrival of many new players looking to harness a portion or share of cloud gold is increasing in rapid numbers. This is leading to a fiercely competitive pricing battle as the CSP's battle for crucial market share.

Sound positive? Well, for the moment, it means lower costs, increased competition, better offers, and generally good value for customers. The challenge becomes real as many of the providers fail to grab sufficient market share or ultimately make enough penetration as a CSP. Some of these will cease cloud services (due to lack of profitability) or will change direction in their service offerings.

Understanding Your Risk Exposure

What risk does this present to you or the organization? How can you address these risks with the view to understanding the risk posture? The following questions should form the basis in understanding the exposure prior to any services engagement:

- Is the provider established for technology?
- Is this cloud service a core business of the provider?
- Where is the provider located?
- Is the company financially stable?

- Is the company subject to any takeover bids or significant sales of business units?

- Is the company outsourcing any aspect of the service to a third party?

- Are there contingencies where key third-party dependencies are concerned?

- Does the company conform?

- Is the company certified against relevant security and professional standards and frameworks?

- How will the provider satisfy relevant regulatory, legal, and other compliance requirements?

- How will the provider ensure the ongoing AIC of your information assets if placed in the cloud environment (where relevant)?

- Are adequate BCDR processes in place?

- Are reports or statistics available from any recent events or incidents affecting cloud services availability?

- Is interoperability a key component to facilitate ease of transition or movement between CSPs?

- Are there unforeseeable regulatory-driven compliance requirements?

These queries should directly influence your decision in terms of cloud services and CSPs. Additionally, efforts made to determine the requirements up front will directly reduce the efforts in defining and selecting the appropriate CSPs and negotiation times and ensuring that the required security controls are in place to meet the organization's needs.

Accountability of Compliance

It is not the CSP's role to determine your requirements and to have a fundamental understanding and appreciation of your business. The role of the CSP is to make services and resources available for your use, not to ensure you are compliant. You can outsource activities and functions; however, you cannot outsource your compliance requirements. You must remain accountable and responsible, regardless of any cloud services used. The organization will be the one affected by the negative outcomes of any violations or breaches of regulatory requirements, not the provider.

Common Criteria Assurance Framework

The Common Criteria (CC) is an international set of guidelines and specifications (ISO/IEC 15408-1:2009) developed for evaluating information security products, with the view to ensuring they meet an agreed-upon security standard for government entities and agencies.[19]

The goal of CC certification is to ensure customers that the products they are buying have been evaluated and that the vendor's claims have been verified by a vendor-neutral third party.

CC looks at certifying a product only and does not include administrative or business processes. Although it views these as beneficial, there are dangers of relying only on technology for robust and effective security.

CSA STAR

Given the distinct lack of cloud-specific security standards and frameworks and the growing requirement for such standards and frameworks to be adopted by CSPs, the CSA launched the STAR[20] initiative at the end of 2011.

The CSA STAR was created to establish a "first step" in displaying transparency and assurance for cloud-based environments. In an effort to ensure adoption and use throughout the cloud-computing industry, the CSA made the STAR a publicly available and accessible registry that provides a mechanism for users to assess the security of the cloud security provider.

Additionally, STAR provides granular levels of detail, with controls specifically defined to address the differing categories for cloud-based services. The use of STAR enables customers to perform a large component of due diligence and allow a single framework of controls and requirements to be utilized in assessing CSP suitability and the ability to fulfill CSP requirements.

At a glance, CSA STAR is broken into three distinct layers, all of which focus on the AIC components (*Figure 6.7*).

- **Level 1, Self-Assessment:** Requires the release and publication of due diligence self-assessment, against the CSA consensus assessment initiative (CAI) questionnaire or CCM

- **Level 2, Attestation:** Requires the release and publication of available results of an assessment carried out by an independent third party based on CSA CCM and ISO27001:2013 or AICPA SOC2

- **Level 3, Ongoing Monitoring Certification:** Requires the release and publication of results related to security-properties monitoring based on the cloud trust protocol (CTP)

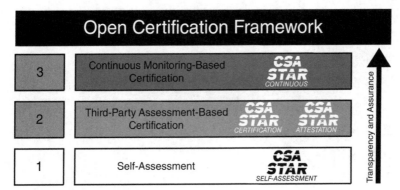

FIGURE 6.7 **CSA STAR's three layers.**

These levels look to address the various demands and requirements based on the levels of assurance. A self-assessment may be sufficient, but others may require third-party verification or continuous assessments and independent verification.

CLOUD COMPUTING CERTIFICATION

According to the ENISA, the Cloud Certification Schemes List (CCSL) provides an overview of different existing certification schemes that might be relevant for cloud-computing customers. CCSL also shows the main characteristics of each certification scheme. For example, CCSL answers questions like these:

- Which are the underlying standards?
- Who issues the certifications?
- Is the CSP audited?
- Who audits it?

The schemes that make up the CCSL are listed here:

- Certified Cloud Service—TUV Rhineland
- CSA Attestation—OCF level 2
- CSA Certification—OCF level 2
- CSA Self Assessment—OCF level 1

- EuroCloud Self-Assessment (ECSA Self-Assessment)
- EuroCloud Star Audit Certification (ECSA Audit)
- ISO/IEC 27001 Certification
- Payment Card Industry Data Security Standard (PCI DSS) v3.1
- LEET Security Rating Guide
- AICPA SOC 1
- AICPA SOC 2
- AICPA SOC 3

According to ENISA, the Cloud Certification Schemes Metaframework (CCSM) is an extension of the CCSL that provides a neutral high-level mapping from the customer's network and information security requirements to security objectives in existing cloud certification schemes. This facilitates the use of existing certification schemes during procurement. The first version of the CCSM was approved and adopted in November 2014.

The online version of the CCSM tool can be accessed at `https://resilience.enisa.europa.eu/cloud-computing-certification/list-of-cloud-certification-schemes/cloud-certification-schemes-metaframework`.

The tool lists 27 CCSM security objectives and then allows the customer to select which ones he wants to cross-reference against the certifications listed in the CCSL. Consider a sample of what the resulting comparison matrix looks like (*Figure 6.8*).

CCSM Security Objectives	Certified Cloud Service – TUV Rhineland	CSA Attestation OCF Level 2	EuroCloud Self-Assessment	ISO/IEC 27001 Certification
Risk Management	•	•	•	
Cloud Data Security	•	•	•	
Cloud Software Security	•	•	•	•
Cloud Monitoring and Log Access	•	•	•	•

FIGURE 6.8 Comparison matrix of CCSL and the CCSM security objectives.

CONTRACT MANAGEMENT

A key and fundamental business activity, amplified by the significant outsourcing of roles and responsibilities, contract management requires adequate governance to be effective and relevant. It involves meeting ongoing requirements, monitoring contract performance, adhering to contract terms, and managing any outages, incidents, violations, or variations to contractual obligations. The role of cloud governance and contract management should not be underestimated or overlooked. So where do you begin?

As a first port of call, consider the initial review and identification of the CSP's ability to satisfy relevant requirements, initial lines of communication, clear understanding and segregation of responsibilities between customer and provider, and penalties and ability to report on adherence and violations of contract requirements. If at this point they are not understood and clearly defined, problems are likely to arise. Remember, the contract is the only legal format to be reviewed and assessed as part of a dispute between the cloud customer and the CSP.

Importance of Identifying Challenges Early

It is essential that any challenges or areas that are unclear should be raised and clarified prior to engagement and signing of contracts between the customer and provider. Why is this important?

- Understanding the contractual requirements forms the organization's baseline and checklist for the right to audit.

- Understanding the gaps allows the organization to challenge and request changes to the contract before signing acceptance.

- The CCSP has an idea of what she is working with and the kind of leverage she will have during the audit.

Documenting the requirements and responsibilities makes it possible to utilize technological components to track and report adherence and variations from contractual requirements. This provides an audit output (report) and allows you to approach the CSP with evidence of variations and violations of the contract.

Prior to signing acceptance of the relevant contracts with the CSP, appropriate organizational involvement across a number of departments is most likely required. This typically includes compliance, regulatory, finance, operations, governance, audit, IT, information security, and legal. Final acceptance typically resides with legal but may be signed off at an executive level from time to time.

Key Contract Components

Depending on your role, inputs, and current focus, the following items usually form the key components of cloud contracts. Given that contracts vary significantly between various CSPs, not all of these may be captured or covered.

This constitutes a typical illustrative list, as opposed to an exhaustive list:

- Performance measurement
- SLAs
- Availability and associated downtime
- Expected performance and minimum levels of performance
- Incident response
- Resolution timeframes
- Maximum and minimum period for tolerable disruption
- Issue resolution
- Communication of incidents
- Investigations
- Capturing of evidence
- Forensic and e-discovery processes
- Civil and state investigations
- Tort law and copyright
- Control and compliance frameworks
- ISO 27001/2
- ISO 27017
- COBIT
- PCI DSS
- HIPAA
- GLBA
- PII
- Data protection
- Safe Harbor
- U.S. Patriot Act
- BCDR

- Priority of restoration
- Minimum levels of security and availability
- Communications during outages
- Personnel checks
- Background checks
- Employee and third-party policies
- Data retention and disposal
- Retention periods
- Data destruction
- Secure deletion
- Regulatory requirements
- Data access requests
- Data protection and freedom of information
- Key metrics and performance related to QoS
- Independent assessments and certification of compliance
- Right to audit (including period or frequencies permitted)
- Ability to delegate third parties to carry out audits on your behalf
- Penalties for nonperformance
- Delayed or degraded performance penalties
- Payment of penalties (supplemented by service or financial payment)
- Backup of media, and relevant assurances related to the format and structure of the data
- Restrictions and prohibiting the use of your data by the CCSP without prior consent or for stated purposes
- Authentication controls and levels of security
- Two-factor authentication
- Password and account management
- Joiner, mover, leaver (JML) processes
- Ability to meet and satisfy existing internal access control policies
- Restrictions and associated NDAs from the CSP related to data and services utilized
- Any other component and requirements deemed necessary and essential

Failing to address any of these components can result in hidden costs being accrued by the cloud customer in the event of additions or amendments to the contract. Isolated and ad hoc contract amendment requests typically take longer to address and may require more resources to achieve than if they are addressed at the outset.

SUPPLY CHAIN MANAGEMENT

Given that organizations have invested heavily to protect their key assets, resources, and intellectual property in recent years, changes to these practices present challenges and complexities. With the supply chain adjusting to include CSPs, security truly is only as good as the weakest link.

Of late, many sizable and well-renowned entities and bodies have been breached and suffered compromises of security due to the extension and inclusion of new entities within their supply chain. Given that many of these are published widely (tenders, awards of contracts, case studies, reference sites, and so on), it makes the supply chain a real and widely targeted threat vector in the security landscape.

How does cloud change this? In truth, *change* is not the most apt term here. The perspective is either an increase or a reduction in risk. This varies for every organization based on their cloud footprint, the length and breadth of cloud use, and the assets and scope of operations. If you use a single CSP as opposed to multiple vendors, this may well form a reduction in risk (not discounting other factors), whereas the migration of high-valued information assets to another provider (with unknown levels of security and assurance) may well constitute an increase in risk and reliance.

Fundamentally, organizations lack clarity, understanding, and awareness of where their suppliers will have dependencies or reliances on third, fourth, or fifth parties. If your provider relies on a single storage provider whose factory, which manufactures 80 percent of its storage devices, is damaged by floods or a natural disaster, that event may affect your organization and its ability to continue to provide business operations. This is a single example of how the supply chain presents risks with which the CCSP must be prepared to contend.

Supply Chain Risk

When looking at supply chain risk, you should take a BCDR mind-set and viewpoint.

- You should obtain regular updates of a clear and concise listing of all dependencies and reliance on third parties, coupled with the key suppliers.

- Where single points of failure exist, these should be challenged and acted upon to reduce outages and disruptions to business processes.

- Organizations need a way to quickly prioritize hundreds or thousands of contracts to determine which of them, and which of their suppliers' suppliers, pose a potential risk. Based on these documented third parties, organizations should perform a risk review to identify, categorize, and determine the current exposure or overall risk ratings versus corporate policies and determine how these risks will be acted upon. Engagement with key suppliers is crucial at this point, as is ensuring that contracts cover such risks or provide a right to audit clause to ascertain and measure relevant risks.

As with risk management, you can take a number of actions to avoid, reduce, transfer, or accept the risk related to cloud computing. The by-product of such an assessment enables the organization to understand supply chain risks, identify assurances or actions required, and work with vendor management to manage appropriate cloud and supply chain risks.

One resource that the CCSP should consider with regard to supply chain risk is NIST SP 800-161. The "Supply Chain Risk Management Practices for Federal Information Systems and Organizations" document, although not focused on cloud environments per se, can help form a baseline of best practices for the organization.[21]

CSA CCM

A useful resource for assisting with supply chain reviews is the CSA CCM. Note that not all risks may be captured as part of the CCM, dependent on your organization, its focus, and its industry.[22] The CCM is designed to provide guidance for cloud vendors and to assist cloud customers with assessing the overall security risk of a CSP. The CSA CCM provides a framework of controls that offers guidance in 13 domains. It offers a ready reference that incorporates other industry-accepted security regulations, standards, and controls frameworks such as the ISO 27001/27002, ISACA COBIT, NIST, PCI, Jericho Forum, and NERC CIP. The CSA CCM framework gives organizations the necessary structure relating to information security tailored to the cloud industry.[23]

The ISO 28000:2007 Supply Chain Standard

In line with previous standards and advice to utilize established and measurable frameworks, the emergence and continued growth of supply chain standards for the measurement of security and resilience continues to gain traction.

Of particular focus is ISO 28000:2007 (Formerly the Publicly Available Specification (PAS) 28000:2005).[24] In line with other ISO security-related management systems, it focuses on the use of PDCA as a lifecycle of continual improvement and enhancement. Other ISO standards that utilize the PDCA model heavily include ISO 27001:2013, ISO 9001, and ISO 14000.

The key objective of ISO 28000:2007 is to assist organizations in the appropriate identification and implementation of controls to protect its people, products, and property (assets). It can be adopted by organizations both large and small, with a reliance or risk exposure related to supply chains. In the world of cloud computing and global computing, that means just about every one of us.

Because ISO 28000:2007 defines a set of security management requirements, the onus is on the organization to establish a security management system (SMS) that meets the standard's requirements. The SMS should then focus on the identification and subsequent risk-reduction techniques associated with the intentional or unintentional disruptions to relevant supply chains.

Organizations can choose to obtain independent certification against ISO 28000:2007 or can conform to the listed requirements.

Independent certification by a third party or recognized certification body requires a review of the following elements:

- Security management policy
- Organizational objectives
- Risk-management programs and practices
- Documented practices and records
- Supplier relationships
- Roles, responsibilities, and relevant authorities
- Use of PDCA
- Organizational procedures and related processes

Given its relatively short lifecycle as an established ISO standard, the uptake in terms of organizations implementing ISO 28000:2007 through to certification has been limited. With the increased awareness and heightened queries from cloud customers related to key dependencies, ISO 28000:2007 looks to continue to grow in terms of adoption.

SUMMARY

When considering the issues that the legal and compliance domain raises, the CCSP needs to be able to focus on many different issues simultaneously. These issues include understanding how to identify the various legal requirements and unique risks associated with the cloud environment with regard to legislation, legal risks, controls, and forensic requirements. In addition, the CCSP must be able to describe the potential personal and data privacy issues specific to PII within the cloud environment. There is a need for clear and concise definition of the process, the methods, and the required adaptions necessary to carry out an audit in a cloud environment. The CCSP also needs to be able to understand the implications of cloud to enterprise risk management. In addition, the CCSP should be able to help the organization achieve the levels of understanding required to address risks through an appropriate audit process. The need to address supply chain management and contract design for outsourced services in a cloud environment is also important.

REVIEW QUESTIONS

1. When does the EU Data Protection Directive (Directive 95/46/EC) apply to data processed?

   A. The directive applies to data processed by automated means and data contained in paper files.

   B. The directive applies to data processed by a natural person in the course of purely personal activities.

   C. The directive applies to data processed in the course of an activity that falls outside the scope of community law, such as public safety.

   D. The directive applies to data processed by automated means in the course of purely personal activities.

2. Which of the following are contractual components that the CCSP should review and understand fully when contracting with a CSP? (Choose two.)

   A. Concurrently maintainable site infrastructure

   B. Use of subcontractors

   C. Redundant site infrastructure capacity components

   D. Scope of processing

3. What does an audit scope statement provide to a cloud service customer or organization?

   A. The credentials of the auditors, as well as the projected cost of the audit

   B. The required level of information for the client or organization subject to the audit to fully understand (and agree) with the scope, focus, and type of assessment being performed

   C. A list of all the security controls to be audited

   D. The outcome of the audit, as well as any findings that need to be addressed

4. Which of the following should be carried out first when seeking to perform a gap analysis?

   A. Define scope and objectives.

   B. Identify potential risks.

   C. Obtain management support.

   D. Conduct information gathering.

5. What is the first international set of privacy controls in the cloud?

   A. ISO/IEC 27032

   B. ISO/IEC 27005

   C. ISO/IEC 27002

   D. ISO/IEC 27018

6. What is domain A.16 of the ISO 27001:2013 standard?

   A. Security Policy Management

   B. Organizational Asset Management

   C. System Security Management

   D. Security Incident Management

7. What is a data custodian responsible for?

   A. The safe custody, transport, storage of data, and implementation of business rules

   B. Data content, context, and associated business rules

   C. Logging and alerts for all data

   D. Customer access and alerts for all data

8. What is typically not included in an SLA?

   A. Availability of the services to be covered by the SLA

   B. Change management process to be used

   C. Pricing for the services to be covered by the SLA

   D. Dispute mediation process to be used

NOTES

[1] See the following for a summary of the attacks and the activities around them:
http://www.zdnet.com/article/cloudflare-how-we-got-caught-in-lulzsec-cia-crossfire/

[2] See the following for a complete copy of the judicial memorandum issued in the case:
https://assets.documentcloud.org/documents/1149373/in-re-matter-of-warrant.pdf

[3] See the following:
http://www.huntonprivacyblog.com/wp-content/files/2013/09/2013-oecd-privacy-guidelines.pdf

[4] See the following: http://www.apec.org/Groups/Committee-on-Trade-and-Investment/~/media/Files/Groups/ECSG/05_ecsg_privacyframewk.ashx

[5] See the following:
`http://eur-lex.europa.eu/LexUriServ/LexUriServ.do?uri=CELEX:31995L0046:en:HTML`

[6] See the following:
`http://eur-lex.europa.eu/LexUriServ/LexUriServ.do?uri=CELEX:32002L0058:en:HTML`

[7] `http://csrc.nist.gov/publications/nistpubs/800-122/sp800-122.pdf` (p. 13)

[8] See the following:
`http://unpan1.un.org/intradoc/groups/public/documents/un-dpadm/unpan044147.pdf`

[9] For points of clarity, consider the following: SOC 1 reporting results in the issuance of SSAE 16 Type 1 or Type 2 reports. SOC 2 reporting utilizes the AICPA AT Section 101 professional standard, resulting in Type 1 or Type 2 reports. SOC 3 reporting utilizes the SysTrust and WebTrust assurance services, also known as the Trust Services, which are a broad-based set of principles and criteria put forth jointly by the AICPA and the CICA.

[10] See the following: `http://www.aicpa.org/Research/Standards/AuditAttest/DownloadableDocuments/AT-00201.pdf`

[11] `https://cloudsecurityalliance.org/star/`

[12] `https://staraudit.org/`

[13] See the following:
`https://www.iso.org/obp/ui/#iso:std:iso-iec:27018:ed-1:v1:en`

[14] See the following for the document "An Executive Overview of GAPP: Generally Accepted Privacy Principles": `http://www.aicpa.org/InterestAreas/InformationTechnology/Resources/Privacy/GenerallyAcceptedPrivacyPrinciples/DownloadableDocuments/10261378ExecOverviewGAPP.pdf`

[15] `https://www.iso.org/obp/ui/#iso:std:iso-iec:27001:ed-2:v1:en`

[16] See the following: `https://www.iso.org/obp/ui/#!iso:std:43170:en`

[17] See the following: `https://www.enisa.europa.eu/activities/risk-management/files/deliverables/cloud-computing-risk-assessment`

[18] See the following:
`http://nvlpubs.nist.gov/nistpubs/Legacy/SP/nistspecialpublication800-146.pdf`

[19] See the following: `https://www.iso.org/obp/ui/#!iso:std:50341:en`
Common Criteria Portal: `https://www.commoncriteriaportal.org/`

[20] `https://cloudsecurityalliance.org/star/`

[21] See the following:
`http://nvlpubs.nist.gov/nistpubs/SpecialPublications/NIST.SP.800-161.pdf`

[22] See the following:
`https://cloudsecurityalliance.org/download/cloud-controls-matrix-v3/`

[23] `https://cloudsecurityalliance.org/research/ccm/`

[24] See the following: `https://www.iso.org/obp/ui/#!iso:std:44641:en`

Answers to Review Questions

DOMAIN 1: ARCHITECTURAL CONCEPTS AND DESIGN REQUIREMENTS

1. Which of the following are attributes of cloud computing?

    A. Minimal management effort and shared resources

    B. High cost and unique resources

    C. Rapid provisioning and slow release of resources

    D. Limited access and service provider interaction

    Answer: A

    Explanation: "Cloud computing is a model for enabling ubiquitous, convenient, on-demand network access to a shared pool of configurable computing resources (e.g., networks, servers, storage, applications, and services) that can be rapidly provisioned and released with minimal management effort or service provider interaction."

    — "The NIST Definition of Cloud Computing"[1]

2. Which of the following are distinguishing characteristics of a managed service provider?

   A. Have some form of a NOC but no help desk.

   B. Be able to remotely monitor and manage objects for the customer and reactively maintain these objects under management.

   C. Have some form of a help desk but no NOC.

   D. Be able to remotely monitor and manage objects for the customer and proactively maintain these objects under management.

   Answer: D

   Explanation: According to the MSP Alliance, typically MSPs have the following distinguishing characteristics:

   - Have some form of NOC service
   - Have some form of help desk service
   - Can remotely monitor and manage all or a majority of the objects for the customer
   - Can proactively maintain the objects under management for the customer
   - Can deliver these solutions with some form of predictable billing model, where the customer knows with great accuracy what her regular IT management expense will be

3. Which of the following are cloud computing roles?

   A. Cloud customer and financial auditor

   B. CSP and backup service provider

   C. Cloud service broker and user

   D. Cloud service auditor and object

   Answer: B

   Explanation: The following groups form the key roles and functions associated with cloud computing. They do not constitute an exhaustive list but highlight the main roles and functions within cloud computing:

   - **Cloud customer:** An individual or entity that utilizes or subscribes to cloud-based services or resources.
   - **CSP:** A company that provides cloud-based platform, infrastructure, application, or storage services to other organizations or individuals, usually for a fee; otherwise known to clients "as a service."

- **Cloud backup service provider:** A third-party entity that manages and holds operational responsibilities for cloud-based data backup services and solutions to customers from a central data center.

- **CSB:** Typically a third-party entity or company that looks to extend or enhance value to multiple customers of cloud-based services through relationships with multiple CSPs. It acts as a liaison between cloud services customers and CSPs, selecting the best provider for each customer and monitoring the services. The CSB can be utilized as a "middleman" to broker the best deal and customize services to the customer's requirements. May also resell cloud services.

- **Cloud service auditor:** Third-party organization that verifies attainment of SLAs.

4. Which of the following are essential characteristics of cloud computing? (Choose two.)

   A. On-demand self service

   B. Unmeasured service

   C. Resource isolation

   D. Broad network access

   Answer: A and D

   Explanation: According to "The NIST Definition of Cloud Computing," the essential characteristics of cloud computing are as follows:

   - **On-demand self-service:** A consumer can unilaterally provision computing capabilities, such as server time and network storage, as needed automatically without requiring human interaction with each service provider.

   - **Broad network access:** Capabilities are available over the network and accessed through standard mechanisms that promote use by heterogeneous thin or thick client platforms (such as mobile phones, tablets, laptops, and workstations).

   - **Resource pooling:** The provider's computing resources are pooled to serve multiple consumers using a multitenant model, with different physical and virtual resources dynamically assigned and reassigned according to consumer demand. There is a sense of location independence in that the customer generally has no control or knowledge over the exact location of the provided resources but may be able to specify location at a higher level of abstraction (such as country, state, or data center). Examples of resources include storage, processing, memory, and network bandwidth.

   - **Rapid elasticity:** Capabilities can be elastically provisioned and released, in some cases automatically, to scale rapidly outward and inward commensurate with

A

ANSWERS TO REVIEW QUESTIONS

demand. To the consumer, the capabilities available for provisioning often appear to be unlimited and can be appropriated in any quantity at any time.

- **Measured service:** Cloud systems automatically control and optimize resource use by leveraging a metering capability at some level of abstraction appropriate to the type of service (such as storage, processing, bandwidth, and active user accounts). Resource usage can be monitored, controlled, and reported, providing transparency for both the provider and the consumer of the utilized service.

5. Which of the following are considered to be the building blocks of cloud computing?

   A. Data, access control, virtualization, and services

   B. Storage, networking, printing, and virtualization

   C. CPU, RAM, storage, and networking

   D. Data, CPU, RAM, and access control

   Answer: C

   Explanation: The building blocks of cloud computing are composed of RAM, CPU, storage, and networking.

6. When using an IaaS solution, what is the capability provided to the customer?

   A. To provision processing, storage, networks, and other fundamental computing resources when the consumer is not able to deploy and run arbitrary software, which can include OSs and applications.

   B. To provision processing, storage, networks, and other fundamental computing resources when the provider is able to deploy and run arbitrary software, which can include OSs and applications.

   C. To provision processing, storage, networks, and other fundamental computing resources when the auditor is able to deploy and run arbitrary software, which can include OSs and applications.

   D. To provision processing, storage, networks, and other fundamental computing resources when the consumer is able to deploy and run arbitrary software, which can include OSs and applications.

   Answer: D

   Explanation: According to "The NIST Definition of Cloud Computing," in IaaS, "the capability provided to the consumer is to provision processing, storage, networks, and other fundamental computing resources where the consumer is able to deploy and run arbitrary software, which can include operating systems and applications. The consumer does not manage or control the underlying cloud infrastructure but has control over operating systems, storage, and deployed applications; and possibly limited control of select networking components (e.g., host firewalls)."[2]

7. When using an IaaS solution, what is a key benefit provided to the customer?

   A. Metered and priced on the basis of units consumed

   B. The ability to scale up infrastructure services based on projected usage

   C. Increased energy and cooling system efficiencies

   D. Transferred cost of ownership

Answer: A

Explanation: IaaS has a number of key benefits for organizations, which include but are not limited to these:

- Usage is metered and priced on the basis of units (or instances) consumed. This can also be billed back to specific departments or functions.

- It has an ability to scale up and down infrastructure services based on actual usage. This is particularly useful and beneficial where there are significant spikes and dips within the usage curve for infrastructure.

- It has a reduced cost of ownership. There is no need to buy assets for everyday use, no loss of asset value over time, and reduced costs of maintenance and support.

- It has a reduced energy and cooling costs along with "green IT" environment effect with optimum use of IT resources and systems.

8. When using a PaaS solution, what is the capability provided to the customer?

   A. To deploy onto the cloud infrastructure provider-created or acquired applications created using programming languages, libraries, services, and tools that the provider supports. The consumer does not manage or control the underlying cloud infrastructure, including network, servers, operating systems, or storage, but has control over the deployed applications and possibly configuration settings for the application-hosting environment.

   B. To deploy onto the cloud infrastructure consumer-created or acquired applications created using programming languages, libraries, services, and tools that the provider supports. The provider does not manage or control the underlying cloud infrastructure, including network, servers, operating systems, or storage, but has control over the deployed applications and possibly configuration settings for the application-hosting environment.

   C. To deploy onto the cloud infrastructure consumer-created or acquired applications created using programming languages, libraries, services, and tools that the provider supports. The consumer does not manage or control the underlying cloud infrastructure, including network, servers, operating systems, or storage, but has control over the deployed applications and possibly configuration settings for the application-hosting environment.

D. To deploy onto the cloud infrastructure consumer-created or acquired applications created using programming languages, libraries, services, and tools that the consumer supports. The consumer does not manage or control the underlying cloud infrastructure, including network, servers, operating systems, or storage, but has control over the deployed applications and possibly configuration settings for the application-hosting environment.

Answer: C

Explanation: According to "The NIST Definition of Cloud Computing," in PaaS, "the capability provided to the consumer is to deploy onto the cloud infrastructure consumer-created or acquired applications created using programming languages, libraries, services, and tools supported by the provider. The consumer does not manage or control the underlying cloud infrastructure including network, servers, operating systems, or storage, but has control over the deployed applications and possibly configuration settings for the application-hosting environment."[3]

9. What is a key capability or characteristic of PaaS?

   A. Support for a homogenous hosting environment

   B. Ability to reduce lock-in

   C. Support for a single programming language

   D. Ability to manually scale

Answer: B

Explanation: PaaS should have the following key capabilities and characteristics:

- **Support multiple languages and frameworks:** PaaS should support multiple programming languages and frameworks, thus enabling the developers to code in whichever language they prefer or the design requirements specify. In recent times, significant strides and efforts have been taken to ensure that open source stacks are both supported and utilized, thus reducing "lock-in" or issues with interoperability when changing CSPs.

- **Multiple hosting environments:** The ability to support a wide variety of underlying hosting environments for the platform is key to meeting customer requirements and demands. Whether public cloud, private cloud, local hypervisor, or bare metal, supporting multiple hosting environments allows the application developer or administrator to migrate the application when and as required. This can also be used as a form of contingency and continuity and to ensure the ongoing availability.

- **Flexibility:** Traditionally, platform providers provided features and requirements that they felt suited the client requirements, along with what suited their service offering and positioned them as the provider of choice, with limited options for the customers to move easily. This has changed drastically, with extensibility and flexibility now afforded to meeting the needs and requirements of developer audiences. This has been heavily influenced by open source, which allows relevant plug-ins to be quickly and efficiently introduced into the platform.

- **Allow choice and reduce lock-in:** PaaS learns from previous horror stories and restrictions, proprietary meant red tape, barriers, and restrictions on what developers could do when it came to migration or adding features and components to the platform. Although the requirement to code to specific APIs was made available by the providers, they could run their apps in various environments based on commonality and standard API structures, ensuring a level of consistency and quality for customers and users.

- **Ability to auto-scale:** This enables the application to seamlessly scale up and down as required to accommodate the cyclical demands of users. The platform will allocate resources and assign these to the application as required. This serves as a key driver for any seasonal organizations that experience spikes and drops in usage.

10. When using a SaaS solution, what is the capability provided to the customer?

   A. To use the provider's applications running on a cloud infrastructure. The applications are accessible from various client devices through either a thin client interface, such as a web browser (for example, web-based email), or a program interface. The consumer does not manage or control the underlying cloud infrastructure, including network, servers, operating systems, storage, or even individual application capabilities, with the possible exception of limited user-specific application configuration settings.

   B. To use the provider's applications running on a cloud infrastructure. The applications are accessible from various client devices through either a thin client interface, such as a web browser (for example, web-based email), or a program interface. The consumer does manage or control the underlying cloud infrastructure, including network, servers, operating systems, storage, or even individual application capabilities, with the possible exception of limited user-specific application configuration settings.

C. To use the consumer's applications running on a cloud infrastructure. The applications are accessible from various client devices through either a thin client interface, such as a web browser (for example, web-based email), or a program interface. The consumer does not manage or control the underlying cloud infrastructure including network, servers, operating systems, storage, or even individual application capabilities, with the possible exception of limited user-specific application configuration settings.

D. To use the consumer's applications running on a cloud infrastructure. The applications are accessible from various client devices through either a thin client interface, such as a web browser (for example, web-based email), or a program interface. The consumer does manage or control the underlying cloud infrastructure, including network, servers, operating systems, storage, or even individual application capabilities, with the possible exception of limited user-specific application configuration settings.

Answer: A

Explanation: According to "The NIST Definition of Cloud Computing," in SaaS, "The capability provided to the consumer is to use the provider's applications running on a cloud infrastructure. The applications are accessible from various client devices through either a thin client interface, such as a web browser (e.g., web-based e-mail), or a program interface. The consumer does not manage or control the underlying cloud infrastructure including network, servers, operating systems, storage, or even individual application capabilities, with the possible exception of limited user-specific application configuration settings."[4]

11. What are the four cloud deployment models?

   A. Public, internal, hybrid, and community

   B. External, private, hybrid, and community

   C. Public, private, joint, and community

   D. Public, private, hybrid, and community

   Answer: D

   Explanation: According to "The NIST Definition of Cloud Computing," the cloud deployment models are as follows:

   ■ "**Private cloud:** The cloud infrastructure is provisioned for exclusive use by a single organization comprising multiple consumers (e.g., business units). It may be owned, managed, and operated by the organization, a third party, or some combination of them, and it may exist on- or off-premises.

- **"Community cloud:** The cloud infrastructure is provisioned for exclusive use by a specific community of consumers from organizations that have shared concerns (e.g., mission, security requirements, policy, and compliance considerations). It may be owned, managed, and operated by one or more of the organizations in the community, a third party, or some combination of them, and it may exist on- or off-premises.

- **"Public cloud:** The cloud infrastructure is provisioned for open use by the general public. It may be owned, managed, and operated by a business, academic, or government organization, or some combination of them. It exists on the premises of the CSP.

- **"Hybrid cloud:** The cloud infrastructure is a composition of two or more distinct cloud infrastructures (private, community, or public) that remain unique entities but are bound together by standardized or proprietary technology that enables data and application portability (e.g., cloud bursting for load balancing between clouds)."[5]

12. What are the six stages of the cloud secure data lifecycle?

   A. Create, use, store, share, archive, and destroy

   B. Create, store, use, share, archive, and destroy

   C. Create, share, store, archive, use, and destroy

   D. Create, archive, use, share, store, and destroy

   Answer: B

   Explanation: As with systems and other organizational assets, data should have a defined and managed lifecycle across the following key stages (*Figure A.1*):

   - **Create:** Generation of new digital content or modification of existing content
   - **Store:** Committing data to storage repository; typically occurs directly after creation
   - **Use:** Data is viewed, processed, or otherwise used in some sort of activity (not including modification)
   - **Share:** Information made accessible to others—users, partners, customers, and so on
   - **Archive:** Data leaves active use and enters long-term storage
   - **Destroy:** Data permanently destroyed using physical or digital means

ANSWERS TO REVIEW QUESTIONS

Domain 1: Architectural Concepts and Design Requirements   449

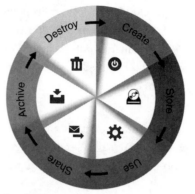

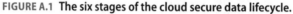

FIGURE A.1 **The six stages of the cloud secure data lifecycle.**

13. What are SOC 1/SOC 2/SOC 3?

    A. Risk management frameworks

    B. Access controls

    C. Audit reports

    D. Software development phases

    Answer: C

    Explanation: An SOC 1 is a report on controls at a service organization that may be relevant to a user entity's internal control over financial reporting. An SOC 2 report is based on the existing SysTrust and WebTrust principles. The purpose of an SOC 2 report is to evaluate an organization's information systems relevant to security, availability, processing integrity, confidentiality, or privacy. An SOC 3 report is also based on the existing SysTrust and WebTrust principles, like a SOC 2 report. The difference is that the SOC 3 report does not detail the testing performed.

14. What are the five Trust Services principles?

    A. Security, Availability, Processing Integrity, Confidentiality, and Privacy

    B. Security, Auditability, Processing Integrity, Confidentiality, and Privacy

    C. Security, Availability, Customer Integrity, Confidentiality, and Privacy

    D. Security, Availability, Processing Integrity, Confidentiality, and Nonrepudiation

    Answer: A

    Explanation: SOC 2 reporting was specifically designed for IT-managed service providers and cloud computing. The report specifically addresses any number of the five so-called Trust Services principles, which follow:

    - **Security:** The system is protected against unauthorized access, both physical and logical.

- **Availability:** The system is available for operation and use as committed or agreed.

- **Processing Integrity:** System processing is complete, accurate, timely, and authorized.

- **Confidentiality:** Information designated as confidential is protected as committed or agreed.

- **Privacy:** Personal information is collected, used, retained, disclosed, and disposed of in conformity with the provider's privacy policy.

15. What is a security-related concern for a PaaS solution?

   A. Virtual machine attacks

   B. Web application security

   C. Data access and policies

   D. System and resource isolation

   Answer: D

   Explanation: PaaS security concerns are focused on the areas shown (*Figure A.2*).

System and Resource Isolations	User Level Permissions	User Access Management	Protection Against Malware/ Backdoors/ Trojans

FIGURE A.2 The PaaS security concerns

DOMAIN 2: CLOUD DATA SECURITY

1. What are the three things that you must understand before you can determine the necessary controls to deploy for data protection in a cloud environment?

   A. Management, provisioning, and location

   B. Function, location, and actors

   C. Actors, policies, and procedures

   D. Lifecycle, function, and cost

   Answer: B

   Explanation: To determine the necessary controls to be deployed, you must first understand the following:

- Functions of the data

- Locations of the data

- Actors upon the data

Once you understand and document these three items, you can design the appropriate controls and apply them to the system to safeguard data and control access to it. These controls can be of a preventive, detective (monitoring), or corrective nature.

2. Which of the following storage types are used with an IaaS solution?

   A. Volume and block

   B. Structured and object

   C. Unstructured and ephemeral

   D. Volume and object

   Answer: D

   Explanation: IaaS uses the following storage types:

   - **Volume storage:** A virtual hard drive that can be attached to a VM instance and be used to host data within a file system. Volumes attached to IaaS instances behave just like a physical drive or an array does. Examples include VMware VMFS, Amazon EBS, Rackspace RAID, and OpenStack Cinder.

   - **Object storage:** Object storage is like a file share accessed via APIs or a web interface. Examples include Amazon S3 and Rackspace cloud files.

3. Which of the following data storage types are used with a PaaS solution?

   A. Raw and block

   B. Structured and unstructured

   C. Unstructured and ephemeral

   D. Tabular and object

   Answer: B

   Explanation: PaaS utilizes the following data storage types:

   - **Structured:** Information with a high degree of organization, such that inclusion in a relational database is seamless and readily searchable by simple, straightforward search engine algorithms or other search operations.

   - **Unstructured:** Information that does not reside in a traditional row-column database. Unstructured data files often include text and multimedia content. Examples include email messages, word processing documents, videos, photos, audio files, presentations, web pages, and many other kinds of business documents. Note that although these sorts of files may have an internal structure, they are still considered unstructured because the data they contain does not fit neatly in a database.

4. Which of the following can be deployed to help ensure the confidentiality of the data in the cloud? (Choose two.)

   A. Encryption

   B. SLAs

   C. Masking

   D. Continuous monitoring

   Answer: A and C

   Explanation: It is important to be aware of the relevant data security technologies you may need to deploy or work with to ensure the AIC of data in the cloud.

   Potential controls and solutions can include the following:

   ■ **Encryption:** For preventing unauthorized data viewing

   ■ **DLP:** For auditing and preventing unauthorized data exfiltration

   ■ **File and database access monitor:** For detecting unauthorized access to data stored in files and databases

   ■ **Obfuscation, anonymization, tokenization, and masking:** Different alternatives for the protection of data without encryption

5. Where would the monitoring engine be deployed when using a network-based DLP system?

   A. On a user's workstation

   B. In the storage system

   C. Near the organizational gateway

   D. On a VLAN

   Answer: C

   Explanation: DLP tool implementations typically conform to the following topologies:

   ■ **DIM:** Sometimes referred to as network-based or gateway DLP. In this topology, the monitoring engine is deployed near the organizational gateway to monitor outgoing protocols such as HTTP, HTTPS, SMTP, and FTP. The topology can be a mixture of proxy based, bridge, network tapping, or SMTP relays. To scan encrypted HTTPS traffic, appropriate mechanisms to enable SSL interception and broker are required to be integrated into the system architecture.

   ■ **DAR:** Sometimes referred to as storage based. In this topology, the DLP engine is installed where the data is at rest, usually one or more storage subsystems and file and application servers. This topology is effective for data discovery and tracking usage but may require integration with network or endpoint-based DLP for policy enforcement.

- **DIU:** Sometimes referred to as client or endpoint based, the DLP application is installed on a user's workstations and endpoint devices. This topology offers insights into how users use the data, with the ability to add protection that network DLP may not be able to provide. The challenge with client-based DLP is the complexity, time, and resources to implement across all endpoint devices, often across multiple locations and significant numbers of users.

6. When using transparent encryption of a database, where does the encryption engine reside?

   A. At the application using the database

   B. On the instances attached to the volume

   C. In a key management system

   D. Within the database

Answer: D

Explanation: For database encryption, you should understand the following options:

- **File-level encryption:** Database servers typically reside on volume storage. For this deployment, you are encrypting the volume or folder of the database, with the encryption engine and keys residing on the instances attached to the volume. External file system encryption protects from media theft, lost backups, and external attack but does not protect against attacks with access to the application layer, the instance's OS, or the database itself.

- **Transparent encryption:** Many database-management systems have the ability to encrypt the entire database or specific portions, such as tables. The encryption engine resides within the database, and it is transparent to the application. Keys usually reside within the instance, although processing and management of them may also be offloaded to an external KMS. This encryption can provide effective protection from media theft, backup system intrusions, and certain database and application-level attacks.

- **Application-level encryption:** In application-level encryption, the encryption engine resides at the application that is utilizing the database. Application encryption can act as a robust mechanism to protect against a range of threats, such as compromised administrative accounts and other database and application-level attacks. Because the data is encrypted before reaching the database, it is challenging to perform indexing, searches, and metadata collection. Encrypting at the application layer can be challenging, based on the expertise requirements for cryptographic development and integration.

7. What are three analysis methods used with data discovery techniques?

   A. Metadata, labels, and content analysis

   B. Metadata, structural analysis, and labels

   C. Statistical analysis, labels, and content analysis

   D. Bit splitting, labels, and content analysis

   Answer: A

   Explanation: Data discovery tools differ by technique and data-matching abilities. Assume you wanted to find credit card numbers. Data discovery tools for databases use a couple of methods to find and then identify information. Most use special login credentials to scan internal database structures, itemize tables and columns, and then analyze what was found. Three basic analysis methods are employed:

   - **Metadata:** Data that describes data; all relational databases store metadata that describes tables and column attributes.

   - **Labels:** Where data elements are grouped with a tag that describes the data. This can be done at the time the data is created, or tags can be added over time to provide additional information and references to describe the data. In many ways, labels are just like metadata but slightly less formal. Some relational database platforms provide mechanisms to create data labels, but this method is more commonly used with flat files, becoming increasingly useful as more firms move to ISAM or quasi-relational data storage, such as Amazon's SimpleDB, to handle fast-growing data sets. This form of discovery is similar to a Google search, with the greater the number of similar labels, the greater likelihood of a match. Effectiveness is dependent on the use of labels.

   - **Content analysis:** In this form of analysis, you investigate the data itself by employing pattern matching, hashing, statistical, lexical, or other forms of probability analysis.

8. In the context of privacy and data protection, what is a controller?

   A. One who cannot be identified, directly or indirectly, in particular by reference to an identification number or to one or more factors specific to his physical, physiological, mental, economic, cultural, or social identity

   B. One who can be identified, directly or indirectly, in particular by reference to an identification number or to one or more factors specific to his physical, physiological, mental, economic, cultural, or social identity

   C. The natural or legal person, public authority, agency, or any other body that alone or jointly with others determines the purposes and means of processing personal data

   D. A natural or legal person, public authority, agency, or any other body that processes personal data on behalf of the customer

Answer: C

Explanation: Where the purposes and means of processing are determined by national or community laws or regulations, the controller or the specific criteria for his nomination may be designated by national or community law.

The customer determines the ultimate purpose of the processing and decides on the outsourcing or the delegation of all or part of the concerned activities to external organizations. Therefore, the customer acts as a controller. In this role, the customer is responsible and subject to all the legal duties that are addressed in the privacy and data protection (P&DP) laws applicable to the controller's role. The customer may task the service provider with choosing the methods and the technical or organizational measures to be used to achieve the purposes of the controller.

9. What is the CSA CSM?

   A. A set of regulatory requirements for CSPs

   B. An inventory of cloud service security controls that are arranged into separate security domains

   C. A set of software development lifecycle requirements for CSPs

   D. An inventory of cloud service security controls that are arranged into a hierarchy of security domains

   Answer: B

   Explanation: The CSA CCM is an essential and up-to-date security controls framework that is addressed to the cloud community and stakeholders. A fundamental richness of the CCM is its ability to provide mapping and cross relationships with the main industry-accepted security standards, regulations, and controls frameworks such as the ISO 27001/27002, ISACA's COBIT, and PCI DSS.

10. Which of the following are common capabilities of IRM solutions?

    A. Persistent protection, dynamic policy control, automatic expiration, continuous audit trail, and support for existing authentication infrastructure

    B. Persistent protection, static policy control, automatic expiration, continuous audit trail, and support for existing authentication infrastructure

    C. Persistent protection, dynamic policy control, manual expiration, continuous audit trail, and support for existing authentication infrastructure

    D. Persistent protection, dynamic policy control, automatic expiration, intermittent audit trail, and support for existing authentication infrastructure

    Answer: A

    Explanation: The following table illustrates key capabilities common to IRM solutions.

Persistent protection	Ensures that documents, messages, and attachments are protected at rest, in transit, and even after they're distributed to recipients
Dynamic policy control	Allows content owners to define and change user permissions (view, forward, copy, or print) and recall or expire content even after distribution
Automatic expiration	Provides the ability to automatically revoke access to documents, emails, and attachments at any point, thus allowing information security policies to be enforced wherever content is distributed or stored
Continuous audit trail	Provides confirmation that content was delivered and viewed and offers proof of compliance with your organization's information security policies
Support for existing authentication security infrastructure	Reduces administrator involvement and speeds deployment by leveraging user and group information that exists in directories and authentication systems
Mapping for repository ACLs	Automatically maps the ACL-based permissions into policies that control the content outside the repository
Integration with all third-party email filtering engines	Allows organizations to automatically secure outgoing email messages in compliance with corporate information security policies and federal regulatory requirements
Additional security and protection capabilities	Allows users additional capabilities such as these: Determine who can access a document Prohibit printing of an entire document or selected portions Disable copy and paste and screen capture capabilities Watermark pages if printing privileges are granted Expire or revoke document access at any time Track all document activity through a complete audit trail
Support for email applications	Provides interface and support for email programs such as Microsoft Outlook and IBM Lotus Notes
Support for other document types	Other document types, besides Microsoft Office and PDF, can be supported as well

11. What are the four elements that a data retention policy should define?

   A. Retention periods, data access methods, data security, and data retrieval procedures

   B. Retention periods, data formats, data security, and data destruction procedures

C. Retention periods, data formats, data security, and data communication procedures

D. Retention periods, data formats, data security, and data retrieval procedures

Answer: D

Explanation: A data retention policy is an organization's established protocol for retaining information for operational or regulatory compliance needs. The objectives of a data retention policy are to keep important information for future use or reference, to organize information so it can be searched and accessed at a later date, and to dispose of information that is no longer needed. The policy balances the legal, regulation, and business data archival requirements against data storage costs, complexity, and other data considerations.

A good data retention policy should define the following:

- Retention periods
- Data formats
- Data security
- Data retrieval procedures for the enterprise

12. Which of the following methods for the safe disposal of electronic records can always be used in a cloud environment?

    A. Physical destruction

    B. Encryption

    C. Overwriting

    D. Degaussing

    Answer: B

    Explanation: To safely dispose of electronic records, the following options are available:

    - **Physical destruction:** Physically destroying the media by incineration, shredding, or other means.

    - **Degaussing:** Using strong magnets for scrambling data on magnetic media such as hard drives and tapes.

    - **Overwriting:** Writing random data over the actual data. The more times the overwriting process occurs, the more thorough the destruction of the data is considered to be.

    - **Encryption:** Using an encryption method to rewrite the data in an encrypted format to make it unreadable without the encryption key.

- **Crypto-shredding:** Because the first three options are not fully applicable to cloud computing, the only reasonable method remaining is encrypting the data. The process of encrypting the data to dispose of it is called digital shredding or crypto-shredding.

  Crypto-shredding is the process of deliberately destroying the encryption keys that were used to encrypt the data originally. Because the data is encrypted with the keys, the data is rendered unreadable (at least until the encryption protocol used can be broken or is capable of being brute-forced by an attacker). To perform proper crypto-shredding, consider the following:

  - The data should be encrypted completely without leaving clear text remaining.
  - The technique must make sure that the encryption keys are totally unrecoverable. This can be hard to accomplish if an external CSP or other third party manages the keys.

13. To support continuous operations, which of the following principles should be adopted as part of the security operations policies?

    A. Application logging, contract and authority maintenance, secure disposal, and business continuity preparation

    B. Audit logging, contract and authority maintenance, secure usage, and incident response legal preparation

    C. Audit logging, contract and authority maintenance, secure disposal, and incident response legal preparation

    D. Transaction logging, contract and authority maintenance, secure disposal, and DR preparation

    Answer: C

    Explanation: To support continuous operations, the following principles should be adopted as part of the security operations policies:

    - **Audit logging:** Higher levels of assurance are required for protection, retention, and lifecycle management of audit logs. They must adhere to applicable legal, statutory, or regulatory compliance obligations and provide unique user access accountability to detect potentially suspicious network behaviors or file integrity anomalies through forensic investigative capabilities in the event of a security breach.

      The continuous operation of audit logging is composed of three important processes:

      - **Detecting new events:** The goal of auditing is to detect information security events. Policies should be created that define what a security event is and how to address it.

- **Adding new rules:** Rules are built to detect new events. Rules allow for mapping of expected values to log files and detect events. In continuous operation mode, rules have to be updated to address new risks.

- **Reducing false positives:** The quality of the continuous operations audit logging depends on the ability to gradually reduce the number of false positives to maintain operational efficiency. This requires constant improvement of the rule set in use.

■ **Contract and authority maintenance:** Points of contact for applicable regulatory authorities, national and local law enforcement, and other legal jurisdictional authorities should be maintained and regularly updated as per the business need (that is, a change in impacted scope or a change in any compliance obligation). This ensures direct compliance liaisons have been established and will prepare for a forensic investigation requiring rapid engagement with law enforcement.

■ **Secure disposal:** Policies and procedures shall be established with supporting business processes and technical measures implemented for the secure disposal and complete removal of data from all storage media. This is to ensure data is not recoverable by any computer forensic means.

■ **Incident response legal preparation:** If a follow-up action concerning a person or organization after an information security incident requires legal action, proper forensic procedures, including chain of custody, should be required for preservation and presentation of evidence to support potential legal action subject to the relevant jurisdictions. Upon notification, impacted customers (tenants) or other external business relationships of a security breach should be given the opportunity to participate as is legally permissible in the forensic investigation.

DOMAIN 3: CLOUD PLATFORM AND INFRASTRUCTURE SECURITY

1. What is a cloud carrier?

   A. A person, organization, or entity responsible for making a service available to service consumers

   B. The intermediary that provides connectivity and transport of cloud services between CSPs and cloud consumers

   C. A person or organization that maintains a business relationship with, and uses service from, CSPs

D. The intermediary that provides business continuity of cloud services between cloud service consumers

Answer: B

Explanation: According to NIST's *Cloud Computing Synopsis and Recommendations*, the following first-level terms are important to define:

- **Cloud service consumer:** Person or organization that maintains a business relationship with, and uses service from, CSPs.

- **Cloud service provider:** Person, organization, or entity responsible for making a service available to service consumers.

- **Cloud carrier:** The intermediary that provides connectivity and transport of cloud services between CSPs and cloud consumers.

In the NIST Cloud Computing reference model, the network and communication function is provided as part of the cloud carrier role. In practice, this is an IP service, increasingly delivered through IPv4 and IPv6. This IP network might not be part of the public Internet.

2. Which of the following statements about SDN are correct? (Choose two.)

   A. SDN enables you to execute the control plane software on general-purpose hardware, allowing for the decoupling from specific network hardware configurations and allowing for the use of commodity servers. Further, the use of software-based controllers permits a view of the network that presents a logical switch to the applications running above, allowing for access via APIs that can be used to configure, manage, and secure network resources.

   B. SDN's objective is to provide a clearly defined network control plane to manage network traffic that is not separated from the forwarding plane. This approach allows for network control to become directly programmable and for dynamic adjustment of traffic flows to address changing patterns of consumption.

   C. SDN enables you to execute the control plane software on specific hardware, allowing for the binding of specific network hardware configurations. Further, the use of software-based controllers permits a view of the network that presents a logical switch to the applications running above, allowing for access via APIs that can be used to configure, manage, and secure network resources.

   D. SDN's objective is to offer a clearly defined and separate network control plane to manage network traffic that is separated from the forwarding plane. This approach permits network control to become directly programmable and distinct from forwarding, allowing for dynamic adjustment of traffic flows to address changing patterns of consumption.

Answer: A and D

Explanation: According to `OpenNetworking.org`, software-defined networking is defined as the physical separation of the network control plane from the forwarding plane, and where a control plane controls several devices.

This architecture decouples the network control and forwarding functions, thus enabling the network control to become directly programmable and the underlying infrastructure to be abstracted for applications and network services. The SDN architecture has the following characteristics:

- **Directly programmable:** Network control is directly programmable because it is decoupled from forwarding functions.

- **Agile:** Abstracting control from forwarding lets administrators dynamically adjust network-wide traffic flow to meet changing needs.

- **Centrally managed:** Network intelligence is (logically) centralized in software-based SDN controllers that maintain a global view of the network, which appears to applications and policy engines as a single, logical switch.

- **Programmatically configured:** SDN lets network managers configure, manage, secure, and optimize network resources quickly via dynamic, automated SDN programs, which they can write themselves because the programs do not depend on proprietary software.

- **Open standards based and vendor neutral:** When implemented through open standards, SDN simplifies network design and operation because instructions are provided by SDN controllers instead of multiple, vendor-specific devices and protocols.

3. With regard to management of the compute resources of a host in a cloud environment, what does a reservation provide?

   A. The ability to arbitrate the issues associated with compute resource contention situations. Resource contention implies that there are too many requests for resources based on the actual available resources currently in the system.

   B. A guaranteed minimum resource allocation that must be met by the host with physical compute resources to allow a guest to power on and operate.

   C. A maximum ceiling for a resource allocation. This ceiling may be fixed, or it may be expandable, allowing for the acquisition of more compute resources through a borrowing scheme from the root resource provider (the host).

   D. A guaranteed maximum resource allocation that must be met by the host with physical compute resources to allow a guest to power on and operate.

Answer: B

Explanation: The use of reservations, limits, and shares provides the contextual ability for an administrator to allocate the compute resources of a host.

A reservation creates a guaranteed minimum resource allocation that must be met by the host with physical compute resources to allow a guest to power on and operate. This reservation is traditionally available for either CPU or RAM, or both, as needed.

A limit creates a maximum ceiling for a resource allocation. This ceiling may be fixed, or it may be expandable, allowing for the acquisition of more compute resources through a borrowing scheme from the root resource provider (the host).

Shares are used to arbitrate the issues associated with compute resource contention situations. Resource contention implies the existence of too many requests for resources based on the actual available resources currently in the system. If resource contention takes place, share values are used to prioritize compute resource access for all guests assigned a certain number of shares. The shares are weighed and used as a percentage against all outstanding shares assigned and in use by all powered-on guests to calculate the amount of resources each guest is given access to. The higher the share value assigned to the guest, the larger the percentage of the remaining resources they are given access to during the contention period.

4. What is the key issue associated with the object storage type that the CCSP has to be aware of?

   A. Data consistency, which is achieved only after change propagation to all replica instances has taken place

   B. Access control

   C. Data consistency, which is achieved only after change propagation to a specified percentage of replica instances has taken place

   D. Continuous monitoring

   Answer: A

   Explanation: The features you get in an object storage system are typically minimal. You can store, retrieve, copy, and delete files, as well as control which users can undertake these actions. If you want the ability to search or to have a central repository of object metadata that other applications can draw on, you generally have to implement them yourself. Amazon S3 and other object storage systems provide REST APIs that allow programmers to work with the containers and objects.

   The key issue that the CCSP has to be aware of with object storage systems is that data consistency is achieved only eventually. Whenever you update a file, you may have to wait until the change is propagated to all the replicas before requests return the latest version. This makes object storage unsuitable for data that changes frequently. However, it provides a good solution for data that does not change much, such as backups, archives, video and audio files, and VM images.

5. What types of risks are typically associated with virtualization?

   A. Loss of governance, snapshot and image security, and sprawl

   B. Guest breakout, snapshot and image availability, and compliance

   C. Guest breakout, snapshot and image security, and sprawl

   D. Guest breakout, knowledge level required to manage, and sprawl

   Answer: C

   Explanation: Although other risks might not appear in virtualized environments as a result of choices made by the architect, implementer, and customer, virtualization risks traditionally are seen as including the following:

   - **Guest breakout:** This occurs when there is a breakout of a guest OS so that it can access the hypervisor or other guests. This is presumably facilitated by a hypervisor flaw.

   - **Snapshot and image security:** The portability of images and snapshots makes people forget that images and snapshots can contain sensitive information and need protecting.

   - **Sprawl:** This occurs when you lose control of the amount of content on your image store.

6. When using a SaaS solution, who is responsible for application security?

   A. Both the cloud consumer and the enterprise

   B. The enterprise only

   C. The CSP only

   D. The CSP and the enterprise

   Answer: D

   Explanation: Implementation of controls requires cooperation and a clear demarcation of responsibility between the CSP and the cloud consumer. Without that, there is a real risk for certain important controls to be absent. For example, IaaS providers typically do not consider guest OS hardening their responsibility.

   Consider this visual responsibility matrix across the cloud environment (*Figure* A.3).

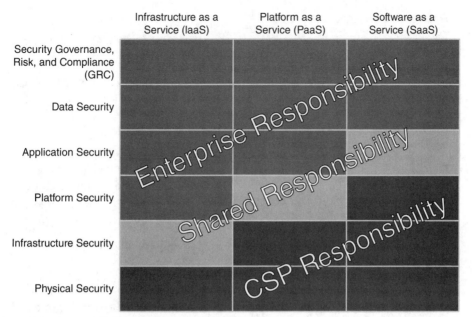

FIGURE A.3 Responsibility matrix across the cloud environment

7. Which of the following are examples of trust zones? (Choose two.)

   A. A specific application being used to carry out a general function such as printing

   B. Segmentation according to department

   C. A web application with a two-tiered architecture

   D. Storage of a baseline configuration on a workstation

   Answer: B and C

   Explanation: A trust zone can be defined as a network segment within which data flows relatively freely, whereas data flowing in and out of the trust zone is subject to stronger restrictions. Some examples of trust zones include demilitarized zones (DMZs); site-specific zones, such as segmentation according to department or function; and application-defined zones, such as the three tiers of a web application.

8. What are the relevant cloud infrastructure characteristics that can be considered distinct advantages in realizing a BCDR plan objective with regard to cloud computing environments?

   A. Rapid elasticity, provider-specific network connectivity, and a pay-per-use model

   B. Rapid elasticity, broad network connectivity, and a multitenancy model

   C. Rapid elasticity, broad network connectivity, and a pay-per-use model

   D. Continuous monitoring, broad network connectivity, and a pay-per-use model

Answer: C

Explanation: Cloud infrastructure has a number of characteristics that can be distinct advantages in realizing BCDR, depending on the scenario:

- Rapid elasticity and on-demand self-service lead to a flexible infrastructure that can be quickly deployed to execute an actual DR without hitting unexpected ceilings.

- Broad network connectivity reduces operational risk.

- Cloud infrastructure providers have resilient infrastructure, and an external BCDR provider has the potential for being experienced and capable because their technical and people resources are being shared across a number of tenants.

- Pay-per-use can mean that the total BCDR strategy can be a lot cheaper than alternative solutions. During normal operation, the BCDR solution is likely to have a low cost.

Of course, as part of due diligence in your BCDR plan, you should validate all assumptions with the candidate service provider and ensure that they are documented in your SLAs.

DOMAIN 4: CLOUD APPLICATION SECURITY

1. What is REST?

   A. A protocol specification for exchanging structured information in the implementation of web services in computer networks

   B. A software architecture style consisting of guidelines and best practices for creating scalable web services

   C. The name of the process that an organization or a person who moves data between CSPs uses to document what he is doing

   D. The intermediary process that provides business continuity of cloud services between cloud consumers and CSPs

   Answer: B

   Explanation: APIs can be broken into multiple formats, two of which follow:

   - **REST:** A software architecture style consisting of guidelines and best practices for creating scalable web services[6]

   - **SOAP:** A protocol specification for exchanging structured information in the implementation of web services in computer networks[7]

2. What are the phases of a software development lifecycle model?

   A. Planning and requirements analysis, defining, designing, developing, and testing

   B. Defining, planning and requirements analysis, designing, developing, and testing

   C. Planning and requirements analysis, defining, designing, testing, and developing

   D. Planning and requirements analysis, designing, defining, developing, and testing

   Answer: A

   Explanation: Following are the phases in all software development lifecycle process models:

   - **Planning and requirements analysis:** Business and security requirements and standards are being determined. This phase is the main focus of the project managers and stakeholders. Meetings with managers, stakeholders, and users are held to determine requirements. The software development lifecycle calls for all business requirements (functional and nonfunctional) to be defined even before initial design begins. Planning for the quality assurance requirements and identification of the risks associated with the project is also done in the planning stage. The requirements are then analyzed for their validity and the possibility of incorporating them into the system to be developed.

   - **Defining:** This phase is meant to clearly define and document the product requirements to place them in front of the customer and get them approved. This is done through a requirement specification document, which consists of all the product requirements to be designed and developed during the project lifecycle.

   - **Designing:** This phase helps in specifying hardware and system requirements and overall system architecture. The system design specifications serve as input for the next phase of the model. Threat modeling and secure design elements should be discussed here.

   - **Developing:** Upon receiving the system design documents, work is divided in modules or units and actual coding is started. This is typically the longest phase of the software development lifecycle. Activities include code review, unit testing, and static analysis.

   - **Testing:** After the code is developed, it is tested against the requirements to make sure that the product is actually solving the needs gathered during the requirements phase. During this phase, unit testing, integration testing, system testing, and acceptance testing are accomplished.

3. When does an XSS flaw occur?

   A. Whenever an application takes trusted data and sends it to a web browser without proper validation or escaping

B. Whenever an application takes untrusted data and sends it to a web browser without proper validation or escaping

C. Whenever an application takes trusted data and sends it to a web browser with proper validation or escaping

D. Whenever an application takes untrusted data and sends it to a web browser with proper validation or escaping

Answer: B

Explanation: XSS flaws occur whenever an application takes untrusted data and sends it to a web browser without proper validation or escaping. XSS allows attackers to execute scripts in the victim's browser, which can hijack user sessions, deface websites, or redirect the user to malicious sites.

4. What are the six components that make up the STRIDE threat model?

    A. Spoofing, tampering, repudiation, information disclosure, DoS, and elevation of privilege

    B. Spoofing, tampering, nonrepudiation, information disclosure, DoS, and elevation of privilege

    C. Spoofing, tampering, repudiation, information disclosure, DDoS, and elevation of privilege

    D. Spoofing, tampering, repudiation, information disclosure, DoS, and social engineering

Answer: A

Explanation: In the STRIDE threat model, the following six threats are considered and controls are used to address the threats:

- **Spoofing:** Attacker assumes identity of subject
- **Tampering:** Attacker alters data or messages
- **Repudiation:** Illegitimate denial of an event
- **Information disclosure:** Information is obtained without authorization
- **Denial of service:** Attacker overloads system to deny legitimate access
- **Elevation of privilege:** Attacker gains a privilege level above what is permitted

5. In a federated environment, who is the relying party, and what does it do?

    A. The relying party is the identity provider; it consumes the tokens that the service provider generates.

    B. The relying party is the service provider; it consumes the tokens that the customer generates.

C. The relying party is the service provider; it consumes the tokens that the identity provider generates.

D. The relying party is the customer; he consumes the tokens that the identity provider generates.

Answer: C

Explanation: In a federated environment, there is an identity provider and a relying party. The identity provider holds all the identities and generates a token for known users. The relying party is the service provider and consumes these tokens.

6. What are the five steps used to create an ASMP?

A. Specifying the application requirements and environment, creating and maintaining the ANF, assessing application security risks, provisioning and operating the application, and auditing the security of the application

B. Assessing application security risks, specifying the application requirements and environment, creating and maintaining the ANF, provisioning and operating the application, and auditing the security of the application

C. Specifying the application requirements and environment, assessing application security risks, provisioning and operating the application, auditing the security of the application, and creating and maintaining the ANF

D. Specifying the application requirements and environment, assessing application security risks, creating and maintaining the ANF, provisioning and operating the application, and auditing the security of the application

Answer: D

Explanation: ISO/IEC 27034-1 defines an ASMP to manage and maintain each ANF. The ASMP is created in five steps:

1. Specifying the application requirements and environment

2. Assessing application security risks

3. Creating and maintaining the ANF

4. Provisioning and operating the application

5. Auditing the security of the application

DOMAIN 5: OPERATIONS

1. At which of the following levels should logical design for data separation be incorporated?

    A. Compute nodes and network

    B. Storage nodes and application

    C. Control plane and session

    D. Management plane and presentation

    Answer: A

    Explanation: Logical design for data separation needs to be incorporated at the following levels:

    - Compute nodes
    - Management plane
    - Storage nodes
    - Control plane
    - Network

2. Which of the following is the correct name for Tier II of the Uptime Institute Data Center Site Infrastructure Tier Standard Topology?

    A. Concurrently Maintainable Site Infrastructure

    B. Fault-Tolerant Site Infrastructure

    C. Basic Site Infrastructure

    D. Redundant Site Infrastructure Capacity Components

    Answer: D

    Explanation: The Uptime Institute is a leader in data center design and management. Their "Data Center Site Infrastructure Tier Standard: Topology" document provides the baseline that many enterprises use to rate their data center designs.

    The document describes a four-tiered architecture for data center design, with each tier being progressively more secure, reliable, and redundant in its design and operational elements. The document also addresses the supporting infrastructure systems that these designs will rely on, such as power generation systems, ambient temperature control, and makeup (backup) water systems. The four tiers are listed in order from left to right (*Figure A.4*).

Tier I: Basic Site Infrastructure	Tier II: Redundant Site Infrastructure Capacity Components	Tier III: Concurrently Maintainable Site Infrastructure	Tier IV: Fault- Tolerant Site Infrastructure

FIGURE A.4 **The Uptime Institute "Data Center Site Infrastructure Tier Standard: Topology"**

3. Which of the following is the recommended operating range for temperature and humidity in a data center?

   A. Between 62° F and 81° F and 40 percent and 65 percent relative humidity

   B. Between 64° F and 81° F and 40 percent and 60 percent relative humidity

   C. Between 64° F and 84° F and 30 percent and 60 percent relative humidity

   D. Between 60° F and 85° F and 40 percent and 60 percent relative humidity

   Answer: B

   Explanation: The American Society of Heating, Refrigeration, and Air Conditioning Engineers (ASHRAE) Technical Committee 9.9 created a widely accepted set of guidelines for optimal temperature and humidity set points in the data center. The guidelines are available as the 2008 ASHRAE Environmental Guidelines for Datacom Equipment. These guidelines specify a required and allowable range of temperature and humidity, as follows:

Low-end temperature	64.4° F (18° C)
High-end temperature	80.6° F (27° C)
Low-end moisture	40% relative humidity and 41.9° F (5.5° C) dew point
High-end moisture	60% relative humidity and 59° F (15° C) dew point

4. Which of the following are supported authentication methods for iSCSI? (Choose two.)

   A. Kerberos

   B. TLS

   C. SRP

   D. L2TP

   Answer: A and C

   Explanation: A number of authentication methods are supported with iSCSI:

   ■ **Kerberos:** A network authentication protocol designed to provide strong authentication for client/server applications by using secret key cryptography. The Kerberos protocol uses strong cryptography so that a client can prove its identity to a server (and vice versa) across an insecure network connection. After a client and server use Kerberos to prove their identity, they can encrypt all their communications to ensure privacy and data integrity as they go about their business.

- **SRP:** A secure password-based authentication and key-exchange protocol that exchanges a cryptographically strong secret as a by-product of successful authentication. This enables the two parties to communicate securely.

- **SPKM1/2:** Provides authentication, key establishment, data integrity, and data confidentiality in an online distributed application environment using a public-key infrastructure. The use of a public-key infrastructure allows digital signatures supporting nonrepudiation to be employed for message exchanges.

- **CHAP:** Used to periodically verify the identity of the peer using a three-way handshake. This is done upon initial link establishment and may be repeated anytime after the link has been established.

5. What are the two biggest challenges associated with the use of IPSec in cloud computing environments?

   A. Access control and patch management

   B. Auditability and governance

   C. Configuration management and performance

   D. Training customers on how to use IPSec and documentation

   Answer: C

   Explanation: The two key challenges with the deployment and use of IPSec follow:

   - **Configuration management:** The use of IPSec is optional, and as such, many endpoint devices connecting to cloud infrastructure do not have IPSec support enabled and configured. If IPSec is not enabled on the endpoint, then depending on the configuration choices made on the server side of the IPSec solution, the endpoint may not be able to connect and complete a transaction if it does not support IPSec.

     CSPs may not have the proper visibility on the customer endpoints or the server infrastructure to understand IPSec configurations. As a result, the ability to ensure the use of IPSec to secure network traffic may be limited.

   - **Performance:** The use of IPSec imposes a performance penalty on the systems deploying the technology. Although the impact to the performance of an average system is small, it is the cumulative effect of IPSec across an enterprise architecture, end to end, that must be evaluated prior to implementation.

6. When setting up resource sharing within a host cluster, which option would you choose to mediate resource contention?

    A. Reservations

    B. Limits

    C. Clusters

    D. Shares

    Answer: D

    Explanation: Within a host cluster, resources are allocated and managed as if they are pooled or jointly available to all members of the cluster. The use of resource-sharing concepts such as reservations limits and shares may be used to further refine and orchestrate the allocation of resources according to requirements that the cluster administrator imposes.

    Reservations guarantee that a certain amount of the cluster's pooled resources will be made available to a specified VM.

    Limits guarantee a certain maximum amount of the cluster's pooled resources will be made available to a specified VM.

    Shares provision the remaining resources left in a cluster when there is resource contention. Specifically, shares allow the cluster's reservations to be allocated and then to address any remaining resources that may be available for use by members of the cluster through a prioritized percentage-based allocation mechanism.

7. When using maintenance mode, which two items are disabled and which item remains enabled?

    A. Customer access and alerts are disabled while logging remains enabled.

    B. Customer access and logging are disabled while alerts remain enabled.

    C. Logging and alerts are disabled while the ability to deploy new VMs remains enabled.

    D. Customer access and alerts are disabled while the ability to power on VMs remains enabled.

    Answer: A

    Explanation: Maintenance mode is utilized when updating or configuring different components of the cloud environment. While in maintenance mode, customer access is blocked, and alerts are disabled. (Logging is still enabled.)

8. What are the three generally accepted service models of cloud computing?

    A. IaaS, DRaaS, and PaaS

    B. PaaS, SECaaS, and IaaS

A

ANSWERS TO REVIEW QUESTIONS

C. SaaS, PaaS, and IaaS

D. Desktop as a service, PaaS, and IaaS

Answer: C

Explanation: According to "The NIST Definition of Cloud Computing," the three service models are as follows:

- **SaaS:** Customers can use the provider's applications running on a cloud infrastructure. The applications are accessible from various client devices through a thin client interface such as a web browser (for example, web-based email) or a program interface. The consumer does not manage or control the underlying cloud infrastructure, including network, servers, OSs, storage, or even individual application capabilities, with the possible exception of limited user-specific application configuration settings.

- **PaaS:** Consumers can deploy onto the cloud infrastructure consumer-created or acquired applications created using programming languages and tools that the provider supports. The consumer does not manage or control the underlying cloud infrastructure, including network, servers, OSs, or storage, but has control over the deployed applications and possibly application hosting environment configurations.

- **IaaS:** The capability provided to the consumer is to provision processing, storage, networks, and other fundamental computing resources where the consumer can deploy and run arbitrary software, which can include OSs and applications. The consumer does not manage or control the underlying cloud infrastructure but has control over OSs, storage, and deployed applications and possibly limited control of select networking components, such as host firewalls.

9. What is a key characteristic of a honeypot?

   A. Isolated, nonmonitored environment

   B. Isolated, monitored environment

   C. Composed of virtualized infrastructure

   D. Composed of physical infrastructure

   Answer: B

   Explanation: A honeypot is used to detect, deflect, or in some manner counteract attempts at unauthorized use of information systems. Generally, a honeypot consists of a computer, data, or a network site that appears to be part of a network but is actually isolated and monitored and that seems to contain information or a resource of value to attackers.

10. What does the concept of nondestructive testing mean in the context of a vulnerability assessment?

   A. Detected vulnerabilities are not exploited during the vulnerability assessment.

   B. Known vulnerabilities are not exploited during the vulnerability assessment.

   C. Detected vulnerabilities are not exploited after the vulnerability assessment.

   D. Known vulnerabilities are not exploited before the vulnerability assessment.

   Answer: A

   Explanation: During a vulnerability assessment, the cloud environment is tested for known vulnerabilities. Detected vulnerabilities are not exploited during a vulnerability assessment (nondestructive testing) and may require further validation to detect false positives.

11. Seeking to follow good design practices and principles, the CCSP should create the physical network design based on which of the following?

   A. A statement of work

   B. A series of interviews with stakeholders

   C. A design policy statement

   D. A logical network design

   Answer: D

   Explanation: The basic idea of physical design is that it communicates decisions about the hardware used to deliver a system. The following is true about a physical network design:

   - It is created from a logical network design
   - It often expands elements found in a logical design

   For instance, a WAN connection on a logical design diagram can be shown as a line between two buildings. When transformed into a physical design, that single line can expand into the connection, routers, and other equipment at each end of the connection. The actual connection media might be shown on a physical design as well as manufacturers and other qualities of the network implementation.

12. What should configuration management always be tied to?

   A. Financial management

   B. Change management

   C. IT service management

   D. D Business relationship management

Answer: B

Explanation: The need to tie configuration management to change management is because change management has to approve any changes to all production systems prior to them taking place. In other words, there should never be a change that is allowed to take place to a Configuration Item (CI) in a production system unless change management has approved the change first.

13. What are the objectives of change management? (Choose all that apply.)

   A. Respond to a customer's changing business requirements while maximizing value and reducing incidents, disruption, and rework.

   B. Ensure that changes are recorded and evaluated.

   C. Respond to business and IT requests for change that will disassociate services with business needs.

   D. Ensure that all changes are prioritized, planned, tested, implemented, documented, and reviewed in a controlled manner.

Answer: A and B

Explanation: Change management has several objectives:

   ■ Respond to a customer's changing business requirements while maximizing value and reducing incidents, disruption, and rework.

   ■ Respond to business and IT requests for change that aligns services with business needs.

   ■ Ensure that changes are recorded and evaluated.

   ■ Ensure that authorized changes are prioritized, planned, tested, implemented, documented, and reviewed in a controlled manner.

   ■ Ensure that all changes to CIs are recorded in the configuration management system.

   ■ Optimize overall business risk; it is often correct to minimize business risk, but sometimes it is appropriate to knowingly accept a risk because of the potential benefit.

14. What is the definition of an incident according to the ITIL framework?

   A. An unplanned interruption to an IT service or a reduction in the quality of an IT service

   B. A planned interruption to an IT service or a reduction in the quality of an IT service

   C. The unknown cause of one or more problems

   D. The identified root cause of a problem

Answer: A

Explanation: According to the ITIL framework, an incident is defined as an unplanned interruption to an IT service or a reduction in the quality of an IT service.

15. What is the difference between BC and BCM?

   A. BC is defined as the capability of the organization to continue delivery of products or services at acceptable predefined levels following a disruptive incident. BCM is defined as a holistic management process that identifies actual threats to an organization and the impacts to business operations that those threats, if realized, will cause. BCM provides a framework for building organizational resilience with the capability of an effective response that safeguards its key processes, reputation, brand, and value-creating activities.

   B. BC is defined as a holistic process that identifies potential threats to an organization and the impacts to business operations that those threats, if realized, might cause. BC provides a framework for building organizational resilience with the capability of an effective response that safeguards the interests of its key stakeholders, reputation, brand, and value-creating activities. BCM is defined as the capability of the organization to continue delivery of products or services at acceptable predefined levels following a disruptive incident.

   C. BC is defined as the capability of the first responder to continue delivery of products or services at acceptable predefined levels following a disruptive incident. BCM is defined as a holistic management process that identifies potential threats to an organization and the impacts to business operations that those threats, if realized, will cause. BCM provides a framework for building organizational resilience with the capability of an effective response that safeguards the interests of its key stakeholders, reputation, brand, and value-creating activities.

   D. BC is defined as the capability of the organization to continue delivery of products or services at acceptable predefined levels following a disruptive incident. BCM is defined as a holistic management process that identifies potential threats to an organization and the impacts to business operations that those threats, if realized, might cause. BCM provides a framework for building organizational resilience with the capability of an effective response that safeguards the interests of its key stakeholders, reputation, brand, and value-creating activities.

Answer: D

Explanation: It is important to understand the difference between BC and BCM:

- **BC:** The capability of the organization to continue delivery of products or services at acceptable predefined levels following a disruptive incident (Source: ISO 22301:2012).

- **BCM:** A holistic management process that identifies potential threats to an organization and the impacts to business operations that those threats, if realized, might cause. It provides a framework for building organizational resilience with the capability of an effective response that safeguards the interests of its key stakeholders, reputation, brand, and value-creating activities (Source: ISO 22301:2012).

16. What are the four steps in the risk management process?

   A. Assessing, monitoring, transferring, and responding

   B. Framing, assessing, monitoring, and responding

   C. Framing, monitoring, documenting, and responding

   D. Monitoring, assessing, optimizing, and responding

   Answer: B

   Explanation: Risk-management processes include framing risk, assessing risk, responding to risk, and monitoring risk.

   Note the four steps in the risk-management process, which includes the risk assessment step and the information and communications flows necessary to make the process work effectively (*Figure A.5*).

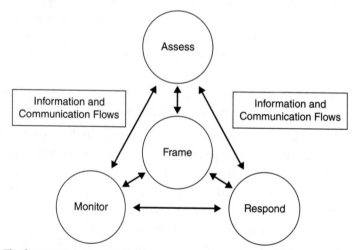

FIGURE A.5 The four steps in the risk-management process
SOURCE: NIST Special Publication 800-39, "Managing Information Security Risk: Organization, Mission, and Information System View"

17. An organization will conduct a risk assessment to evaluate which of the following?

   A. Threats to its assets, vulnerabilities not present in the environment, the likelihood that a threat will be realized by taking advantage of an exposure, the impact that the exposure being realized will have on the organization, and the residual risk

B. Threats to its assets, vulnerabilities present in the environment, the likelihood that a threat will be realized by taking advantage of an exposure, the impact that the exposure being realized will have on another organization, and the residual risk

C. Threats to its assets, vulnerabilities present in the environment, the likelihood that a threat will be realized by taking advantage of an exposure, the impact that the exposure being realized will have on the organization, and the residual risk

D. Threats to its assets, vulnerabilities present in the environment, the likelihood that a threat will be realized by taking advantage of an exposure, the impact that the exposure being realized will have on the organization, and the total risk

Answer: C

Explanation: An organization will conduct a risk assessment (or risk analysis) to evaluate the following:

- Threats to its assets
- Vulnerabilities present in the environment
- The likelihood that a threat will be realized by taking advantage of an exposure (or probability and frequency when dealing with quantitative assessment)
- The impact that the exposure being realized will have on the organization
- Countermeasures available that can reduce the threat's ability to exploit the exposure or that can lessen the impact to the organization when a threat is able to exploit a vulnerability
- The residual risk, or the amount of risk that is left over when appropriate controls are properly applied to lessen or remove the vulnerability

An organization may also document evidence of the countermeasure in a deliverable called an exhibit or evidence. An exhibit can provide an audit trail for the organization and, likewise, evidence for any internal or external auditors that may have questions about the organization's current state of risk. Why undertake such an endeavor? Without knowing which assets are critical and which would be most at risk within an organization, it is not possible to appropriately protect those assets.

18. What is the minimum and customary practice of responsible protection of assets that affects a community or societal norm?

   A. Due diligence

   B. Risk mitigation

   C. Asset protection

   D. Due care

ANSWERS TO REVIEW QUESTIONS

Domain 5: Operations   479

Answer: D

Explanation: Due diligence is the act of investigating and understanding the risks the company faces. A company practices due care by developing security policies, procedures, and standards. Due care shows that a company has taken responsibility for the activities that take place within the corporation and has taken the necessary steps to help protect the company, its resources, and employees from possible risks. So due diligence is understanding the current threats and risks and due care is implementing countermeasures to provide protection from those threats. If a company does not practice due care and due diligence pertaining to the security of its assets, it can be legally charged with negligence and held accountable for any ramifications of that negligence.

19. Within the realm of IT security, which of the following combinations best define risk?

A. Threat coupled with a breach

B. Threat coupled with a vulnerability

C. Vulnerability coupled with an attack

D. Threat coupled with a breach of security

Answer: B

Explanation: A vulnerability is a lack of a countermeasure or a weakness in a countermeasure that is in place. A threat is any potential danger that is associated with the exploitation of a vulnerability. The threat is that someone, or something, will identify a specific vulnerability and use it against the company or individual. A risk is the likelihood of a threat agent exploiting a vulnerability and the corresponding business impact.

20. SLE is calculated by using which of the following?

A. Asset value and ARO

B. Asset value, LAFE, and SAFE

C. Asset value and exposure factor

D. LAFE and ARO

Answer: C

Explanation: SLE must be calculated to provide an estimate of loss. SLE is defined as the difference between the original value and the remaining value of an asset after a single exploit. The formula for calculating SLE is as follows:

SLE = asset value (in $) × exposure factor (loss due to successful threat exploit, as a %)

Losses can include lack of availability of data assets due to data loss, theft, alteration, or DoS (perhaps due to business continuity or security issues).

21. What is the process flow of digital forensics?

    A. Identification of incident and evidence, analysis, collection, examination, and presentation

    B. Identification of incident and evidence, examination, collection, analysis, and presentation

    C. Identification of incident and evidence, collection, examination, analysis, and presentation

    D. Identification of incident and evidence, collection, analysis, examination, and presentation

Answer: C

Explanation: The figure illustrates the process flow of digital forensics (*Figure A.6*). Cloud forensics can be defined as applying all the processes of digital forensics in the cloud environment.

FIGURE A.6 **Proper methodologies for forensic collection of data**

In the cloud, forensic evidence can be collected from the host or guest OS. The dynamic nature and use of pooled resources in a cloud environment can affect the collection of digital evidence.

The process for performing digital forensics includes the following phases:

- **Collection:** Identifying, labeling, recording, and acquiring data from the possible sources of relevant data, while following procedures that preserve the integrity of the data.

- **Examination:** Forensically processing collected data using a combination of automated and manual methods, and assessing and extracting data of particular interest, while preserving the integrity of the data.

- **Analysis:** Analyzing the results of the examination, using legally justifiable methods and techniques, to derive useful information that addresses the questions that were the impetus for performing the collection and examination.

- **Reporting:** Reporting the results of the analysis, which may include describing the actions used, explaining how tools and procedures were selected, determining what other actions need to be performed (such as forensic examination of additional data sources, securing of identified vulnerabilities, improvement of existing security controls), and providing recommendations for improvement to policies, procedures, tools, and other aspects of the forensic process.

DOMAIN 6: LEGAL AND COMPLIANCE ISSUES

1. When does the EU Data Protection Directive (Directive 95/46/EC) apply to data processed?

   A. The directive applies to data processed by automated means and data contained in paper files.

   B. The directive applies to data processed by a natural person in the course of purely personal activities.

   C. The directive applies to data processed in the course of an activity that falls outside the scope of community law, such as public safety.

   D. The directive applies to data processed by automated means in the course of purely personal activities.

   Answer: A

   Explanation: Directive 95/46/EC of the European Parliament and of the Council of October 24, 1995, on the protection of individuals with regard to the processing of personal data and on the free movement of such data, regulates the processing of personal data within the European Union. It is designed to protect the privacy and protection of all personal data collected for or about citizens of the European Union, especially as it relates to the processing, using, or exchanging of such data. The data protection directive encompasses the key elements from article 8 of the European Convention on Human Rights, which states its intention to respect the rights of privacy in personal and family life, as well as in the home and in personal correspondence. This directive applies to data processed by automated means and data contained in paper files. It does not apply to the processing of data in these instances:

   - By a natural person in the course of purely personal or household activities

   - In the course of an activity that falls outside the scope of community law, such as operations concerning public safety, defense, or state security

   The directive aims to protect the rights and freedoms of persons with respect to the processing of personal data by laying down guidelines determining when this processing is lawful.

2. Which of the following are contractual components that the CCSP should review and understand fully when contracting with a CSP? (Choose two.)

A. Concurrently maintainable site infrastructure

B. Use of subcontractors

C. Redundant site infrastructure capacity components

D. Scope of processing

Answer: B and D

Explanation: From a contractual, regulated, and PII perspective, the following should be reviewed and fully understood by the CCSP with regard to any hosting contracts (along with other overarching components within an SLA):

- **Scope of processing:** Clear understanding of the permissible types of data processing should be provided. The specifications should also list the purpose for which the data can be processed or utilized.

- **Use of subcontractors:** Understanding where any processing, transmission, storage, or use of information will occur. A complete list should be drawn up including the entity, location, rationale, form of data use (processing, transmission, and storage), and any limitations or nonpermitted uses. Contractually, the requirement for the procuring organization to be informed as to where data has been provided or will be utilized by a subcontractor is essential.

- **Deletion of data:** Where the business operations no longer require information to be retained for a specific purpose (that is, not retaining for convenience or potential future uses), the deletion of information should occur in line with the organizations data retention policies and standards. Data deletion is also of critical importance when contractors and subcontractors no longer provide services or when a contract is terminated.

- **Appropriate or required data security controls:** Where processing, transmission, or storage of data and resources is outsourced, the same level of security controls should be required for any entry's contracting or subcontracting services. Ideally, security controls should be of a higher level (which is the case for a large number of cloud computing services) than the existing levels of controls; however, this is never to be taken as a given in the absence of confirmation or verification. Additionally, technical security controls should be unequivocally called out and stipulated in the contract; they are applicable to any subcontractors as well.

- **Locations of data:** To ensure compliance with regulatory and legal requirements, the CCSP needs to understand the location of contractors and subcontractors. She must pay particular attention to where the organization is located and where operations, data centers, and headquarters are located. The CCSP needs to know where information is being stored, processed, and transmitted. Finally, any contingency or continuity requirements may require failover to different geographic locations, which can affect or violate regulatory or contractual requirements. The CCSP should fully understand these and accept them prior to engagement of services with any contractor, subcontractor, or CSP.

- **Return or restitution of data:** For both contractors and subcontractors where a contract is terminated, the timely and orderly return of data has to be required both contractually and within the SLA. Format and structure of data should be clearly documented, with an emphasis on structured and agreed-upon formats being clearly understood by all parties. Data retention periods should be explicitly understood, with the return of data to the organization that owns the data, resulting in the removal or secure deletion on any contractors' or subcontractors' systems or storage.

- **Right to audit subcontractors:** Right to audit clauses should allow for the organization owning the data (not possessing) to audit or engage the services of an independent party to ensure that contractual and regulatory requirements are being satisfied by either the contractor or the subcontractor.

3. What does an audit scope statement provide to a cloud service customer or organization?

   A. The credentials of the auditors, as well as the projected cost of the audit

   B. The required level of information for the client or organization subject to the audit to fully understand (and agree) with the scope, focus, and type of assessment being performed

   C. A list of all the security controls to be audited

   D. The outcome of the audit, as well as any findings that need to be addressed

   Answer: B

   Explanation: An audit scope statement provides the required level of information for the client or organization subject to the audit to fully understand (and agree with) the scope, focus, and type of assessment being performed. Typically, an audit scope statement includes the following:

   - General statement of focus and objectives
   - Scope of audit (including exclusions)
   - Type of audit (certification, attestation, and so on)
   - Security assessment requirements
   - Assessment criteria (including ratings)
   - Acceptance criteria
   - Deliverables
   - Classification (confidential, highly confidential, secret, top secret, public, and so on)

The audit scope statement can also catalog the circulation list, along with key individuals associated with the audit.

4. Which of the following should be carried out first when seeking to perform a gap analysis?

   A. Define scope and objectives.

   B. Identify potential risks.

   C. Obtain management support.

   D. Conduct information gathering.

   Answer: C

   Explanation: Numerous stages are carried out prior to commencing a gap analysis review. Although they can vary depending on the review, common stages include the following:

   1. Obtain management support from the right managers.

   2. Define the scope and objectives.

   3. Plan an assessment schedule.

   4. Agree on a plan.

   5. Conduct information gathering exercises

   6. Interview key personnel.

   7. Review supporting documentation.

   8. Verify the information obtained.

   9. Identify any potential risks.

   10. Document the findings.

   11. Develop a report and recommendations.

   12. Present the report.

   13. Sign off and accept the report.

   The objective of a gap analysis is to identify and report on any gaps or risks that may affect the AIC of key information assets. The value of such an assessment is often determined based on what you did not know or for an independent resource to communicate to relevant management or senior personnel such risks, as opposed to internal resources saying what you need or should be doing.

5. What is the first international set of privacy controls in the cloud?

   A. ISO/IEC 27032

   B. ISO/IEC 27005

C. ISO/IEC 27002

D. ISO/IEC 27018

Answer: D

Explanation: ISO/IEC 27018 addresses the privacy aspects of cloud computing for consumers. ISO 27018 is the first international set of privacy controls in the cloud.

ISO 27018 was published by the ISO on July 30, 2014, as a new component of the ISO 27001 standard. ISO 27018 sets forth a code of practice for protection of PII in public clouds acting as PII processors. CSPs adopting ISO/IEC 27018 must operate under five key principles:

- **Consent:** CSPs must not use the personal data they receive for advertising and marketing unless expressly instructed to do so by the customers. In addition, a customer should be able to employ the service without having to consent to the use of her personal data for advertising or marketing.

- **Control:** Customers have explicit control over how CSPs are to use their information.

- **Transparency:** CSPs must inform customers about items such as where their data resides. CSPs also need to disclose to customers the use of any subcontractors who will be used to process PII.

- **Communication:** CSPs should keep clear records about any incident and their response to it, and they should notify customers.

- **Independent and yearly audit:** To remain compliant, the CSP must subject itself to yearly third-party reviews. This allows the customer to rely upon the findings to support her own regulatory obligations.

Trust is key for consumers leveraging the cloud; therefore, vendors of cloud services are working toward adopting the stringent privacy principles outlined in ISO 27018.

6. What is domain A.16 of the ISO 27001:2013 standard?

   A. Security Policy Management

   B. Organizational Asset Management

   C. System Security Management

   D. Security Incident Management

   Answer: D

   Explanation: The following domains make up the ISO 27001:2013, the most widely used global standard for ISMS implementations:

   A.5—Security Policy Management

   A.6—Corporate Security Management

   A.7—Personnel Security Management

A.8—Organizational Asset Management

A.9—Information Access Management

A.10—Cryptography Policy Management

A.11—Physical Security Management

A.12—Operational Security Management

A.13—Network Security Management

A.14—System Security Management

A.15—Supplier Relationship Management

A.16—Security Incident Management

A.17—Security Continuity Management

A.18—Security Compliance Management

7. What is a data custodian responsible for?

A. The safe custody, transport, storage of data, and implementation of business rules

B. Data content, context, and associated business rules

C. Logging and alerts for all data

D. Customer access and alerts for all data

Answer: A

Explanation: The following are key roles associated with data management:

- **Data subject:** This is an individual who is the focus of personal data.

- **Data controller:** This is a person who either alone or jointly with other persons determines the purposes for which and the manner in which any personal data is processed.

- **Data processor:** In relation to personal data, this is any person other than an employee of the data controller who processes the data on behalf of the data controller.

- **Data stewards:** These people are commonly responsible for data content, context, and associated business rules.

- **Data custodians:** These people are responsible for the safe custody, transport, data storage, and implementation of business rules.

- **Data owners:** These people hold legal rights and complete control over a single piece or set of data elements. Data owners can also define distribution and associated policies.

8. What is typically not included in an SLA?

   A. Availability of the services to be covered by the SLA

   B. Change management process to be used

   C. Pricing for the services to be covered by the SLA

   D. Dispute mediation process to be used

   Answer: C

   Explanation: Within an SLA, the following contents and topics should be covered as a minimum:

   - Availability (for example, 99.99 percent of services and data)
   - Performance (for example, expected response times versus maximum response times)
   - Security and privacy of the data (for example, encrypting all stored and transmitted data)
   - Logging and reporting (for example, audit trails of all access and the ability to report on key requirements and indicators)
   - Disaster recovery expectations (for example, worse-case recovery commitment, RTO, MPTD)
   - Location of the data (for example, ability to meet requirements or consistent with local legislation)
   - Data format and structure (for example, data retrievable from provider in readable and intelligent format)
   - Portability of the data (for example, ability to move data to a different provider or to multiple providers)
   - Identification and problem resolution (for example, help desk/service desk, call center, or ticketing system)
   - Change-management process (for example, updates or new services)
   - Dispute-mediation process (for example, escalation process and consequences)
   - Exit strategy with expectations on the provider to ensure smooth transition

NOTES

[1] http://nvlpubs.nist.gov/nistpubs/Legacy/SP/nistspecialpublication800-145.pdf (p. 6)

[2] http://nvlpubs.nist.gov/nistpubs/Legacy/SP/nistspecialpublication800-145.pdf (p. 7)

[3] http://nvlpubs.nist.gov/nistpubs/Legacy/SP/nistspecialpublication800-145.pdf (p. 6)

[4] http://nvlpubs.nist.gov/nistpubs/Legacy/SP/nistspecialpublication800-145.pdf (p. 6)

[5] http://nvlpubs.nist.gov/nistpubs/Legacy/SP/nistspecialpublication800-145.pdf (p. 7)

[6] http://en.wikipedia.org/wiki/Representational_state_transfer

[7] http://en.wikipedia.org/wiki/SOAP

A

ANSWERS TO REVIEW QUESTIONS

APPENDIX **B**

CCSP™

Glossary

A

All-or-Nothing-Transform with Reed-Solomon (AONT-RS)
Integrates the AONT and erasure coding. This method first encrypts and transforms the information and the encryption key into blocks in a way that the information cannot be recovered without using all the blocks. Then it uses the information dispersal algorithm (IDA) to split the blocks into m shares that are distributed to different cloud storage services (the same as in Secret Sharing Made Short [SSMS]).

Anonymization
The act of permanently and completely removing personal identifiers from data, such as converting personally identifiable information (PII) into aggregated data.

Anything as a Service (XaaS)
XaaS refers to the growing diversity of services available over the Internet via cloud computing as opposed to being provided locally, or on-premises.

Apache CloudStack
An open source cloud computing and infrastructure as a service (IaaS) platform developed to help IaaS make creating, deploying, and managing cloud services easier by providing a complete stack of features and components for cloud environments.

Application Normative Framework (ANF)
A subset of the organizational normative framework (ONF) that contains only the information required for a specific business application to reach the targeted level of trust.

Application Programming Interfaces (APIs)
A set of routines, standards, protocols, and tools for building software applications to access a web-based software application or web tool.

Application Virtualization
Software technology that encapsulates application software from the underlying operating system (OS) on which it is executed.

Authentication
The act of identifying or verifying the eligibility of a station, originator, or individual to access specific categories of information. Typically, a measure designed to protect against fraudulent transmissions by establishing the validity of a transmission, message, station, or originator.

Authorization
The granting of right of access to a user, program, or process.

B

Bit Splitting
Usually involves splitting up and storing encrypted information across different cloud storage services.

Business Impact Analysis (BIA)
An exercise that determines the impact of losing the support of any resource to an organization, establishes the escalation of that loss over time, identifies the minimum resources needed to recover, and prioritizes the recovery of processes and supporting systems.

C

Chain of Custody

(1) The identity of persons who handle evidence between the time of commission of the alleged offense and the ultimate disposition of the case. It is the responsibility of each transferee to ensure that the items are accounted for during the time they are in his possession, that they are properly protected, and that there is a record of the names of the persons from whom he received the items and to whom he delivered those items, together with the time and date of such receipt and delivery.

(2) The control over evidence. Lack of control over evidence can lead to its being discredited completely. Chain of custody depends on being able to verify that evidence could not have been tampered with. This is accomplished by sealing off the evidence so that it cannot in any way be changed and providing a documentary record of custody to prove that the evidence was at all times under strict control and not subject to tampering.

Cloud Administrator

This individual is typically responsible for the implementation, monitoring, and maintenance of the cloud within the organization or on behalf of an organization (acting as a third party).

Cloud App (Cloud Application)

Short for cloud application, *cloud app* is the phrase used to describe a software application that is never installed on a local computer. Instead, it is accessed via the Internet.

Cloud Application Architect

Typically responsible for adapting, porting, or deploying an application to a target cloud environment.

Cloud Application Management for Platforms (CAMP)

A specification designed to ease management of applications—including packaging and deployment—across public and private cloud computing platforms.

Cloud Architect

Someone who determines when and how a private cloud meets the policies and needs of an organization's strategic goals and contractual requirements from a technical perspective.

Also responsible for designing the private cloud, being involved in hybrid cloud deployments and instances, and having a key role in understanding and evaluating technologies, vendors, services, and other skillsets needed to deploy the private cloud or to establish and function the hybrid cloud components.

Cloud Backup Service Provider

A third-party entity that manages and distributes remote, cloud-based data backup services and solutions to customers from a central data center.

Cloud Backup Solutions

Enable enterprises or individuals to store their data and computer files on the Internet using a storage service provider rather than storing the data locally on a physical disk, such as a hard drive or tape backup.

Cloud Computing

A type of computing, comparable to grid computing, that relies on sharing computing resources rather than having local servers or personal devices to handle applications.

GLOSSARY

Cloud Computing Accounting Software

Accounting software that is hosted on remote servers.

Cloud Computing Reseller

A company that purchases hosting services from a cloud server hosting or cloud computing provider and then resells them to its own customers.

Cloud Data Architect

Ensures the various storage types and mechanisms utilized within the cloud environment meet and conform to the relevant service-level agreements (SLAs) and that the storage components are functioning according to their specified requirements.

Cloud Database

A database accessible to clients from the cloud and delivered to users on demand via the Internet.

Cloud Developer

Focuses on development for the cloud infrastructure. This role can vary from client tools or solutions engagements through systems components. Although developers can operate independently or as part of a team, regular interactions with cloud administrators and security practitioners are required for debugging, code reviews, and relevant security assessment remediation requirements.

Cloud Enablement

The process of making available one or more of the following services and infrastructures to create a public cloud computing environment: cloud provider, client, and application.

Cloud Management

Software and technologies designed for operating and monitoring the applications, data, and services residing in the cloud. Cloud management tools help to ensure a company's cloud computing–based resources are working optimally and properly interacting with users and other services.

Cloud Migration

The process of transitioning all or part of a company's data, applications, and services from onsite premises behind the firewall to the cloud, where the information can be provided over the Internet on an on-demand basis.

Cloud Operating System (OS)

A phrase frequently used in place of platform as a service (PaaS) to denote an association to cloud computing.

Cloud Portability

The ability to move applications and their associated data between one cloud provider and another or between public and private cloud environments.

Cloud Provider

A service provider who offers customers storage or software solutions available via a public network, usually the Internet.

Cloud Provisioning

The deployment of a company's cloud computing strategy, which typically first involves selecting which applications and services will reside in the public cloud and which will remain onsite behind the firewall or in the private cloud.

Cloud Server Hosting

A type of hosting in which hosting services are made available to customers on demand via the Internet. Rather than being provided by a single server or virtual server, cloud server hosting services are provided by multiple connected servers that comprise a cloud.

Cloud Services Brokerage (CSB)

Typically a third-party entity or company that looks to extend or enhance value to multiple customers of cloud-based services through relationships with multiple cloud service providers (CSPs). It acts as a liaison between cloud services customers and CSPs, selecting the best provider for each customer and monitoring the services.

Cloud Storage

The storage of data online in the cloud, wherein a company's data is stored in and accessible from multiple distributed and connected resources that comprise a cloud.

Cloud Testing

Load and performance testing conducted on the applications and services provided via cloud computing—particularly the capability to access these services—to ensure optimal performance and scalability under a variety of conditions.

Compute

The compute parameters of a cloud server are the number of central processing units (CPUs) and the amount of random access memory (RAM).

Content Delivery Network (CDN)

A service where data is replicated across the global Internet.

Control

Acts as a mechanism to restrict a list of possible actions down to allowed or permitted actions.

Corporate Governance

The relationship between the shareholders and other stakeholders in the organization versus the senior management of the corporation.

Crypto-Shredding

The process of deliberately destroying the encryption keys that were used to encrypt the data originally.

D

Database Activity Monitoring (DAM)

A database security technology for monitoring and analyzing database activity that operates independently of the database management system (DBMS) and does not rely on any form of native (DBMS-resident) auditing or native logs such as trace or transaction logs.

Database as a Service (DBaaS)

In essence, a managed database service.

Data Loss Prevention (DLP)

Auditing and preventing unauthorized data exfiltration.

Data Masking

A method of creating a structurally similar but inauthentic version of an organization's data that can be used for purposes such as software testing and user training.

Degaussing

Using strong magnets for scrambling data on magnetic media such as hard drive and tapes.

Demilitarized Zone (DMZ)

Isolates network elements such as email servers that, because they can be accessed from trustless networks, are exposed to external attacks.

Desktop as a Service (DaaS)

A form of virtual desktop infrastructure (VDI) that a third party outsources and handles.

Digital Rights Management (DRM)

Focuses on security and encryption to prevent unauthorized copying, thus limiting distribution to only those who pay.

Dynamic Application Security Testing (DAST)

The process of testing an application or software product in an operating state.

E

e-Discovery

e-Discovery refers to any process in which electronic data is sought, located, secured, and searched with the intent of using it as evidence.

Encryption

An overt secret writing technique that uses a bidirectional algorithm in which humanly readable information (referred to as plaintext) is converted into humanly unintelligible information (referred to as ciphertext).

Encryption Key

A special mathematical code that allows encryption hardware and software to encode and then decipher an encrypted message.

Enterprise Application

Software that a business uses to assist in solving problems.

Enterprise Risk Management

The set of processes and structures to systematically manage all risks to the enterprise.

Eucalyptus

An open source cloud computing and infrastructure as a service (IaaS) platform for enabling AWS-compatible private and hybrid clouds.

F–G

Federal Information Processing Standard (FIPS) 140-2

A National Institute of Standards and Technology (NIST) publication written to accredit and distinguish secure and well-architected cryptographic modules produced by private-sector vendors who seek to or are in the process of having their solutions and services certified for use in U.S. government departments and regulated industries that collect, store, transfer, or share data that is deemed to be sensitive but not classified as top secret.

Federated Identity Management (FIM)

An arrangement that can be made among multiple enterprises allowing subscribers to use the same identification data to obtain access to the networks of all enterprises in the group.

Federated Single Sign-On (SSO)

A system that allows a single user authentication process across multiple information technology (IT) systems or even organizations. SSO is a subset of federated identity management (FIM), as it relates only to authentication and technical interoperability.

H

Hardware Security Module (HSM)
A device that can safely store and manage encryption keys. This can be used in servers, data transmission, protection of log files, and more.

Homomorphic Encryption
Enables processing of encrypted data without the need to decrypt the data. It allows the cloud customer to upload data to a cloud service provider (CSP) for processing without the requirement to decipher the data first.

Hybrid Cloud Storage
A combination of public cloud storage and private cloud storage in which some critical data resides in the enterprise's private cloud whereas other data is stored and accessible from a public cloud storage provider.

I–J

Identity and Access Management (IAM)
The security discipline that enables the right individuals to access the right resources at the right times for the right reasons.

Identity Provider
Responsible for (a) providing identifiers for users looking to interact with a system, (b) asserting to such a system that such an identifier presented by a user is known to the provider, and (c) possibly providing other information about the user that is known to the provider. This can be achieved via an authentication module that verifies a security token that can be accepted as an alternative to repeatedly and explicitly authenticating a user within a security realm.

Infrastructure as a Service (IaaS)
A model that provides a complete infrastructure (servers and internetworking devices) and allows companies to install software on provisioned servers and control the configurations of all devices.

ISO/IEC 27034-1
Represents an overview of application security. It introduces definitions, concepts, principles, and processes involved in application security.

K–L

Key Management
The generation, storage, distribution, deletion, archiving, and application of keys in accordance with a security policy.

M

Management Plane
The plane that controls the entire infrastructure. Because parts of it are exposed to customers independent of the network location, it is a prime resource to protect.

Masking
A weak form of confidentiality assurance that replaces the original information with asterisks or Xs.

Mean time between failure (MTBF)
The measure of the average time between failures of a specific component or part of a system.

Mean time to repair (MTTR)
The measure of the average time it should take to repair a failed component or part of a system.

Mobile Cloud Storage

A form of cloud storage that applies to storing an individual's mobile device data in the cloud and providing the individual with access to the data from anywhere.

Multifactor Authentication

A method of computer access control that a user can pass by successfully presenting authentication factors from two or more independent credentials: what the user knows (password), what the user has (security token), and what the user is (biometric verification).

Multitenant

Multiple customers using the same public cloud.

N

National Institute of Standards and Technology (NIST) SP 800-53

A NIST publication written to ensure that appropriate security requirements and security controls are applied to all U.S. federal government information and information management systems.

Nonrepudiation

The assurance that a specific author actually did create and send a specific item to a specific recipient and that it was successfully received. With assurance of nonrepudiation, the sender of the message cannot later credibly deny having sent the message, nor can the recipient credibly claim not to have received it.

O

Obfuscation

The convoluting of code to such a degree that even if the source code is obtained, it is not easily decipherable.

Object Storage

Additional metadata, such as content type, redundancy required, and creation date, that is stored for a file. These objects are accessible through application programming interfaces (APIs) and potentially through a web user interface (UI).

Online Backup

Leverages the Internet and cloud computing to create an attractive offsite storage solution with little hardware requirements for any business of any size.

Organizational Normative Framework (ONF)

A framework of so-called containers for all components of application security best practices catalogued and leveraged by the organization.

P

Personal Cloud Storage

A form of cloud storage that applies to storing an individual's data in the cloud and providing the individual with access to the data from anywhere.

Personal Data

Any information relating to an identified or identifiable data subject; an identifiable person is one who can be identified, directly or indirectly, in particular by reference to an identification number or to one or more factors specific to his physical, physiological, mental, economic, cultural, or social identity.

Personally Identifiable Information (PII)

Information that can be traced back to an individual user, such as name, postal address, or email address. Personal user preferences tracked by a website via a cookie are also considered personally identifiable when linked to other PII you provide online.

Platform as a Service (PaaS)
A category of cloud computing services that provides a computing platform and a solution stack as a service. It provides a way for customers to rent hardware, operating systems (OSs), storage, and network capacity over the Internet from a cloud service provider (CSP).

Private Cloud Project
Used by organizations to enable their information technology (IT) infrastructures to become more capable of quickly adapting to continually evolving business needs and requirements.

Private Cloud Storage
A form of cloud storage in which the enterprise data and cloud storage resources reside within the enterprise's data center and behind the firewall.

Public Cloud Storage
A form of cloud storage in which the enterprise and storage service provider are separate and the data is stored outside the enterprise's data center.

Q

Quality of Service (QoS)
The capability of a network to provide better service to selected network traffic over various technologies, including Frame Relay, Asynchronous Transfer Mode (ATM), Ethernet and 802.1 networks, synchronous optical networking (SONET), and Internet protocol (IP)–routed networks that may use any or all of these underlying technologies.

R

Record
A data structure or collection of information that must be retained by an organization for legal, regulatory, or business reasons.

Redundant Array of Independent Disks (RAID)
An approach to using many low-cost drives as a group to improve performance. Also provides a degree of redundancy that makes the chance of data loss remote.

Request for Proposal
A solicitation, often made through a bidding process by a company, looking to secure goods or services from an external vendor.

S

Sandbox
A testing environment that isolates untested code changes and outright experimentation from the production environment or repository, in the context of software development, including web development and revision control.

Security Alliance's Cloud Controls Matrix
A framework to enable cooperation between cloud consumers and cloud providers on demonstrating adequate risk management.

Security Assertion Markup Language (SAML)
A version of the SAML standard for exchanging authentication and authorization data between security domains.

Security Information and Event Management (SIEM)
A method for analyzing risk in software systems.

Service-Level Agreement (SLA)
A formal agreement between two or more organizations: one that provides a service and the other that is the recipient of the service. It may be a legal contract with incentives and penalties.

B

GLOSSARY

Software as a Service (SaaS)

A distributed model in which software applications are hosted remotely by a vendor or cloud service provider (CSP) and made available to customers over network resources.

Software-Defined Networking (SDN)

A broad and developing concept addressing the management of the various network components. The objective is to provide a control plane to manage network traffic on a more abstract level than through direct management of network components.

Static Application Security Testing (SAST)

A set of technologies designed to analyze application source code, byte code, and binaries for coding and design conditions that are indicative of security vulnerabilities.

Storage Cloud

The collection of multiple distributed and connected resources responsible for storing and managing data online in the cloud.

STRIDE Threat Model

Derived from an acronym for the following six threat categories: spoofing identity, tampering with data, repudiation, information disclosure, denial of service (DoS), and elevation of privilege.

T–U

TCI Reference Architecture

A methodology and a set of tools that enable security architects, enterprise architects, and risk management professionals to leverage a common set of solutions that fulfill their common needs to be able to assess where their internal IT and their cloud providers are in terms of security capabilities. Allows them to plan a roadmap to meet the security needs of their business.

Tokenization

The process of replacing sensitive data with unique identification symbols that retain all the essential information about the data without compromising its security.

V

Vendor Lock-In

Highlights where a customer may be unable to leave, migrate, or transfer to an alternate provider due to technical or nontechnical constraints.

Vertical Cloud Computing

The optimization of cloud computing and cloud services for a particular vertical (such as a specific industry) or specific-use application.

Virtual Machine Introspection (VMI)

A VMI helps to mitigate risk and ensure that a virtual machine's (VM's) security baseline is not modified over time. It provides an agentless method to examine all aspects of a VM from its physical location and its network settings to the installed operating systems (OSs), patches, applications, and services being used.

Virtualization Technologies

Enable cloud computing to become a real and scalable service offering due to the savings, sharing, and allocation of resources across multiple tenants and environments.

W–Z

Web Application Firewall (WAF)

An appliance, server plug-in, or filter that applies a set of rules to a hypertext transfer protocol (HTTP) conversation. Generally, these rules cover common attacks such as cross-site scripting (XSS) and SQL injections.

APPENDIX C

Helpful Resources and Links

The following links were verified before the release of these materials. However, (ISC)² cannot guarantee their accuracy after release. Please do further research as necessary.

- APEC Privacy Framework:
  `http://www.apec.org/Groups/Committee-on-Trade-and-Investment/~/media/Files/Groups/ECSG/05_ecsg_privacyframewk.ashx`

- Application-Level Denial of Service Attacks and Defenses:
  `https://media.blackhat.com/bh-dc-11/Sullivan/BlackHat_DC_2011_Sullivan_Application-Level_Denial_of_Service_Att_&_Def-wp.pdf`

- Basel Accord II: `http://www.bis.org/publ/bcbs128.pdf`

- Behavior Change When Working with Pass-Through Disks in Windows Server 2012 Failover Clusters: `https://blogs.technet.microsoft.com/askcore/2013/01/24/behavior-change-when-working-with-pass-through-disks-in-windows-server-2012-failover-clusters/`

- CERT Software Engineering Institute: Carnegie Mellon University: Insider Threat: `http://www.cert.org/insiderthreat/`

- CleverSafe:
  `http://www.cleversafe.com/overview/how-cleversafe-works`

- Cloud Computing Security Risk Assessment:
  `http://www.enisa.europa.eu/activities/risk-management/files/deliverables/cloud-computing-risk-assessment`

- Cloud Data Protection Cert: `http://clouddataprotection.org/cert`
- Cloud Data Security Lifecycle:
  `https://securosis.com/blog/data-security-lifecycle-2.0`
- Common Criteria: `http://www.commoncriteriaportal.org/cc/`
- CSA: Cloud Controls Matrix Downloads: `https://cloudsecurityalliance.org/research/ccm/#_downloads`
- CSA: Cloud Controls Matrix v1.4:
  `https://cloudsecurityalliance.org/download/cloud-controls-matrix-v1-4/`
- CSA: Cloud Controls Matrix Working Group:
  `https://cloudsecurityalliance.org/research/ccm/`
- CSA: Data Loss Prevention: `https://downloads.cloudsecurityalliance.org/initiatives/secaas/SecaaS_Cat_2_DLP_Implementation_Guidance.pdf`
- CSA: EAWG Enterprise Architecture Whitepaper: `https://downloads.cloudsecurityalliance.org/initiatives/eawg/EAWG_Whitepaper.pdf`
- CSA: Privacy Legal Agreement Working Group:
  `https://cloudsecurityalliance.org/research/pla/`
- CSA: SecaaS Implementation Guidance: Category 1 // Identity and Access Management: `https://downloads.cloudsecurityalliance.org/initiatives/secaas/SecaaS_Cat_1_IAM_Implementation_Guidance.pdf`
- CSA: SecaaS Implementation Guidance: Category 8 // Encryption:
  `https://downloads.cloudsecurityalliance.org/initiatives/secaas/SecaaS_Cat_8_Encryption_Implementation_Guidance.pdf`
- CSA: Security Guidance for Critical Areas of Focus in Cloud Computing v3.0:
  `https://downloads.cloudsecurityalliance.org/initiatives/guidance/csaguide.v3.0.pdf`
- CSA: Security, Trust & Assurance Registry (STAR):
  `https://cloudsecurityalliance.org/star/`
- CSA: STAR Certification Guidance Document: Auditing the Cloud Controls Matrix: `https://downloads.cloudsecurityalliance.org/initiatives/ocf/STAR_Cert_Auditing_the_CCM.pdf`
- CSA: TCI Reference Architecture:
  `https://downloads.cloudsecurityalliance.org/initiatives/tci/TCI_Reference_Architecture_v2.0.pdf`
- CSA: Top Threats Working Group: The Notorious Nine Cloud Computing Threats in 2013: `https://downloads.cloudsecurityalliance.org/initiatives/top_threats/The_Notorious_Nine_Cloud_Computing_Top_Threats_in_2013.pdf`

- EU: Directive on Privacy and Electronic Communications:
  `http://www.dataprotection.ro/servlet/ViewDocument?id=201`
- EU Data Protection Regulation Tracker:
  `http://www.huntonregulationtracker.com/legislativescrutiny/`
- FedRAMP: `https://www.fedramp.gov/`
- FTC: `http://www.ftc.gov/`
- HP Digital Safe: `http://www8.hp.com/us/en/software-solutions/digital-safe-cloud-archiving/`
- Information Splitting in Cloud Storage Services: `http://mariusaharonovich.blogspot.co.il/2013/12/introduction-use-of-cloudcomputing.html`
- InfoWorld: IBM's Homomorphic Encryption Could Revolutionize Security: `http://www.infoworld.com/t/encryption/ibms-homomorphic-encryption-could-revolutionize-security-233323`
- ISO 27001:2013: `https://www.iso.org/obp/ui/#iso:std:iso-iec:27001:ed-2:v1:en`
- ISO/IEC 27037:2012: `http://www.iso.org/iso/catalogue_detail?csnumber=44381`
- KMIP: `https://www.oasis-open.org/committees/tc_home.php?wg_abbrev=kmip`
- Luhn Test of Credit Card Numbers: `http://rosettacode.org/wiki/Luhn_test_of_credit_card_numbers`
- NIST: Cloud Computing Synopsis and Recommendations: `http://nvlpubs.nist.gov/nistpubs/Legacy/SP/nistspecialpublication800-146.pdf`
- NIST: Complete Listing of All NIST FIPS Documentation: `http://csrc.nist.gov/publications/PubsFIPS.html`
- NIST: Definition of Cloud Computing: `http://nvlpubs.nist.gov/nistpubs/Legacy/SP/nistspecialpublication800-145.pdf`
- OAUTH: `http://oauth.net/2/`
- OAuth 2.0 Authorization Framework: `http://tools.ietf.org/html/rfc6749`
- OWASP: Logging Cheat Sheet: `https://www.owasp.org/index.php/Logging_Cheat_Sheet`
- OWASP: Top Ten Project: `https://www.owasp.org/index.php/Category:OWASP_Top_Ten_Project`
- PCI DSS Version 3.1: `https://www.pcisecuritystandards.org/documents/PCI_DSS_v3-1.pdf`

- PCI SSC Data Security Standards Overview:
  `https://www.pcisecuritystandards.org/security_standards/pci_dss.shtml`

- "Secret Sharing Made Short" by Hugo Krawcyzk:
  `http://www.cs.cornell.edu/courses/cs754/2001fa/secretshort.pdf`

- VMware's Guidance on Using RDMs:
  `http://pubs.vmware.com/vsphere-60/topic/com.vmware.ICbase/PDF/`
  `vsphere-esxi-vcenter-server-601-storage-guide.pdf`

Index

Numbers

3DES (Triple DES), 35

A

abuse of services, 219
access controls
    decision-making process, 180–181
    remote access, 304–305
        deployment methods, 279–281
    security countermeasures and,
        171–172
access decisions, 179–180
access management, 179, 223
accounting for resources, 179
access. *See* data access
AES (Advanced Encryption Standard), 35
AIC (availability, integrity, and
    confidentiality), 176
air management considerations, 251
aisle separation and containment
    considerations, 252–253
ANF (Application Normative
    Framework), 233, 492
anonymization, 103, 453, 492
answers to review questions, 441–489
AONT-RS (All-or-Nothing-Transform
    with Reed-Solomon), 492
Apache CloudStack, 7, 492
APEC (Asia-Pacific Economic
    Cooperation) framework, 369–370

APIs (Application Programming
    Interfaces), 492
    gateway, 227
    insecure, 219
    insecurity, 45
    REST, 208–209
    SOAP, 208–209
application deployment
    cloud readiness, 210
    documentation, lack, 211
    guidelines, lack, 211
    integration, pitfalls, 211
    on-premises infrastructure
        and, 210
    pitfalls, 209–212
    training and, 210
application development
    access controls, function-level, 216
    authentication, 216
    component vulnerabilities,
        216–217
    CSRF, 216
    data exposure, 216
    data sensitivity, 208
    direct objects, indirect references, 216
    encryption
        data at rest, 212
        data in transit, 212
        data masking, 212
    forwards, 217
    Framework Core, 217
    injection, 215

clustered hosts
  DRS (distributed resource
    scheduling), 274
  resource sharing
clustered storage
  loosely coupled, 275
  tightly coupled, 275
COBIT (Control Objectives for Information
  and Related Technology), 6
communication
  distributed IT and, 412–413
  protections, 173–174
communication management
  customers, 353
  five Ws and one H, 351
  partners, 351–352
  regulators, 353–354
  SLAs, 353
  stakeholders, 354
  vendors, 351–352
community cloud, 25, 449
compliance issues, review question
  answers, 482–488
compute, 495
configuration
  automation, 174
  reduction in time, 61
configuration management, 310
content analysis, 455
continual service improvement
  management, 321
continuous operations, 146–147, 171
contract maintenance, 460
control, 495
controls, 173
  automation, 171
  CCA CCM, 307
copyrights, 367
corporate governance, 495
COSO (Committee of Sponsoring
  Organizations of the Treadway
  Commission), 6
cost-benefit analysis, 60–62

countermeasures for security, 170–171
  access controls, 171–172
  continuous uptime, 171
  control automation, 171
Country-Specific Legislation and Regulations
  Related to PII Data Privacy, and Data
  protection, 373
CPU (central processing unit), 16
create phase (lifecycle), 82
criminal law, 367
Critical Controls for Effective Cyber-
  Defense, 295–296
CRM (customer relationship management),
  6
cross-border transfers, 374
cryptography, 33
  encryption, 33–34
    data at rest, 35
    data in motion, 34–35
  erasure, 41
  key management, 35–36
    approaches, 36
  SSL (secure sockets layer), 227
  TLS (transport layer security), 227
  VPN (virtual private network), 227
crypto-shredding, 138–139, 459, 495
CSB (cloud services brokerage), 12, 443, 495
CSO (chief security officer), 81
CSP (cloud service provider), 3–4, 12, 442
CTO (chief technology officer), 81

D

DaaS (desktop as a service), 496
DAM (database activity monitoring),
  226, 495
DAR (data at rest), 94, 453
  development and, 212
  encryption, 228
DAST (dynamic application security testing),
  234, 496
data access, 84
data at rest, 35

HTTP (hypertext transfer protocol), 93
HTTPS (hypertext transfer protocol secure), 34, 93
HVAC considerations, 250, 253
hybrid cloud, 24–25
hybrid cloud storage, 9, 449, 497
hypervisor, 42, 162–163

I

IaaS (infrastructure as a service), 4, 10, 18–19, 48–50, 474, 497
   event sources, 142
   object storage, 88
   volume storage, 88
IAM (identity and access management), 222–223, 497
   access management, 39
   authorization, 39
   centralized directory services, 38
   deprovisioning, 37–38
   privileged user management, 38–39
   provisioning, 37–38
ID (Identify), ID.AM (Asset Management), 217–218
identification, managing, 178
identity management, 179, 223
identity providers, 497
identity repository, access management and, 223
IDS (intrusion detection system), 174, 290–291
IETF (Internet Engineering Task Force), 266
incident management
   events *versus* incidents, 315
   incident classification, 316–317
   objective, 315
   plan, 316
   process example, 317
   purpose, 315
incidents, 10
information and governance types, 56–57
information security management, 310

infrastructure
   physical, 278–279
   physical environment, 157–158
   security, review question answers, 460–466
intellectual property rights, 367
interfaces, insecurity, 45
international law, 366–367
international regulations, 374
IPSec (IP security), 35, 269–270
IPSs (intrusion prevention systems), 174
IRM solutions, 134–136, 456–457
iSCSI (Internet small computer system interface), 256
   implementation, 257–258
ISMS (information security management system), 405
   internal
      ISO 27001:2013 domains, 406
      repeatability, 406–407
      standardization, 406–407
      value of, 405–406
ISO (International Organization for Standardization), 62–63
   ISO/IEC 27002:2013, 64
   ISO/IEC 27017:2015, 64
   SOC 1/SOC 2/SOC 3, 64–65
ISO 27001:2013 domains, 406
ISO/IEC 27017:2015, 368
ISO/IEC 27018, 403–404
ISO/IEC 27034-1, 232, 497
ISO/IEC 27050-1, 377–378
isolation of network, 266
ISVs (independent system vendors), 278
ITaaS (IT as a service), 278
ITIL (Information Technology Infrastructure Library), 26–27
ITSM solutions, 308

J–K

Jericho Forum Cloud Cube Model, 27

Kerberos, 257, 471–472

key management, 35–36, 497
key regulations, 173
KIMP (Key Management Interoperability Protocol), 100
KMS (Key Management Service), 36
KVM (kernel-based virtual machine), 265–266

L

labels, 455
languages, 446
layered security
 IDS (intrusion detection), 289
  HIDs, 290
  IPS combination, 291–292
  NIDs, 289–290
 IPSs, 290–291
LDAP (Lightweight Directory Access Protocol), 38
legal issues, 374–375
 auditing
  conducting, 402–403
  external audits, 392–393
  goals, 401
  information gathering, 397–398
  internal audits, 392–393
  objectives, 401
  reporting, 393–396
  scope, 398–402
  virtualization and, 396–397
 business requirements, 425–426
 CCSL (Cloud Certification Schemes List), 429–430
 contract design and, 425
 contract management, 431–434
 contractual obligations, 374
 copyrights, 367
 criminal law, 367
 cross-border transfers, 374
 doctrine of proper law, 367
 e-Discovery, 375–377
 enforcable governmental requests, 367
 Federal laws, 373

GLBA (Gramm-Leach-Bliley Act), 372
HIPAA, 372
intellectual property rights, 367
international conflicts, 365–366
international law, 366–367
international regulations, 374
 outsourcing and, 425
PII, 378–379, 498
 Argentina, 385
 Australia, 388–390
 breach reporting, 380–381
 CCM, 129–132
 contractual, 379–383
 controls, 128–129
 European Union, 383–384
 Ireland, 384–385
 New Zealand, 388–390
 regulated, 380
 Russia, 390
 Switzerland, 391–392
 United Kingdom, 384–385
 United States, 387–388
piracy law, 367
privacy laws, 367
regional regulations, 374
restatement conflict of laws, 368
review question answers, 482–488
standards, 373
state law, 367, 373
supply chain management, 434–436
tort law, 367–368
vendor management
 CC (Common Criteria) framework, 427–428
 compliance and, 427
 CSA STAR, 428–429
 risk exposure and, 426–427
legal requirements, 373–374
licensing, costs, 61
Linux, security baseline, 302–303
location of data. See data location
lock-in, reduction, 447
log analysis, 306–307

log capture, 293–295, 306–307
log management, 293–395
logical design, 298
    access control, remote access, 304–305
    OS baselines and, 305
    OS guest
        backups, 305–307
        restores, 305–307
    risk management, 323
loosely coupled clustered storage, 275
LulzSec, 366
LUN (logical unit number), 90, 256

M

maintenance, reduction in time, 61
maintenance mode, 276
malicious insiders, 219
managed service provider, 10
management plan, 164–166, 296–297,
    307, 497
    maintenance, 297
    orchestration, 297–298
masking, 453, 497
measured service, 14, 444
media sanitization
    cryptographic erasure, 41
    data overwriting, 41
    vendor lock-in, 40
metadata, 455
mobile cloud storage, 10, 498
MSP (managed service provider), 3–4
MTAs (message transfer agents), 34
MTBF (mean time between failure), 10, 497
MTTR (mean time to repair), 10, 497
multifactor authentication, 225–226, 498
multitenant, 10, 498

N

network
    access control, 159
    address allocation, 159
    bandwidth, 160
    filtering, 160

    functionality, 159–160
    infrastructure and, 279
    isolation, 266
    OS, guest, 303
    OS hardening, 301–303
    rate limiting, 160
    routing, 160
    SDN (software-defined networking), 160
    secure, building, 300–301
    security, controls, 306–308
    standalone hosts, 271–273
    threat identification, 270–271
network security, 32–33
NICs (network interface cards), 259
NIDS (network intrusion detection system),
    289–290
NIST Cloud Technology Roadmap
    auditability, 31–32
    availability, 29
    compliance, 32
    governance, 30–31
    interoperability, 28
    performance, 30
    portability, 28
    privacy, 29–30
    resiliency, 30
    security, 29
    SLAs, 31
NIST Risk Management Framework, 6
NIST (National Institute of Standards and
    Technology) SP 800-53, 498
    cloud computing definition, 3
nodes, 10
nonrepudiation, 147–148, 498

O

OAuth, 224
obfuscation, 453, 498
object storage, 164, 452, 498
on-demand self-service, 12–13, 443
ONF (organizational normative framework),
    232–233, 498
online backup, 10, 498

oversubscription, 257
RAID, 163
SSDs (solid-state drives), 163
structured, 452
targets, 256
unstructured, 452
storage cloud, 11, 500
store phase (lifecycle), 82
STRIDE threat model, 220–221, 468, 500
system and subsystem production
   certification
     CC, 69–70
     FIPS 140-2, 70–71
     FIPS levels, 71–72
system availability, 276–277
system protections, 173–174

T

TCI reference architecture, 500
TCO (total cost of ownership), 62
temperature and humidity
   considerations, 250
testing
   BCDR, 197–198
     full-interruption, 200–201
     full-scale, 200–201
     functional drill, 199–200
     objectives, 196–197
     parallel test, 199–200
     simulation, 199
     structured walk-through, 199
     tabletop exercise, 199
     walk-through drill, 199
   DAST (dynamic application security
     testing), 235
   OWASP recommendations, 236
   penetration testing, 235–236
   RASP (runtime application self-
     protection), 235
   SAST (static application security
     testing), 234
   secure code reviews, 236
   vulnerability assessment, 235–236

threat modeling
   APIs, 221
     supply chain, 221–222
   open source software, 222
   STRIDE, 220–221
threats
   API insecurity, 45
   data breaches, 43–44
   data loss, 44–45
   DoS (denial of service), 46
   due diligence insufficiency, 47
   hijacking, 45
   insiders, malicious, 46
   interface insecurity, 45
   service abuse, 46
   shared technology, 47
tightly coupled clustered storage, 275
TLS (transport layer security), 227, 266, 268
TOGAF (The Open Group Architecture
   Framework), 27
tokenization, 103–105, 228, 453, 500
tort law, 367–368
training, application deployment and, 210
transition scenario, 14–15
transparent encryption, 454
trust zones, 177
TSL (transport layer security), 34

U

use phase (lifecycle), 82
utilities, 61

V

VDI (virtual desktop infrastructure), 9
vendor lock-in, 40–41, 500
vendors, communicating with, 351–352
vertical cloud computing, 11, 500
virtual host, 11
virtual switches, best practices, 259–260
virtualization
   application virtualization, 229–230, 492
   auditing and, 396–397
   cloud server, 161

W–Z